CULT HORROR FILMS

CULT HORROR FILMS

From *Attack of the 50 Foot Woman* to *Zombies of Mora Tau*

by WELCH EVERMAN

A CITADEL PRESS BOOK

Published by Carol Publishing Group

Copyright © 1993 by Welch Everman
All rights reserved. No part of this book may be reproduced in any form, except by a newspaper or magazine reviewer who wishes to quote brief passages in connection with a review.

A Citadel Press Book
Published by Carol Publishing Group
Citadel Press is a registered trademark of Carol Communications, Inc.
Editorial Offices: 600 Madison Avenue, New York, N.Y. 10022
Sales and Distribution Offices: 120 Enterprise Avenue, Secaucus, N.J. 07094
In Canada: Canadian Manda Group, P.O. Box 920, Station U, Toronto, Ontario M8Z 5P9
Queries regarding rights and permissions should be addressed to Carol Publishing Group, 600 Madison Avenue, New York, N.Y. 10022

Carol Publishing Group books are available at special discounts for bulk purchases, for sales promotions, fund-raising, or educational purposes. Special editions can be created to specifications. For details, contact Special Sales Department, Carol Publishing Group, 120 Enterprise Avenue, Secaucus, N.J. 07094

Designed by A. Christopher Simon

Manufactured in the United States of America

10 9 8 7 6 5 4 3 2 1

Library of Congress Cataloging-in-Publication Data

Everman, Welch D., 1946-
    Cult horror films : offbeat thrillers from Attack of the fifty foot woman to Zombies of Nora Tau / by Welch Everman.
      p. cm.
    "A Citadel Press book."
    ISBN 0-8065-1425-6 (pbk.)
    1. Horror films. 2. Low budget motion pictures. I. Title.
PN1995.9.H6E88   1993
791.43'61—dc20   93-11664
                                                             CIP

To my sons,
Charlie and Johnnie.
Thanks, guys.

Acknowledgments

Very special thanks to Leslie Flemming, dean of the College of Arts and Humanities, and to Harvey Kail, chair of the Department of English, University of Maine, for encouragement and research assistance that made this book possible.

Special thanks also to Eric Caidin and the good people at Hollywood Book and Poster for locating and graciously providing stills from *Attack of the 50 Foot Woman, Barn of the Naked Dead, Blood Feast, Creature of the Walking Dead, Don't Look in the Basement, Fiend Without a Face, The Giant Gila Monster, The Hideous Sun Demon, I Was a Teenage Werewolf, It Came From Beneath the Sea, It Conquered the World, Phantom From Space, Plan 9 From Outer Space, The Satanic Rites of Dracula, Them!, The Toolbox Murders, The Unearthly, Zombies of Mora Tau.* I don't know what I would have done without their help.

And thanks to Steve Wegnur at MGM/UA for providing stills from MGM/UA Home Video releases; to Plus*Video* of Bangor, Maine, for coming up with some really obscure titles on video; to my students Brad Finch, Lyman Feero, Matt Sweeney, and Chris Goldrup, who, for better or worse, share my taste in films and who have spent long hours talking with me about the movies; to Allan J. Wilson, editor at Citadel Press, who believed in this project in the first place; to my wife, Liz, and my sons, Charlie and Johnnie, for putting up with all the screaming coming from the TV; and thanks, Mom, for letting me stay up to watch *Horror Theater* when I was a kid.

PHOTO CREDITS

A.D.P. Productions
Allied Artists
American International Pictures
Amicus Productions
Amulet Pictures, Ltd.
Anglo-Amalgamated
Associated Distributors, Inc.
AVCO Embassy Pictures
Box Office Spectaculars
Budd Rodgers, Inc.
Cal-Am Productions
Cambist Films
Cinema Shares
Cinemation Industries
Cinerama Releasing
Columbia Pictures
Constitution Films, Inc.
Crown International Pictures
DCA Productions
Dimensions Pictures
Diplomat Pictures
Fabtrax Films
Film Ventures International
Filmakers Releasing Organization
Fulvia Cinematografica
Genini Film Distributing Company
Goldstone Films
Group 1 Films
Hallmark Releasing
Hammer Productions
Hemisphere Productions
Independent-International Pictures
International Amusement Corporation
Joseph Brenner Associates
King Brothers
McLendon Radio Pictures
MGM/United Artists/Steve Wegnur
New World Pictures
Orion Pictures

Pacemaker Films	Translor/Black Lion Productions	Warner Brothers
Pacific International	20th Century Fox	Woolner Brothers
Paragon Pictures	Twenty-Four Horses Company	World Amusements
Phil-Am Enterprises, Ltd.	Twin World	Zopix Company
Republic Pictures	United Film Distribution Company	
Toho Productions	Valiant Films Corporation	

Contents

Introduction	1
THE FILMS	9
Alice, Sweet Alice	11
Amityville 3-D	12
The Asphyx	14
The Astro-Zombies	16
Attack of the 50 Foot Woman	19
Audrey Rose	22
Barn of the Naked Dead	25
The Beast Within	28
Ben	31
Beyond the Door	33
Blacula	36
Blood Feast	39
Blood Orgy of the She-Devils	40
The Bride	42
Brides of Blood	45
The Brood	47
The Corpse Grinders	49
Count Dracula's Great Love	53
Craze	55
The Crazies	59
Creature of the Walking Dead	61
Curse of the Devil	64
Daughters of Darkness	68
Dementia 13	72
The Devil's Nightmare	74
The Devil's Wedding Night	79
Donovan's Brain	82
Don't Look in the Basement	86
Dracula vs. Frankenstein	88
Dracula's Dog	93
Fiend Without a Face	95
Frankenstein's Castle of Freaks	98
Freaks	103
From Beyond the Grave	105
The Fury	109
The Giant Gila Monster	111
Godzilla on Monster Island	114
Gorgo	118
He Knows You're Alone	122
The Hideous Sun Demon	125
Hillbillys in a Haunted House	127
House of Whipcord	130
I Eat Your Skin	132
I Was a Teenage Werewolf	133
Invasion of the Body Snatchers	136
It Came From Beneath the Sea	139
It Conquered the World	141
It Lives Again	142
Lady Frankenstein	145
Land of the Minotaur	147
Legend of the Wolf Woman	150
Mania	153
The Manitou	156
Mansion of the Doomed	159
Mary, Mary, Bloody Mary	162

The Mask	165	Tentacles	200
The Mind Snatchers	172	The Terror	202
Mother's Day	176	Them!	204
Nightmare in Wax	178	Tombs of the Blind Dead	206
Phantom From Space	180	The Toolbox Murders	208
The Pit	181	Torso	209
Plan 9 From Outer Space	185	Torture Dungeon	211
Queen of Blood	186	Trap Them and Kill Them	213
The Satanic Rites of Dracula	188	The Undying Brain	214
Satan's Cheerleaders	189	The Unearthly	217
Scream and Scream Again	191	The Vampire Lovers	218
Shock Waves	193	Werewolf of Washington	220
Slithis	195	Wolfen	222
Squirm	197	Zombies of Mora Tau	225

In *The Hideous Sun Demon*, the creature (actor Robert Clarke under the makeup) is so frightening that he even scares himself—in fact, he seems to have wet his pants. This is what cult horror films are all about. *(Courtesy Hollywood Book and Poster)*

INTRODUCTION

What Is a Cult Horror Film?

The phrase *cult horror film* has come to mean "bad horror film," and that's a bit unfair—but only a bit. The truth is that, yes, most movies that are called cult horror films *are* bad, and that's certainly true for most of the movies discussed in this book. They have minimal budgets, they are poorly written and directed, the production values are near zero, and the acting is appalling. A lot of these films, though, are so bad they're good—or at least they're funny. Take a look at *Werewolf of Washington*, *Dracula's Dog*, or *Blood Orgy of the She Devils* and you'll see what I mean. On the other hand, some of these movies—like *Hillbillys in a Haunted House* and *Tentacles*—are so bad they really *are* bad, and others—such as *The Mind Snatchers*, *The Asphyx*, and *Donovan's Brain*—are very good, low budgets and all.

In other words, cult horror films are not necessarily bad, and even when they are, they aren't necessarily a total loss. What these films seem to have in common is that they're all kind of offbeat, kind of weird, kind of strange. Brains float in fish tanks, giant creatures level major metropolitan areas, presidential advisers turn into werewolves, and vampire dogs roam the countryside in search of victims. Some cult horror films are mindless copies or very conscious rip-offs of bigger-budget movies, while others are so original and so idiosyncratic that they hardly make any sense at all.

Maybe it's easier to say what cult horror films are not.

Cult horror films, first of all, are not for everybody. Horror movies are always popular—it is very likely that nobody has ever lost money making one of these films. But the word *cult* suggests a small group of loyal fans, so a cult horror film would seem to be one made strictly for the horror audience, the audience that will literally watch anything as long as it's a horror flick. By this definition, blockbuster hits such as *The Exorcist*, the *Alien* series, and *Bram Stoker's Dracula* would not be cult horror films because they are made to appeal to a more general audience. On the other hand, only a true horror film fanatic would sit through *Satan's Cheerleaders* or *The Corpse Grinders*.

Cult horror films, then, are not classics and never will be. Classic horror films are those that have influenced the entire history of horror movies—James Whale's *Frankenstein*, Tod Browning's *Dracula*, George Waggner's *The Wolf Man*, and so on. It isn't very likely, however, that movies like *Dracula vs. Frankenstein*, *Mansion of the Doomed*, or *The Vampire Lovers* will have any lasting effects on the genre.

And, for the most part, cult horror films are not products of the big Hollywood studios. The vast majority are independent productions, and a lot of them were not made in the Untied States. When connoisseurs of cinema talk about foreign films, they usually mean movies like *Kagemusha*, *Juliet of the Spirits*, *Christiane F.*, or *Jules and Jim*. When cult horror film fans talk about foreign films, they mean *Godzilla on Monster Island* (Japan), *Curse of the Devil* (Spain), *Torso* (Italy), *Mary, Bloody Mary* (Mexico), or *Brides of Blood* (the Philippines).

In his essay "The Work of Art in the Age of Mechanical Reproduction," German philosopher Walter Benjamin wrote that the object of cult worship is invested with an aura, an indefinable something that sets it apart from ordinary objects, making it special, unique, one of a kind (in *Illuminations*, Hannah Arendt, ed., Harry Zahn, trans., New York: Schocken Books, 1969, p. 226). The aura defines a religious object—the relic of a saint or the place where a miracle has occurred. In our own time, objects of art are also invested with the same kind of aura—it's the aura that makes a Picasso painting different from a cheese knife, a coffee cup, or any other mass-produced object. Cult horror films seem to have auras, too, something that makes them special—though, in many cases, the aura is more like an aroma and not a particularly good one.

For example, a horror film might become special because it marks one of the first efforts by an actor or a director who would later go on to bigger, better, or at least different things. Roger Corman's movie *The Terror* is a cult film partly because of Jack Nicholson's early appearance in a starring role. A brief appearance by Tom Hanks in *He Knows You're Alone* adds a lot to an otherwise pedestrian slasher flick, and *Donovan's Brain*—already a fine film—gets an aura boost from the presence of Nancy Davis, who would become First Lady Nancy Reagan. *Dementia 13* is an early and impressive

London falls beneath the relentless onslaught of an angry mother dinosaur in *Gorgo*.

effort by director Francis Ford Coppola, and *Land of the Minotaur*—a loser on almost every count—can boast of a musical score by Brian Eno. Well, everybody has to start somewhere.

A horror film might also gain special cult status because it features a late appearance by a fading star—Richard Basehart and Gloria Grahame in *Mansion of the Doomed* or Yvonne DeCarlo and John Ireland in *Satan's Cheerleaders*. And the presence of a name horror star—Boris Karloff, Bela Lugosi, or Lon Chaney Jr.—might

add a bit of an aura even to low-budget quickies such as *The Terror, Plan 9 From Outer Space,* or *Hillbillys in a Haunted House.*

A cult horror film might have something else going for it, something to set it apart. It might be the first of its kind, as *Blood Feast* is the first film to offer not only gallons of blood but also exposed entrails for our entertainment. Or it might be in 3-D or involve audience participation or simply present a new idea for a monster, such as the killer babies in the *It's Alive* series or the living dead Knights Templar in *Tombs of the Blind Dead* and its sequels. Or, for a variety of reasons, it might be weird enough or good enough or perverse enough or awful enough to stand out from the crowd.

The cult horror film, then, is unique and yet marginal at the same time. In general, most of what happens in popular culture happens in the margins. For every Madonna, there are hundreds of sleazy-nightclub singers working in out-of-the-way joints all over America, and for every blockbuster horror hit like *The Exorcist,* there are hundreds of marginal copies such as *Beyond the Door* and *House of Exorcism.*

But these marginal horror movies are interesting and popular, too—not with a mass audience but with the core of horror fans. And what is popular must say what we want it to say. Otherwise, we wouldn't like it.

So cult horror films must say what we want them to say, though we may not be readily aware of what these films are really saying to us. Still, every now and then, it might do us some good to take seriously what we would not normally take seriously and ask these cult horror movies what they are all about.

Most horror filmmakers don't have a particular message in mind—they just want to make a buck. The best way to do that is to copy films that have already made a buck. That's why John Carpenter's *Halloween* led to an enormous wave of mad-slasher clones that are still being cranked out today. But even the most mindless copy of a successful horror film—even the copy of a copy and the copy of a copy of a copy—says something, whether the makers of the movie know it or not.

For instance, virtually all horror films are basically conservative. Think for a moment of how the horror film works. In the beginning, things are okay. Then something unusual turns up—a vampire, a werewolf, an alien, a monster of some sort, a guy in a hockey mask—and everything is a mess. But someone figures out how to solve the problem, and in the end, things are pretty much as they were in the beginning.

This basic horror-film formula assumes that the way things are is the way things ought to be, and so the goal of the movie is to get everything back to the way it was, back to normal. This is a fundamentally conservative view of the world. Horror films are often conservative in more specific ways: for example, in their treatment of women as helpless, powerless victims or in their view of anyone who is different as dangerous and deserving of death.

On the other hand, these same movies often raise important questions about the way things are. Many horror films question authority or reject it outright. It isn't at all unusual to see the government, the military, the police, and scientists depicted as ineffectual or evil. Beginning in the 1970s, the ecological horror film started questioning the way we were treating Earth. During that same decade, the true horror-film heroine

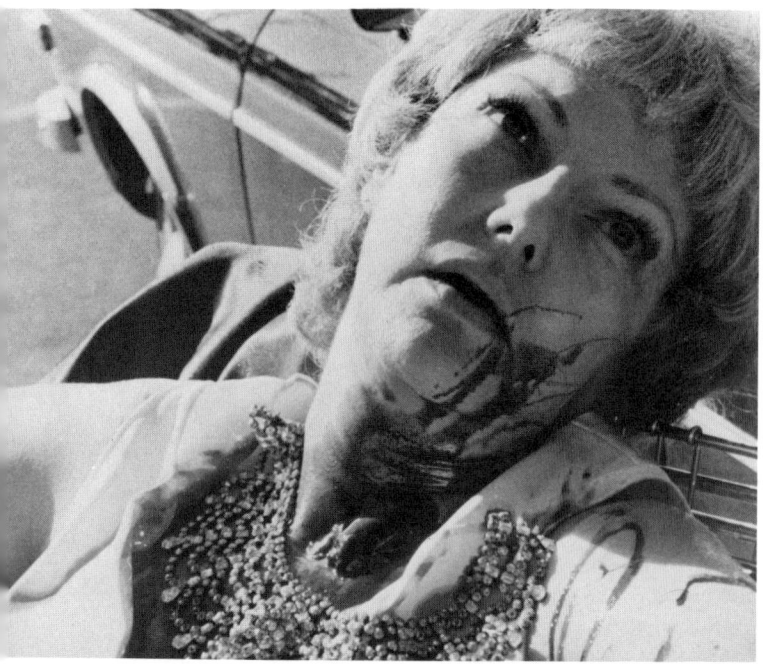

A victim in the hilarious *Werewolf of Washington*.

began to emerge—the woman who could deal with the problems that had once been the province solely of men.

Any particular horror movie can be offering a number of mixed and contradictory messages—for example, that women ought to be helpless, but if they are, they deserve whatever happens to them, or that nuclear weapons are really bad and can create monsters, but when we use them against the monsters they have created, then these weapons are really good. As Stephen King points out in his book on the horror genre, *Danse Macabre* (New York: Berkley Books, 1983, p. 177), it isn't unusual for a particular horror movie to be conservative, even reactionary, and liberal, even revolutionary, at the same time.

Cult Horror Films is an effort to look seriously—and often, not very seriously—at a number of such movies to try to figure out what it is that they are saying to us. It's also an effort to decide whether we want these movies to be saying what they are saying. In some cases, while watching these films—many of them for the zillionth time—I was shocked and often embarrassed to realize

It's *Dracula's Dog*.

George Barrows (in the ape costume), John Carradine, and Lon Chaney Jr. make up part of the all-star cast in the appalling *Hillbillys in a Haunted House*.

Sir Hugo Cunningham (Robert Stephens) gets acid thrown in his face while his assistant Giles (Robert Powell) looks on in the remarkable film *The Asphyx*.

The Frankenstein monster (John Bloom) battles with Count Dracula (Zandor Vorkov) in the appropriately titled *Dracula vs. Frankenstein*.

A modern-day vampire (that's John Carradine's hand holding the razor) finds another victim in the Mexican production of *Mary, Bloody Mary*.

A typically gruesome scene from the Italian slasher film *Torso*. Carla Brait is the killer's latest victim.

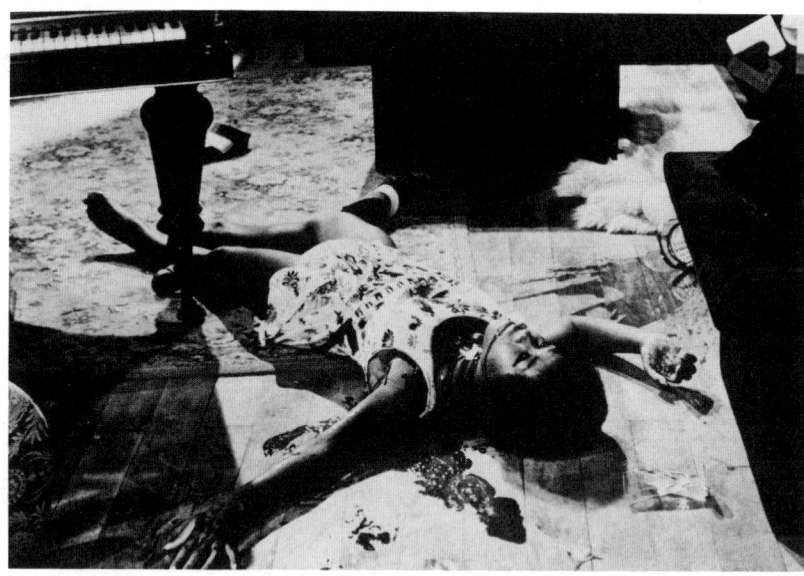

Jack Nicholson stars with Sandra Knight, along with Boris Karloff, in *The Terror*.

what it was that these seemingly innocuous movies wanted to tell me. In other cases, I was pleasantly surprised.

Cult Horror Films is something of an encyclopedia, and the reader is invited to use it that way. The book isn't intended to be read from cover to cover, though you can do so if you wish. But it's probably more useful if you just dip into it here and there to see what you can come up with.

For each film, I've included some basic information: alternate titles, names of the director, producer, and screenwriter, cast members, the company that originally produced and/or released the movie, and the company that has released it on videocassette. One of my rules in selecting the films to be discussed was that they have to be available on video so that, when you found something of interest, you would at least have the chance of seeing it.

Be aware, however, that although all of these films have been available on video at one time or another, they might not be easy to find. Movies on videocassette go out of print quickly nowadays, and even though I've tried to provide up-to-date information, it might be out-of-date by the time you read this.

Even so, video rental shops tend to keep horror films on their shelves for a long time even as they unload their copies of last month's blockbuster, because the horror films continue to go out. You can find copies of out-of-print horror videos, but you might have to go to the more out-of-the-way, mom-and-pop stores to do so.

After a plot summary, each entry offers an analysis of the film, an effort to discover what it is that the particular movie might be saying to us, whether it really intends to

William Campbell stars as a brooding and possibly homicidal artist in director Francis Ford Coppola's excellent *Dementia 13*.

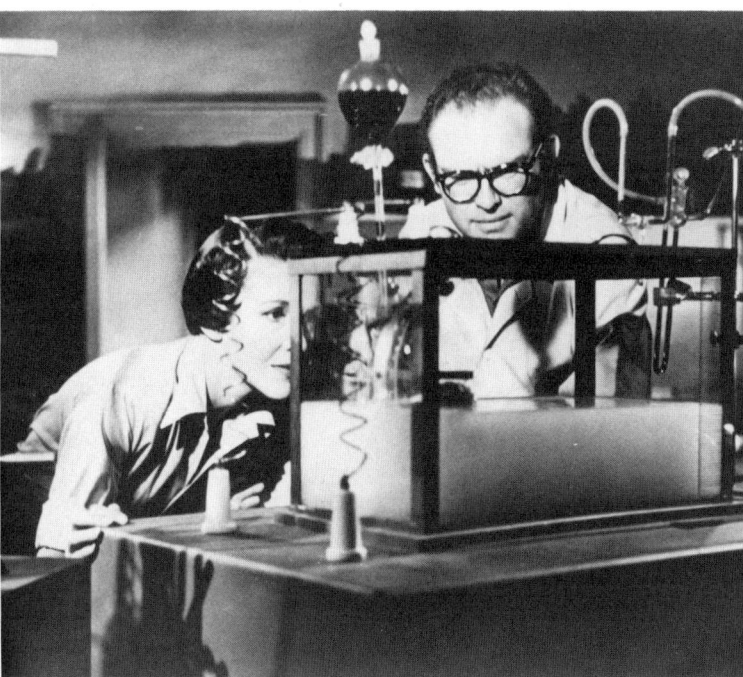

Long before she took up residence in the White House as the first lady, Nancy Davis spent time with Gene Evans studying *Donovan's Brain*. *(Courtesy MGM/UA Home Video)*

Another lovely woman falls victim to *Blacula* (William Marshall).

Harry Archer (William Hudson) has to come to grips with his wife Nancy (Allison Hayes) in *Attack of the 50 Foot Woman*. *(Courtesy Hollywood Book and Poster)*

say anything or not. Of course, for any given film, there are any number of possible readings, and the analyses I offer here are mine. Please feel free to disagree.

Now I know what some of you are thinking: Hey, where's *Robot Monster?* Where's *Wrestling Women vs. the Aztec Mummy?* Where's *Incredibly Strange Creatures Who Stopped Living and Became Mixed-Up Zombies?* If I've skipped over your favorite cult horror movie, you have my apologies. There are literally thousands of bizarre, offbeat thrillers out there, and so, for every one that I decided to include, I had to pass over many, many more.

In general, I have tried to avoid the obvious choices, although the likes of *Attack of the 50 Foot Woman* and *Plan 9 From Outer Space* seemed unavoidable. I've also tried to provide a good mix, without focusing too exclusively on any one era or subgenre—you could easily do an entire book on cult horror films of the 1950s or the history of the offbeat vampire movie. And I've tried to include, along with the many movies produced in the United States, a good number of films from other countries.

In the end, though, the list of films discussed here is my list and no one else's. These are my favorites—and my least favorites. These are the movies about which I felt I had something to say. I hope some of your favorites are here, too, and that you will also discover some movies that perhaps you didn't know about before and will want to see.

And now it's time for a confession. I love these movies, all of them, even the ones I hate. That might seem like a contradiction, but if you are a fan of cult horror films, you know exactly what I mean. I saw my first horror movie more than thirty-five years ago, and I haven't been able to get enough of them since.

So enjoy. I know I have.

WELCH EVERMAN
March 1993

A psychedelic scene from *The Mask,* a 3-D cult horror goodie.

THE FILMS

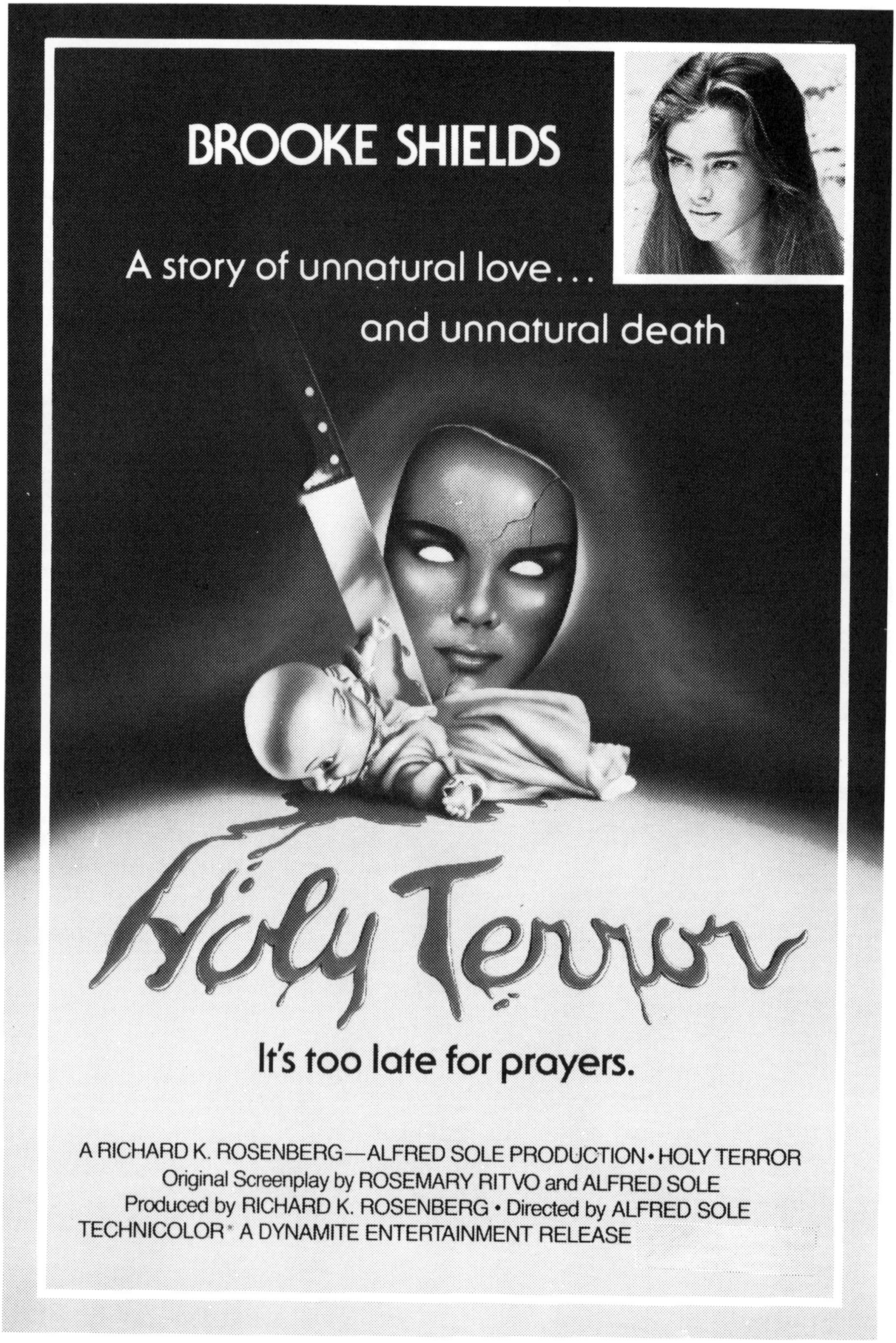

When *Alice, Sweet Alice* was rereleased as *Holy Terror*, the ads made it look as if Brooke Shields were the star. In fact, Shields's character dies about ten minutes into the film.

Alice, Sweet Alice

ALTERNATE TITLES:

*Communion,
Holy Terror*

1977

Director: Alfred Sole; *Producer:* Richard K. Rosenberg; *Screenplay:* Rosemary Ritvo and Alfred Sole

CAST:
Linda Miller, Tom Signorelli, Louisa Horton, Paula Sheppard, Mildred Clinton, Rudolph Willrich, Brooke Shields

ORIGINAL RELEASE: Allied Artists
VIDEO: Goodtimes and others

This was ten-year-old Brooke Shields's first film, and though video releases give her top billing, she is not the star. In fact, her character dies in the first ten minutes. The real star of this powerful and disturbing film is Paula Sheppard in the title role.

The action is set in Paterson, New Jersey, and takes place in the early 1960s, to judge by the cars, the picture of JFK on the wall of the police station, and the Latin Mass. Alice is a very disturbed twelve-year-old who wears a Halloween mask to scare people and torments her sister, Karen (Shields). On the day of her first Communion, Karen is strangled and set on fire in church by a small figure wearing Alice's mask and a yellow raincoat. Detective Brenner (Tom Signorelli) suspects Alice, and so does her aunt Annie (Jane Lowry).

Admittedly, Alice was jealous of her sister and does not seem bothered by her death. Her mother, Catherine Spages (Linda Miller), and her father are divorced, but Dad (Niles McMaster) returns to town for Karen's funeral and to find out what happened to his daughter. While he is there, Aunt Annie is stabbed in the leg by the figure in the raincoat and mask, and when she tells the police that Alice attacked her, the little girl is locked up in a juvenile mental facility.

Alice's father is murdered, too, and Alice is cleared and released. The identity of the murderer is still a mystery to the police, but we now know that the crimes have been committed by Mrs. Tredoni (Mildred Clinton), a fervent Catholic who cooks and cleans for the priests of the parish and who is particularly attached to Father Tom (Rudolph Willrich), Catherine's brother. She believes that Tom's family is distracting him from his duties ("Father belongs to the Church") and that Catherine, who was pregnant with Alice when she was married and who is now divorced, is a sinner who must be punished.

Finally, Brenner finds out about Mrs. Tredoni and tries to stop her, but first she manages to stab Father Tom to death during Mass. In the end, it is clear that, though Alice did not commit any of the crimes, she is certainly as insane as Mrs. Tredoni and will probably do something equally horrible one day.

Clearly, *Alice, Sweet Alice* is a reply to William Friedkin's 1973 blockbuster hit *The Exorcist*. In that film, when Regan O'Neal is possessed by Satan, the medical and psychiatric sciences fail to help her. So does

Father Damien Karras, who is both a priest and a psychiatrist and, therefore, very much a product of the new, socially relevant Church of the seventies. Regan's salvation comes from Father Merrin, the representative of the old Catholic Church of the Latin Mass, who is untainted by modern, liberal beliefs. *The Exorcist* insists that conservative Catholicism is the only effective agent against evil in the world.

Alice, Sweet Alice says just the opposite. Like Regan, Alice is also a disturbed twelve-year-old, but her attachment to icons and her Catholic school uniform suggest that the Church is the cause of her problems, not the cure. The film also suggests that Catholicism creates the fanatical Mrs. Tredonis of the world and that it is helpless in the face of real evil. When the police follow Tredoni to Mass at the end of the movie, Father Tom tells them he will get her to give herself up. "I can handle her," he says, just before she kills him. While Karen is being murdered in the opening sequence, the camera shows the statues of the saints and Christ looking on but doing nothing.

Alice, Sweet Alice is an overtly anti-Catholic film and will be offensive to a lot of people on that basis. It is also remarkably well made and a strong antidote to movies like *The Exorcist*, which offer simplistic solutions to the problems of the world. In *Alice, Sweet Alice*, nothing is simple, and in the end, nothing has been solved.

Amityville 3-D

ALTERNATE TITLE:

Amityville: The Demon

1983

Director: Richard Fleischer; *Producer:* Stephen F. Kesten; *Screenplay:* William Wales

CAST:
Tony Roberts, Tess Harper, Robert Joy, Candy Clark, Lori Loughlin, Meg Ryan

ORIGINAL RELEASE: Orion Pictures
VIDEO: Vestron Home Video

The Amityville Horror and its various sequels are okay, but my favorite is *Amityville 3-D* because ... well, it's in 3-D. Even in the videocassette from Vestron, which isn't in 3-D—you can watch it without the special glasses— you still get the effect of flies buzzing in your face, hands

Melanie (Candy Clark) is one of the first to be terrorized by the house in *Amityville 3-D*.

John Baxter (Tony Roberts), the new owner of the Amityville house, invites psychic researcher Elliott West (Robert Joy) and his crew to investigate the strange goings-on there.

Elliott (Robert Joy) loses his scientific objectivity when he comes face-to-face with the demon from the pit.

reaching out of the screen, and all that good three-dimensional stuff.

After all the problems people have had with the house in Amityville, who would buy the place? John Baxter (Tony Roberts), investigative reporter for *Reveal* magazine, that's who. After all, he isn't superstitious, and it's a real steal.

John first comes to Amityville with his photographer, Melanie (Candy Clark), to expose the Caswells (John Beal and Leora Dana) an elderly couple who have been operating a spiritualist scam out of the house. His friend, Dr. Elliott West (Robert Joy), is also interested in the house because he is a psychic investigator, and after all, there's a pit in the basement that's supposed to be the gateway to hell.

Recently divorced from Nancy (Tess Harper), John plans to quit his job and retreat to Amityville to write his novel. It isn't long before Melanie suspects that "something weird is going on here," but John merely laughs at her. He's so sure the house is safe that he lets his teenage daughter Susan (Lori Loughlin) visit him and pick out a room for herself—of course, she chooses the room upstairs where all the flies hang out, and things sort of go downhill from there.

The real estate dealer (John Harkins) who sold John the house dies mysteriously. Then Melanie dies. Then Susan dies, and when Nancy sees her daughter's ghost in the house, Elliott decides to investigate for psychic phenomena in hopes of setting Susan's spirit free. In the

John (Tony Roberts) and his soon-to-be-ex-wife Nancy (Tess Harper) are attacked by the Amityville house.

end, he confronts the demon from the pit, who hauls him down into hell in exchange for Susan and the house collapses (again) and explodes, killing off the psychic investigators—apparently, they tampered with things they were not supposed to know. John and Nancy survive and so do the flies, indicating that the evil will live on, at least for a few more sequels.

The film is effective mostly because of its professional cast. Roberts, Harper, and Clark are talented performers who don't always get to show what they can do, and *Amityville 3-D* even features Meg Ryan in a small part as Susan's libido-driven friend: "You know you can have sex with a ghost?"

In his book *Danse Macabre,* Stephen King refers to the original Amityville movie as an economic horror film, and that analysis applies to *Amityville 3-D* as well. It's a story many people known firsthand. They buy an old house, and as soon as they move in, the furnace goes and the pipes burst and the whole place needs to be rewired, etc., etc. Before they know it, they owe everybody in town and the roof still leaks.

If misery really does love company, then, for homeowners, watching *Amityville 3-D* is a relief, because, no matter how badly your own house is treating you, it isn't *this* bad. Suddenly a leaky radiator just doesn't seem quite so serious.

The Asphyx

1972

Director: Peter Newbrook; *Producer:* John Brittany; *Screenplay:* Brian Comport;

CAST:
Robert Stephens, Robert Powell, Jane Lapotaire

ORIGINAL RELEASE: Paragon Pictures
VIDEO: Interglobal Home Video

In 1875, Sir Hugo Cunningham (Robert Stephens), well-known British philanthropist and gentleman scientist, makes an important discovery. As a reasearcher in psychic phenomena, he takes photographs of people at the moment of death and discovers a strange smudge in all of his pictures. He assumes that he has photographed the soul as it leaves the body. Later, however, when he inadvertently photographs the death of his son, Clive (Ralph Arliss), in a boating accident, he learns that the smudge is really a picture of the Asphyx—the spirit of death, according to ancient Greek mythology. Apparently, each living creature has its own Asphyx, which comes for it at the very instant it is about to die. Somehow, the blue crystals Sir Hugo uses to generate light for his photography enable him not only to make the Asphyx visible and to capture it on film but also to immobilize it.

Working with his foster son, Giles (Robert Powell), Sir Hugo manages to immobilize and capture the Asphyx of a guinea pig. With its Asphyx sealed away in a tiny cage, trapped by the blue light, the guinea pig is now immortal because the spirit of its death cannot get to it. "But can we snare a human Asphyx?" Giles wants to know.

Hugo devises a sort of electric chair, and sitting in it, he invites his own Asphyx to come calling. When it does, Giles and Hugo's daughter, Christina (Jane Lapotaire), trap it in the blue light and lock it away in the family burial vault. Now, no matter what happens to him, Sir Hugo cannot die.

Hugo decides to immortalize Giles and Christina as well. He rigs up a guillotine for his daughter and manages to trap her Asphyx, but in the process, something goes wrong and she is decapitated. She is still alive, however—even with the spirit of her death safely tucked away, she can still suffer pain and physical damage—so Hugo releases her Asphyx and lets her die.

Giles is so overcome by grief and guilt that he purposely sabotages the experiment designed to give him immortal life, blowing up Sir Hugo's lab in the process. Alone, Hugo accepts his fate—"damned to eternal guilt, damned to eternal remorse"—and goes into the world with his immortal guinea pig, "my everlasting friend."

The film catches up with him in London about a hundred years later. He is now a ragged bum and very, very old—it seems that having your Asphyx locked up doesn't prevent aging. In the closing sequence, he is caught between two colliding cars and virtually cut in two—but he still lives.

There are a lot of logical problems here. For example, since Hugo's electric chair is so effective in the effort to trap his Asphyx, why does he use a guillotine on Christina and a gas chamber on Giles? Why not stick with what works? And what about the Asphyx itself? If every human being and every guinea pig has its own Asphyx, is that also true for every ant, every blade of grass? What about a tree? Does every leaf have its own Asphyx? And where do these zillions and zillions of Asphyxes hang out while they're waiting for us to die?

In fact, though, these questions only come to mind after the film is over, because the performances are so strong and the pacing so intense that, while you're watching *The Asphyx,* it is absolutely convincing. Even the fact that the Asphyx itself is clearly a puppet doesn't make any difference. The movie is excellent.

Obviously, *The Asphyx* is a variation on the old mad-scientist theme, but it addresses issues that don't

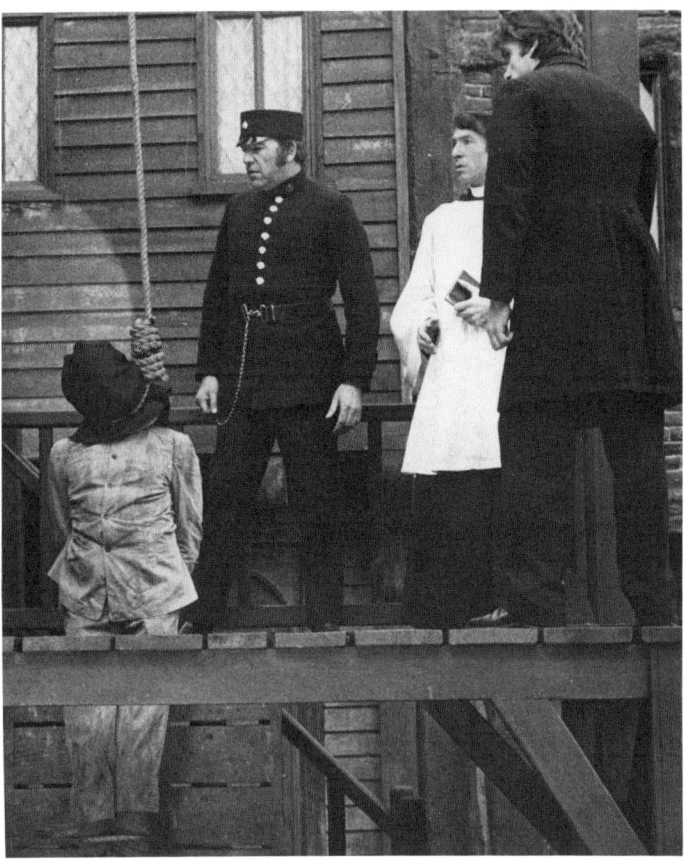

Sir Hugo manages to photograph and to freeze the Asphyx at a public execution.

In the lab, Sir Hugo (Robert Stephens, left) and Giles (Robert Powell) trap the Asphyx of a guinea pig, making it immortal.

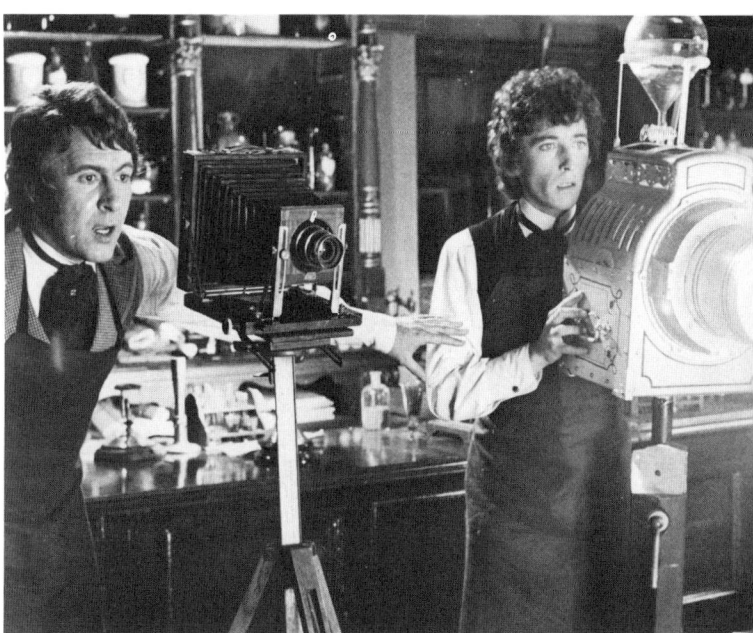

Sir Hugo (Robert Stephens, left) immortalizes himself with the help of Giles (Robert Powell) and a homemade electric chair.

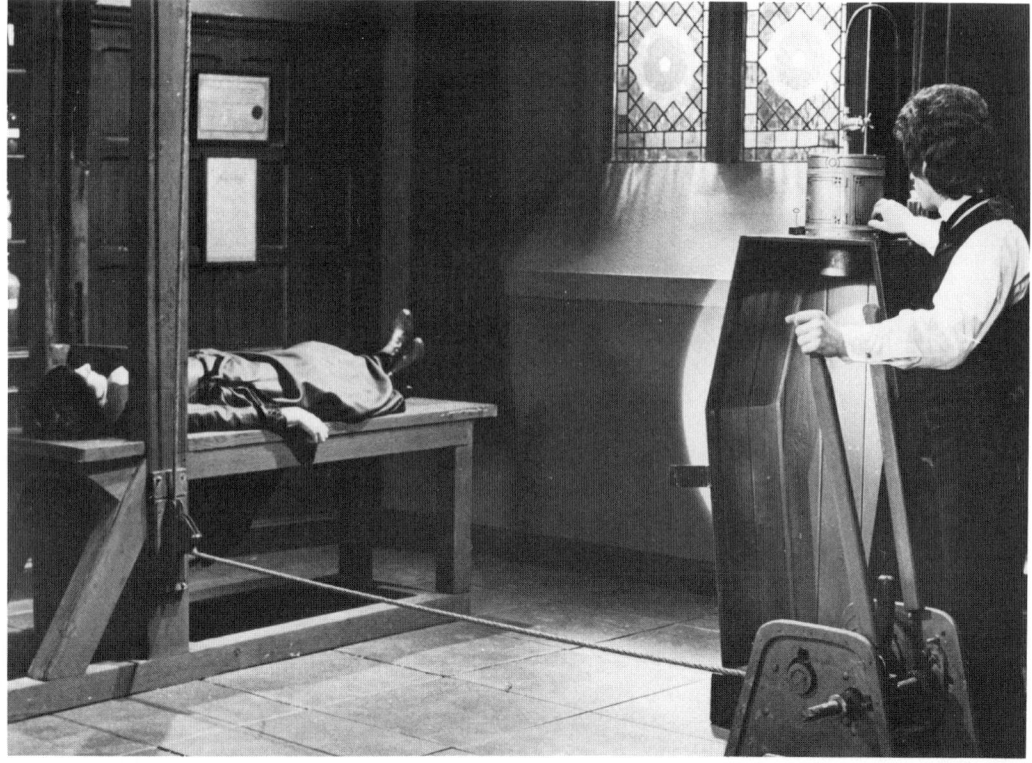

Giles (Robert Powell) helps in the effort to immortalize Hugo's daughter, Christina (Jane Lapotaire), using a guillotine. It doesn't work, in *The Asphyx*.

usually come up in more pedestrian movies. Early on, Sir Hugo says, "Privilege means power, and we must never abuse that power." Of course, he does abuse the power he has—that's the whole point of the film—and it would be easy to write him off as just another mad scientist if he were depicted as self-serving, power mad, and evil.

But he isn't. In fact, he is always shown as a good, kind man who is caught up in something beyond his control, and his goal is simply to protect the ones he loves from death. In other words, while most scientists in horror films are clearly rotten and certainly not people we would want to identify with, Sir Hugo is a lot like us. That's disturbing, because if a nice guy like Hugo can become lost in a tragic drive for power that eventually costs him all that he loves, something like that could happen to us, too.

The Asphyx is a well-made, well-acted, and intelligent film that does what very few horror films do—it makes us stop and think.

The Astro-Zombies

1968

Director/producer: Ted V. Mikels; *Screenplay:* Wayne Rogers and Ted V. Mikels

CAST:
John Carradine, Wendell Corey, Tura Satana, Rafael Campos, Vincent Barbi, William Bagdad, Rod Wilmoth

ORIGINAL RELEASE: Geneni Film Distributing Company
VIDEO: WorldVision Home Video

Though *Astro-Zombies* is not Ted V. Mikels's best movie—personally, I much prefer *The Corpse Grinders*—it is probably his best-known work, thanks to the presence of two cult horror film stars: Tura Satana (who also appears in Mikels's *Doll Squad* and Russ Meyer's *Faster, Pussycat! Kill! Kill!*) and John Carradine (who seems to be in 96.7 percent of all the cult horror movies ever made.) Even so, *Astro-Zombies* does not have a lot to recommend it.

Murders are being committed, and human organs are being stolen. Who could be the cause of these atrocities? Well, it's Dr. DeMarco (Carradine), your typical mad scientist, who is working in his basement to develop a superhuman race of Astro-Zombies and who needs parts. As a typical mad scientist, DeMarco has a typical assistant, Franchot (William Bagdad), who, in his off-hours, is permitted to conduct "experiments" of his own, which seem to involve the gratuitous torture of lovely young women. Everyone needs a hobby.

At the same time, Satana is the evil head of an evil spy

Tura Satana is the evil spy in an evening gown in *Astro-Zombies*.

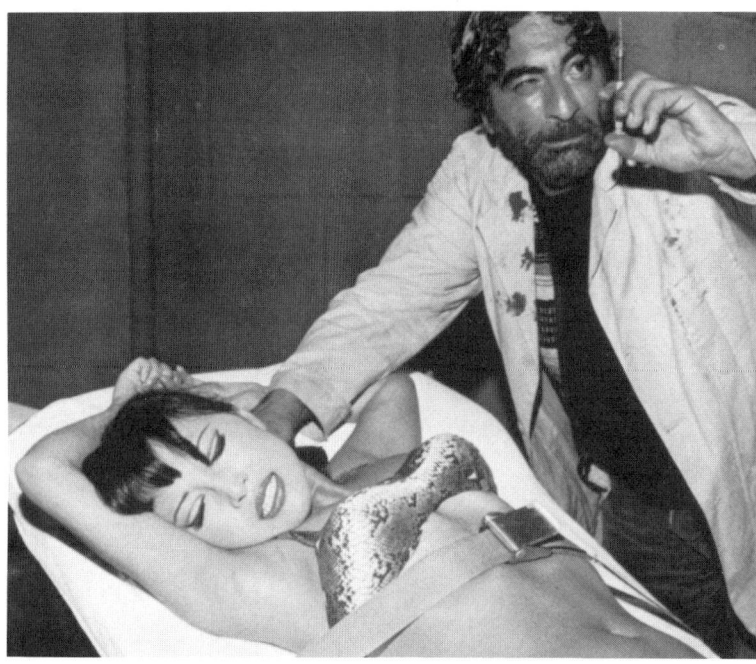

Franchot (William Bagdad), Dr. DeMarco's assistant, prepares for one of his "experiments."

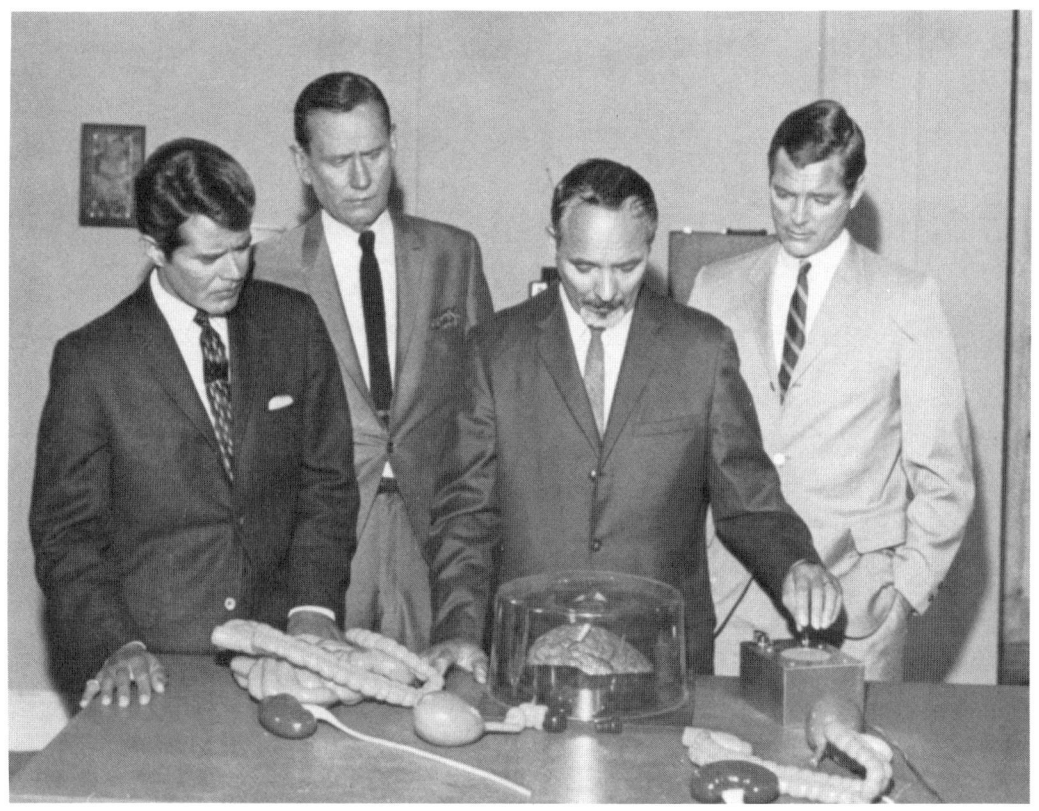

Holman (Wendell Corey, second from left) and his cohorts study some obviously plastic human organs in their effort to track down the spies.

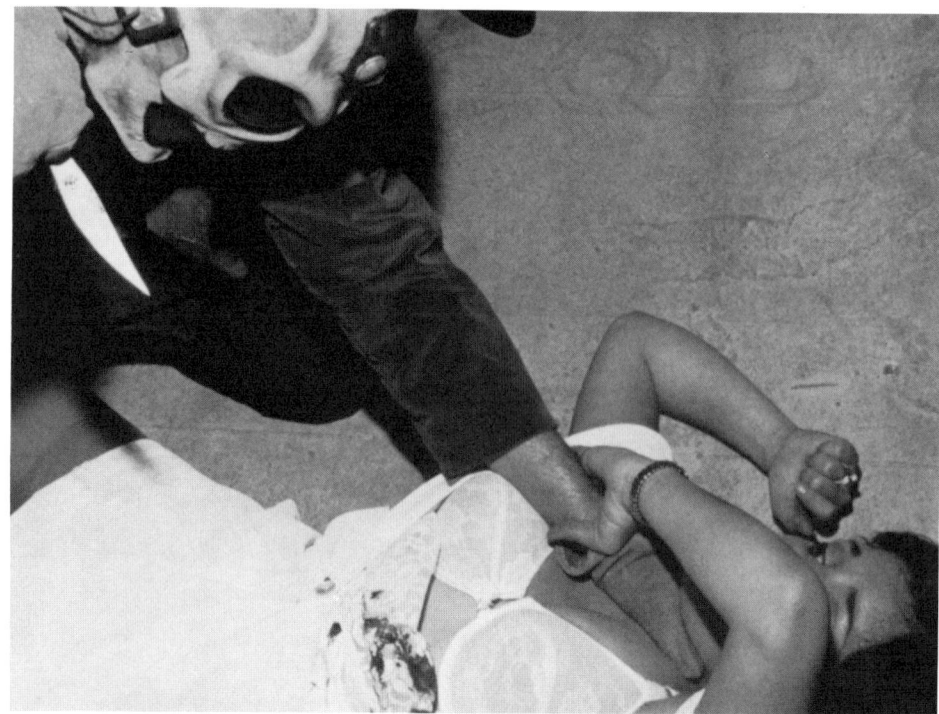

The Astro-Zombie (Rod Williams) runs amok.

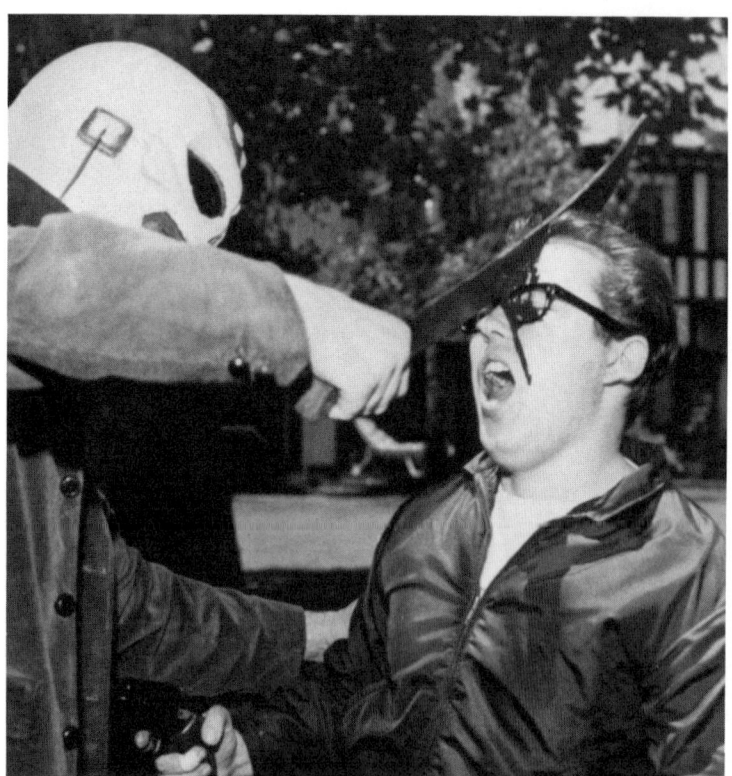

More mayhem from the Astro-Zombie (Rod Williams).

The Astro-Zombie (Rod Williams) puts an end to the nefarious schemes of Tura Satana.

ring bent on gaining the secret of the Astro-Zombies so her evil country can create an evil army of these monsters and turn them loose on America. Satana is the kind of spy who wears an evening gown for almost every occasion—even when she's simply murdering someone—but even so, we in the audience know that she really isn't very classy. She employs two thugs, the brutal Tiros (Vincent Barbi) and the gleeful, knife-wielding Juan (Rafael Campos), to do her dirty work.

Holman of the CIA (Wendell Corey) is after the spy lady, who is after DeMarco, who is after more parts, and things become pretty confusing pretty quickly, especially when a completed but unbalanced Astro-Zombie (Rod Wilmoth) escapes and begins slaughtering the neighborhood. Well, eventually, the spy lady shoots DeMarco, then gets electrocuted by the Astro-Zombie, who, in turn, gets his power shut off, and the world is safe for democracy once again.

Astro-Zombies has all the elements of a 1950s horror film. Unfortunately, it came along about ten years too late. At a time when public sentiment was turning against American involvement in Southeast Asia, Mikels's movie seems to be trying to convince viewers that evil foreign spies are everywhere—Satana's character is certainly supposed to be Chinese or even Vietnamese—and that we have to put our trust and faith in our own spy network, the very people who got us involved in Vietnam in the first place. If *Astro-Zombies* doesn't hold up very well for viewers today, that's probably because it didn't hold up even for viewers in 1968, who were already too sophisticated to accept the film's mindless clichés.

Best scene: The Astro-Zombie runs on solar power—for all his faults, Dr. DeMarco seems to want his creatures to have a minimal negative impact on the environment. One night, though, the zombie is out too late in the dark, and his batteries run down. He has to go back to DeMarco's basement for a recharge, all the while holding a flashlight to the solar collectors on his forehead to keep himself going. This bit is a riot.

Note: Yes, the Wayne Rogers who coscripted this atrocity with Mikels is the Wayne Rogers from *M*A*S*H* on television. At least things got better for him.

Attack of the 50 Foot Woman

1958

Director: Nathan Hertz; *Producer:* Bernard Woolner; *Screenplay:* Mark Hanna

Harry (William Hudson) and Nancy Archer (Allison Hayes) have a less than ideal marriage in *Attack of the 50 Foot Woman*. Note the size of Nancy's diamond pendant. *(Courtesy Hollywood Book and Poster)*

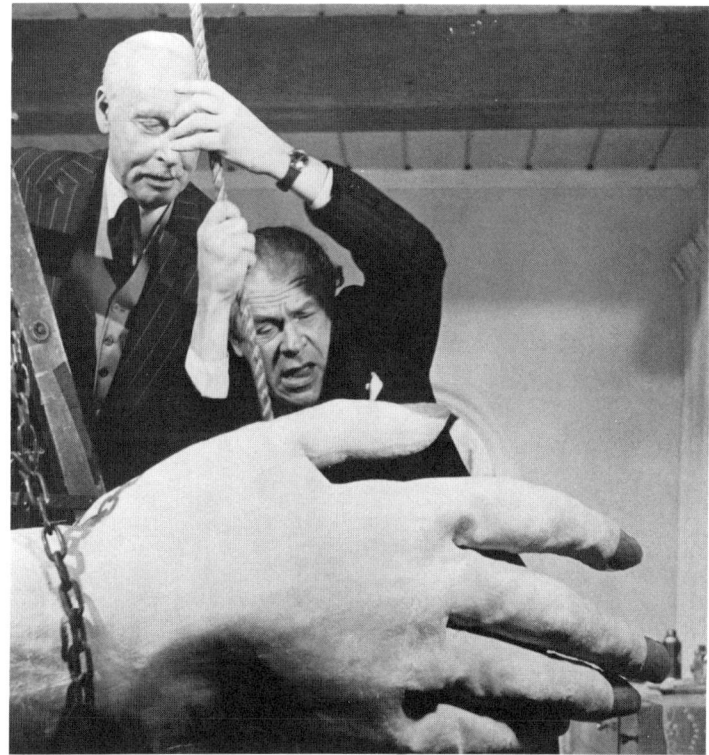

Dr. Cushing (Roy Gordon) and Dr. von Loeb (Otto Waldid) try to restrain Nancy after she becomes the fifty-foot woman. *(Courtesy Hollywood Book and Poster)*

The giant from outer space attacks Sheriff Dubbitt (George Douglas). *(Courtesy Hollywood Book and Poster)*

Nancy (Allison Hayes) gets her revenge against Harry (William Hudson), her cheating husband. *Courtesy Hollywood Book and Poster)*

CAST:
Allison Hayes, William Hudson, Yvette Vickers

ORIGINAL RELEASE: Allied Artists
VIDEO: Key Home Video

When people talk about bad 1950s horror films, this is one of those they always discuss, and that's a bit unfair. The fact is, *Attack of the 50 Foot Woman* has something going for it. Yes, the plot is stupid. Yes, the special effects are abysmal. Yes, the actors often seem to be embarrassed about taking part in this project. But the movie does offer two of the premier 1950s scream queens, Allison Hayes (*The Unearthly, Zombies of Mora Tau, The Hypnotic Eye*) and Yvette Vickers (*Attack of the Giant Leeches*), and that's got to be worth something.

Hayes plays Nancy Archer, a beautiful socialite who is incredibly wealthy but miserable. (Those of us who aren't rich always like to think that those who *are* rich are unhappy, though why they would be is anybody's guess.) Her husband, Harry (William Hudson), who seems to be drunk most of the time, is running around with Honey Parker (Vickers) and he doesn't care who knows about it. Mrs. Archer is inconsolable because she still loves him, and so she, too, seems to be drunk most of the time.

One night after an argument, she storms out of the house, drives to a deserted highway, and almost runs into a gigantic flying saucer, which contains a huge bald alien who looks remarkably like Ike Eisenhower. The alien tries to steal her diamond necklace—it seems he needs diamonds to run his spaceship—and in the process, he scratches her neck and infects her with an alien disease that makes her grow to a height of fifty feet (hence the title of the film).

With her newfound power, the now very large Mrs. Archer invades the town (inexplicably clad in a bikini), destroying a number of buildings in her search for her husband. She smashes through the roof of the bar where Harry hangs out, killing Honey in the process, clutches him in her enormous fist, and carries him around kicking and screaming until she bumps into some high-tension wires and is electrocuted, along with her wayward love.

Most horror films present us with women who are helpless victims and who need a male hero to save them. But there are no such women in this movie, and that's refreshing. It is even possible to view *Attack of the 50 Foot Woman* as an early feminist flick, but it is, more likely, an expression of a 1950s society's fear of women who do not know their place. The movie suggests that, if a woman happens to come by a bit of power, she will use it to destroy the local community and crush her lover to bits—hardly a flattering image but one that still shows up in a lot of more contemporary films.

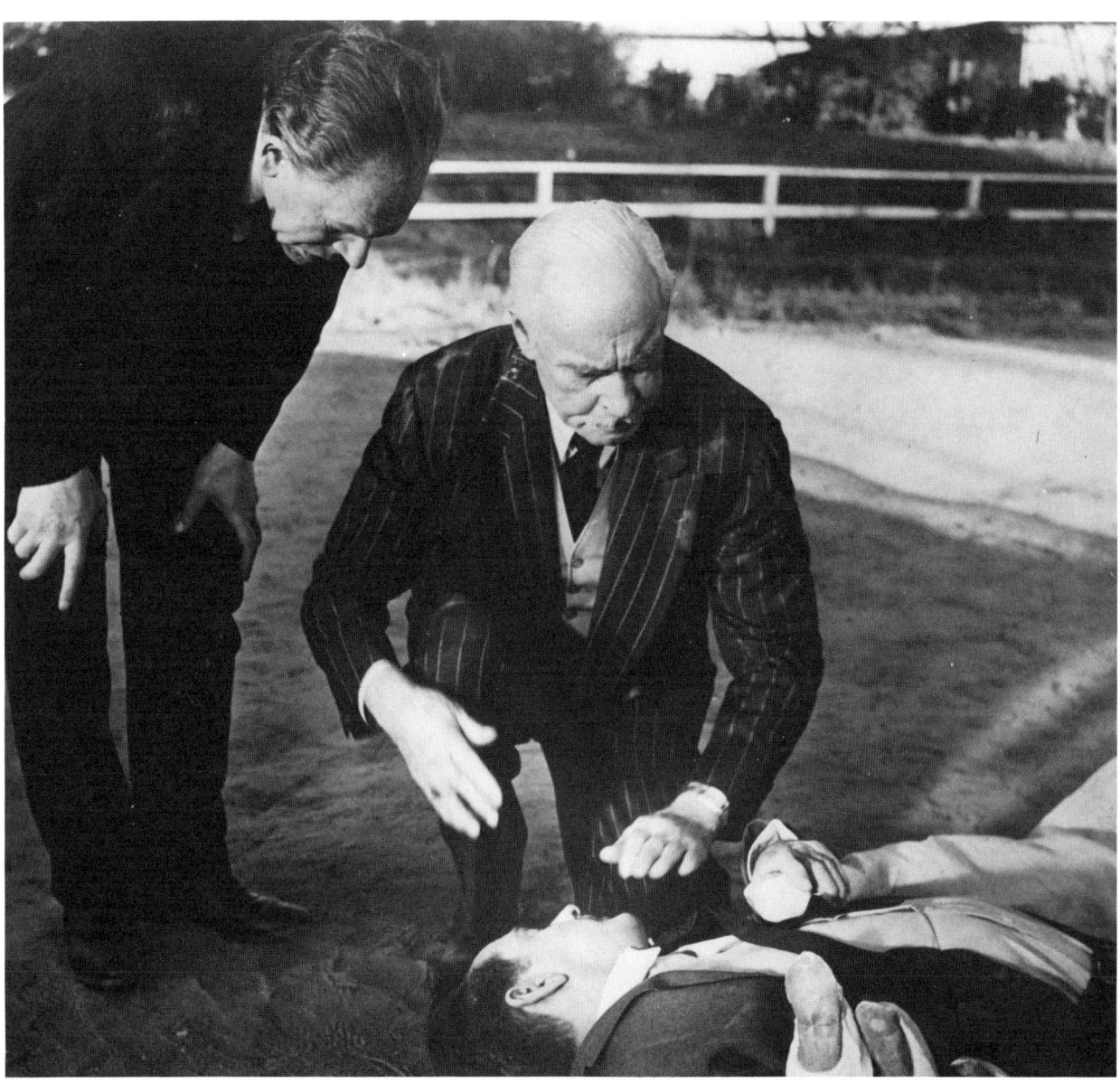

Dr. von Loeb (Otto Waldid) and Dr. Cushing (Roy Gordon) examine the lifeless corpses of Harry (Willian Hudson) and Nancy (Allison Hayes) at the end of *Attack of the 50 Foot Woman*. (Courtesy Hollywood Book and Poster)

Audrey Rose

1977

Director: Robert Wise; *Producers:* Joe Wizan and Frank de Felitta; *Screenplay:* Frank de Felitta

CAST:
Marsha Mason, Anthony Hopkins, John Beck, Susan Swift, Norman Lloyd, Robert Walden

ORIGINAL RELEASE: United Artists
VIDEO: MGM/UA Home Video

Here's another bizarre film that owes its very existence to *The Exorcist*, although, with a cast like this and a director like Robert Wise *(The Day the Earth Stood Still, The Haunting, West Side Story, The Sound of Music)*, *Audrey Rose* could hardly be called just another mindless *Exorcist* rip-off. Even so, the similarities are hard to ignore—the eleven-year-old girl who seems to be possessed by something that is not herself, the confused and worried mother, the stranger who arrives on the scene with all the answers. We've seen all this before. But, as Elliot Hoover (Anthony Hopkins) points out, there is one significant difference between the two films: "We're not talking about possession. We're talking about reincarnation."

The Templetons are a happy, well-to-do New York family—father Bill (John Beck), mother Janice (Marsha Mason), and daughter Ivy (Susan Swift)—until a stranger begins to stalk them. Some of the most terrifying scenes come early on when Janice sees the man hanging around Ivy's school and their apartment building. Bill reports the stalker to the police, but because the man has never done anything to harm anyone, there is nothing the law can do.

The Templetons—Janice (Marsha Mason), Ivy (Susan Swift), and Bill (John Beck)—have a little reincarnation problem in *Audrey Rose*.

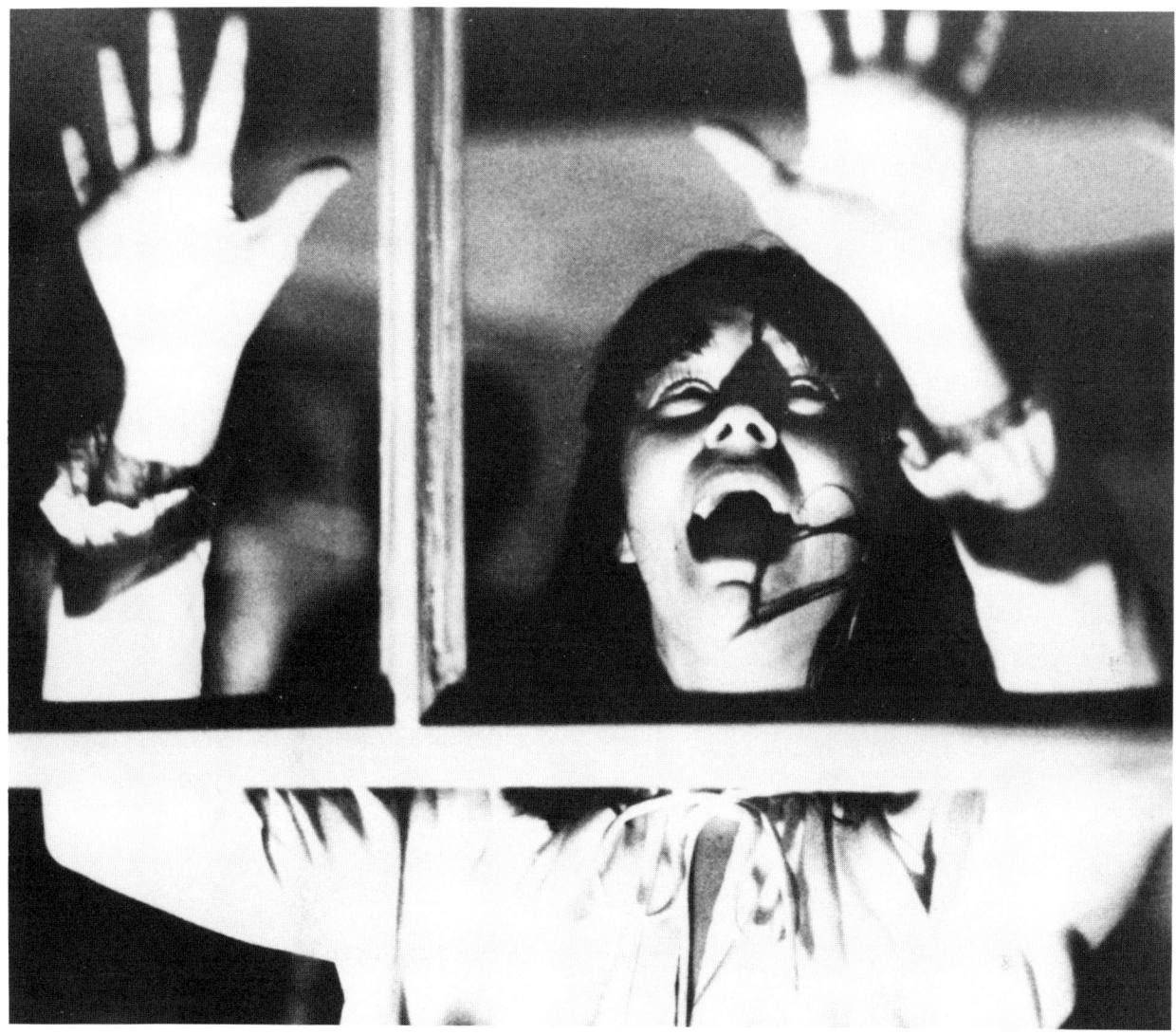
Ivy (Susan Swift) burns her hands on a cold window, reliving the fiery death of her previous incarnation.

At last, the stranger contacts the Templetons, introduces himself as Elliot Hoover, and politely asks if they can meet and talk. They do, and Hoover tells them about the death of his wife and daughter, Audrey Rose, in an auto accident eleven years before. Later, a psychic told him that his daughter was still alive, that she had been reincarnated, and he believes this. In fact, according to what the psychic said, Hoover is convinced that Ivy Templeton is the reincarnation of Audrey Rose.

The Templetons don't take this seriously, despite the fact that Ivy has a history of fits and night terrors. Their lawyer, however, urges them to invite Hoover to their home where he will be present as a witness to hear Hoover's demands. But, in fact, his wishes are very simple: "I'd just like the chance to see Ivy occasionally."

While he is in the apartment, Ivy has another fit and burns her hands on the cold glass of a window, reliving the moment in which Audrey Rose died in the burning car. Hoover comforts her by calling her Audrey Rose, and Janice begins to believe his story, though Bill does not.

Then things become even more complicated. "Your daughter is in mortal danger," Hoover tells Janice. "My daughter's soul returned too soon." Apparently, the soul that Ivy and the late Audrey Rose share wants to return to death so it can prepare for yet another life.

At last, again during one of her fits, Hoover takes Audrey Rose out of her parents' apartment after a fight with Bill. Hoover is arrested and charged with kidnapping. The rest of the film is the trial, in which defense attorney Brice Mack (Robert Walden) tries to convince the jury that Hoover is not a kidnapper because Ivy really

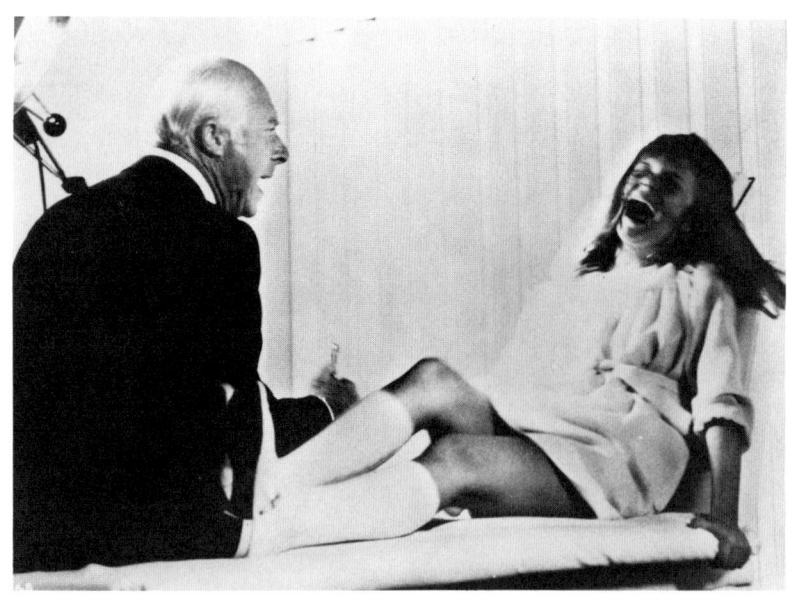

Dr. Lipscomb (Norman Lloyd) takes Ivy (Susan Swift) back to her former life through hypnosis.

In the final moments of her new life, Ivy Templeton (Susan Swift) becomes *Audrey Rose*.

is the reincarnation of his daughter. We hear the testimony of Indian mystics and other experts, but the clincher comes when Mack asks Janice, "Do you believe that your daughter, Ivy, is the reincarnation of Mr. Hoover's daughter, Audrey Rose?" Janice says, "Yes."

The district attorney calls for a test of the child under hypnosis, but this works too well. While she is hypnotized, Ivy *becomes* Audrey Rose at the moment of her death, and psychiatrist Lipscomb (Norman Lloyd) is unable to snap her out of it. Amazingly, Ivy/Audrey Rose dies—again. If you believe in reincarnation, this is a happy ending—"Her soul is set free," as Elliot says. But if you don't, the closing sequence to the film is depressing.

Audrey Rose, like *The Exorcist*, addresses the fears of every parent who has ever looked at his or her child and said, Who is this person? Kids do strange and crazy things; that's simply a fact. *The Exorcist* explains this by saying that they might be possessed. *Audrey Rose* explains it by saying they might be the reincarnation of somebody else. But the truth is that they're just being kids, and such simplistic, mystical explanations of their behavior don't get us very far.

The performances in *Audrey Rose* are remarkable—Hopkins is particularly compelling—but the movie does what no work of fiction should ever do. It preaches. In fact, it is little more than propaganda for reincarnation, with endless lectures by Hoover and other experts on how it works and how true it is. The movie simply tells us what to think, as if we were incapable of thinking for ourselves. Whether reincarnation really *is* true or not is beside the point. Propaganda makes for boring films, and in the end, that's what *Audrey Rose* is.

Barn of the Naked Dead

ALTERNATE TITLE:

Terror Circus

1973

Director/producer: Gerald Cormier; *Screenplay:* Roman Valenti and Ralph Harolde

CAST:
Andrew Prine, Manuella Thiess, Sherry Alberoni, Gyl Roland

ORIGINAL RELEASE: Twin World

VIDEO: Midnight Video

Here's another horror movie that doesn't live up to its title. There is a barn, and by the end of the film, there are a lot of dead people. But no one ever gets naked. So where does the title come from? Probably the writers felt that *Barn of the Clothed Dead* just didn't have enough zip.

Three showgirls are on their way to Las Vegas when their car breaks down in the desert. A guy named Andre (Andrew Prine) offers to let them use the phone in his nearby house, but when they get there, he adds the three to the collection of young women he keeps chained in the barn.

Andre is kind of a circus nut, and he trains the women to do tricks and stage performances for which he wears a ringmaster's outfit, sporting a whip, which he uses liberally throughout the film. Whenever one of his "animals" proves to be untrainable or tries to escape, he paints her with calves' blood, turns her out into the

Andre (Andrew Prine) studies one of the women he holds prisoner in the *Barn of the Naked Dead*. (Courtesy Hollywood Book and Poster)

Andre (Andrew Prine) decides that Simone (Manuella Thiess) is his mother come back to him at last. *(Courtesy Hollywood Book and Poster)*

desert, and sets his caged mountain lion loose. We never find out how he gets it back in the cage again.

So what's Andre's problem? If you've seen *Psycho*, you already know that the basic trouble is with his mother, who left young Andre and Dad long ago. Andre has to keep his women prisoner so they, too, will not run away.

Andre's father is still around, but there's a problem with him, too. The farm is on a nuclear weapons test site, and thanks to the radioactivity, Dad is now a raving, homicidal mutant. Andre keeps him locked in the shed, but the old boy escapes now and then to slaughter campers and hunters in the area.

Derrick, the showgirls' agent, is worried because they didn't show up for their job in Vegas, and he files a report with the police, then goes looking for them himself. It seems that he is their only hope.

Meanwhile, Andre decides that one of his new tenants, Simone (Manuella Thiess), is his mother returned to him, and so he unchains her and takes her into the house, giving her the opportunity to escape. He catches

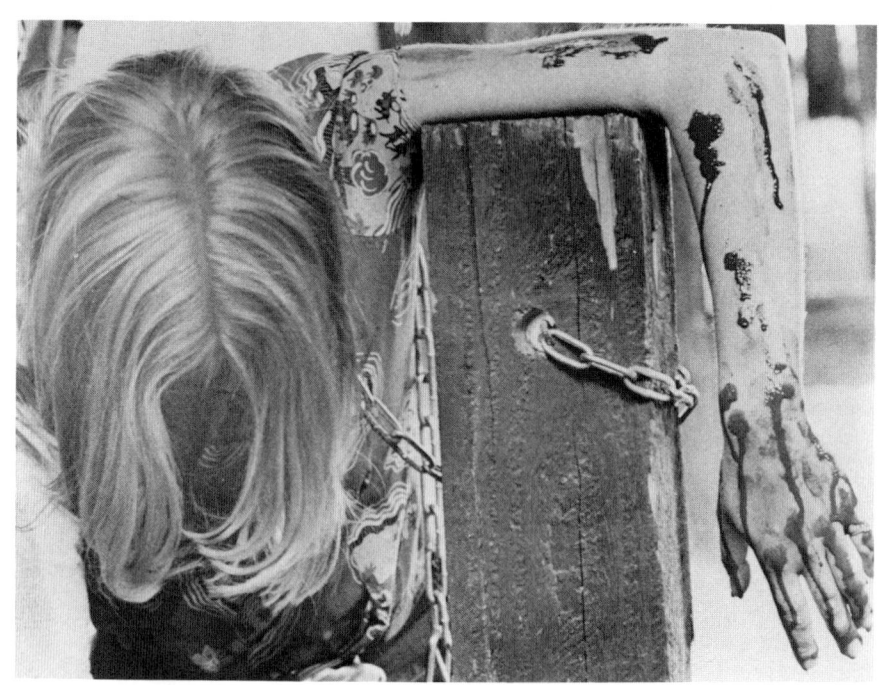

One of Andre's victims. *(Courtesy Hollywood Book and Poster)*

Simone (Manuella Thiess) looks on as Andre (Andrew Prine) gets into more mischief. *(Courtesy Hollywood Book and Poster)*

her again, but Dad breaks loose and kills both Andre and Simone. Then he proceeds to the barn, where he slaughters just about everybody, including the other two showgirls. Surprisingly, Derrick and the police arrive too late to save any of the main characters, and at the end of the film, Andre's mutant dad is still running loose in the desert.

Andre's radioactive dad shows up for the big finish in *Barn of the Naked Dead*.
(*Courtesy Hollywood Book and Poster*)

While a lot of mainstream movies suggest that solid family values are the solution to all our problems, a lot of horror films like this one say that it is the family that is the *cause* of our troubles. If only Andre's mom hadn't run off, and if only his father hadn't refused to move the old homestead from that nuclear test site, everything would probably be okay. The truth is that, in many cases, a film like *Barn of the Naked Dead* is exactly right in what it says about families, and in this sense it is a more honest movie than most.

On the other hand, *Barn of the Naked Dead* pretends to disapprove of what it shows again and again in graphic detail—the physical abuse of women. There is an effort to espouse a phony feminism here. One of the captives says, "He wants to control us. He's like all the other men." Simone points out, "We're not the animals—you are." But this is all pretense. Nobody watches a movie called *Barn of the Naked Dead* in hopes of getting a feminist message. What happens here is that the movie allows us to enjoy the whippings and the torture, and the brief nod to feminism allows us not to feel guilty afterward.

Barn of the Naked Dead is a terrible movie with bad acting and virtually no production values, but it would be a little bit better if it were content simply to be what it is—a piece of junk.

The Beast Within

1982

Director: Phillipe Mora; *Producers:* Harvey Bernhard and Gabriel Katzka; *Screenplay:* Tom Holland

CAST:

Ronny Cox, Bibi Besch, Paul Clemens, Don Gordon, L. Q. Jones, Meshach Taylor, Kitty Ruth Moffat, Logan Ramsey

ORIGINAL RELEASE: United Artists
VIDEO: MGM/UA Home Video

Maybe there should be an Academy Award for the most outlandish premise in a motion picture. If there were, *The Beast Within* would certainly have taken the Oscar in that category for 1982. Even so, the performances and the special effects are so good that you probably won't care how zany and illogical this film really is.

To the best of my knowledge, this is the only were-cicada movie on record. What's a were-cicada? Well, it's a man who turns into a giant cicada, one of those insects that makes a singing noise and that poets seem to be so fond of. And how do you become a were-cicada? Do you have to be bitten by another were-cicada?

In fact, it's not quite that simple. One evening, Eli and Caroline MacCleary (Ronny Cox and Bibi Besch) are driving through rural Mississippi when their car gets stuck. Eli goes for help, and Caroline is attacked and raped by a thing that has just escaped from the basement of a nearby house.

Seventeen years later, the MacClearys' son, Michael (Paul Clemens), the product of that rape, suddenly becomes deathly ill. Doctors think it might be hereditary, so Eli and Caroline, who have never told Michael the truth about his conception, go back to where it happened to find the rapist and, hopefully, to save their son's life.

The MacClearys don't learn much, except that everyone in town seems to be hiding something. Meanwhile, Michael leaves the hospital and follows his parents. He keeps having visions of the house where the thing was kept locked up, even though he's never been there, and these weird cicada sounds keep coming out of him for no particular reason. That night, he arrives in the small town where his parents are also staying, bites the local newspaper owner to death, and meets Amanda (Kitty Ruth Moffat), a teenage girl who will be his first love. When he meets up with Eli and Caroline, they are amazed to see how healthy he seems, and a doctor's tests show that his illness is gone.

Michael does really seem a lot better, but something is still wrong, because at night he keeps going out and killing members of the Curwin family that runs this small Mississippi town. He also begins to speak in the voice of someone named Billy Connor, saying things like, "I came back for 'em—all the Curwins. . . . It took me seventeen years, like the cicadas, but I came back."

Finally, in an incredible transformation scene, Michael bursts through his skin—"just like a cicada"—and goes on a final rampage as a giant bug. Fearing for his life, Judge Curwin (Don Gordon), the leader of the

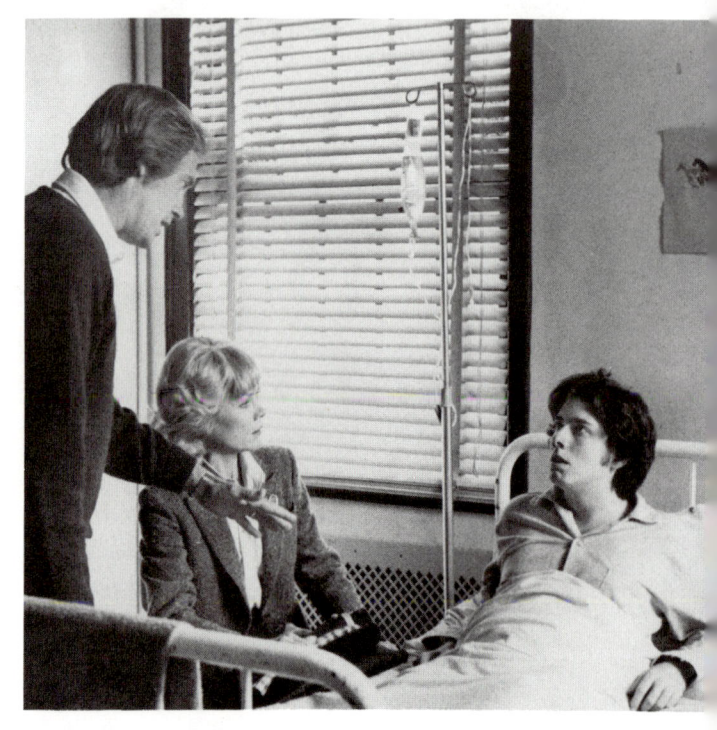

Eli MacCleary (Ronny Cox) and his wife, Caroline (Bibi Besch), are worried about their son, Michael (Paul Clemens), who seems to be suffering from an inherited illness in *The Beast Within*. (*Courtesy MGM/UA Home Video*)

Something from the swamp has possessed Michael MacCleary (Paul Clemens). *(Courtesy MGM/UA Home Video)*

clan, begs Sheriff Pool (L. Q. Jones), Deputy Herbert (Meshach Taylor of TV's *Designing Women*), and the MacClearys to protect him and tells them what really happened.

The judge's brother Lionel (Logan Ramsey), the town undertaker, thought sex was sinful, and so, when he caught local stud Billy Connor with his wife, Lionel killed her, then locked Billy up in the basement of his home and fed him the body of his dead lover, which Billy ate, once he became hungry enough. As the undertaker, Lionel could keep feeding Billy human flesh—the sheriff discovers three dozen skeletons in a mass grave in the local bog, all of them gnawed upon—while the judge and the other Curwins covered everything up. Eventually, Billy became an inhuman monster, and it was he who escaped that fateful night and raped Caroline, producing not only a child but a strange kind of reincarnation of himself. That night, Billy also killed and ate Lionel.

What does this have to do with cicadas? Who knows.

Anyway, the judge's story comes to an end when Michael, now completely transformed, arrives and pulls Curwin's head off. Then the cicada chases Amanda, who is now the last of the Curwins, and rapes her, making sure Billy Connor's legacy will continue. Eli and Caroline arrive, and the mother shoots and kills her only son.

All of this seems to make perfect sense while you're watching it, but afterward a lot of questions crop up. Why did Lionel keep feeding Billy human flesh, and why would eating people turn Billy into a cicada-person? Why not a june bug or a killer bee or a seven-year locust? And what happened to Billy? What's it all about?

This movie owes a lot to the classic werewolf tales, to *The Wolf Man* and particularly to the British film *Curse of the Werewolf* in which lycanthropy is also hereditary and the main character is also the product of a rape perpetrated by a man who has been wrongfully impris-

29

oned and reduced to the status of an animal. Like the werewolf, Michael the were-cicada is not responsible for what he is, and we sympathize with him.

In our modern American culture, we don't consider heredity to be important. After all, according to the American dream, anyone—no matter how lowly his or her origin might be—can succeed. We tend to dislike people who are born with the proverbial silver spoon, and we particularly love those rags-to-riches stories in which someone from a disadvantaged background makes it big. Heredity is a European concept—the divine right of kings and all that—and it is a concept that Americans did away with early in our history.

And yet, in recent years, Americans have developed a real desire to get to know their roots, to discover where they came from, to get a sense of their heritage. Why? Maybe because the very notion of the American dream cuts people off from their history and their traditions by making the future more important than the past, by discounting where you've been in favor of where you're going. Maybe, in our constant orientation toward the future, we Americans feel that we've missed something important.

Getting back to one's roots is what *The Beast Within* is all about, though the movie suggests that it might not be such a good idea. Even so, the fact that we can respond to this film indicates that we suspect heredity might be important after all, that perhaps individuals don't have complete control over their destinies.

Whether we are right or wrong about that, of course, is anybody's guess. But it makes for a hell of a horror film.

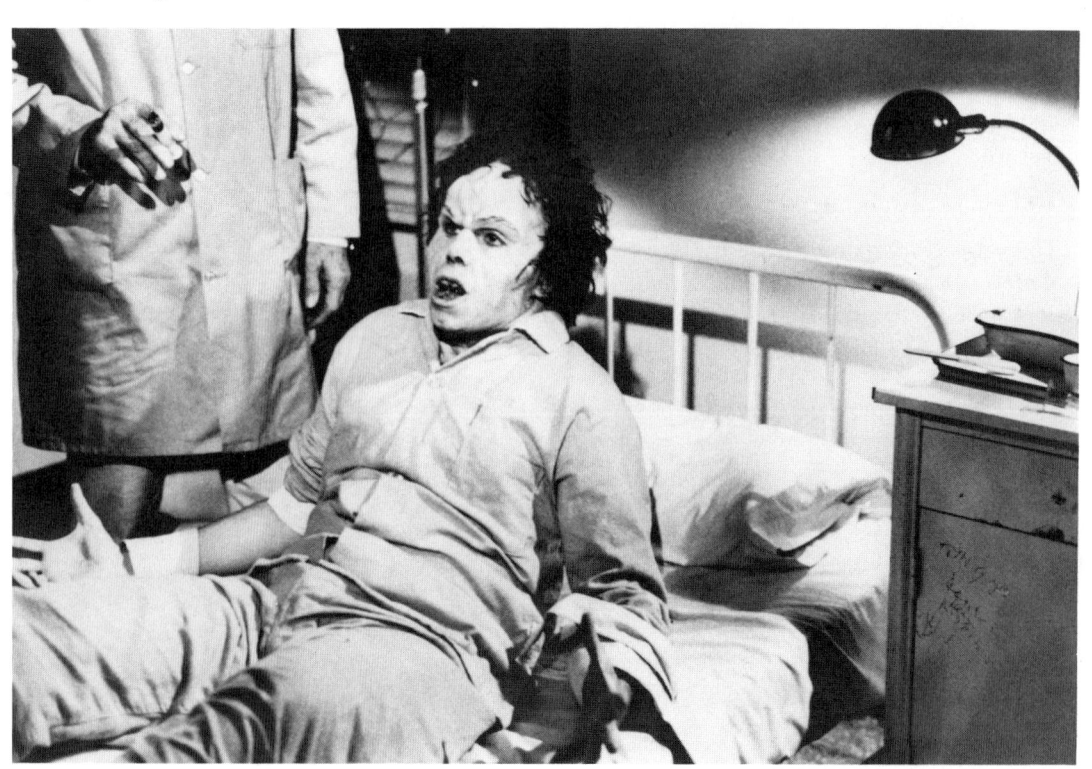

Michael (Paul Clemens) becomes a murderous lunatic who seeks revenge against the entire Curwin clan. *(Courtesy MGM/UA Home Video)*

The transformation from teenage boy to teenage cicada begins. *(Courtesy MGM/UA Home Video)*

Ben

1972

Director: Phil Karlson; *Producer:* Mort Briskin; *Screenplay:* Gilbert Ralston

CAST:
Lee Harcourt Montgomery, Joseph Campanella, Arthur O'Connell, Rosemary Murphy, Meredith Baxter

ORIGINAL RELEASE: Cinerama Releasing
VIDEO: Prism Entertainment

The idea behind this sequel was, if you liked *Willard*, you'll love *Ben*. In fact, however, if you really did like *Willard*, you'll probably hate *Ben*. *Willard*, you might remember, was a striking and terrifying film about a very disturbed young man who trains rats to deal with his problems and his enemies, though, in the end, his rat army proves to be too independent for him to control. *Ben*, on the other hand, is nothing more than a sentimental boy-and-his-rat story. Though it was in theatrical release, it has a made-for-TV feel to it, probably because it is so mindless and so completely safe for public consumption.

The beginning of *Ben* is the best part because it recapitulates what happened in *Willard*, using scenes from the original film. Then it's all downhill. Detective Kirtland (Joseph Campanella) is investigating the killings from the first movie, though he and his cohorts are not prone to believe that there is an army of killer rats loose in the city.

Danny Garrison (Lee Montgomery) knows better, though. Danny is a little kid who lives with his mother (Rosemary Murphy) and sister, Eve (Meredith Baxter), in a fatherless family, and he is lonely. On top of that, he has a heart condition, and he is terminally cute. But he is also very talented. For one thing, he can play "Moonlight Sonata" on the harmonica. He is a puppeteer and a composer, too, who writes the maudlin love theme "Ben's Song" as a tribute to his friendship with the leader of the rat army.

Yes, Danny meets Ben when the rat comes into the Garrison house looking to hide out from the cops, and the two become fast and eternal friends. Danny even talks about Ben to his mother and sister and, later, to Kirtland, but, of course, everyone believes that Ben is only an imaginary playmate. But we know different. We see Danny and Ben snuggling together in bed at night

Danny Garrison (Lee Harcourt Montgomery) and his new friend *Ben*—another boy-and-his-rat story.

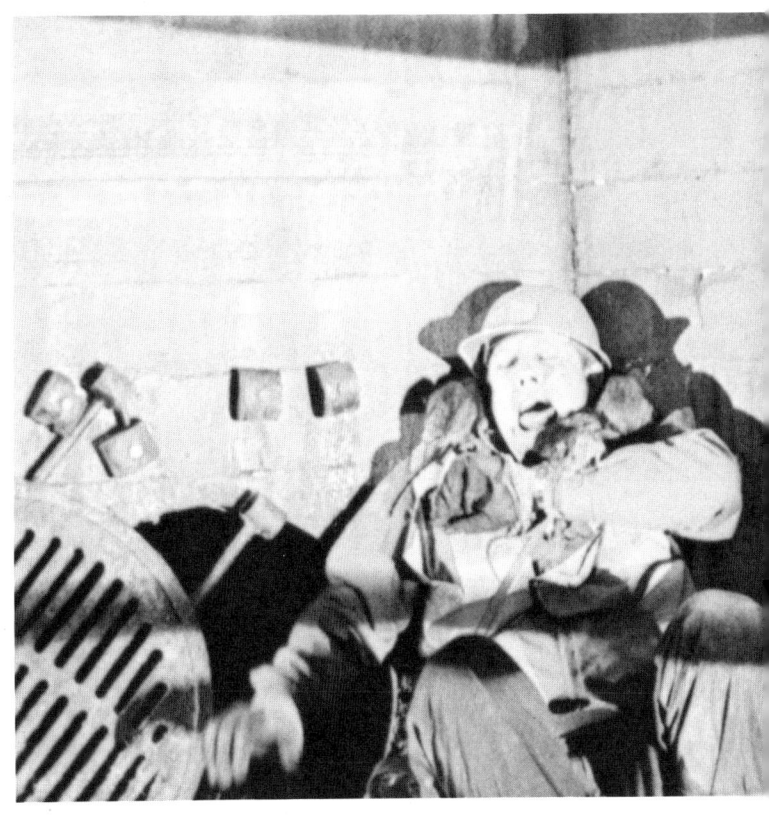

Ben's army of rats claims another victim in the sewer.

and kissing. We see Danny giving Ben rides on his toy train. We see Ben and his rat buddies save Danny from the local bully. We even see Danny make a rat puppet that performs the cheery song "Start the Day" for Ben's entertainment.

Oh, this is awful!

Eventually, the police realize that there really is an army of rats running amok, and they take to the sewers with flamethrowers and fire hoses. Sickly Danny goes to the sewers, too, to save Ben—"You're the best friend I ever had"—and sister Eve goes after Danny. The two kids are almost killed in the battle between cops and rats, but they manage to escape.

The rats are wiped out, but the wounded Ben makes his way back to the Garrison home where Danny promises to nurse him back to health and to be his buddy forever. The big question at the end of the film is, Will Danny become the next Willard?

The answer is no. Danny is too sweet ever to become another Willard, and Ben has been humanized through his friendship with the kid, so he really doesn't want to eat people anymore. We humans are safe.

Though *Ben* is the sequel to *Willard,* it manages to undermine everything the original film tried to say. In *Willard,* it is clear that humans do not have dominion over the animal world. Human civilization is at the mercy of the rats, and if they decide to take over, there doesn't seem to be much that we can do about it in our defense. In *Ben,* on the other hand, the authorities manage to wipe out the rats pretty easily, and the transformation of Ben from rat leader to household pet indicates that we humans really are superior to the

Danny (Lee Harcourt Montgomery) goes down to the sewer to meet Ben's pals.

The star of the show—Ben.

animals after all, because what they really want is to be like us. In effect, *Ben* takes an intelligent, thoughtful film such as *Willard* and simply cancels it out.

By the way, "Ben's Song," sung by a young Michael Jackson, was a hit single and was even nominated for an Academy Award. It is, to my knowledge, the only love theme to a rat that ever had a shot at winning an Oscar.

Beyond the Door

ALTERNATE TITLES:

Chi Sei?,
The Devil Within Her,
Who?

1975

Director: Ovidio Assonitis (Oliver Hellman); *Producers:* Edward L. Montoro, Ovidio Assonitis, Giorgio Rossi; *Screenplay:* Roberto d'Ettare Piazzoli, Richard Barrett

CAST:
Juliet Mills, Richard Johnson, Gabriele Lavia, Dana Colin Jr.

ORIGINAL RELEASE: Film Ventures International
VIDEO: Video Treasures

In the field of popular culture, general wisdom has it that, if you want to make some money, simply do a mindless copy of something that has already made some money. This is precisely what director Ovidio Assonitis does for a living—he makes simpleminded clones of other people's films. His *Tentacles,* for instance, is a rip-off of *Jaws.* With *Beyond the Door,* however, he decided to take that extra step. Here, he rips off *The Exorcist* and *Rosemary's Baby* in the same flick. Now there's an idea that's a surefire winner. The problem is that, since he never makes up his mind which of the two films he is copying at any given moment, the result in *Beyond the Door* is a hopeless mishmash that never makes any sense.

Somehow, Assonitis manages to get American and British stars to appear in his atrocities, and he often shoots in California, importing an Italian supporting cast. *Beyond the Door* features Juliet Mills of the famous theatrical family and Richard Johnson, whose film work ranges from the sublime (Robert Wise's *The Haunting*) to the grotesque (Lucio Fulci's *Zombie*).

The movie opens with a voice-over by Johnson, who claims to be the devil himself and who warns us of the reality of things unseen: "That stranger sitting in the seat next to you could be . . ." Wow, is that scary or what?

This opening suggests that Johnson's character is Satan, but, in fact, he is one of the devil's minions named Dimitri. It seems that, some years ago, Dimitri's car went off a cliff, and in that moment, he sold his soul to Satan for ten years more of life. The ten years are almost up, so he and his master strike a new deal involving a pregnant woman.

The woman is Jessica Barrett (Mills), who has a husband, Robert (Gabriele Lavia), and two kids and who is pregnant again, despite the fact that she's been on the pill. She isn't particularly thrilled with the prospect of another child. As she tells her husband, "This baby, I feel as though it's suffocating me, trying to kill me."

Her doctor, George, says that the fetus is growing at a remarkable rate—in fact, she will come to term in a matter of days. Now strange things start to happen—Jessica breaks an aquarium, levitates herself, eats a banana peel she finds on the street, vomits up the conventional green stuff, talks in voices other than her own, and turns her head around 180 degrees. Why is this happening? Because most of it happened in *The Exorcist,* that's why.

33

In *Beyond the Door,* Jessica Barrett (Juliet Mills) is pregnant with a very special baby.

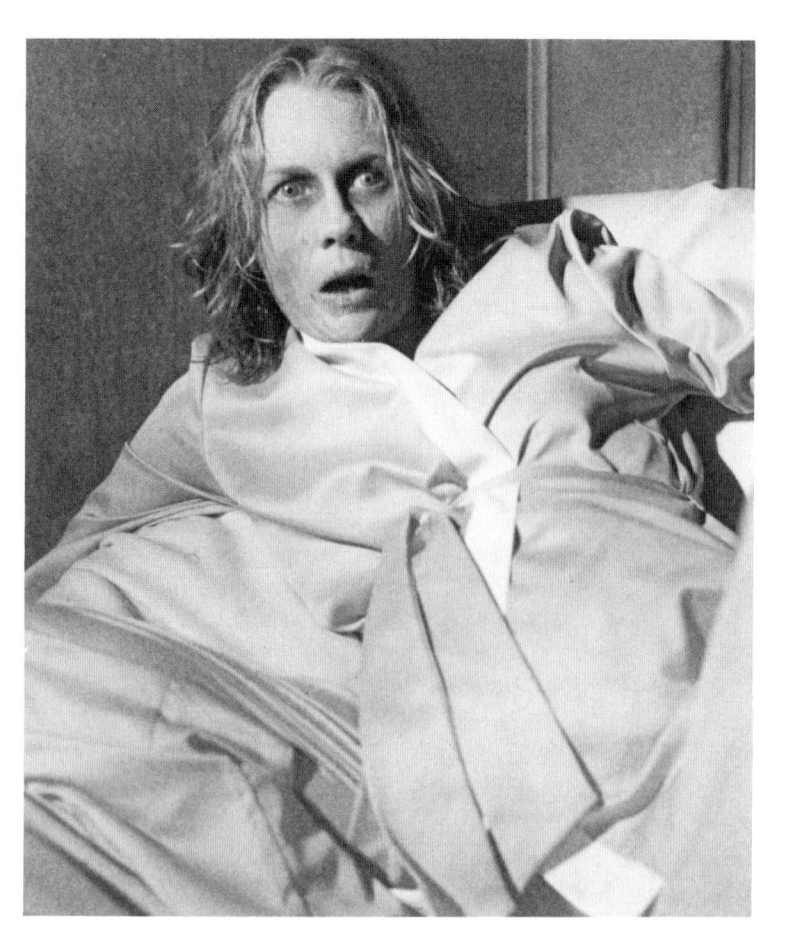

And what does Dimitri have to do with all of this? That isn't very clear. At one point, Jessica says that she met Dimitri once, years ago, and found him fascinating. According to Dimitri, though, they were lovers for a long time before she met her husband, Robert. In any case, Dimitri calls upon Robert and offers his help: "I would like to save her and the child." For absolutely no reason at all, Robert rejects the medical advice of his best friend, George (David Colin, Jr.), and agrees immediately to let his wife's ex-lover solve the family's problems. Wouldn't you?

But what is Dimitri up to here? He claims that he only wants to help the woman he once loved. On the other hand, as we know, he works for Satan, so he can't be all good. As it turns out, he isn't. According to his deal with the devil, he was supposed to supply a pure woman—Jessica—so the devil could impregnate her and be born into the world—this is the *Rosemary's Baby* part of the film. In return, Dimitri would be given more life on earth.

In the end, however, as Jessica explains in the devil's voice, it was all a joke. Satan was merely toying with

Jessica (Juliet Mills) is possessed by the devil—this leads to the usual green vomit and head-spinning.

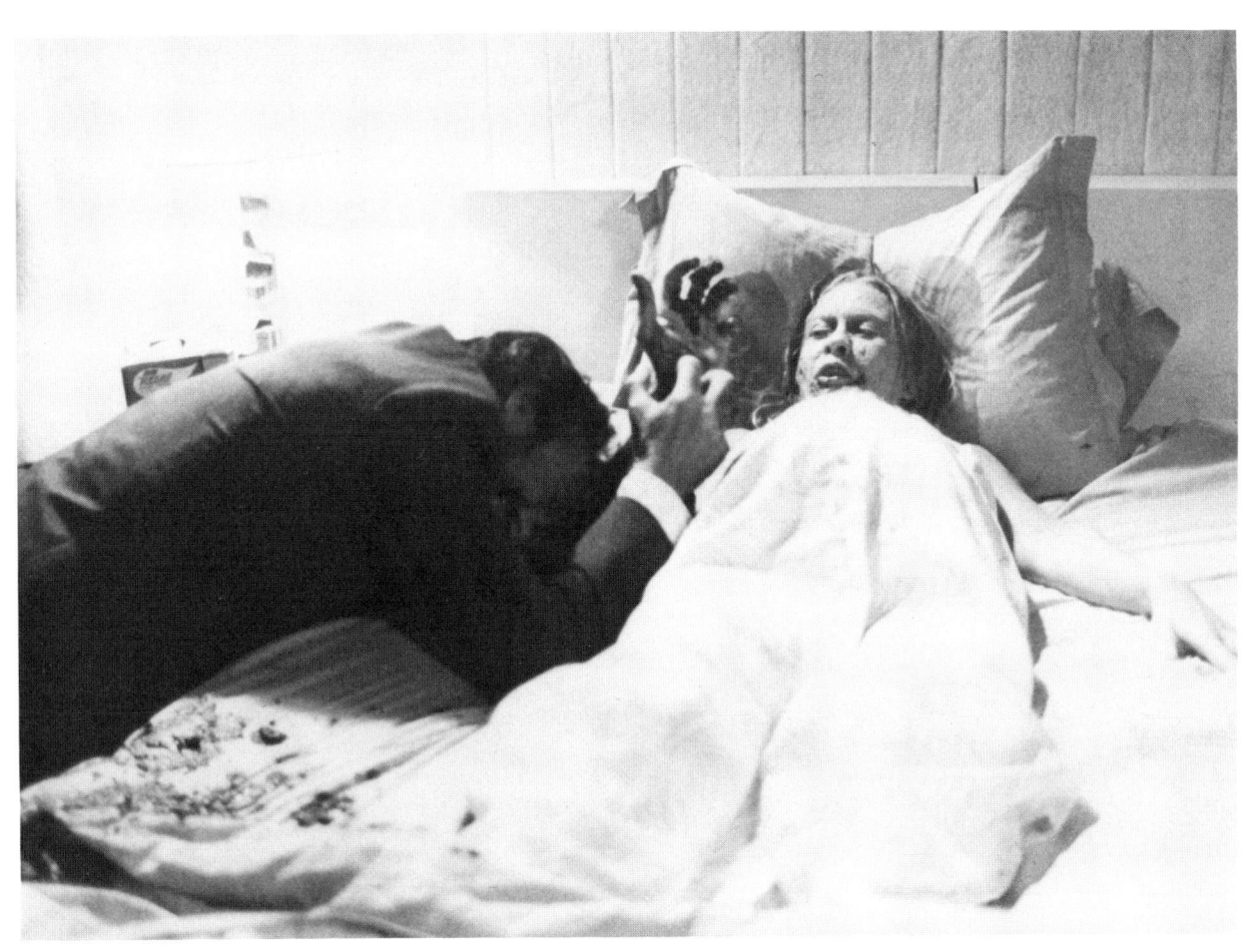

Dimitri (Richard Johnson) arrives at Jessica's (Juliet Mills) bedside to help deliver the baby devil.

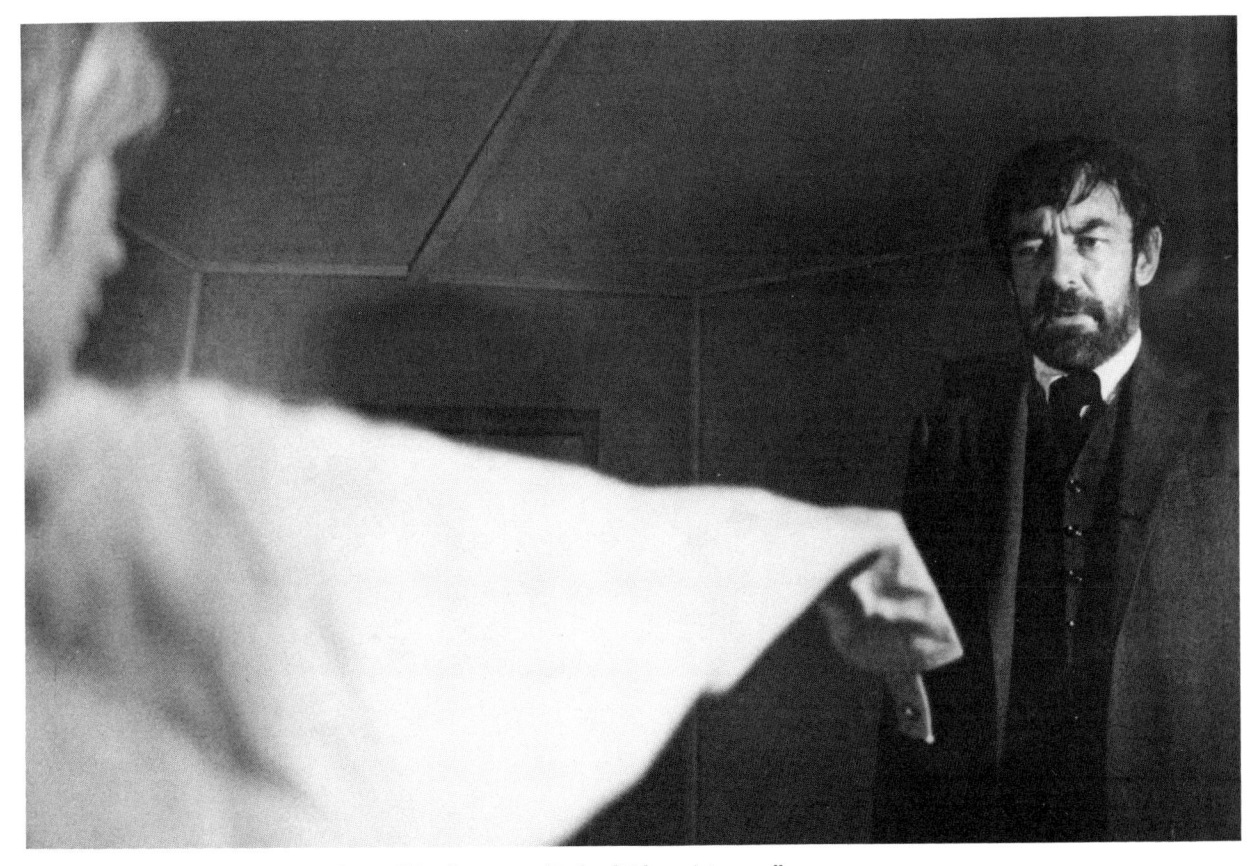

Speaking in Satan's voice, Jessica (Juliet Mills) tells Dimitri (Richard Johnson) it was all a gag in *Beyond the Door*.

Dimitri, tormenting him. The prince of darkness has no intention of being incarnated or of giving Dimitri more life, and so Dimitri's car—which, apparently has been falling off that cliff for the past ten years—finally hits bottom. Dimitri dies and is damned, the baby is stillborn, and Jessica returns to normal, although, at the end, it seems that her son Ken is possessed. The devil explains that, on occasion, he constructs plots to torment people like Dimtri for his own amusement. I'm glad someone was amused by all this.

This plot makes no sense, of course. Assonitis and his cohorts were so eager to get to the special effects in this film, they overlooked the need for a coherent story to tie those special effects together. So when the kids' toys come to life or when a rocking chair starts rocking by itself, all we can do is wonder whether what we are seeing on the screen has anything to do with anything.

The surprising thing about almost all *Exorcist* clones—and about *The Exorcist,* too, for that matter—is that they depict Satan as such a wimp. The idea, of course, is that we should be frightened of him—he is, after all, the prince of darkness and the universal principle of evil—and yet he never seems to be able to do much more than make people say bad words and spit up pea soup. Maybe it's comforting to think that evil is such a feeble, trivial force, but it's hardly frightening. And a glance at this morning's front page ought to convince anyone that the real evil in the world is far from trivial.

Blacula

1972

Director: William Crain; *Producer:* Joseph T. Naar; *Screenplay:* Joan Torres and Raymond Koenig

CAST:
William Marshall, Vonetta McGee, Denise Nicholas, Thalmus Rasulala, Gordon Pinsent

ORIGINAL RELEASE: American International Pictures
VIDEO: HBO Cannon Home Video

In the 1970s, Hollywood remembered, after a lapse of some thirty years, that there was a black moviegoing audience out there, and so was born the "blaxploitation" film. Unfortunately, many white filmmakers merely tapped into black steoreotypes, and the results were often simply embarrassing (if you've ever seen Rudy Ray Moore in *The Human Tornado* or *Disco Godfather,* you

Count Dracula (Charles Macaulay) is taken with Mamuwalde's wife (Vonetta McGee) in *Blacula.*

know what I mean). Sometimes these films were downright dangerous as they glorified black drug dealers and pimps who were able to outwit white cops.

Blacula, which certainly makes the top ten list of most ridiculous movie titles, is among the best of the blaxploitation films. It's scary, funny, and emotionally moving, and this is so mostly thanks to the work of Shakespearean actor William Marshall in the title role. Marshall also appeared in the sequel, *Scream, Blacula, Scream,* and later he was the King of Cartoons on TV's *Pee-wee Herman Show*.

In 1780, African prince Mamuwalde (William Marshall) and his wife, Luva (Vonetta McGee), tour Europe to visit nobles to gain support for an end to the slave trade. They come to Castle Dracula, where the prince discovers that Dracula (Charles McCauley) is not only a racist ("Slavery has merit, I believe") but a vampire. The prince offends him, and Dracula infects him with the curse of vampirism and locks him in a secret tomb with Luva, who is left to die while Mamuwalde is condemned to live on and on.

Almost two hundred years later, American interior

Dr. Gordon Thomas (Thalmus Rasulala) and Lieutenant Peters (Gordon Pinsent) are baffled by a series of vampire-style murders.

Blacula himself (William Marshall).

Sam (Elisha Cook), the one-armed morgue attendant, is victimized by one of Blacula's victims.

Gordon (Thalmus Rasulala) and Michelle (Denise Nicholas) dig up the grave of their friend Billy (Rick Metzler) and discover that he is one of the living dead.

Lieutenant Peters (Gordon Pinsent), Michelle (Denise Nicholas), and Gordon (Thalmus Rasulala) look on as Blacula (William Marshall) disintegrates in the rays of the morning sun.

decorators buy up the contents of Dracula's castle and ship them to Los Angeles where Mamuwalde, now Blacula, is set free. He soon meets Tina (McGee again), the reincarnation of Luva, and offers her eternal life with him.

Meanwhile, Dr. Gordon Thomas (Thalmus Rasulala), working with the police, is trying to solve a number of strange murders. He figures out that a vampire is at work in Los Angeles and eventually discovers that Tina's new friend is behind the killings. Thomas and Lt. Jack Peters (Gordon Pinsent) go after Blacula and find Tina, already vampirized and in her coffin. They put an end to her, and filled with grief—"I've lived again to lose you twice"— Blacula walks out into the sunlight and dies.

The film is effective, not only because the ending is so unexpected, but because *Blacula* does what blaxploitation movies were supposed to do—it offers blacks as strong role models cast outside of the traditional stereotypes. The characters here are positive, intelligent, and well developed. This is particularly true for Mamuwalde/Blacula, who changes from a monster to a painfully human figure. It is too bad that Marshall worked only twice in the horror genre. Like Christopher Lee, he is both dignified and imposing, with a strikingly beautiful and elegant voice. It would have been interesting to see what he might have done if he had been given the chance.

Blood Feast

1963

Director: Herschell Gordon Lewis; *Producer:* David F. Friedman; *Screenplay:* A. Louise Downe

CAST:
Connie Mason, Thomas Wood, Mal Arnold

ORIGINAL RELEASE: Box Office Spectaculars
VIDEO: Continental Home Video

Let me tell you a story. It's the summer of 1963. I'm a teenager, and I'm tooling down the road in my Dodge convertible on my way to the pool hall to meet my buddies. I pass the drive-in, and when I glance out my car window, I see—larger than life on the gigantic silver screen—a guy tearing out a woman's heart in glorious color. "Wow," I say to myself, "I never saw *that* in a movie before."

And that, of course, was the whole point.

Blood Feast was the first real gore film, and it was yet

Blood Feast is one of the few horror films ever made that actually lives up to its advertising. *(Courtesy Hollywood Book and Poster)*

another effort on the part of former English professor H. G. Lewis to show on-screen what Hollywood either could not or would not show. Lewis began his movie career doing nudist-camp films with lots of volleyball matches, but *Blood Feast* introduced something unthinkable into the movies—not just blood but exposed entrails. And amazingly, Lewis asked us to like it, even to laugh at it.

Wealthy socialite Suzette Fremont (Connie Mason, a 1963 *Playboy* Playmate) is having a birthday. Her mother wants something unique for the party, and caterer Fuad Ramses (Mal Arnold) proposes a special Egyptian feast that has not been prepared in five thousand years. Mrs. Fremont (Lyn Bolton) goes for it, not knowing that the feast calls for body parts from a number of young women. Ramses spends most of the film collecting what he will need—a leg here, a tongue there—until he is tracked down by Suzette's policeman boyfriend Pete Thornton (Thomas Wood). The caterer tries to escape by hiding in a garbage truck, but he is accidentally ground up with the rest of the trash.

Herschell Gordon Lewis is to cinema what Henry Miller is to literature—both men spit in the eye of their respective art forms. Like Miller's novels, Lewis's films are enormously energetic and excessive, despite the fact that they are obviously shot with one camera and one microphone on incredibly low budgets. His performers are almost unbelievably bad—you'd think he could make a better film just by picking people off the street at random. In *Blood Feast*, Connie Mason gives new meaning to the word *amateur,* and yet, in spite of her failings (or perhaps because of them), Lewis uses her again in *2,000 Maniacs*.

Lewis seems to revel in the kind of tasteless incompetence that Andy Warhol and his minions would later call camp. But Lewis isn't camp. Lewis is Lewis, and there is no other director quite like him. He manages to be funny and disgusting and offensive and thoroughly enjoyable, all at the same time. *Blood Feast* is extremely violent, even by contemporary standards, and yet it is never grim or serious. It is fun the way a roller-coaster ride is fun, and while, in good conscience, it is impossible to recommend his films, you must see them to know what all the fuss is about.

Blood Orgy of the She-Devils

1973

Director/producer/screenplay: Ted V. Mikels

CAST:
Lila Zaborin, Victor Izay, Tom Pace, Leslie McRae, William Bagdad

ORIGINAL RELEASE: Geneni Film Distributing Company
VIDEO: World Video

No film could possibly live up to this title, and the movie that actually has this title—brought to you by the director of *The Corpse Grinders* and *Astro-Zombies* and the producer of *The Undertaker and His Pals* and *The Worm Eaters*—doesn't even come close. There is almost no blood, definitely no orgy, and absolutely no plot.

There *are* she-devils, though. The movie is a collec-

Mara (Lila Zaborin), the head of the witches' coven, accepts an assignment to kill a United Nations ambassador using her evil arts in *Blood Orgy of the She-Devils*.

Mark (Tom Pace) and Lorraine (Leslie McRae) consult with Dr. Helsford (Victor Izay) to find out what can be done about the witches.

tion of more or less related scenes involving Mara (Lila Zaborin), the head of a coven of scantily clad young witches who attend sabbats and sacrifice men to various demons. Mara also holds the occasional séance in which her Indian guide speaks through her to her assembled guests—not surprisingly, the guide talks like Tonto, because, according to Hollywood wisdom, Indians can never learn to speak proper English: "No take big shiny bird cross big waters."

Lorraine (Leslie McRae) and Mark (Tom Pace), the young lovers of the film, attend one of these séances and report their findings to Dr. Helsford (Victor Izay), Mark's theology professor, who is an expert in witchcraft and the occult. Helsford delivers lectures on the topic over drinks and games of chess, explaining the differences between black magic and white magic, and he warns the two to be careful.

Meanwhile, Mara accepts a contract from a sleazy-looking guy to kill a United Nations ambassador by using her black arts. She does, but then the sleazy guy has Mara killed, or so it seems. But Mara is reincarnated, first as a black cat, then as her old self, and she uses voodoo to get her revenge against her would-be assassins.

In between these various events, Mara shows clients images of their past lives, thus allowing for some historical flashbacks, and she also just sort of hangs around the house, doing incantations with her male assistant Toruke (William Bagdad). Finally, during another sabbat, Helsford gathers three more professors together and they exorcise the demons from Mara's home. The coven members kill each other off, and though Mara tries to escape in the form of a bat, Helsford and his boys capture and burn her.

This is another of those movies in which women who want power are depicted as evil, because, of course, the power they want is power over men. Helsford talks about black magic and white magic, and at the end of the movie we see what he means—evil black magic is magic exercised by women, and good white magic is the province of men.

Early on, during one of his interminable lectures, Helsford condemns the barbaric witch-hunts of past ages, and this gives Mikels the opportunity to offer a flashback that shows a young accused "witch" being tortured with long needles then burned alive while her child is whipped before her eyes—apparently, though Helsford disapproves of such methods, Mikels still thinks they're fun to watch. In the end, though, Helsford and his male cohorts don't mind condemning a dozen or so young witches to death—Lorraine among them—for the good of humanity.

It doesn't make any sense, but what do you expect from a film entitled *Blood Orgy of the She-Devils?*

The Bride

1985

Director: Franc Roddam; *Producer:* Victor Drai; *Screenplay:* Lloyd Fonvielle

CAST:
Sting, Jennifer Beals, Clancy Brown, David Rappaport, Anthony Higgins, Geraldine Page

ORIGINAL RELEASE: Columbia Pictures
VIDEO: RCA/Columbia Home Video

This film offers the occasional nod to its sources, the Universal Frankenstein series that spanned the thirties and forties, in particular James Whale's *Bride of Frankenstein* from 1935, but clearly the intent here is to make, at long last, a "serious" Frankenstein film. *The Bride* proves that, if there is anything worse than a horror movie with nothing to say, it's a horror flick that is desperately trying to say something serious.

Baron Frankenstein (Sting)—in this film, his name, for some reason, is Charles—has already made his monster when the movie opens. Now he's working on a mate (Jennifer Beals) for the creature. As she comes to life, the lab explodes and Charles carries her to safety, wrongly assuming that the male monster has died in the fire.

Frankenstein must have learned a lot between creations, because his first creature is pretty ugly, but his second try results in a beautiful young woman, and he decides to keep her for himself. Like any good romantic, he claims to be profeminist and tells his friend Clerval (Anthony Higgins); "Think of it. She might be made into anything. . . . I might make the new woman—independent, free, as bold and as proud as a man." He names her Eva, after the first woman, and tells her that she is an amnesia victim who was found in the woods and that he has taken it upon himself to care for her.

The film shifts back and forth between Eva's life with Charles and the male creature's life on the road where he meets a dwarf named Rinaldo (David Rappaport), joins a circus, and becomes quite a success. His new friend names him Viktor (which, of course, was Baron Frankenstein's name in the original novel, though in

Baron Charles Frankenstein (Sting) and his assistant create *The Bride* (Jennifer Beals), the perfect woman.

Eva (Jennifer Beals) comes to life, thanks to the efforts of Frankenstein (Sting).

James Whale's *Frankenstein* of 1931, his name, for some reason, is Henry). Things go well until Rinaldo is murdered. Viktor avenges his friend's death and has to run for it.

Meanwhile, Eva is becoming the independent woman Charles thought he wanted, but the baron is having second thoughts about all this feminism stuff. For one thing, his creation is interested in a young cavalry officer, not in him, and this makes him jealous. Even worse, she keeps throwing his own philosophy in his face: "A woman should do as she pleases, just like a man. You taught me that." Clerval states the case perfectly when he says, "The trouble with free women, Charles, is that they're free to despise us."

At last, Charles tells her who she is and where she came from, and she learns of the existence of another creature like her, now supposedly dead. Viktor, of course, is still alive but in jail, charged with murder. But there is a telepathic link between Viktor and Eva because . . . well, that's never explained. Anyway, Charles tries to force himself on his female creation, but Viktor

Eva (Jennifer Beals) doesn't know who she really is.

Viktor (Clancy Brown), Frankenstein's monster, finds a friend in Rinaldo (David Rappaport).

escapes from prison in time to rescue her and throw Frankenstein from the top of the castle tower. Now Viktor is suddenly a lot better looking, because . . . well, that's never explained either. But apparently, free of their creator, the two will live happily ever after and maybe raise some little monsters of their own.

All the time you're watching this movie, you're pretty sure there's something profound going on, but it's hard to know what that might be. There's the feminist message, of course, but that sort of cancels itself out in the end when Eva discovers that, no matter how independent she might be, she still needs a man in her life, even if he's a monster. In fact, when Charles attacks her, proud, bold, and independent Eva faints, and it's up to the male hero, Viktor, to save her, which is exactly what happens in almost every horror movie.

So what could this film be saying? That Frankenstein tampered with things man was not meant to know? That you should always be nice to monsters because, who knows, you may be one yourself? The film must be pretty deep, because everybody in *The Bride* acts as if there's

A fire in the lab threatens Baron Frankenstein (Sting) and Eva (Jennifer Beals) in *The Bride*.

something heavy going down, and, let's face it, no movie would be this boring without offering some kind of life-enhancing message as a reward for sitting through it. If you figure out what that message might be, drop me a line, will ya?

Brides of Blood

ALTERNATE TITLES:

*Brides of the Beast,
Grave Desires,
Island of Living Horrors,
Blood Brides*

1968

Directors: Eddie Romero and Gerrardo de Leon; *Producer:* Eddie Romero

CAST:
Kent Taylor, Beverly Hills, John Ashley, Eva Darren, Mario Montenegro, Oscar Keesee

ORIGINAL RELEASE: Hemisphere Pictures
VIDEO: Regal Home Video

Filipino producer/director Eddie Romero—no relation to George Romero of *Night of the Living Dead* fame—is responsible for this one, the first in his "Blood Island" series.

Dr. Paul Henderson (Kent Taylor), his sexy wife Carla (Beverly Hills), and Peace Corp volunteer Jim Farrell (John Ashley) arrive on Blood Island in the Pacific to discover that all is not well there. As village leader Acadio explains, "We have gone back to primitive ways." These primitive ways include a lottery held every day or so to choose young women who are tied naked to crosses and left as sacrifices for the Evil One, a monster that has the villagers living in fear. The Evil One uses the young women for his sexual gratification, which involves tearing them to pieces. According to Alla (Eva Darren), Acadio's granddaughter, "This is how he satisfies himself."

Scientist Henderson is there to see what effects, if any, the atomic bomb tests of the late 1940s have had on the local plant and animal life. He discovers that trees, plants, and some crabs and insects turn into monstrous creatures by night, only to return to normal in the daylight. "It seems that some living organisms on this island are undergoing drastic mutations." The people on

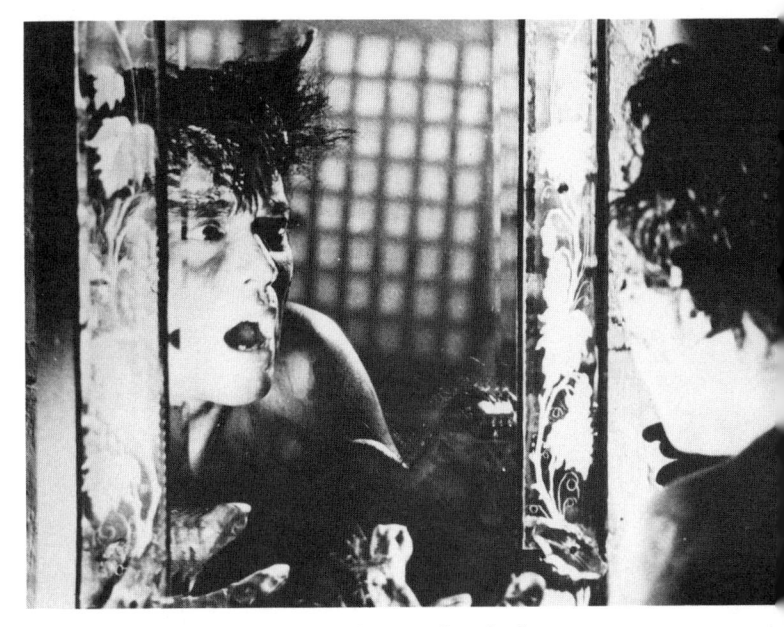

Esteban Powers (Mario Montenegro) discovers that, thanks to a dose of radioactivity, he is the beast of Blood Island.

Carla Henderson (Beverly Hills) is assaulted in the jungle by the monster (Mario Montenegro).

Esteban (Mario Montenegro), after the transformation.

In *Brides of Blood,* the natives indulge in the fertility rites that got them in trouble in the first place.

the island are not affected, however, because they were relocated there after the nuclear tests.

Yet, one islander was exposed to radiation. Esteban Powers (Mario Montenegro) is the local patron, a cultured man who lives in a mansion with an army of dwarf servants and an ugly overseer named Goro (Oscar Keesee). Powers seems to be unaffected by his encounter with radioactivity, except for occasional attacks that he calls migraines. He offers the Hendersons his hospitality, and they accept.

Soon Alla draws the black stone in the lottery—it's amazing that there are any young women left in the village by this time—and is turned out as a sacrifice to the Evil One. Farrell saves her and takes her to Powers's compound for protection from the villagers, who believe the Evil One has been offended.

The monster runs amok again, dismembering Carla in the process, but this time Farrell manages to convince the villagers to go after the thing with torches and burn it. In the end, to no one's surprise, we discover that the Evil One was Esteban all the time. Like the flora and fauna on the island, he mutated into a monster at night and returned to himself by day. With the problem solved, Farrell and the villagers get back to turning Blood Island into a tropical paradise.

The antinuke message is obvious enough, but the image of third-world people is more interesting. Romero's film implies that the villagers on Blood Island were doing the right thing—giving up their culture and becoming more like the Americans—when the Evil One showed up and caused a setback. According to Alla: "We have returned to the ways of our ancestors, and we are not too proud of it." Once the Peace Corp guy shows them that their ignorant and dangerous beliefs are wrong, they get back on track and do what they ought to do—Blood Island becomes another American colony.

There is even the implication that the villagers have brought the Evil One on themselves. Yes, Esteban is a monster because of radioactive testing, but his sexual appetites are only an extension of the natives' fertility rites, which we witness in the film. Clearly, the movie urges that this obsession with sex is dangerous. Carla is a nymphomaniac, and in the end, when she is torn to pieces by Esteban, the look on her face indicates that she is finally getting what she wants. The young island women who are sacrificed to the Evil One seem to be getting what's coming to them, too, because they also participate in the mating rituals, which, like other "primitive ways," ought to be stopped, now that the Peace Corp has arrived.

According to the film, third-world people who cannot or will not become Americanized deserve whatever punishment comes their way. The fact that *Brides of Blood* was made in a third-world country by a third-world producer/director makes this message all the more disturbing.

The Brood

1979

Director/screenplay: David Cronenberg; *Producer:* Claude Heroux

CAST:
Oliver Reed, Samantha Eggar, Art Hindle, Cindy Hinds

ORIGINAL RELEASE: New World Pictures
VIDEO: Embassy Home Video

For a long time, David Cronenberg has been turning out horrifying films about the ways in which the human body might be used and abused by science and technology, and *The Brood* is certainly one of these. Dr. Hal Raglan (Oliver Reed) is a famous psychologist/guru whose Institute of Psychoplasmics is dedicated to curing patients by getting them to bring their inner angers out of themselves in the form of welts, bruises, and other growths on their bodies. Nola Carveth (Samantha Eggar) is his prize

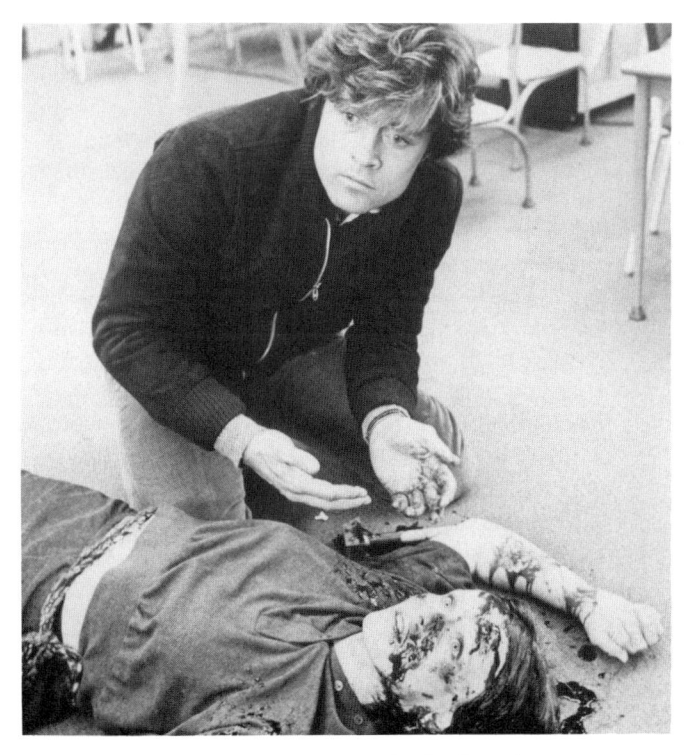

Frank Carveth (Art Hindle) finds that his daughter's teacher (Susan Hogan) has been murdered by *The Brood*.

Nola Carveth (Samantha Eggar) has been undergoing a strange transformation.

pupil because she develops the power to give birth to deformed kids ("They're the children of her rage") who exist independently of her and who kill whenever she is upset. During the course of the film, they wipe out her divorced parents—apparently, the mother abused Nola when she was a child—and a teacher she thinks is having an affair with her husband, Frank (Art Hindle).

The Carveths have a little daughter, Candice (Cindy Hinds), and Frank suspects Nola of beating her when she visits at the Institute, though in fact the child is being abused by the brood whenever Mom gets mad. But Frank is afraid that, if he files for divorce, Nola will get custody of their daughter. So he sets out to prove that Raglan is a fraud in order to establish legal grounds for keeping Candy away from the Institute and Nola.

The kids kidnap Cindy, and in the effort to get her away from her mutant brothers and sisters, Raglan is killed, though Frank puts an end to the problem by strangling Nola, for without her rage to support them, the members of the brood die. Candy is rescued, but the marks on her arm at the end of the film suggest that she has inherited her mother's ability.

The Brood is an effective indictment of pop and fad psychology, which, according to the film, is not only dangerous but also fails to deal with real problems, in this case child abuse, which is passed on from generation to generation. But there is more than this going on here.

In a man's world, women still wield one vital power—the power to reproduce, though of course they can't do this alone. But what if they could? What if women could have children on their own, by their own decision, without the male having to take part? They would then hold supreme power because they could decide whether the human race would continue or not.

Interestingly, *Frankenstein* and all the movies ever based on that familiar story deal with the same issue, but from a different perspective. The story of Frankenstein tells of a man who tries to "give birth" on his own, without the need for a woman, and of course the tale shows the disastrous consequences of going against the natural order of things. In *The Brood*, it is a woman who challenges this natural order.

But the analogy doesn't hold because, more often than not, the male Frankenstein figure is destroyed by his creation. Nola isn't; she is killed by her husband, the man whose position she has taken over, the man she has made superfluous, and in a horror film, the woman who tries to assume the power of the male is evil and must be put to death. In the end, *The Brood* blames women for all the

Dr. Raglan (Oliver Reed) is attacked by his own creations.

Candice (Cindy Hinds) is at the mercy of *The Brood*.

trouble. It was Nola's mother who abused her, Nola who (indirectly) abuses Candy, and Candy who will abuse her own children. In this film, women are a threat and must be kept in their place. The world only becomes normal/good when the men—in this case, Frank—are in control.

The Corpse Grinders

1971

Director/producer: Ted V. Mikels; *Screenplay:* Arch Hall and Joseph L. Cranston

CAST:
Sean Kenney, Monika Kelly, Sanford Mitchell, J. Byron Foster, Ray Dannis, Warren Ball

ORIGINAL RELEASE: Geneni Releasing Corporation
VIDEO: World Video

Despite the fact that there are millions of cat lovers in the world, the media almost always give cats a bad rap. Think about Sylvester and Tweety, Mr. Jinx and Pixie and Dixie, or Tom and Jerry. And now this . . .

There is a wave of mysterious and apparently unmotivated cat attacks against people in the city, and when nurse Angie Robinson's (Monika Kelly) gentle and loving kitty assaults her boyfriend, Dr. Howard Glass (Sean Kenney), the two get suspicious.

What we know and what Angie and Howard have to find out is that a certain Mr. Landau (Sanford Mitchell)

Caleb (Warren Ball) is the caretaker of
Fairwell Acres in *The Corpse Grinders*.

and his partner Maltby (J. Byron Foster) have been grinding up human bodies at the Lotus Cat Food factory and using the meat in their product, which has become the meal of choice for cats in the know. This explains the attacks on people, of course; the cats have developed a taste for human flesh. It makes you wonder why dogs don't attack horses, doesn't it?

Landau has a number of suppliers, including some very strange morticians and Caleb (Warren Ball), groundskeeper at Farewell Acres, who robs graves and sells the meat by weight to the Lotus company: "That's 833 pounds we got tonight. Makes a total of 2,485 pounds they owe me for, at twenty cents a pound."

Howard and Angie become more involved when an elderly woman is killed by her cat. Howard does an autopsy on the animal and discovers human flesh in its stomach. Meanwhile, the production line at Lotus has to shut down temporarily for lack of "ingredients." Landau solves the problem by putting Willie (Charles Fox), his cleanup man, into the grinder, and this leads him to an important realization: "The world is full of ingredients."

Just how did Landau and Maltby come up with the idea of feeding people to cats? Like so many great

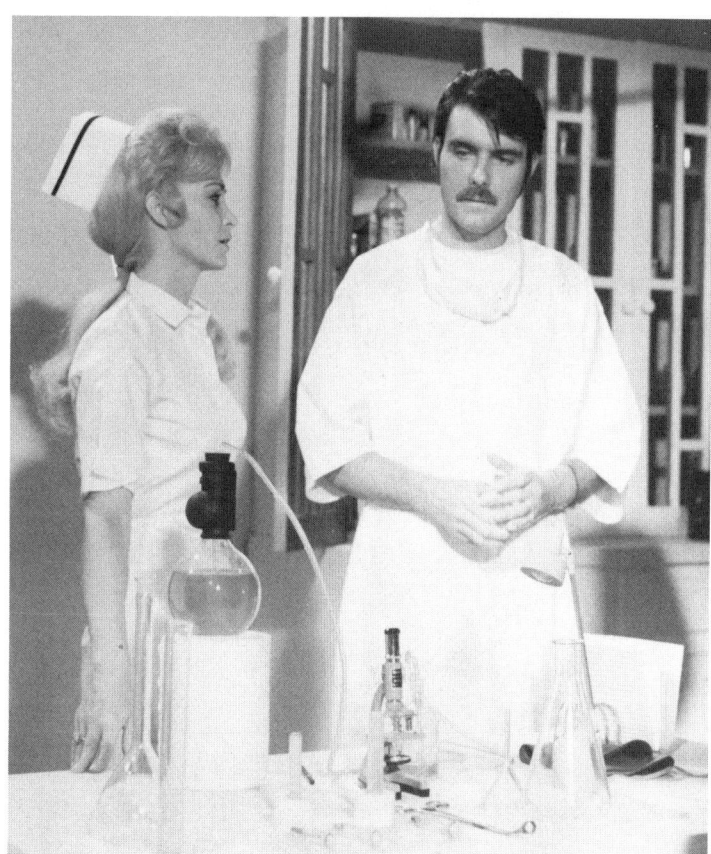

Nurse Angie Robinson (Monika Kelly) and Dr. Howard Glass (Sean Kenney) are puzzled by the recent wave of cat attacks against humans.

51

Maltby (J. Byron Foster) and Landau (Sanford Mitchell) buy corpses from Caleb (Warren Ball) to grind into cat food at their factory.

Maltby (J. Byron Foster) catches Angie (Monika Kelly) spying at the factory and plans to put her into the corpse grinder. Note the nearby trash can full of "ingredients."

discoveries, it was an accident. Financier Carlton Babcock (Ray Dannis) was the owner of the Lotus company, and Landau and Maltby were his managers. When Babcock decided to close down the factory, there was an argument, and Maltby killed him. To get rid of the body, Landau put him in the grinder. The rest is history. "That added ingredient turned out to be a delicacy to felines."

Eventually, however, Landau and Maltby get greedy. Landau kills Caleb rather than paying up what he owes. Maltby catches Angie sneaking around the factory and gets ready to leave town with the company profits, but Landau kills him, too, and puts him in the grinder. Howard and a private investigator who has been looking for Babcock arrive in time to save Angie from the same fate, and Landau is shot to death.

Horror films like *The Stuff* suggest that big corporations don't necessarily make consumer welfare a top priority when it comes to turning a profit, and *The Corpse Grinders* makes the same point about small, independent companies like Lotus Cat Food, which, apparently, are willing to foist anything off on the public, just to make a quick buck. Business is business, as they say, and as Landau explains, "We're businessmen."

But, of course, as an independent film director and producer of such movies as *Astro-Zombies, Blood Orgy of the She-Devils,* and *The Corpse Grinders,* Ted V. Mikels is a small businessman, too. That's enough to make you stop and think.

Count Dracula's Great Love

ALTERNATE TITLES:

*Gran Amor del Conde Dracula,
Dracula's Great Love,
Vampire Playgirls*

1972

Director: Javier Aguirre; *Producer:* F. Laura Polop; *Screenplay:* Jacinto Molina (Paul Naschy) and Javier Aguirre

CAST:
Paul Naschy, Haydee Politoff, Rossana Yanni, Mirta Miller, Ingrid Garbo, Vic Winner

ORIGINAL RELEASE: Cinema Shares
VIDEO: Sinister Cinema

Twenty years before Francis Ford Coppola directed the blockbuster hit *Bram Stoker's Dracula,* this Spanish production was trying to remake the vampire tale into a love story. Unfortunately, Paul Naschy is hopelessly miscast in the role of Dracula. He is built like a professional wrestler, which makes him perfect for his series of werewolf movies but all wrong for the suave, distinguished vampire. Even so, Naschy always gets the girls in his movies because, under his real name, Jacinto Molina, he's the guy who writes the screenplays.

In the opening sequence, two deliverymen bring a large wooden box to the abandoned Kargos Clinic in Transylvania, located just down the street from Castle Dracula. Looking for something to steal, they open the crate and discover a coffin containing only a skeleton. Suddenly, one of them is attacked by a vampire. The other gets an ax in his head and rolls down a flight of stairs. Apparently, the director really liked this scene, because it repeats in slow motion more than half a dozen times as the opening credits roll.

Four young women and a man are riding along the road near Castle Dracula when their carriage loses a wheel. Their driver is killed, and they go to the clinic for help, where they meet Dr. Wendell Marlow (Naschy), a scientist who has recently bought the place. He offers to put them up until they can get a carriage to take them back to the city.

Next morning, while the doctor is away (it seems he's never around during the daylight hours) and lovers Imre (Vic Winner) and Marlene (Ingrid Garbo) are off on their own, Senta (Rosanna Yanni), Elke (Mirta Miller), and Karen (Haydee Politoff) explore the clinic. In the library, they find the diary of a certain Prof. Van Helsing and learn about Dracula. It seems that the prince of darkness can never really die—given the number of Dracula movies that have been made over the years, we should certainly know this by now. But Dracula can only attain his full powers by finding a virgin who loves him so completely that she will give herself to him by her own choice. Her blood will then be used to resurrect Dracula's daughter, Countess Rhodna, and the three will rule as the royal family of the undead.

The Count's recent converts (Rossana Yanni, Vic Winner, and Ingrid Garbo) roam Castle Dracula in search of victims in *Count Dracula's Great Love.*

This isn't Count Dracula's great love, though she seems a likely prospect.

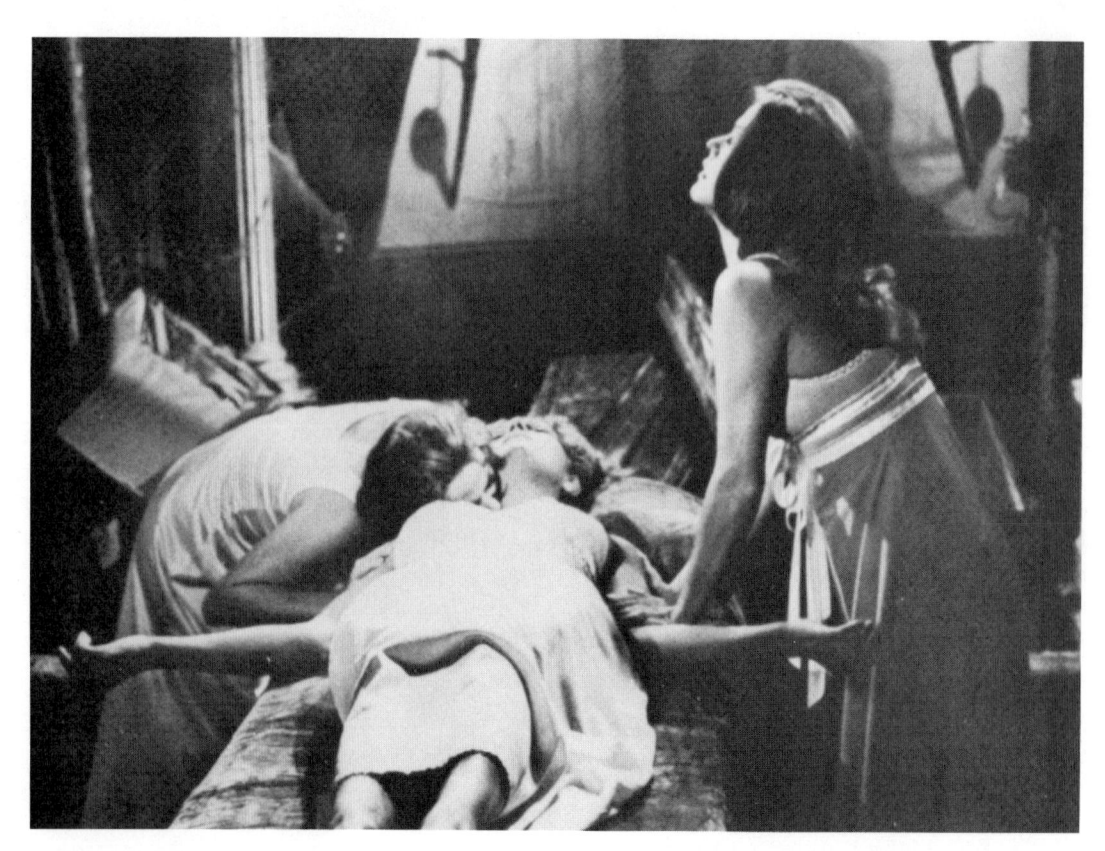

Marlene (Ingrid Garbo) and Elke (Mirta Miller) bring Senta (Rossana Yanni) into the vampire fold.

If this sounds unnecessarily confusing, well, that's just the way Naschy's movies are. In any case, things start to happen pretty quickly. Imre is attacked by the vampire delivery man—remember him?—and becomes a vampire himself. He then vampirizes his lover, Marlene, who vapirizes Elke. The two vampire women, working together, convert Senta. By now, the clinic is so full of vampires that, at one point, they start attacking each other.

Meanwhile, Marlow and Karen go for a walk in the garden and get to know each other. She asks him what he thinks of all these Transylvanian vampire legends, and he says, rather cryptically, that the price of immortality is "horror and eternal loneliness." All this vampire theory becomes practice moments later, when Imre, the deliveryman, and Senta attack Karen, and Marlow has to destroy them.

Karen admits her love for Marlow, but then she learns the truth. Marlow is really Count Dracula, and for the first time he, too, is in love. This is his big chance to come to his full power and revive his daughter, who is the skeleton we met in the opening scene. Unfortunately, Karen doesn't love him enough to go along with all this, and as Dracula makes clear, "I love you, but I cannot obligate you to share my destiny." So he packs Rhodna's body away carefully and destroys Elke and Marlene by chaining them outside in the sunlight. Then, with the words, "For the first time, love brings a finish to the life of Dracula," he stakes himself in the heart.

There is some good stuff here, particularly the slow-motion scenes of the vampire women drifting through the catacombs under the clinic. The basic problem,

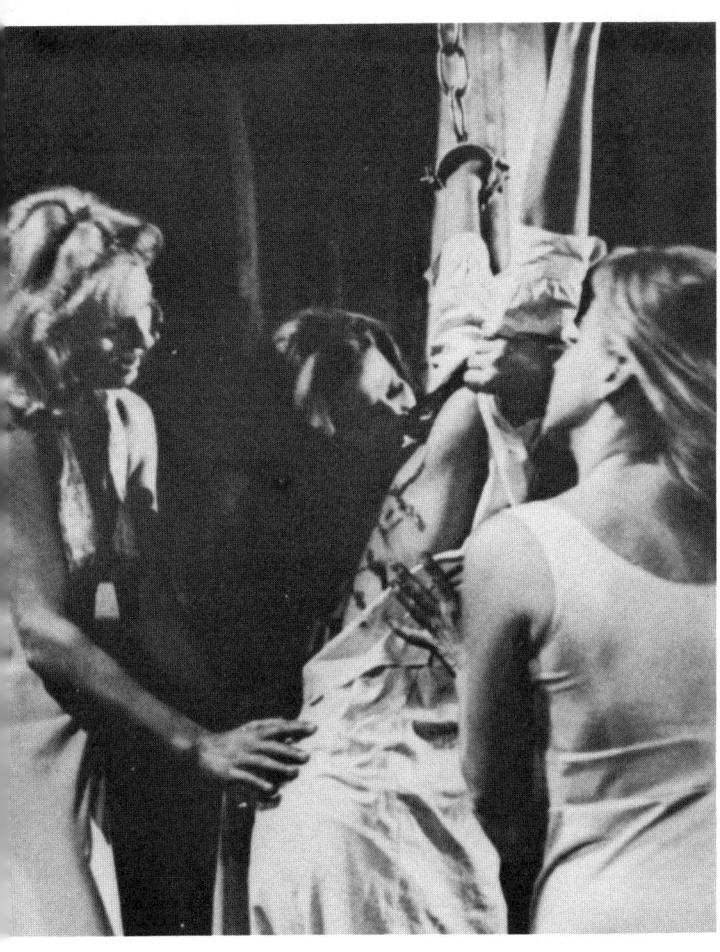

The vampire women strike again in *Count Dracula's Great Love*.

however—and this is a problem with Coppola's *Dracula*, too—is that the vampire story isn't a love story. It's a sex story, a lust story. As a vile seducer or a wild beast, Dracula works, but as a lover, he is just too soft to be frightening. Early in this film, we actually see Marlow free a cute little bunny from a trap, and after that it's hard to take the guy seriously as the prince of darkness.

The best vampire movies remind us that our own sexuality is often bestial. The difference between the vampire and the rest of us is that we keep our bestiality under control and he doesn't. In return, we can give and receive love and he can't. Sometimes we envy the vampire because he lives beyond the rules that confine us, but we are also frightened by him, as we are frightened by the potential violence in ourselves. But if the vampire can love and be loved, too, if he is just like us, then what's the point?

Craze

ALTERNATE TITLE:

The Infernal Idol

1974

Director: Freddie Francis; *Producer:* Herman Cohen; *Screenplay:* Aben Kandel and Herman Cohen

CAST:

Jack Palance, Diana Dors, Julie Ege, Dame Edith Evans, Hugh Griffith, Trevor Howard, Suzy Kendall, Martin Potter, Michael Jayston

ORIGINAL RELEASE: Warner Brothers
VIDEO: Burbank Video

Jack Palance probably deserved an Oscar for his performance in *Shane* back in the fifties, but he had to wait until the nineties to actually get one. In between, he acted in a lot of strange movies, from Dan Curtis's made-for-TV *Dracula* to Jesus Franco's *Justine*, loosely based on the novel by the Marquis de Sade. In this modest British film, he heads an all-star cast and delivers one of the weirdest performances of his varied career.

Palance is Neal Mottram, owner of an antique shop in London and high priest of a coven that meets in his basement to worship an African idol named Chuku. After one such meeting, an expelled member of the group shows up, claiming that she was the original owner of the idol and that Mottram has stolen her position as head of the coven. During a struggle, she falls on Chuku's spear and is killed. "Here is your sacrifice," Mottram tells the African god.

The police find the body of the woman in the river and come around to the antique shop to question Mottram and his nervous associate, Ronnie (Martin Potter), because they found Mottram's name in her address book. Then Ronnie overhears him praying to Chuku for money and realizes that his boss is the murderer. Ronnie doesn't go for this black magic stuff—"I don't beieve"—but he is impressed when Mottram finds gold coins hidden in an antique desk. "I told you, Ronnie, Chuku is a generous god . . . . Do the sacrifice and get the reward."

Now that he knows the sacrifices work, Mottram picks up a tourist named Helena (Julie Ege) in a bar, takes her home, and kills her in the basement. Again, he comes into money unexpectedly when two customers pay a fortune for some fake Ming vases he has had in stock for years.

Neal Mottram (Jack Palance) pays homage to the idol of the African god Chuku in *Craze*.

Mottram decides to sacrifice his rich old aunt Louise (Dame Edith Evans), so he concocts an elaborate plan, using a business trip and an old girlfriend, Dolly Newman (Diana Dors), as his alibi. This really isn't much of a challenge for Chuku, because, as Louise's only heir, Mottram inherits a fortune automatically, and it seems he would have done so even without help from the idol, but Mottram is a devoted worshiper, and he still pays homage to his god—"Your humble subject lives in your shadow."

The police question Neal, whose name has now cropped up in two recent murders. Sergeant Wall (Michael Jayston) is convinced that Mottram is the killer, but Superintendent Bellamy (Trevor Howard) isn't so sure. The cops investigate Neal's alibi, which holds up, but Dolly informs Wall of Mottram's interest in black magic, and this convinces the sergeant that he is right in his suspicions. He decides to have Mottram and the antique shop watched.

Even though he is now a wealthy man, Mottram still isn't satisfied, so he calls on a hooker named Sally (Suzy Kendall) and sacrifices her, too. Meanwhile, Ronnie has just about had enough of this black magic mumbo jumbo. He goes down to the basement of the antique shop and takes an ax to Chuku, and when Mottram arrives to stop him, he stabs his boss in the arm with a spear.

In a fit of rage, Mottram tosses Ronnie out of the shop window. The police come in and are threatened with an ax by Mottram until one of them shoots. Dying, he throws himself on Chuku's spear and mutters, "Your last sacrifice."

Palance is marvelously maniacal as Mottram, but the rest of this impressive cast is wasted here. Griffith and Evans have only bit parts, and Howard simply walks through his role as if he were on his way to somewhere else. The story isn't bad, though the film never explains what drew Mottram to Chuku in the first place, and an

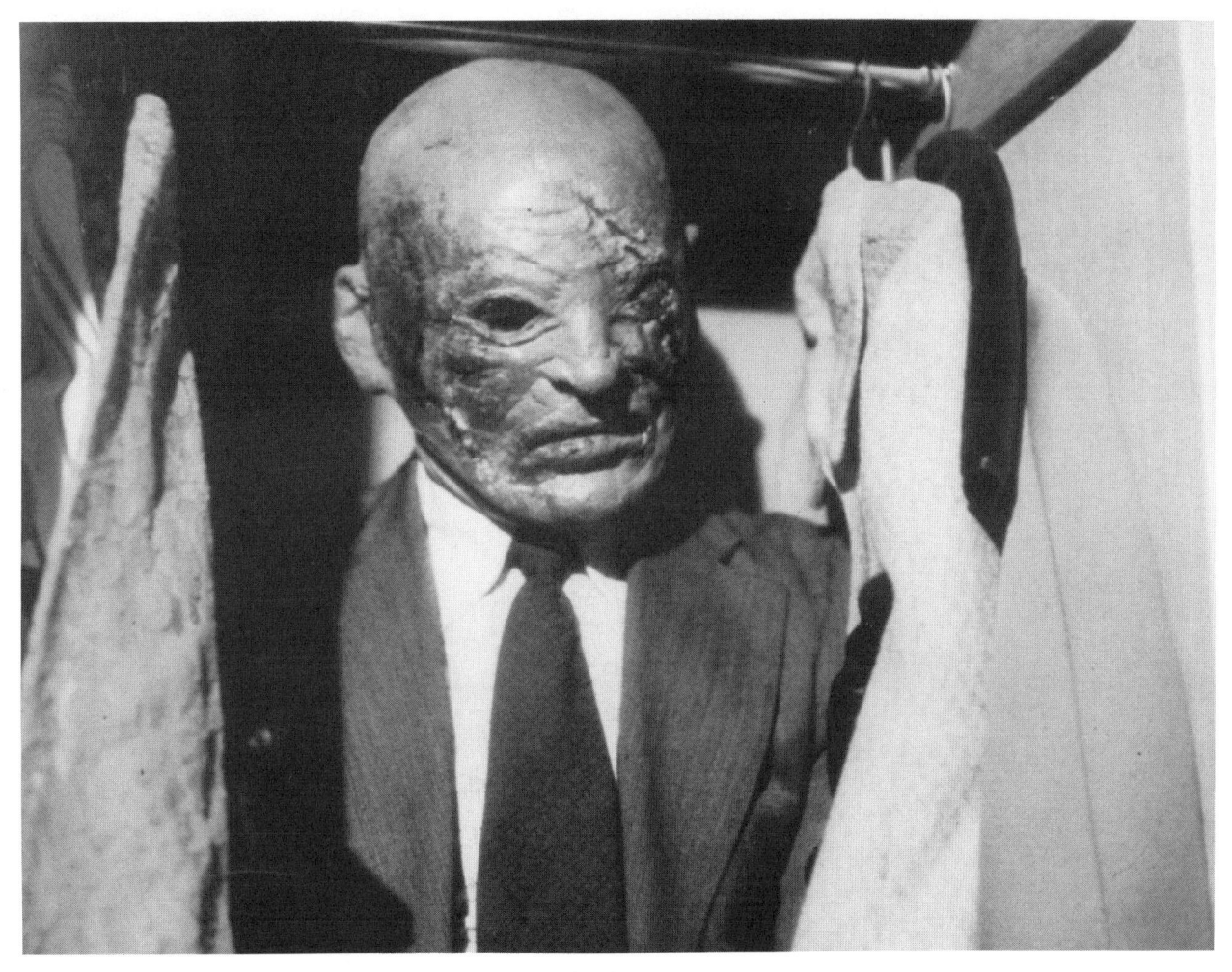

No, it's not a monster. It's Mottram (Jack Palance) wearing a mask as he prepares to jump out of a closet and scare his poor aunt Louise to death.

Mottram (Jack Palance) offers Sally the prostitute (Suzy Kendall) as a sacrifice to Chuku.

Ronnie (Martin Potter) has had enough of Neal's black magic and attacks Chuku with an ax.

enormous amount of screen time is devoted to his intricate plot to kill his aunt Louise. On top of that, the scenes in which he and his coven chant in Latin to an *African* god are more than a bit strange. Still, Palance's performance makes the whole thing worthwhile as he moves convincingly from menacing understatement to overt lunacy, depending upon the situation.

Like a lot of other British horror films, *Craze* warns viewers about the dangers of foreign influences, especially influences from "the colonies." The idea of imperialism—British or otherwise—is to make the natives we have conquered more like us, not to let ourselves become more like them. Mottram's great crime is not murder—it is giving up his European values in favor of the values of darkest Africa, a place that is traditionally depicted as a pit of evil in horror films.

On this basis, *Craze* is a chauvinistic and insulting movie, but not as bad as director Francis's film of 1975, *The Ghoul,* never put into theatrical release in the United States but available on videocassette. In that movie, the son of a diplomat in the foreign service comes

Ronnie throws a spear that finds its mark in *Craze*.

under the influence of a cult in India and, as a result, turns into a cannibal who can eat nothing but human flesh. The notion that there are cannibal cults in a country like India is absurd, of course, but the message is perfectly clear: not only do we have nothing to learn from other cultures but also to attempt to do so is to court disaster.

This isn't exactly the kind of thinking that promotes global understanding.

The Crazies

ALTERNATE TITLE:

Code Name: Trixie

1973

Director/screenplay: George A. Romero; *Producer:* Alvin C. Croft

CAST:

Lane Carroll, W. G. McMillan, Harold Wayne Jones, Lloyd Hollar, Richard Liberty, Richard France, Harry Spillman

ORIGINAL RELEASE: Cambist Films
VIDEO: Vista Home Video

After his success with *Night of the Living Dead*, George Romero fell on hard box-office times, and that's unfortunate, because *The Crazies* is a fine film and speaks directly to its historical moment.

A military plane carrying a new biological weapon crashes outside the small western-Pennsylvania town of Evans City, and the population is infected with a plague for which there is no antidote. The army immediately seals off the town, hoping to contain not only the plague but also the fact that such a weapon exists. Civilians are rounded up in their homes at gunpoint by soldiers wearing white, antiseptic uniforms and gas masks, and a plane carrying an atomic bomb is stationed overhead, just in case extraordinary methods are necessary "to burn out the infected area," in the words of one government official.

The virus makes those infected go insane before they die, and many turn violent. There are soon murders all over town, and armed warfare breaks out between the soldiers and townspeople who do not want to be captured—or who, perhaps, have already gotten the bug. Military personnel become infected as well, and soon the entire town is a battlefield.

David (W. G. McMillan), his pregnant soon-to-be-wife, Judy (Lane Carroll), and their friend Clank (Harold Wayne Jones) escape the roundup and try to find out what is going on. David and Clank are Vietnam veterans—David was a Green Beret—and so when they must defend themselves against soldiers who have orders to kill anyone trying to escape or anyone obviously infected with the virus, the two do a good job.

Meanwhile, Colonel Peckem (Lloyd Hollar) is trying to maintain some sense of order in the town. In Washington, officials are trying to come up with cover stories to explain to the press what is happening. Dr. Watts

A special military unit begins to round up the citizens of a Pennyslvania town that has been infected by a top-secret biological weapon in George Romero's *The Crazies*.

The soldiers have orders to shoot anyone who offers resistance or anyone who seems to be infected by the disease and to burn the bodies.

Judy (Lane Carroll) and David (W. G. McMillan) manage to escape the military roundup for a little while.

(Richard France), one of the creators of the virus, is in Evans City looking for an antidote. What he needs is someone who has a natural immunity to the disease, but so far, he has had no luck.

As happens so often in Romero's films, things do not end well. Clank gets sick and sacrifices himself for his friends. Judy also contracts the disease and is killed by the locals. Dr. Watts finds his antidote, but he is killed before he can deliver it to Colonel Peckem. David is captured, and though he has good reason to believe that he has a natural immunity to the plague, he doesn't tell anyone, preferring to let everyone die of the disease. And Peckem finds out that, after all his efforts, it seems likely that the plague has spread beyond Evans City already and could infect the entire country, even the entire world.

The Crazies is very much a Vietnam-era film, made in a time when American civilians and military personnel were considering the very real possibility that our government officials and top brass don't always have our best interests at heart. Romero creates a mini–Vietnam

The soldiers shoot down another helpless citizen in the Vietnam-era thriller *The Crazies*.

War in Evans City. The town has been invaded by force, the people don't know why, and the military personnel "haven't even been told why they're here," according to Peckem's assistant, Major Ryder (Harry Spillman). Most of the soldiers are good, ordinary guys, though some steal fishing rods and other things from the local houses or loot the bodies of the dead before they're burned. Peckem and Ryder just seem to be doing their jobs, but their commanding officers—who are nowhere near Evans City—hamstring their efforts again and again. And, in the end, everyone—civilian and military alike—is expendable. As Clank says, "The army's nobody's friend. We know. We've been in."

Though the actors are clearly professional and the production values are higher, *The Crazies* doesn't have the raw impact of *Night of the Living Dead*. It is often heavy-handed—Romero seems to do better when he doesn't have a specific message to sell. Even so, this is a powerful and frightening film about a nation that is losing faith in its values, and that makes it as relevant today as it was in the seventies.

Creature of the Walking Dead

ALTERNATE TITLE:

La Marca del Muerto

1960/1965

Director: Fernando Cortés (Frederic Corte); *Producers:* Jerry Warren, Cesar Santos Galindo and Alfredo Ripstein Jr.; *Screenplay:* Alfredo Varela Jr. and Fernando Cortés; *Story:* José Maria Fernández Unsáin

CAST:

Fernando Casanova (Rock Madison), Sonia Furio (Ann Wells), Pedro dé Agguillon, Katherine Victor, Bruno Ve Sota, Willard Gross

ORIGINAL RELEASE: A.D.P. Productions
VIDEO: Goodtimes Home Video

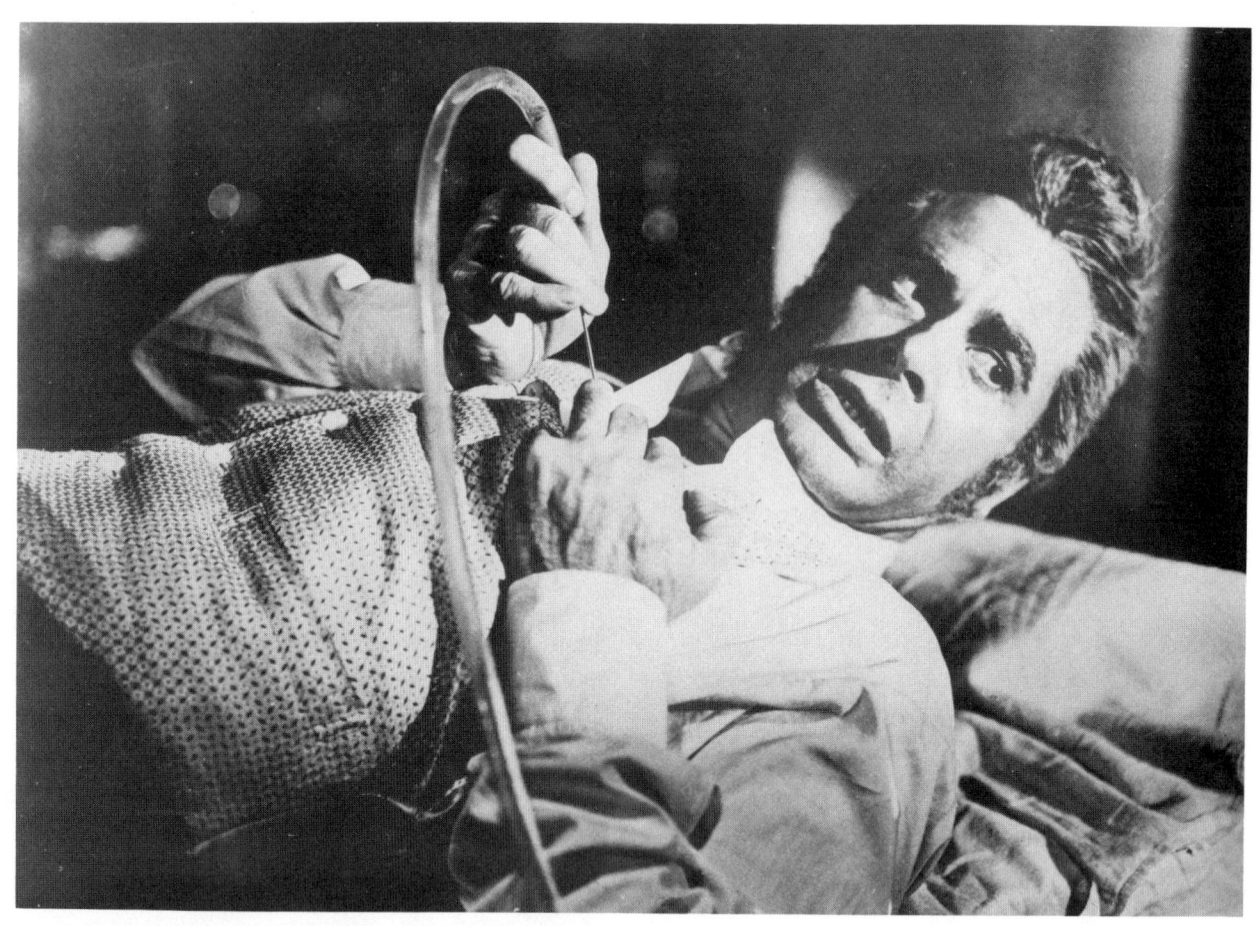

Dr. John Malthus (Fernando Casanova, aka Rock Madison) injects himself with the eternal-life fluid just as the police come for him in *Creature of the Walking Dead*. *(Courtesy Hollywood Book and Poster)*

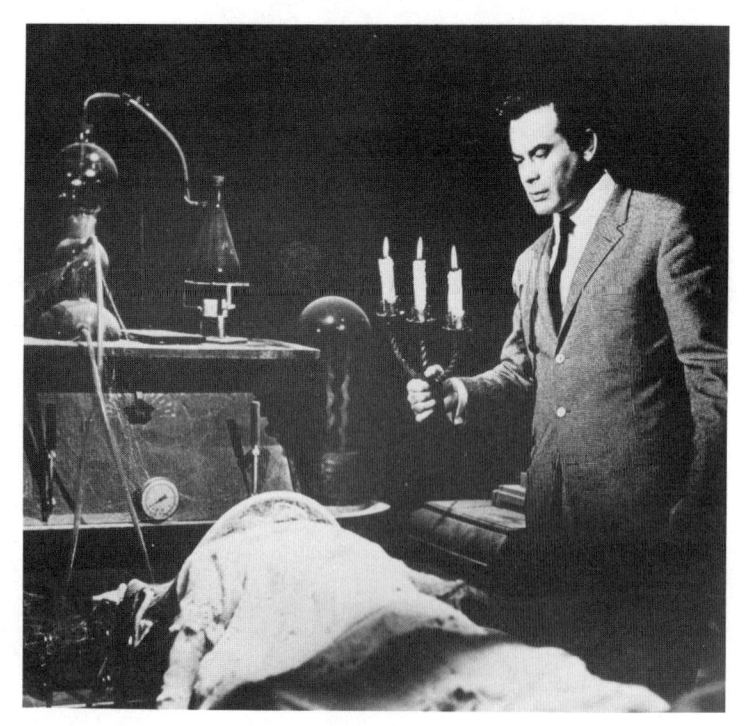

Dr. Martin Malthus (Fernando Casanova/Rock Madison) discovers his great-grandfather's laboratory in his ancestral home. *(Courtesy Hollywood Book and Poster)*

This is a bad film. This is a very bad film, and even if you have a high tolerance for bad films, you'll still find this one pretty hard to take. It was made in Mexico under the title *La Marca del Muerto*, and there is every reason to suspect that even the original version wasn't very good. But then schlockmeister Jerry Warren got hold of it in 1965, chopped it up, and inserted some new footage in English featuring Bruno Ve Sota (*Attack of the Giant Leeches*) and other American actors, who mostly sit around explaining to each other what's going on in the Mexican part of the film. It isn't clear why Warren shot the new scenes; it does seem that huge chunks of the original movie are missing, but the new additions don't do much to make up for that. Warren also changed the names of everyone involved—for the American version, Casanova became Rock Madison, Furio became Ann Wells, and director Cortes became Frederic Corte. Probably this was supposed to convince viewers that *Creature of the Walking Dead* was a high-class Hollywood production. Still it doesn't take long to figure out that some of the characters in this flick are badly dubbed, others are not, and the people from one part of the film never come into contact with people from the other.

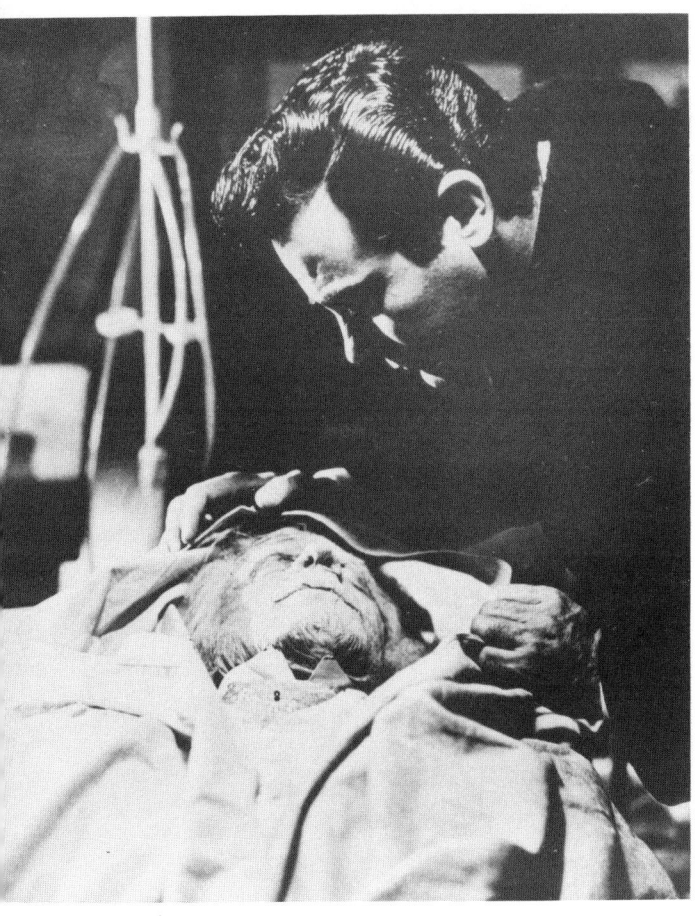

Martin (Fernando Casanova/Rock Madison) uncovers the corpse of his late grandfather in hopes of returning the old boy to life. (*Courtesy Hollywood Book and Poster*)

The year is 1881, and Dr. John Malthus (Casanova/Madison), like any self-respecting mad scientist, is in search of eternal life. He grabs a young woman off the street, spirits her away to his secret laboratory, and kills her in preparation for the great experiment that will make him immortal. Unfortunately, he is captured by the police and hanged before he can work out all the details.

Now it's the present, and Dr. Martin Malthus (Casanova/Madison again), great-grandson of John, is a nice young physician who inherits his ancestor's estate. There he discovers the hidden laboratory, some skeletons locked in jail cells, and Grandpa's notes. Of course, he immediately goes to the family crypt and steals the old man's body. Then he gets a woman from somewhere—she simply appears on his operating table—and uses her blood to revive Dr. John. Luckily, this process doesn't kill the woman, and Grandpa locks her in one of the cells for later use. Then he begins teaching his great-grandson the secrets of life and death.

Martin is engaged to Beth (Furio/Wells), who doesn't like the fact that her fiancé is suddenly ignoring her in favor of his research. Meanwhile, John continues his experiments, and Martin steals drugs and plasma for him from the local hospital. Even with all his new modern equipment, however, the effects of John's resurrection are temporary. He turns into a walking corpse and has to get a new female victim and fix himself up with her blood. When Martin objects to his methods, Grandpa locks his great-grandson in one of the cells and takes his place. Even Beth doesn't notice the difference.

Eventually, and not unexpectedly, John decides to use Beth's blood to revive himself once again, but Martin escapes from his cell to save her. This leads to the big fight—Martin the humanitarian against his own evil-scientist self—which leads to the big lab fire that spells the end of Dr. John Malthus.

In almost all horror movies, science is evil. Scientists are evil, too, primarily because they aren't like us—they do things we can't do, understand things we don't understand, and say things in their own secret language that, to us, makes no sense. Science and scientists are strange and foreign to most of us nonscientists, so of course they must be bad. In all its mindlessness, however, *Creature of the Walking Dead* hits upon an interesting version of this idea. Here, science is worse than evil—it's a kind of communicable disease.

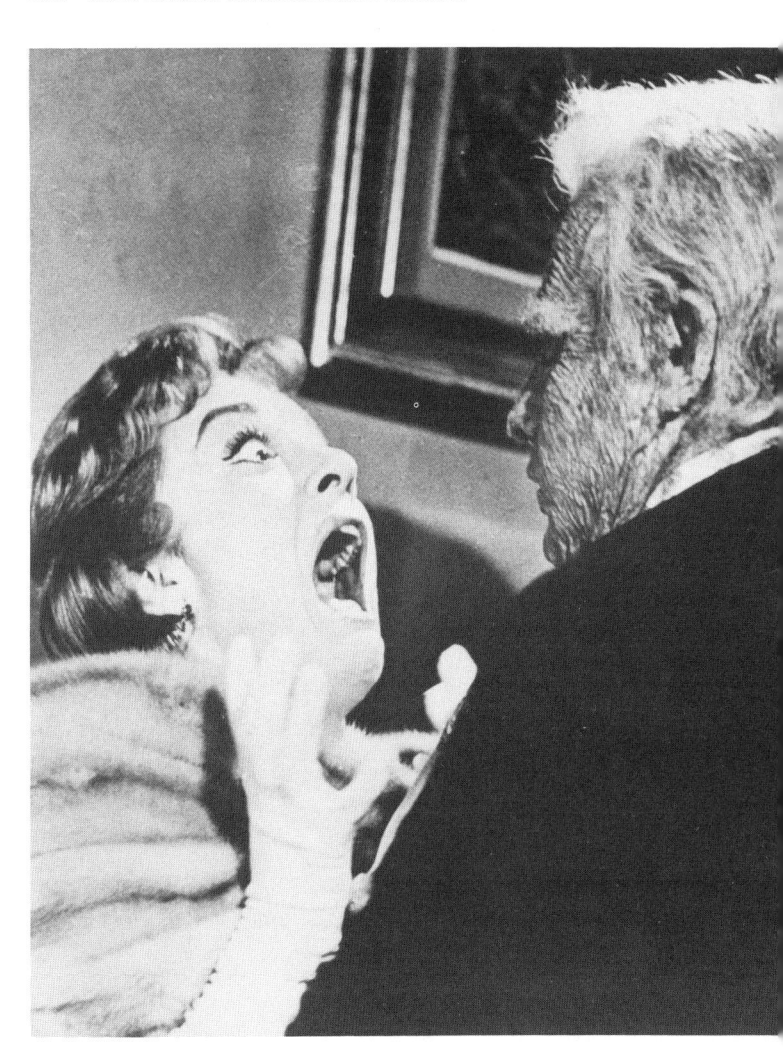

Beth (Sonia Furio, aka Ann Wells) is shocked to see John Malthus (Fernando Casanova/Rock Madison) as he really is. (*Courtesy Hollywood Book and Poster*)

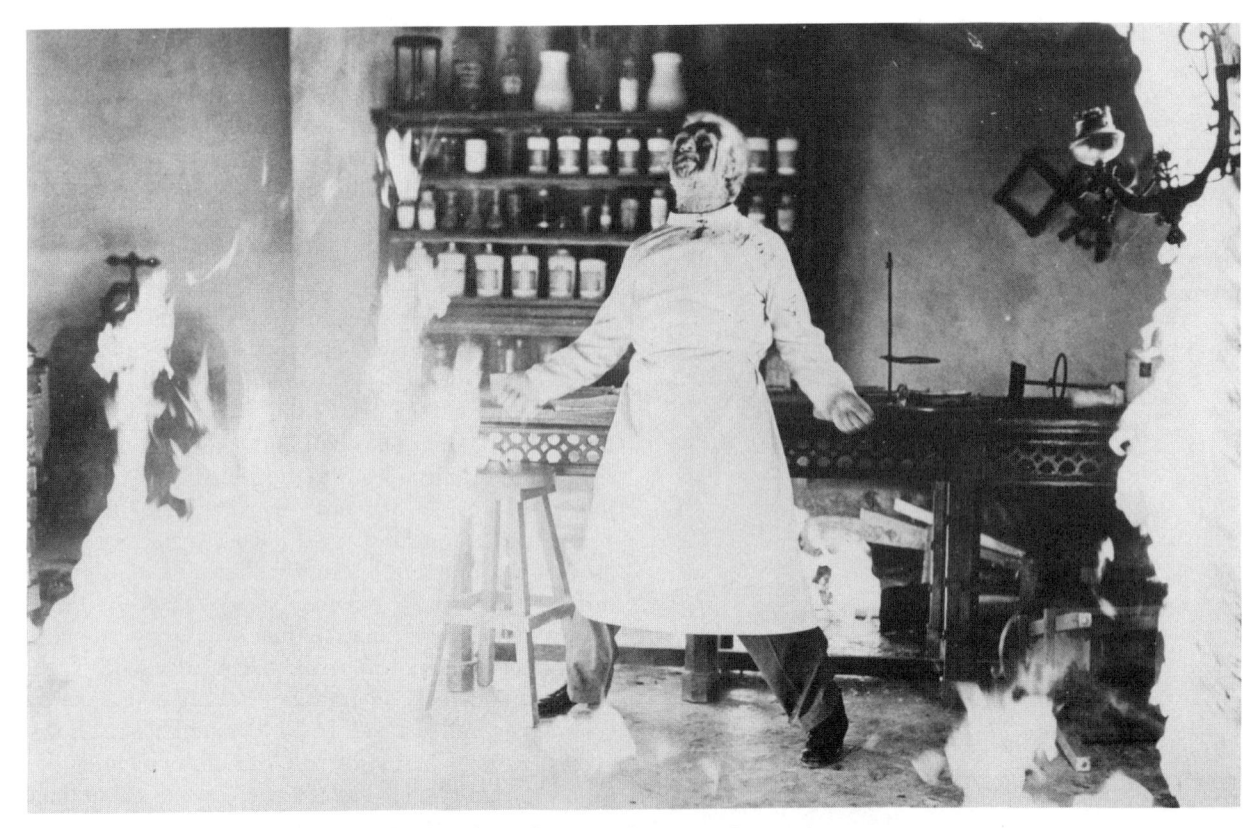

Just as the captain always goes down with his ship, the mad scientist always goes down with his lab, and that's exactly what John Malthus (Fernando Casanova/Rock Madison) does in *Creature of the Walking Dead*. (Courtesy Hollywood Book and Poster)

Without question, Dr. Grandpa is a villain, but in the beginning, Martin isn't an evil scientist. He's a good guy, a helpful physician, and he's engaged to a nice girl. But as soon as he finds Grandpa's notes, he becomes infected. "As a scientist, of course, I was greatly intrigued."

Fortunately, Martin manages to pull himself together, to cure himself, but the message is clear. Scientists can become evil because science itself is evil, and any contact with science is dangerous. So, kids, don't feel bad about cutting those chemistry classes—you're doing the right thing. And for goodness' sake, burn that biology textbook before it's too late.

Curse of the Devil

ALTERNATE TITLE:

El Retorno de la Walpurgis

1973

Director: Charles (Carlos) Aured; *Producer:* Luis Gomez; *Screenplay:* Jacinto Molina (Paul Naschy)

CAST:
Paul Naschy, Faye (Fabiola) Falcon, Maria Silva, Maritza Olivares, Ana Farra

ORIGINAL RELEASE: Goldstone Productions
VIDEO: United Home Video

Curse of the Devil is Spanish actor Paul Naschy's seventh film as the werewolf, and it is certainly one of his best efforts, probably because there are no abominable snowmen, mummies, or vampire women lurking about, as there are in some of his other lycanthropic flicks. In fact, this one owes a lot to the classic films in the genre—*Werewolf of London*, *The Wolf Man*, *Curse of the Werewolf*—without being simply a copy of any of them.

The movie opens in the good old days when knighthood was in flower. Naschy, in white armor, plays Sir Daninsky, who engages a satanist knight, in black armor, and defeats him. Daninsky then invades the dead knight's castle during a Black Mass, hauls all the practitioners outside, hangs them, and burns the evil knight's evil wife at the stake. While she is going up in smoke, she proclaims the curse of the title, which is that, someday, another Daninsky will kill another descendant of the dead knight, and then all Daninskys to come will be in for it.

Cut to the nineteenth century in the Carpathian Mountains. Waldemar (Naschy again), the current heir to the Daninsky name and fortune, joins the hunt to help villagers kill a wolf that has been terrorizing the countryside. He spots the wolf and shoots, but though he's sure he hit it, the animal doesn't fall. His butler and helper, Boris, knows a thing or two about the occult, so he hands Waldemar a rifle loaded with a silver bullet, and this time, when Daninsky shoots, the wolf goes down. But when they search for the body, they discover the corpse of a man, a Gypsy new to the area. The tragedy is declared a hunting accident, but we know better.

When Sir Daninsky (Paul Naschy) executes a coven of satanists, one of them puts the curse of the devil on him.

Waldemar is devastated by the incident, but he doesn't know that the dead Gypsy was a descendant of the evil knight and that now the curse is in effect. The Gypsies send the beautiful Ilona (Maritza Olivares) to seduce Waldemar, and one night in bed, she inflicts a wound on his chest, using the fangs from a wolf's skull. The wound takes the shape of the pentagram, and we all know what that means.

Meanwhile, a maniac named Janos has broken out of the local prison and is roaming through the countryside, so when a few of the locals are brutally murdered, the police blame the escaped killer. And there are other newcomers to the area: engineer Lazlo from Budapest, his blind wife, and his two lovely daughters, Kenya (Faye Falcon) and Maria (Maria Silva). Kenya and Waldemar hit it off right away, but she can tell that he is tormented about something.

Waldemar is a werewolf, of course, and he is responsible for the killings, though he doesn't remember the incidents except as vague dreams. His housekeeper, Melissa (Ana Farra), who is really more of a mother than

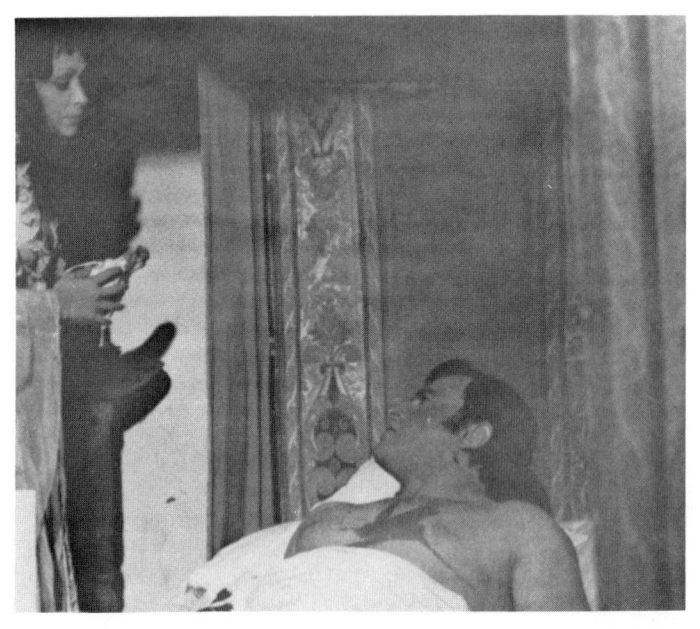

Ilona (Maritza Olivares), the lovely Gypsy girl, uses a wolf's skull to wound Waldemar Daninsky (Paul Naschy), thus turning him into a werewolf.

Waldemar, the werewolf (Paul Naschy).

Mrs. Daninsky (Faye Falcon) and her son visit Waldemar's grave. The boy still bears the Daninsky curse, the curse of the devil.

a housekeeper to him, helps to cover up the truth. But Kenya's blind mother, who is from the mountains originally, knows that a werewolf is at large, and she tells her daughter that a lycanthrope can only die if he is stabbed in the heart with a silver dagger by a woman who loves him enough to set him free—in this movie, it's a lot tougher to get rid of a werewolf than it used to be.

Eventually, after Waldemar kills Kenya's sister, her father, her mother, the local cop, and a lot of other people, it's hard to overlook what is really going on. Kenya prepares the silver dagger and puts an end to Waldemar's little problem. But she is pregnant, and we know that Waldemar's son will bear the curse as well.

What makes almost any werewolf movie particularly disturbing is the fact that the person afflicted with the curse usually does nothing to bring it on himself. In the original *Wolf Man,* Lou Chaney Jr. as Larry Talbot becomes a werewolf because he is bitten by one while trying to help a young woman who is being attacked—in other words, not only does he do nothing to deserve his curse, but also becoming a werewolf is his "reward" for performing a heroic act. This is unfair, of course, and it suggests that anyone might become a werewolf just by being in the wrong place at the wrong time.

Curse of the Devil derives most of its power from this same unsettling notion. Certainly it is not Waldemar's fault that, four-hundred years before he was born, his ancestor wiped out a satanic cult, which probably seemed like a pretty good idea at the time. And, of course, being marked by the fangs of a wolf's skull wasn't Waldemar's idea either. Essentially, thanks to the curse, he is born to be a werewolf for the same reason that some people are born deformed or blind or diseased—for no good reason.

Most of Naschy's movies are more than a little bizarre and take some getting used to, but *Curse of the Devil* is a courageous and terrifying film because it tells us not what we would like to believe but what we know is true—that bad things happen to innocent people who simply don't deserve them, and that is truly frightening.

Daughters of Darkness

ALTERNATE TITLES:

*Le Rouge aux Lèvres,
The Promise of Red Lips*

1971

Director: Harry Kumel; *Producers:* Alain Guilleaume and Paul Collet; *Screenplay:* Harry Kumel, J.J. Amiel and Pierre Drouot

CAST:
Delphine Seyrig, John Karlen, Daniele Ouimet, Andrea Rau, Paul Esser, Georges Jamin, Fons Rademakers

ORIGINAL RELEASE: Geneni Releasing Corporation
VIDEO: Continental Home Video

Every now and then, a horror film goes beyond itself and becomes something else—possibly even a work of art. This happens with Tony Scott's remarkable movie *The Hunger*. It also happens with Harry Kumel's *Daughters of Darkness*, to which *The Hunger* owes an enormous debt.

Daughters of Darkness, shot in Belgium with an international cast, is a visually beautiful vampire film that might not be a vampire film at all. Stefan (John Karlen of TV's *Dark Shadows* series and *Cagney & Lacy*) and Valerie (Daniele Ouimet) are newlyweds traveling by train to catch a boat to England. Because of an unexpected delay, they are forced to stay at an elegant seaside resort that is almost deserted in the off-season.

Though they are married, Stefan and Valerie don't know each other very well. He doesn't seem in any hurry to get to his home in England with his new bride or even to tell his mother that he is married. We find out later that his "mother" is actually an older, homosexual lover who has been keeping him for years. And, indeed, we find out much more about Stefan, too—none of it very good.

That same evening, Countess Elisabeth Bathory (Delphine Seyrig) and her lover/companion Ilona (Andrea Rau) also arrive at the hotel, where the elderly clerk claims to remember her previous visit some forty years earlier. This is impossible, of course, because she is no more than thirty or thirty-five. "My mother, perhaps," the countess explains.

Elisabeth and Ilona have a strange relationship. In fact, Ilona is more like a piece of the countess's property than a lover. When the younger woman makes the rather cryptic comment "I won't be able to wait another night," the countess says, "Yes, you will, because I want you to." She holds some power over Ilona, and it becomes clear early on that she wants to gain power over the newlyweds, too.

The lovers leave the hotel for a day trip to nearby Rouge where there have been some murders recently. Three women have been found, drained of blood. Stefan and Valerie arrive in time to see the police taking away a fourth victim, and Stefan is fascinated. "It gave you

The newlyweds, Valerie (Daniele Ouimet) and Stefan (John Karlen), on board the train in *Daughters of Darkness*.

pleasure," Valerie says later. "You actually enjoyed seeing that dead girl's body."

Back at the hotel, Stefan is also fascinated by Elisabeth, who claims to be descended from the original Countess Bathory, who sacrificed hundreds of young women in the sixteenth century in the belief that, if she bathed in their blood, she would remain young. There is the suggestion, of course, that Elisabeth *is* that countess, still young and now a vampire.

Valerie is repulsed by the countess's decadence and only wants to leave, though she can't get Stefan to go

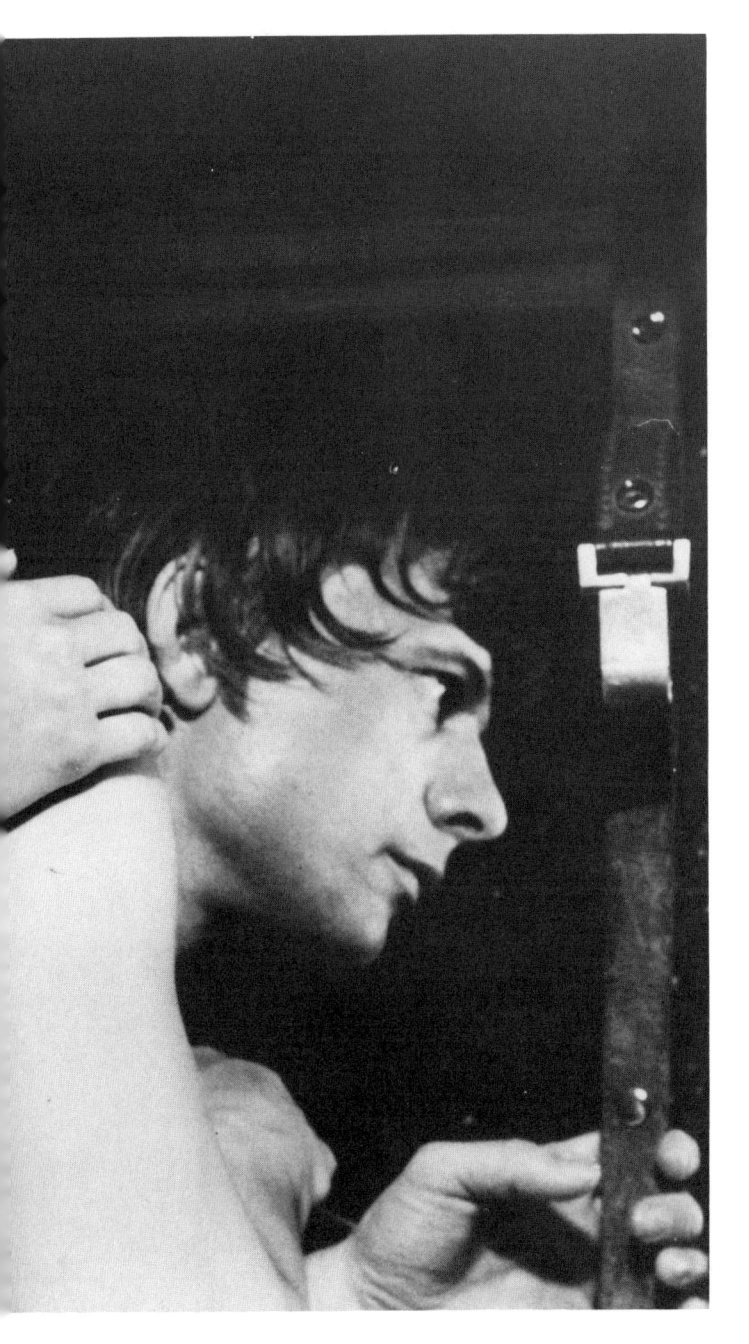

Stefan (John Karlen) cuts himself while shaving—a foreshadowing of things to come.

with her. One night, after he beats and degrades her, Valerie tries to escape to the train station, but Elisabeth stops her and explains, "He dreams of making out of you what every man dreams of making out of every woman—a slave, an object of pleasure."

At the same time, following Elisabeth's directions, Ilona has gone to Stefan's room to seduce him. This proves to be easy, but afterward, when Stefan tries to pull her into the shower with him, she refuses and struggles against him—remember, vampires can be destroyed by running water. Stefan thinks she is only being playful, but when Ilona falls on a straight razor and dies, it doesn't seem funny anymore.

Elisabeth takes Valerie back to the hotel to show her what Stefan is up to, and when they discover Ilona dead, it is the women who take over. Stefan doesn't know what is going on, but Elisabeth and Valerie decide to dispose of the body by burying it on the beach, leaving the helpless man to do nothing more than dig the hole and fill it in again.

Back at the hotel, Valerie spends the night with Elisabeth. In the morning, it is Stefan who is eager to leave and Valerie who wants to stay. "I'd like to go with you," she explains, "but it's too late."

Stefan and Elisabeth argue over Valerie, who seems to

Elisabeth (Delphine Seyrig) ties a choker around Valerie's (Daniele Ouimet) neck to hide the telltale marks.

be in a sort of trance. "I am a man," he shouts, "and she is mine." "Valerie will do as I tell her," Elisabeth claims. Eventually, the problem is resolved when the women kill Stefan and drink his blood.

Leaving the body behind, the two women speed away in Elisabeth's car—"Faster! We must arrive before day." But Valerie is driving too fast. She loses control and crashes, and Elisabeth, thrown from the car, is impaled on a tree branch, putting an end to her.

In the final sequence, however, Valerie is at another resort with another young couple, seducing them with the same words Elisabeth spoke earlier in the film.

Though the symbolism is sometimes a bit heavy-handed, *Daughters of Darkness* raises some interesting questions to which there are no answers. Are these people vampires or only normal but depraved human beings? More important, what is the nature of their various relationships? There is no love in this film, only efforts by one person to control another.

Stefan obviously wants to control Valerie. Elisabeth

warns her of this, though certainly the countess wants the same thing—to control her new lover as she controlled Ilona. Stefan himself is controlled by his "mother," and in the end, Valerie has replaced Elisabeth and now seeks control over others.

Daughters of Darkness suggests that, in our world, this is the nature of human relationships—male/female, female/female, or male/male. Love is meaningless. One either controls or is controlled; one is either master or slave, and the only way to keep from being a slave is to become the master.

If true, this is a tragic commentary on the way we live.

Valerie (Daniele Ouimet, left) and Elisabeth (Delphine Seyrig)—the daughters of darkness.

Dementia 13

ALTERNATE TITLE:

The Haunted and the Hunted

1963

Director/screenplay: Francis Ford Coppola; *Producer:* Roger Corman

CAST:
William Campbell, Luana Anders, Bart Patton, Mary Mitchell, Patrick Magee, Peter Read, Eithne Dunn

ORIGINAL RELEASE: American International Pictures/Filmgroup
VIDEO: Video Classics, Sinister Cinema, and others

Francis Ford Coppola knows how to make big-budget wonders such as *The Godfather* and *Bram Stoker's Dracula*, but *Dementia 13*—made for $22,000—is proof that he doesn't need that kind of heavy backing to turn out a marvelous film.

In the opening sequence, John Haloran (Peter Read) and his wife, Louise (Luana Anders), are out for an evening's boating on an Irish lake. Louise is upset because John's wealthy mother has just changed her will, leaving everything to charity in the name of her dead daughter, Kathleen. Louise wants a piece of the action, but, as John points out, "You're only a member of the family as long as you're my wife." So, when John dies of a heart attack, Louise dumps his body overboard and pretends that he has just gone to New York on business. The shots of John's body sinking slowly in the water are really chilling and set us up for what is to come.

The Halorans have returned to their ancestral castle for the annual memorial service for Kathleen, who drowned in a pond on the estate seven years before. Billy (Bart Patton) is the youngest son. His brother Richard (William Campbell), a neurotic sculptor, is there with his American fiancée, Kane (Mary Mitchell). Lady Haloran (Eithne Dunn) is the matriarch of the clan, and the weird Dr. Caleb (Patrick Magee), the family physician, rounds out the company.

Lady Haloran is obsessed with Kathleen—clearly, she prefers her dead daughter to any of her live children—and Louise tries to win her over by claiming to have seen

Kane (Mary Mitchell) and artist Richard Haloran (William Campbell) are reunited in his studio in Francis Ford Coppola's *Dementia 13*.

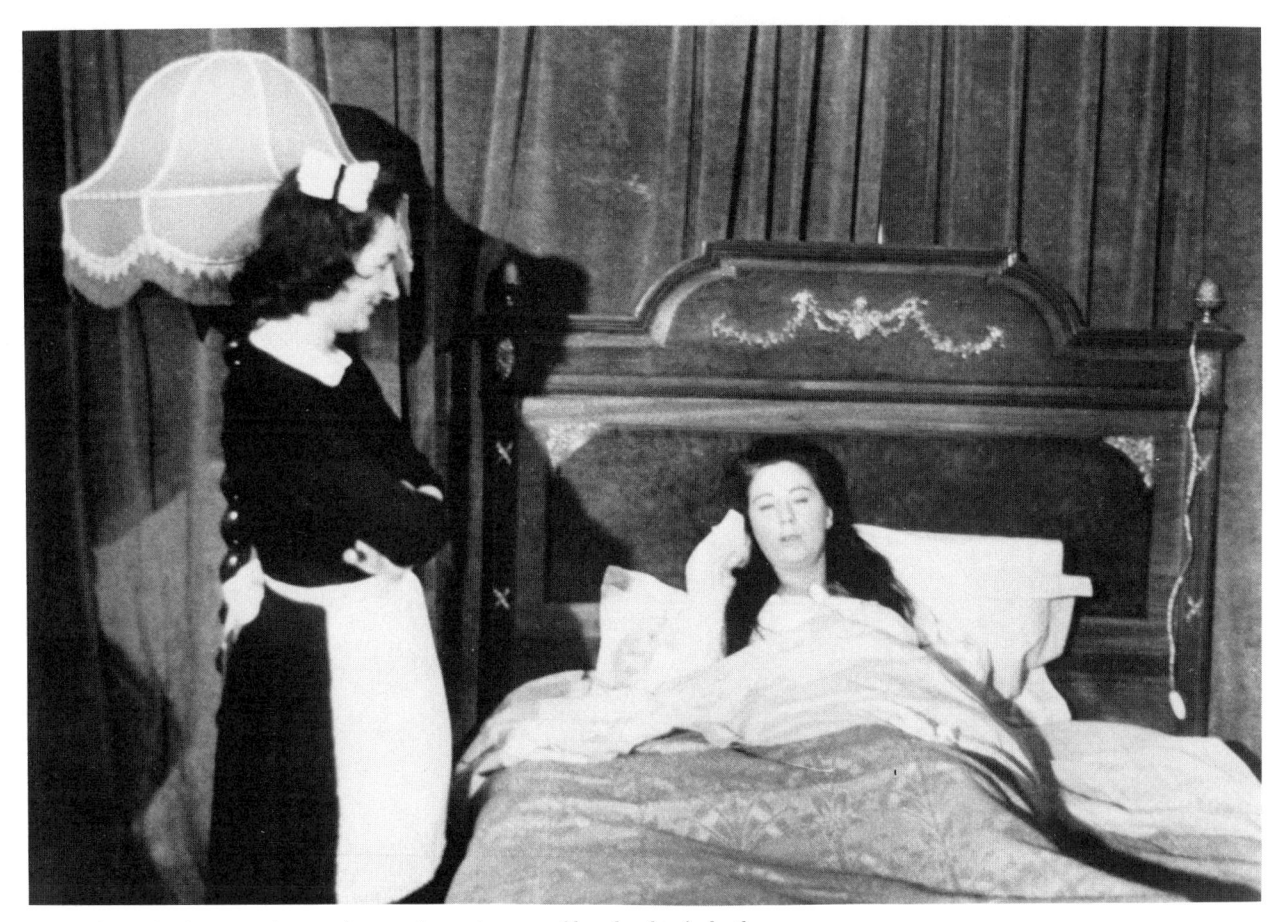

Lady Haloran (Eithne Dunn) is stricken on the anniversary of her daughter's death.

Kathleen's ghost. In fact, Louise is trying to drive Lady Haloran crazy in hopes of discrediting the will. She even plants some of Kathleen's old toys in the pond as proof that the child's spirit has returned, but before she can profit from her little trick, someone brutally murders her with an ax, then hides her body.

The ax attacks continue. A local poacher is decapitated, and Lady Haloran is attacked, too, though she survives. Richard and Kane are married at the castle as planned, but during the reception, Dr. Caleb starts poking around the grounds and discovers the corpse of Louise and a wax dummy of Kathleen, dressed in the dead child's clothes. When brother Billy sees the dummy, he freaks out and starts swinging an ax around, forcing Caleb to shoot him. It seems that mild-mannered Billy was the accidental cause of Kathleen's death seven years before, and by creating a dummy of her and protecting her from discovery—by killing Louise and the poacher—he has been trying to work off his guilt.

This is an effective horror/mystery story that works right up to the end when Caleb uses Billy's ax to smash the dummy of Kathleen. Nothing is obvious here, and since all the Halorans and Dr. Caleb himself are crazy,

Dr. Justin Caleb (Patrick Magee) fears for the sanity of the entire Haloran clan—he's a bit strange himself.

The wedding between Kane (Mary Mitchell) and Richard leads to the discovery of the murderer's identity in *Dementia 13*.

it's almost impossible to guess who the killer is until the final sequence, because everyone in the film is a legitimate suspect. With its creepy castle, its dark, brooding atmosphere, its often bizarre dialogue, and some sudden and violent murders, *Dementia 13* has a lot going for it.

The movie sets up an interesting contrast between the Old World and the New. In America, we tend to overlook or even reject the past in favor of the present, but in Europe it's often the other way round. At Haloran Castle, tradition and the past rule in the person of Lady Haloran. As Billy explains, "Castle Haloran is haunted . . . by Kathleen." Billy and Richard are Irish, too, but both were educated in America. Kane and Louise are also Americans, and none of these people with their roots in the New World can understand why Lady Haloran can't forget about Kathleen and simply get on with it.

In a very real sense, though, Lady Haloran is right. The past *does* continue to influence the present, and it would be foolish to ignore that fact. Certainly, the past influences Billy, who—like his mother—cannot simply forget. *Dementia 13* suggests that to be obsessed with the past is dangerous, but to try to forget it completely is also risky because, whether we of the New World like it or not, our personal, family, and cultural histories are what make us who we are in the here and now.

The Devil's Nightmare

ALTERNATE TITLES:

*La Plus Longue Nuit du Diable,
The Longest Night of the Devil,
Vampire Playgirls*

1971

Director: Jean Brismée; *Producer:* Charles Lecocq; *Screenplay:* Patrice Rhomm, Charles Lecocq, André Hunebelle, and Jean Brismée

CAST:
Erika Blanc, Jean Servais, Daniel Emilfork, Jacques Monseu, Ivana Novak, Luciene Raimberg

ORIGINAL RELEASE: Hemisphere Pictures
VIDEO: New Horizons

This Belgian/Italian spooky-castle film is really pretty good, not because the plot is particularly original but because the pacing and atmosphere make it work in spite of its shortcomings.

It is 1945, and Baron von Runberg (Jean Servais), dressed in a Nazi officer's uniform, awaits the birth of his child. Allied planes are passing overhead, and bombs are falling everywhere, but the baron doesn't seem to notice. Then he hears a baby cry and goes to the bedroom to find his wife dead. The child is a girl. With a grim look on his face, the baron pulls out a dagger and stabs the newborn to death.

Twenty-five years later, a tour bus with a driver and six passengers passes through the area looking for a place to spend the night. A man in black (Daniel Emilfork) directs them to the castle where, strangely, they find rooms waiting for them. The seven meet Hans the butler (Jacques Monseu), Martha the housekeeper (Ivana Novak), and the baron himself, who, over dinner, tells them the story of his twelfth-century ancestor who sold his soul to the devil. As a result, the family is cursed, and the oldest daughter in each generation becomes a succubus—a kind of sexy living-dead female spirit that commits foul deeds. Fortunately, the baron has no children, and his brother, Rudolph, was killed in the war, so the family line will soon end and, with it, the curse.

Another visitor arrives that night. Lisa Miller (Erika Blanc) has come to call on Martha, and she arrives at the dinner table dressed in a skin tight, open-front outfit that turns everybody's head, including that of Sorel (Luciene Raimberg), a young novice priest who has yet to take his final vows.

Everyone goes to bed, and one by one, Lisa kills them off after transforming herself from a sexy woman into a bluish walking corpse. Finally, Sorel is the last remaining tourist, but he uses a cross to ward off the succubus, then makes his way to the sanctuary of a nearby chapel.

Now the devil appears, and what do you know, he is the same man in black who directed the tourists to the castle in the first place. It seems that, unbeknownst to the baron, his brother, Rudolph, and housekeeper Martha had a child together—Lisa—and so the curse has continued despite von Runberg's efforts to bring it to an end.

The devil claims to possess the souls of Lisa's six victims, and being a heroic type, Sorel offers to trade his soul for theirs. He signs the pact, then awakens in his bed. Was it all a dream?

Maybe so, because everyone is alive again at breakfast. The baron goes outside to practice fencing with Hans, but there is an accident, and von Runberg is mortally wounded.

Lisa (Erika Blanc) arrives unexpectedly at Castle von Rumberg in *The Devil's Nightmare*.

The bus leaves, but Sorel stays behind with the baron and Lisa. Then, as the young priest looks on from the ramparts of the castle, the bus goes over a cliff, killing everyone on board. Why? Who knows? Has Sorel really sold his soul to the devil? Who knows? Is Lisa really a succubus? Who knows?

Despite the murky ending, *The Devil's Nightmare* has something going for it. The seven passengers on the bus represent the seven deadly sins, and Lisa makes sure that each is committing his or her deadly sin at the moment of death, thus insuring everybody's eternal damnation. So, for example, Max, the driver, represents gluttony, and Lisa feeds him a sumptuous dinner until he chokes. Nancy Foster, one of the tourists, is greedy, and she drowns in a pool of gold dust in the basement. Corinne represents lust, and she is killed while having sex with Nancy's husband, Howard. This idea is a nice touch, something I haven't seen before.

The Devil's Nightmare suggests something that is very rare in movies about Satan and satanists—namely, that the devil is stronger than the forces of good. The novice priest is the representative of good here, but Sorel also represents the deadly sin of pride because he believes he can beat the devil at his own game. This makes him a lot less heroic than most horror film heroes and gives the

Sorel (Lucien Raimbourg), the novice priest, is tempted by visions of Lisa (Erika Blanc).

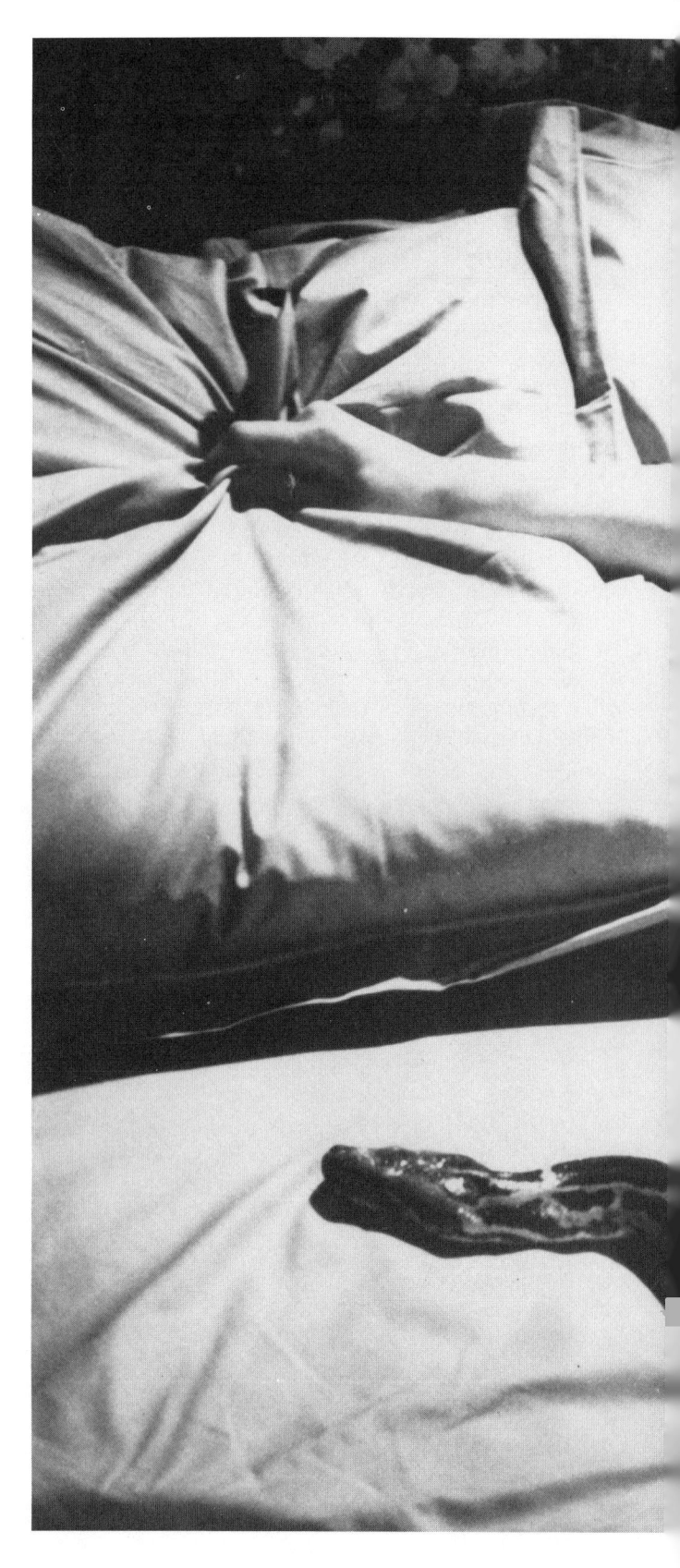

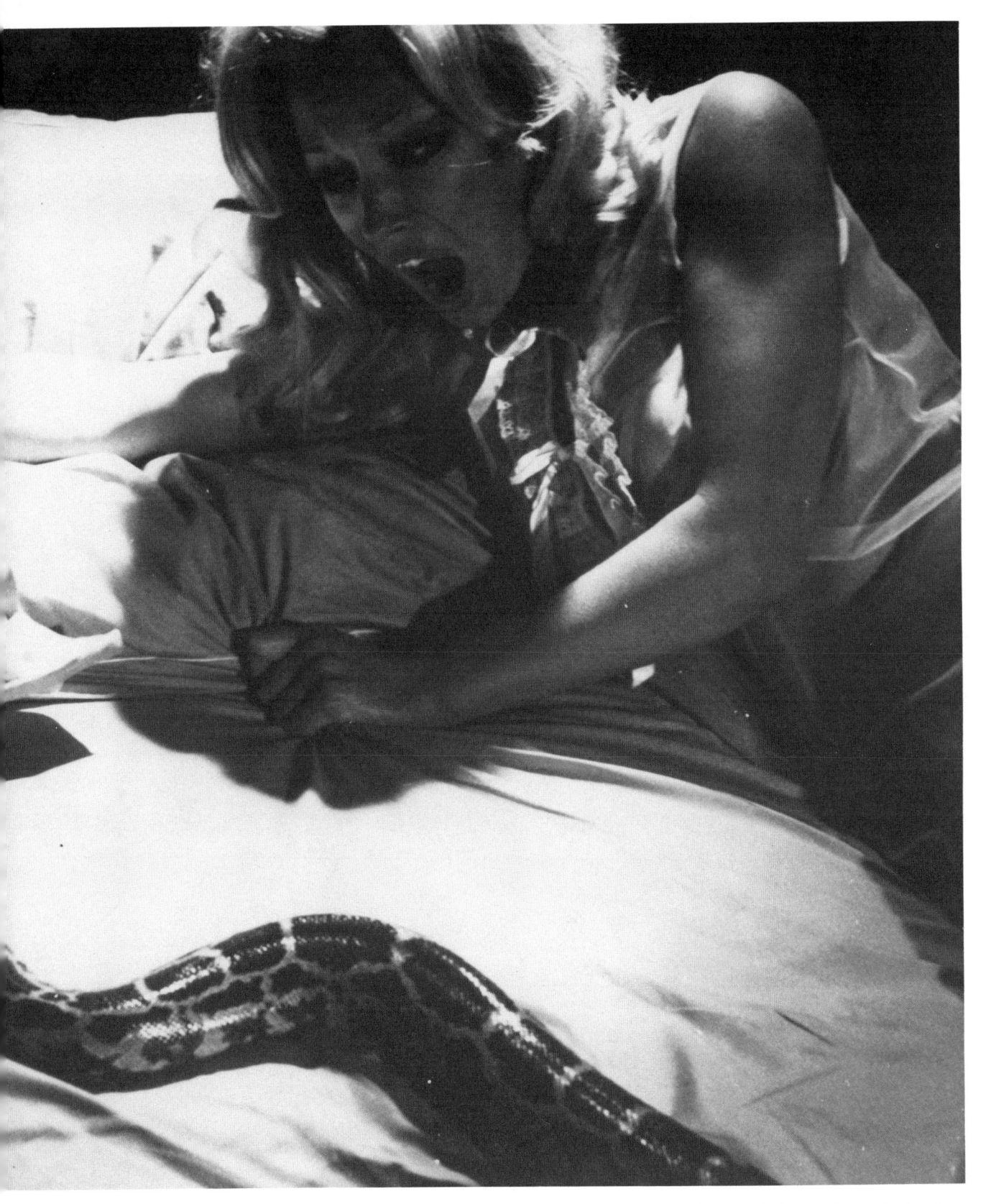

Regine is killed by a snake in her bed as punishment for her sins.

movie a dark feeling, as if the forces of evil are somehow destined to win out over humankind despite the efforts of the heroes we traditionally look to for help.

In short, *The Devil's Nightmare* seems to say that we live in a world where evil can run amok and where there are no heroes capable of stopping it—something the newspapers seem to say every day, too. It's a frightening thought.

Lisa (Erika Blanc) as her real self.

The Devil's Wedding Night

ALTERNATE TITLES:

*Il plenilunio delle Vergini,
The Full Moon of the Virgins*

1973

Director: Paul Solvay; *Producer:* Ralph Zucker; *Screenplay:* Ralph Zucker and Alan M. Harris

CAST:
Mark Damon, Sarah Bay (Rosalba Neri), Esmeralda Barros (Miriam Barrios), Ciro Papas (Stan Papps), Alexander Getty

ORIGINAL RELEASE: Dimension Pictures
VIDEO: VCI

The title of this Italian production is a bit misleading because the devil never actually gets married in the film. In fact, there is no wedding at all. The movie has almost everything else, though. *The Devil's Wedding Night* seems to work under the assumption that, if you put in lots of stuff, every viewer will find something he or she likes. So there is the old good-twin/bad-twin routine, a cult of satanists, an Egyptian amulet, a reference to the Karnsteins (the vampire family in J. S. LeFanu's *Carmilla*), a trip to Castle Dracula in Transylvania, a zombie, and a female vampire who turns out to be Dracula's widow. Countess Dracula drinks blood, of course, but she also takes baths in it, just like the real Elisabeth Bathory, the sixteenth-century Hungarian noblewoman who was convicted of killing some six-hundred young women in the belief that literal bloodbaths would keep her eternally young. For fans of Richard Wagner's operas, there is also the Ring of the Nibelungen. And there's lots of nudity. If you're wondering how all this fits neatly into one plot—well, it doesn't.

Karl Schiller (Mark Damon) is a young scholar who is in quest of the long-lost Ring of the Nibelungen, apparently the most powerful magical object there is. "The possessor of the ring may have power over all mankind . . ." Of course, Karl is a good guy who doesn't want that kind of power; he wants to put the ring in a museum. But his evil twin brother, Franz (Damon again), does want power over all mankind, so he takes Karl's Egyptian talisman that is supposed to protect him from supernatural forces and rides off to Castle Dracula in Transylvania where the ring was last seen.

Franz Schiller (Mark Damon) searches Dracula's castle for the Ring of the Nibelungen in *The Devil's Wedding Night*.

Franz's twin brother, Karl (Mark Damon), puts an end to the vampire monster (Ciro Papas) who serves as Countess Dracula's bodyguard.

There he spends the usual night at the inn where he meets the innkeeper's sexy daughter and gets all the usual warnings about not going to the castle. It seems the Night of the Virgin Moon is coming up. That's the night when, every fifty years, five virgins from the village are mysteriously called to Castle Dracula and never heard of again. "I don't take these tales very seriously," Franz says, which seems to be the case, because he carelessly leaves his protective amulet behind at the inn and goes on to the castle anyway.

There he meets Countess de Vries (Sarah Bay), who is really Countess Dracula, and he comes under her spell. Meanwhile, Karl arrives in Transylvania to search for his brother. He gets his amulet back from the innkeeper's daughter, meets the countess, and discovers that Franz is now a vampire, the reincarnation of the original Count Dracula. Karl is just in time for the Night of the Virgin Moon when Countess Dracula uses the Ring of the Nibelungen to summon the naked virgins who will be sacrificed in a Black Mass. Of course, the innkeeper's daughter is among them.

Karl kills his brother, then takes his place at the Mass, where he grabs an ax and decapitates all the hooded satanists who have gathered for the occasion. Then,

Countess Dracula (Sarah Bay) celebrates the Black Mass in *The Devil's Wedding Night*.

using his Egyptian amulet, he defeats Countess Dracula by cutting off her ring hand. It seems, then, that, despite the fact that the Ring of the Nibelungen is supposedly the most powerful magical object in the world, the talisman is even more powerful, and since Karl already had that in his possession at the beginning of the movie, why did he bother with this whole trip to Transylvania in the first place? And if the ring really does offer its possessor "power over all mankind," if it could be used to rule the world, why does Countess Dracula only use it to summon a handful of virgins to the castle once every fifty years? Oh, well . . .

In the end, everything seems to be okay, but somehow the innkeeper's daughter is now a vampire, too, and she kills Karl. The mysterious stranger (Alexander Getty) who has been cropping up like a running gag throughout the film and who might be the devil ends up with the ring.

What we have here is the usual thing. Countess Dracula is the woman who is open about her carnal desires—in fact, during the course of the movie, she has sex with almost everybody, including Franz, her zombie housekeeper Lara (Esmeralda Barros), and herself. In horror films, and in popular culture generally, the

Lara (Esmeralda Barros), Countess Dracula's zombie housekeeper, meets a bad end in *The Devil's Wedding Night*.

woman who is sexually aggressive is depicted as evil and dangerous to men, and that is certainly the case here. Franz loses control of himself because of the countess, and the same thing almost happens to Karl. The countess wants to be in control of things, and in a male-dominated world, that is not permitted. The worst thing is that Countess Dracula's sexual liberation seems to be contagious. The nice, submissive, virginal innkeeper's daughter also becomes sexually aggressive by the end of the film, and this costs Karl his life. If Countess Dracula had been allowed to continue in her evil ways, she and women like her might have taken over the world.

As usual, the only way to deal with a woman who wants power is to kill her. That is exactly what our hero does, and the film tells us that he has done the right thing. So, women in the audience, be warned. If you want to be more than an innkeeper's daughter in this world, you're in for a lot of trouble.

Donovan's Brain

1953

Director/screenplay: Felix Feist; *Producer:* Tom Gries

CAST:
Lew Ayres, Gene Evans, Nancy Davis, Steve Brodie

ORIGINAL RELEASE: United Artists
VIDEO: MGM/UA Home Video

This is the granddaddy of all brain movies and still the best. It isn't the first brain movie, though; in fact, it is basically a remake of *The Lady and the Monster*, which appeared in 1944. Both films were based on the novel *Donovan's Brain* by Curt Siodmak, who also wrote the

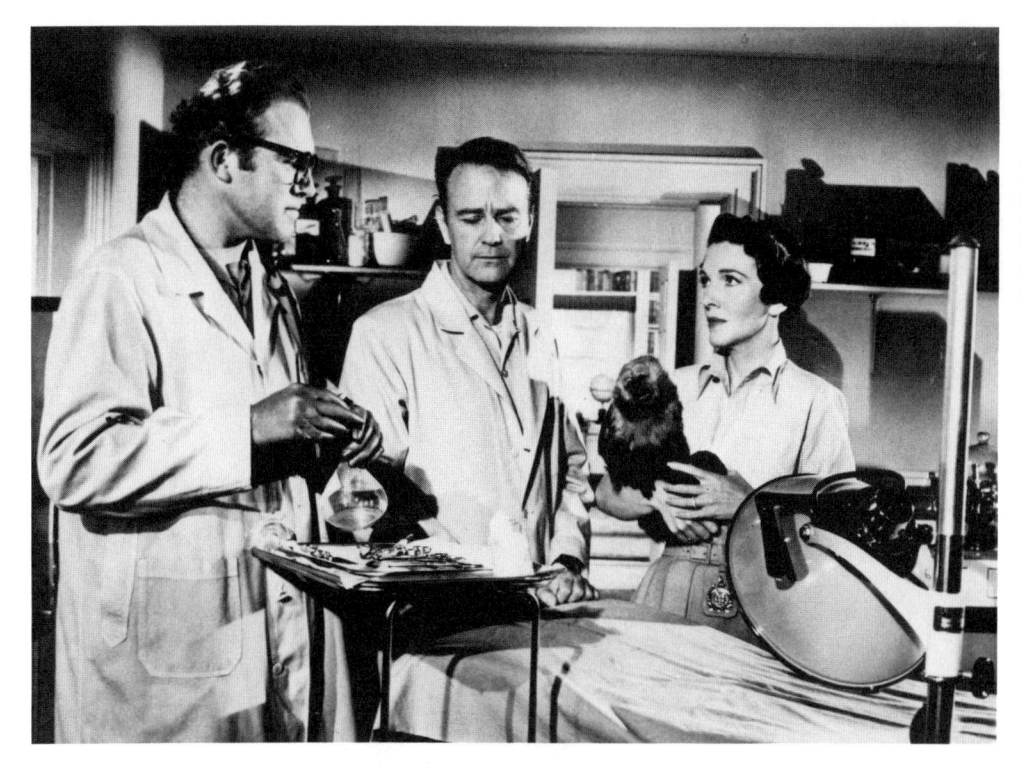

Decades before she became First Lady Nancy Reagan, Nancy Davis was Jan Cory, sympathetic wife of Dr. Patrick Cory (Lew Ayres) and friend to Dr. Frank Schratt (Gene Evans) in *Donovan's Brain*. (*Courtesy MGM/UA Home Video*)

Jan (Nancy Davis), Patrick (Lew Ayres), and Frank (Gene Evans) finally succeed in keeping a monkey's brain alive outside its body. (*Courtesy MGM/UA Home Video*)

screenplay for *The Wolf Man* and other horror films. But the 1953 version offers such a strong cast and such a literate script that it is hard to imagine a better treatment of the basic idea. *Donovan's Brain* still holds up beautifully, even after more than four decades.

Dr. Patrick Cory (Lew Ayres) and Dr. Frank Schratt (Gene Evans) are doing brain research. More specifically, they are trying to remove a monkey's brain and keep it alive outside the body, though the reason for these experiments is never really made clear except that it is being done "for the good of humanity." Assisting them is Pat's wife, Jan, played by Nancy Davis, who shortly before making this film had become Mrs. Ronald Reagan.

The experiment with the monkey is successful—"A brain without a body, alive!"—and that same day, the trio of scientists get another unexpected opportunity. A small plane crashes in the area, and Cory and Schratt are

Jan Cory (Nancy Davis) is terrified to realize that her husband (Lew Ayres) has been possessed by the brain of millionaire Warren H. Donovan. (Courtesy MGM/UA Home Video)

called upon to help. There is only one survivor, multimillionaire Warren H. Donovan, and though it doesn't look as if he has much of a chance, he is taken to Cory's house where the doctors operate. As expected, Donovan dies. But then Pat has an idea. "Science can use Donovan's brain," he says, and though Frank and Jan object at first—"What an idea, stealing a man's brain"—they go along with the operation to remove the brain and keep it alive in a tank in the lab.

The death of Donovan gets a lot of media attention—he was, after all, a famous if somewhat shady businessman and one of the wealthiest men in the world—but Pat and Frank manage to keep their experiment a secret. Then they run into free-lance journalist Herbie Yocum (Steve Brodie), who asks to take pictures of the operating table where Donovan died. Pat agrees for fear that Yocum might become suspicious, and while he is in Cory's lab, Herbie takes a picture of the brain in the tank.

The experiment is a terrific success. Donovan's brain absorbs nourishment and even begins to grow, and Pat's equipment shows that it is thinking, though it is impossible to determine what its thoughts might be. But Dr. Cory has another idea: telepathy. "Donovan's brain is giving out thoughts. All I have to do is use my brain to receive them."

Frank doesn't think it will work, but Pat begins to study up on Donovan and learns that he really was an unscrupulous man who did anything for money, never gave to charities, and had been the target of an income tax evasion case for many years. But you have to get your brains where you can find them, so Pat sits down in front of the tank and tries to open his mind to Donovan's. Eventually, he collapses, and in a trancelike state, he writes a note in Donovan's handwriting with Donovan's signature.

Frank and Jan fear that Pat is going off the deep end, but the next day the brain takes possession of Cory again, causing him to limp as Donovan did. By now, the brain is completely in control of the good doctor, who is free only when Donovan sleeps.

Cory charters a plane to the city where he takes Donovan's favorite suite in his favorite hotel, closes out a bank account for $27,000 that Donovan kept under a false name, buys equipment to boost the brain's power, and orders half a dozen suits like the ones Donovan always wore. He also takes up Donovan's nefarious business deals and blackmail plots where the millionaire left off.

Pat runs into Yocum, who has put everything together and knows that Donovan's brain is still alive. Cory buys him off temporarily, but he knows that this means trouble.

Eventually, the brain hypnotizes Yocum and forces him to kill himself. Frank tries to shoot the brain in its tank—"It's unnatural, unholy"—but is forced to shoot himself instead. In a moment when the brain is asleep, however, Cory manages to make a tape recording for Jan with instructions on how the brain might be destroyed. He tells her to fasten a line from the lightning rod on the roof to the brain's apparatus. She does, and just as the brain has decided to kill her off, too, a storm comes on, and a bolt of lightning puts an end to Warren H. Donovan.

Donovan's Brain is, of course, a "tampering with things man was not meant to know" film, but it has some unusual twists that set it apart from the ordinary mad-scientist flick. For one thing, Pat Cory isn't an evil man. He is a nice guy with a nice wife, nice friends, and high ideals. In the end, he admits, "I did many foolish things," but that could happen to anyone. In short, he's a lot like us, and he only does evil deeds when he is under the control of the brain.

In fact, it isn't really science that is evil in this movie; it's big business. That is a theme that would become common in the seventies but that was almost unheard of in the conservative fifties when what was good for big business was good for America and becoming a self-made millionaire was everybody's American dream. The Donovan character ought to be a hero, but instead, as one newspaper account has it, "Donovan carried to an extreme the independence of the self-made man."

Donovan's Brain says in so many words what lots of ordinary 1950s Americans probably thought but never said—that what is good for big business might not be so good for the rest of us and that our financial and government leaders might simply be looking out for themselves. The Donovans of the world might be controlling us, as the brain controlled Cory, and not necessarily for our welfare.

Perhaps this is why the film was so popular in its own day and why it holds up so well after all these years.

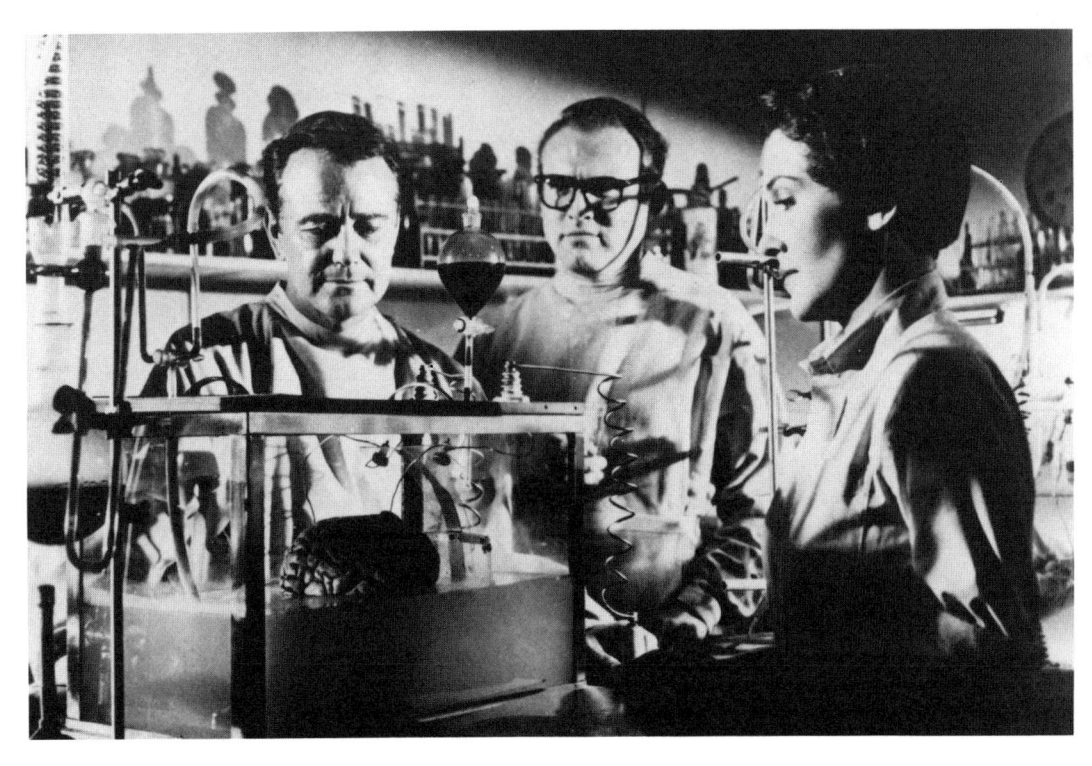

The trio of scientists (Lew Ayres, Gene Evans, Nancy Davis) study *Donovan's Brain.* (*Courtesy MGM/UA Home Video*)

Don't Look in the Basement

1973

Director/producer: S. F. Brownrigg; *Screenplay:* Tim Pope

CAST:

Rosie Holotik, William Bill McGhee, Harryette Warren, Ann MacAdams, Gene Ross, Hugh Feagin, Michael Harvey, Rhea MacAdams

ORIGINAL RELEASE: Hallmark Releasing
VIDEO: Gorgon Video

Nurse Charlotte Beal (Rosie Holotik) reports for her new job at Dr. Stephens's (Michael Harvey) experimental psychiatric clinic, only to find out that Stephens has died since her interview and his assistant Dr. Masters (Ann MacAdams) is now in charge. As you might expect, the place is full of crazy people, including Sergeant Jaffee (Hugh Feagin), a veteran who still thinks he's at war, Jennifer the nymphomaniac (Harryette Warren), Judge Oliver W. Cameron (Gene Ross), and others, including Sam (William Bill McGhee), the stereotypical big strong guy with the mind of a child.

Something is clearly wrong in the clinic, as Nurse Beal suspects right from the beginning, although, as an experienced psychiatric nurse, you'd think she wouldn't

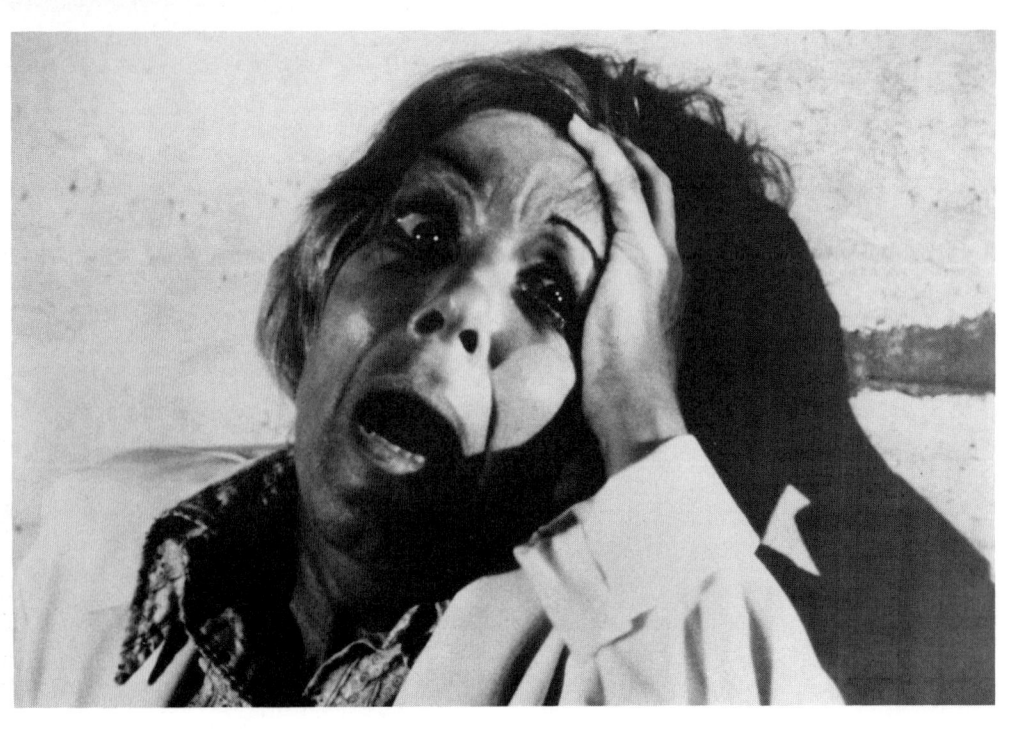

Judge Oliver W. Cameron (Gene Ross) takes the law into his own hands—as well as an ax—in the opening sequence of *Don't Look in the Basement*. (*Courtesy Hollywood Book and Poster*)

Dr. Masters (Ann MacAdams) is as crazy as everybody else in the asylum—maybe even crazier. (*Courtesy Hollywood Book and Poster*)

86

be so freaked out by the patients. In any case, someone starts committing evil deeds around the house. Mrs. Callingham (Rhea MacAdams), a creepy old woman, has her tongue cut out. A visiting repairman is murdered. Then so are some of the inmates.

Beal eventually figures out that the looneys have taken over the asylum. Dr. Stephens was axed to death by Judge Cameron before the nurse arrived, and his body is hidden in the basement—which is why we aren't supposed to look down there. Dr. Masters really was Stephens's assistant, but she has since gone off the deep end herself, and she is the one who has been committing the murders. Finally, the inmates kill her, Beal escapes, and good-natured Sam takes an ax to all the remaining cast members, apparently in hopes of putting an end to all this and getting to the final credits.

Most horror films offer us some kind of warning, but the "Don't" movies of the 1970s are particularly insistent about this—*Don't Answer the Phone, Don't Go in the Woods, Don't Be Afraid of the Dark, Don't Open the Door* (another Brownrigg effort), *Don't Go in the House, Don't Look Now, Don't Eat Your Vegetables* (I made that one up), *Don't Open the Window,* and so on. After seeing all these films, there really isn't much left for you to do.

In his book *Danse Macabre,* Stephen King wisely states that, if there were no such thing as death, there would be no horror films. I would add that, if there were no such thing as insanity, there would certainly be fewer horror movies. Insanity scares us, not only because it makes people act strangely and sometimes dangerously but also because it's something that seemingly could happen to anyone. Part of the definition of insanity—at least in the movies— is that, if you are insane, you don't

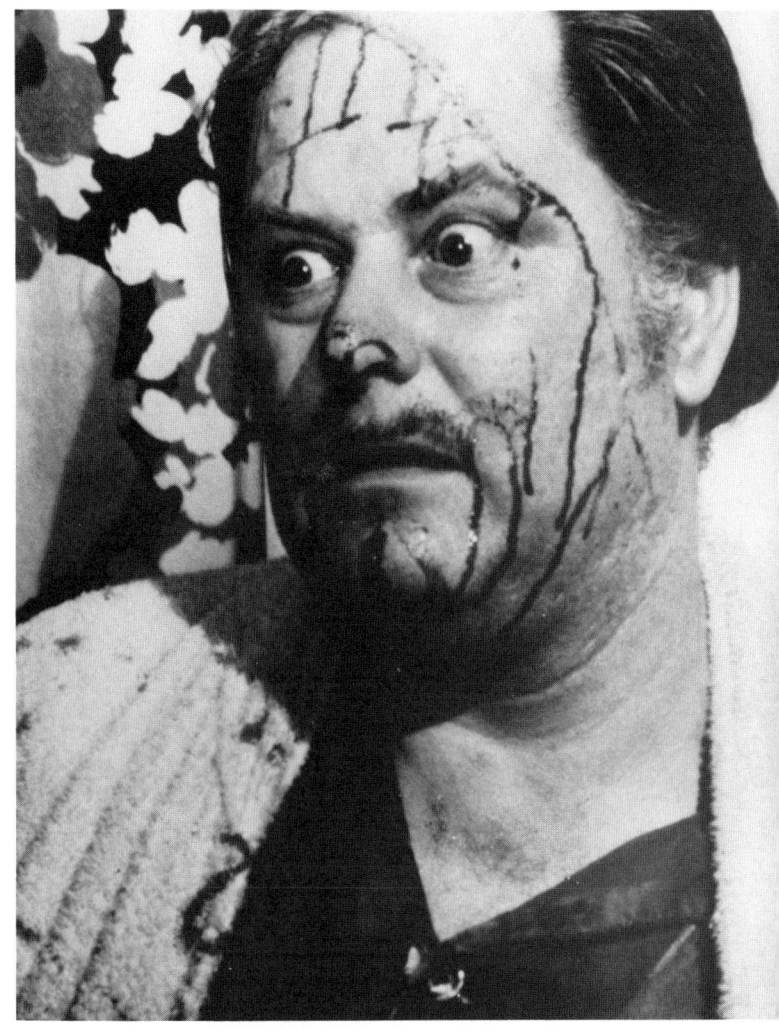

The judge (Gene Ross) sees that the end is in sight. (*Courtesy Hollywood Book and Poster*)

Sam (William Bill McGhee) helps nurse Charlotte Beal (Rosie Holotik) escape before the final massacre. (*Courtesy Hollywood Book and Poster*)

Nothing in her training as a psychiatric nurse has prepared Charlotte (Rosie Holotik) for what she experiences in *Don't Look in the Basement*. (Courtesy Hollywood Book and Poster)

know it. You think you're normal. You think your perception of reality is correct. In *Psycho*, Norman Bates thinks he's normal, and the inmates of Dr. Stephens's clinic think they're normal, too. I think I'm normal, but I could be hopelessly out of my mind and not be aware of it.

Also, insanity is scary because often crazy people don't seem to be crazy. Again, Norman Bates seems normal enough, and so does Dr. Masters in *Don't Look in the Basement*. So anybody might be insane without our even knowing it until it's too late. On top of that, this film suggests that some of those professionals we depend on and trust, such as judges or psychiatrists, might be over the edge. Now that's a frightening idea. It makes you stop and think. But don't think about it too much because it's enough to drive you nuts.

Dracula vs. Frankenstein

ALTERNATE TITLES:

*Blood of Frankenstein,
They're Coming to Get You*

1971

Director: Al Adamson; *Producers:* Al Adamson and Samuel M. Sherman; *Screenplay:* William Pugsley and Samuel M. Sherman

CAST:
J. Carrol Naish, Lon Chaney Jr., Regina Carrol, John Bloom, Zandor Vorkov, Anthony Eisley, Russ Tamblyn, Jim Davis, Forrest J. Ackerman, Angelo Rossitto, Anne Morrell, Greydon Clark

ORIGINAL RELEASE: Independent-International Pictures
VIDEO: VidAmerica

Al Adamson will do just about anything to fill up ninety minutes of screen time, and here he brings together Dr. Frankenstein, his monster, Count Dracula, and an enormous cast in a plot that is so unnecessarily complicated and murky that, in the end, almost nothing makes sense. *Dracula vs. Frankenstein* marks the final screen appearance of Naish (*The Beast With Five Fingers* and countless movies and TV shows) and one of the last of Chaney (*The Wolf Man, Son of Dracula*, and many lesser films). Both of them deserved much better. So did the late Jim Davis of *Dallas* fame and Russ Tamblyn, who, between *West Side Story* and *Twin Peaks*, was in a lot of very bad flicks such as this one.

Judith Fontaine (Adamson's wife, Regina Carrol) is a nightclub singer whose sister Joanie (Maria Lease) has disappeared in the hippie community of Venice, California. Judith goes looking for her, despite warnings from police sergeant Martin (Jim Davis) not to, and there she meets aging bohemian Mike Howard (Anthony Eisley), two hippies name Samantha and Strange, and Dr. Duray (J. Carrol Naish), who runs a house of horrors arcade on the boardwalk.

Duray is really the last of the Frankensteins, and he and his assistants, Groton (Lon Chaney, Jr.) and the dwarf Grazbo (Angelo Rossitto), are busy decapitating young women, then putting them back together and bringing them to life. Why they are doing this is never clear, though Frankenstein keeps saying something about a serum he is developing. In any case, Joanie is one of his victims.

One night, Frankenstein has a visitor. It's Count Dracula (Zandor Vorkov), who always speaks as if he's in an echo chamber and who, again for no particular reason, has dug up and stolen the body of the original Frankenstein monster (John Bloom), which has been

Sometime between *West Side Story* and *Twin Peaks*, Russ Tamblyn played the biker Rico in *Dracula vs. Frankenstein*.

buried in a Venice graveyard for years. What the creature was doing in California is anybody's guess.

Frankenstein revives his ancestor's creation and uses it to get revenge on his professional rival Dr. Beaumont (Forrest J. Ackerman). Groton is still taking time off from the doctor's experiments to ax people under the boardwalk—he gets hippie/biker/punk Rico (Russ Tamblyn) and his gang of no-goods, who really serve no purpose in this movie at all. Meanwhile, Judith and Mike have traced Joanie to the "creature emporium" where Frankenstein and his cronies try to use them in experiments, too. During the fight that follows, the dwarf falls on an ax, Frankenstein accidentally decapitates himself with the guillotine in his exhibition, and Groton is shot by Sergeant Martin.

It looks as if Judith's problems are solved, but then she is captured by Dracula, who wants to turn her into his vampire bride. Mike almost saves her, but in the only unexpected moment in this film, Dracula zaps the hero with a ray from his magical ring and burns him to a crisp.

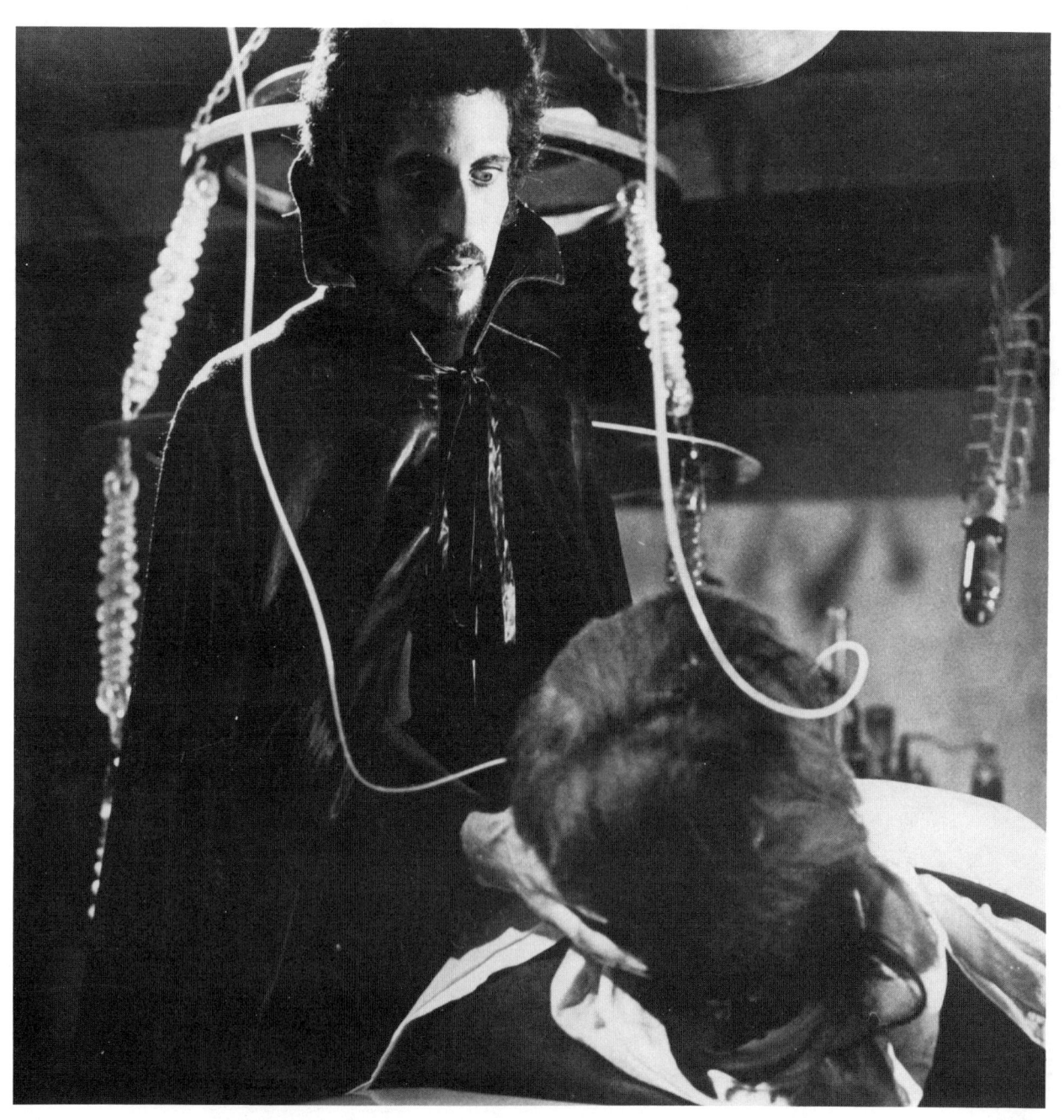

In Dr. Duray's laboratory on the amusement park pier, Count Dracula (Zandor Vorkov) revives the original Frankenstein monster—again.

The Frankenstein monster (John Bloom) is back.

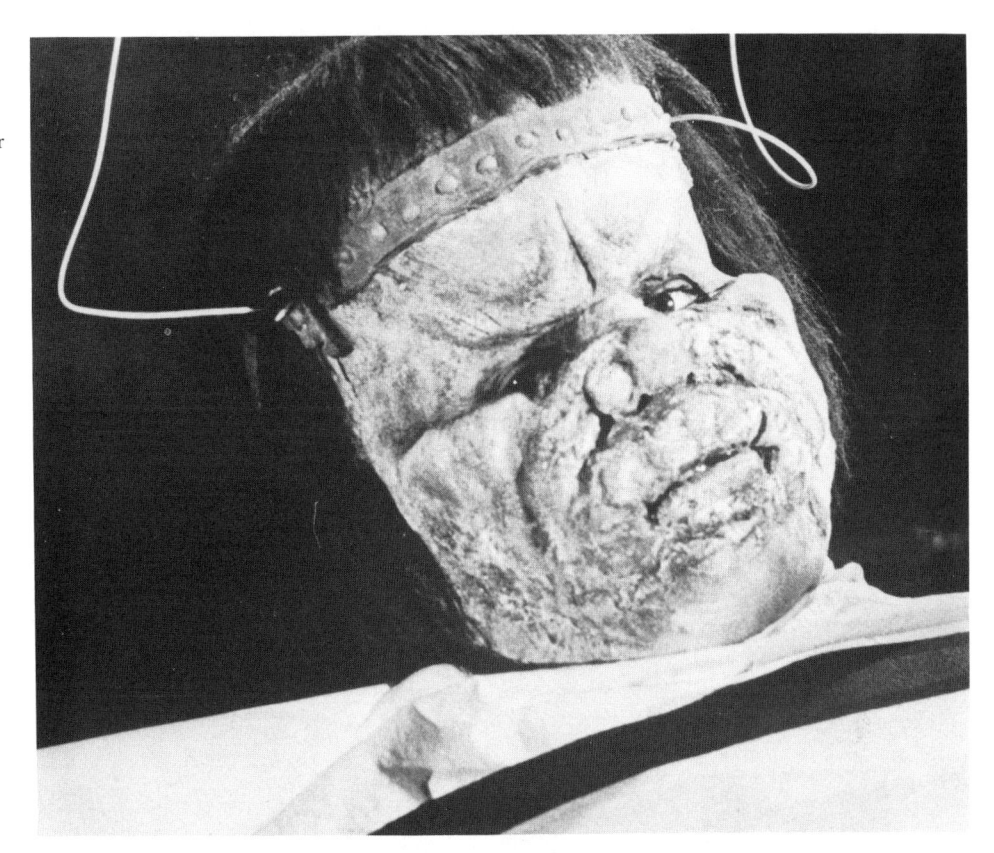

In one of this movie's bondage scenes, Count Dracula (Zandor Vorkov) captures Judith (Regina Carrol).

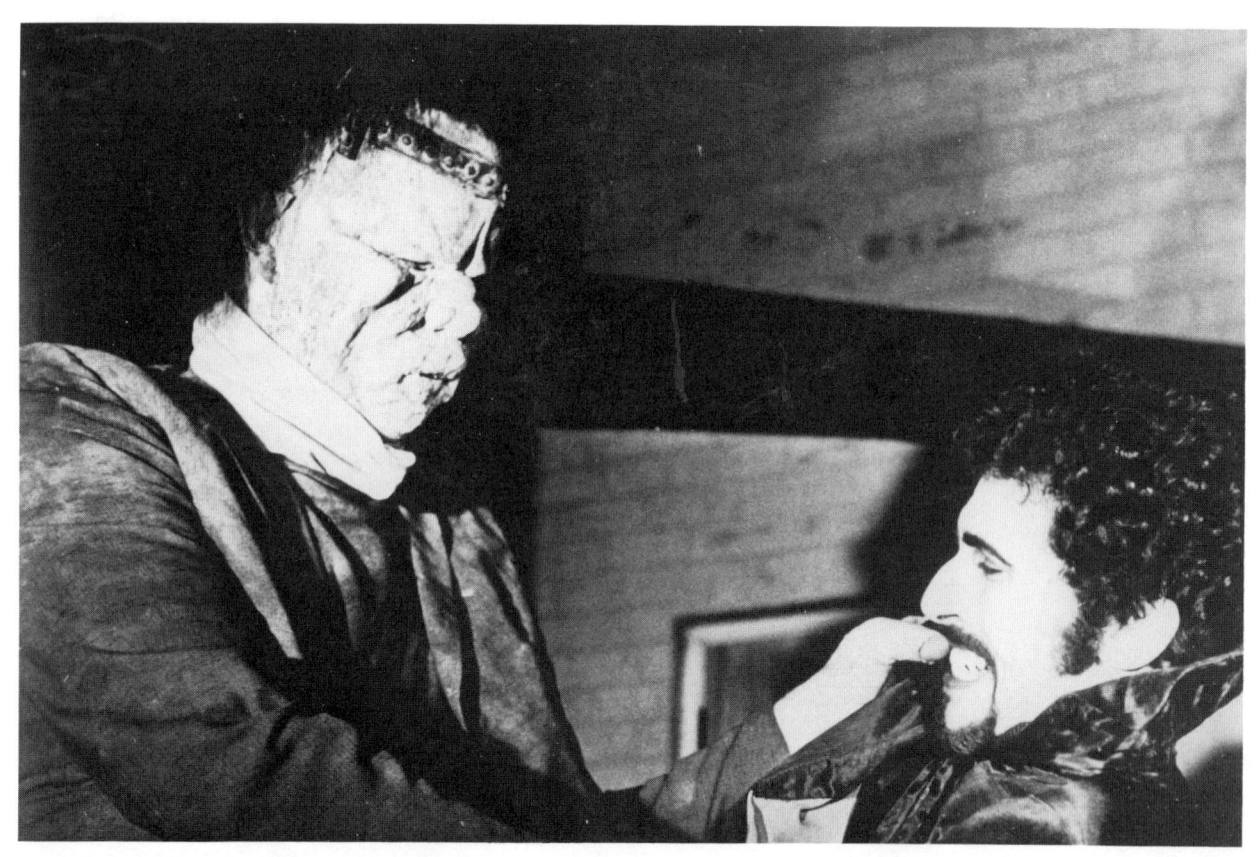

The final showdown between the monster (John Bloom) and Dracula (Zandor Vorkov)—a fitting ending for a film entitled *Dracula vs. Frankenstein*.

But before the vampire can transform Judith into one of the living dead, the Frankenstein monster takes a liking to her, too. As the title suggests, the movie ends with the big fight between Dracula and the monster, and Dracula wins by pulling off both the monster's arms, then his head—it seems the original Dr. Frankenstein's stitching just didn't hold up. The fight has taken a lot out of the Count, however, and he can't make it back to his coffin in time, so he disintegrates in the morning sun.

And that's that.

If this sounds confusing, you should actually watch the film and listen to the characters talk on and on, saying things that make absolutely no sense. Frankenstein and Dracula chat about some comet that is passing overhead, a plague that struck the Venice area many years before, an accidental fire in Frankenstein's lab—all things that seem to have nothing to do with anything that's going on. And no one ever talks about what you really want to know. When you watch one of Adamson's movies, you always feel as if a reel is missing and that, if you could just see it, it would explain everything. But this film is as it is, and Adamson's attitude seems to be take it or leave it.

In general, horror films are conservative, but a lot of movies from the Vietnam era—*The Crazies, The Mind Snatchers, Deathdream*—were sympathetic to the counterculture movement of the time. *Dracula vs. Frankenstein* is not. When the hippie named Strange talks about the protest to be held in Venice that night, Samantha (Anne Morrell) asks, "What are we protesting?" Strange (Greydon Clark) replies, "Who knows, but I bet it'll be fun."

In fact, according to this movie, Dr. Frankenstein is kind of a hippie himself. When he says things like "I believe we should all experience life with a natural spontaneity," he is spouting counterculture philosophy. When he tells Judith that, after he experiments on her, she "will be spiritually released," it sounds as if he's talking about an LSD trip. And since we know that Dr. Frankenstein is evil, the entire counterculture with its protests against the war in Vietnam and its civil rights and women's liberation movements must be evil, too.

As it turns out, it is Sergeant Martin of the local police who has the answer as to why bad things happen in the world and why people fall victim to them. He says, "These people want these things to happen." In other words, people like Joanie and Mike who are not necessarily satisfied with the way things are, are simply asking for trouble. So are people like Judith who want to solve their problems and take control of their lives.

The moral of the story is: Be content with the status quo, know your place and stay there, don't ask questions, don't challenge authority, and nothing bad will happen to you. This is a lie, of course, but you couldn't expect anything different from an appalling film like *Dracula vs. Frankenstein*.

Dracula's Dog

ALTERNATE TITLE:

Zoltan, Hound of Dracula

1978

Director: Albert Band; *Producers:* Charles Band and Frank Ray Perilli; *Screenplay:* Frank Ray Perilli

CAST:
Michael Pataki, Jan Shutan, Reggie Nalder, José Ferrer, John Levin

ORIGINAL RELEASE: Crown International Pictures
VIDEO: Thorn EMI/HBO and United Home Video

Yes, there really is a movie entitled *Dracula's Dog*, and it's about what you would expect. Even the talents of such veteran performers as José Ferrer and Michael Pataki can't help to save this one.

Soviet soldiers in Rumania discover the crypt of the Draculas and accidentally unearth Zoltan, the dog of the title. He, in turn, pulls the stake from the heart of Veidt Smit (Reggie Nalder), Count Dracula's manservant from the good old days. Unfortunately, the two can't manage to bring their master back from the dead this time, but both are compelled to serve a Dracula, so they must begin the search for any of the count's living descendants.

Michael Drake (Pataki) is the last surviving member of the Dracula clan, and he lives in Los Angeles with his wife (Jan Shutan) and kids. Like so many Americans, though, he has lost touch with his European roots—even his name has been anglicized—and he doesn't know that he is linked, as it were, by blood to the infamous Count Dracula. But he is going to find out.

Using his power to hypnotize other dogs, Zoltan gains information about where he can find his new master, and together with Veidt, he makes his way to California. Meanwhile, Inspector Branco (Ferrer), the Van Helsing character in this film, is on the trail of Zoltan and Veidt and tries to enlist Michael's aid in dealing with the undead menace. At the same time, Zoltan is spreading

Michael Pataki could be the most unconvincing Dracula ever in *Dracula's Dog*.

Zoltan, Hound of Dracula, listens for his master's voice.

vampirism through the canine and human population of California. Is the West Coast doomed?

Needless to say, this film is hilarious, though, in all honesty, it's hard to know whether it is supposed to be funny or not. The movie seems to take itself seriously, but of course it's impossible to watch it with a straight face. For example, in one sequence, Zoltan attacks the Drakes' new puppy. Finding the poor little creature dead, Michael and his son Steve (John Levin) bury it out back. But, when night falls, the puppy—now a chubby little vampire dog with sad eyes and droopy ears—digs itself out of its grave and goes bounding across a field in search of victims, wagging its cute little tail in the moonlight.

Now that's funny!

One thing that horror films often do well is to frighten us by questioning the truisms we live by, those little proverbial bits of wisdom that make life seem so simple. For example, most movies tell us that "love conquers all," but in many horror films—in *Night of the Living Dead*, say, or *Invasion of the Body Snatchers*—this doesn't hold true, and that's unsettling. We all know that "childhood is a time of innocence," but in films like *The Children* or *Village of the Damned* or *The Innocents* or *Children of the Corn*, this proves not to be the case. Movies like these make us question what we think we know, and that is frightening but probably useful and healthy, too.

The Long, Dark Night and *Dogs* challenge the long-standing assumption that "a dog is man's best friend" by doing for the canine realm what Hitchcock's *The Birds* did for our feathered friends. *Dracula's Dog* puts a new

Veidt Smit (Reggie Nalder), Count Dracula's manservant, rises from the tomb and goes looking for a new job.

twist on this idea. Zoltan is certainly his late master's best friend, but that very fact makes him everybody else's worst enemy. He offers his friendship and loyalty to Michael Drake, but this doesn't seem like the kind of canine companionship that anyone human might want. There seems to be a lot of potential here. Handled differently—and perhaps with a different title—*Dracula's Dog* could have been a pretty effective and frightening movie.

But it isn't.

Fiend Without a Face

1958

Director: Arthur Crabtree; *Producer:* John Croydon; *Screenplay:* Herbert J. Leder

Inspector Branco (José Ferrer) tries to explain what's going on to Michael Drake (Michael Pataki) in *Dracula's Dog*.

Young Barbara Griselle (Kim Parker) enlists the townsfolk to help her find out who or what murdered her brother in *Fiend Without a Face*. (*Courtesy Hollywood Book and Poster*)

One of the locals has his brain partially sucked out by an invisible monster. (*Courtesy Hollywood Book and Poster*)

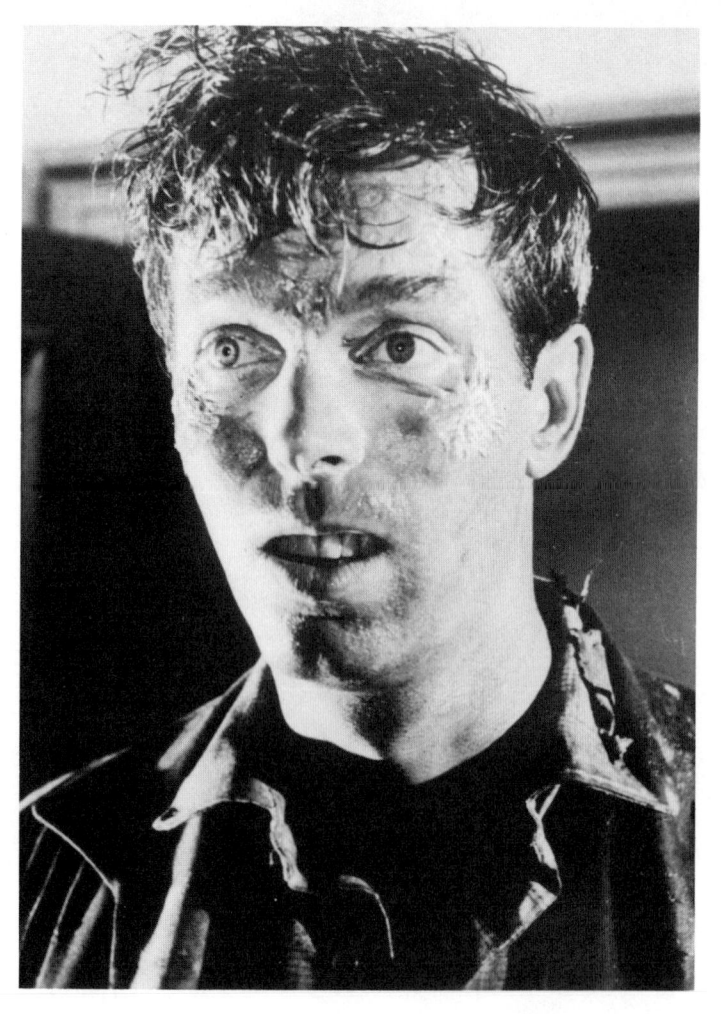

CAST:
Marshall Thompson, Kynaston Reeves, Kim Parker, Stanley Maxted, Terence Kilburn

ORIGINAL RELEASE: Anglo Amalgamated/MGM
VIDEO: Republic Home Video

When there are a number of unexplained civilian deaths in the neighborhood of a U.S./Canadian radar base in Manitoba, Maj. Jeff Cummings (Marshall Thompson) investigates. He finds that each victim has two punctures at the base of the head and that the brain and spinal cord have been removed, "sucked out like an egg through those two holes." Because the base uses nuclear power to boost its radar capabilities, the locals blame the deaths on radiation, but Cummings has another theory. "It's as if some mental vampire were at work."

This isn't the major's only problem, however. Someone has been draining off power from the base's nuclear reactor. Interestingly enough, there is a retired scientist in the area, Professor Walgate (Kynaston Reeves), who is an expert on atomic energy and psychic phenomena—a strange combination, to say the least—and who, as it turns out, is behind the whole mess. Walgate has been experimenting with thought materialization, using electricity to boost his brainpower. By borrowing nuclear energy from the base, he has managed to create living mental beings that can survive and multiply by draining the brains of the living. At first, these creatures are invisible, but when they manage to boost the power of the nuclear reactor, they appear as disembodied brains that slink around on their spinal-cord tails.

Walgate did not intend to create these monsters, but it's too late now for apologies. In the end, the brains attack Cummings, Walgate, his assistant Barbara Griselle (Kim Parker), and some others in Barbara's house, and this is the scene we've all been waiting for. The brains are mortal, at least, and the humans use guns and axes to dispatch them in a real bloodbath. *Fiend Without a Face* is an early attempt at gore cinema, and when shot, stabbed, or chopped, the brains spill enormous amounts of blood with a *glub-glub* sound that is almost as disgusting as the slurping noise they make whenever a victim's skull is drained. Cummings finally manages to shut down the nuclear reactor, and without their source of energy, the brains melt into sludge, but not before Walgate gets what's coming to him. The survivors live happily ever after.

This is one of the first films to address the issue of nuclear *energy* rather than nuclear weapons, and that's interesting. The bomb was the negative result of nuclear science, but atomic energy was supposed to be the positive side. *Fiend Without a Face* says that nuclear

Maj. Jeff Cummings (Marshall Thompson) finds Professor Walgate's pipe in the crypt and realizes that the old boy has been up to something. (*Courtesy Hollywood Book and Poster*)

Barbara (Kim Parker) and Jeff (Marshall Thompson) call on Professor Walgate (Kynaston Reeves) and demand an explanation of recent weird events. (*Courtesy Hollywood Book and Poster*)

power can be a gift to mankind, but also a danger if it falls into the wrong hands. Today, our society still seems to have its doubts about whether nuclear energy is in the right hands or not.

Frankenstein's Castle of Freaks

ALTERNATE TITLES:

*El Castello dell'Orrore,
House of Freaks*

1973

Director: Robert Oliver; *Producer:* Robert Randall; *Screenplay:* Mario Francini

Jeff (Marshall Thompson), Barbara (Kim Parker), the professor (Kynaston Reeves), and some of the men from the local base are attacked by the brain monsters. (*Courtesy Hollywood Book and Poster*)

Jeff (Marshall Thompson) blasts a few of the brain monsters at the nuclear power station in the closing moments of *Fiend Without a Face*. (*Courtesy of Hollywood Book and Poster*)

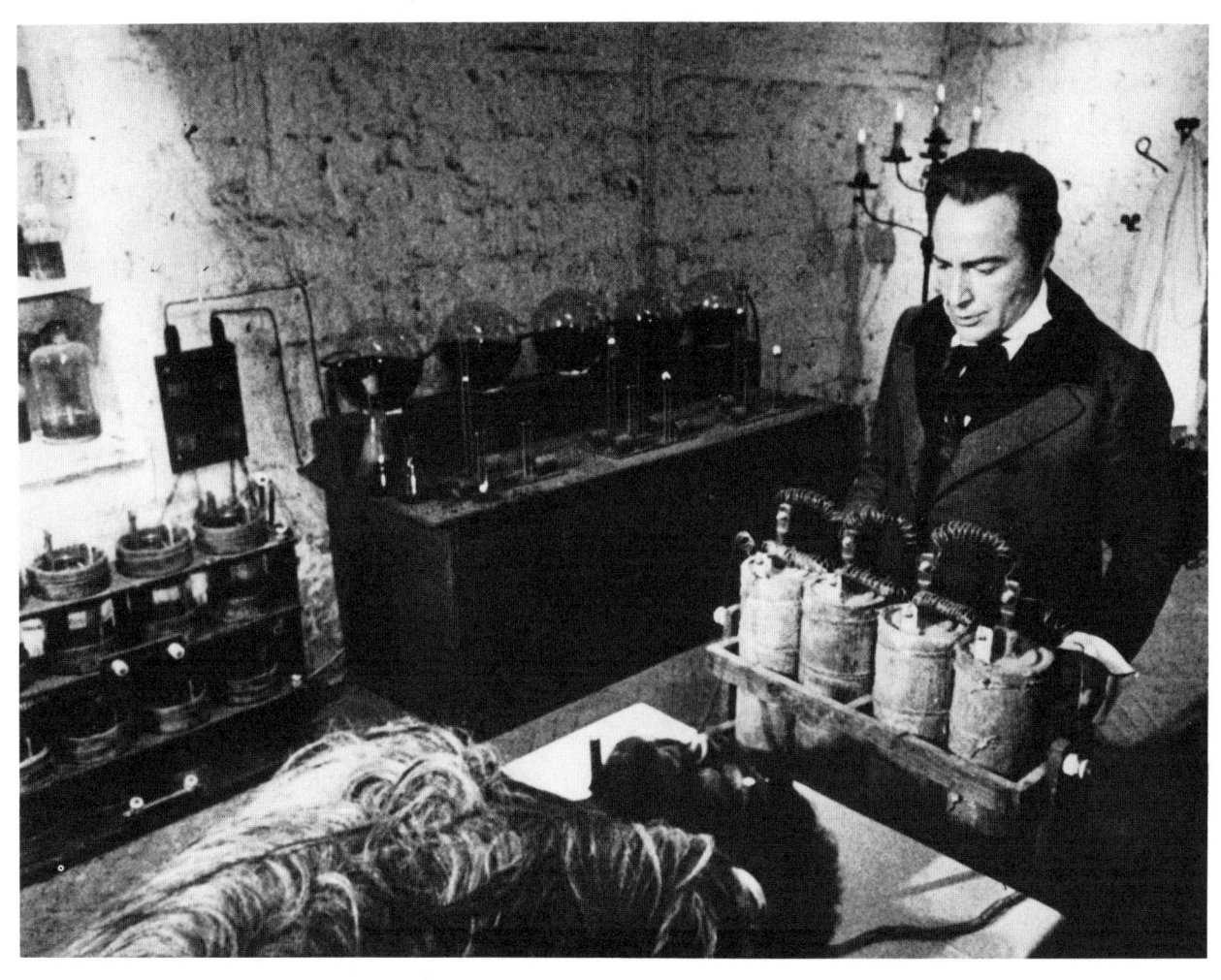

Count Frankenstein (Rossano Brazzi) plans to bring a dead Neanderthal man back to life.

CAST:
Rossano Brazzi, Michael Dunn, Edmund Purdom, Simone Blondell, Christiane Royce, Boris Lugosi, Alan Collins

ORIGINAL RELEASE: Cinerama Releasing

VIDEO: Magnum Home Video, Catalina Home Video, and Sinister Cinema

It's amazing to realize how many film careers get started in disastrous movies like this one—and how many careers end there. This made-in-Italy production of *Frankenstein's Castle of Freaks* pretty much marks the end of the road for one time matinee idol Rossano Brazzi—it's a far cry from *South Pacific*, not to mention Edmund (*The Student Prince*) Purdom.

Some movies must be seen to be believed. This one is so terrible that even seeing it won't necessarily convince you that it exists. Why would anyone think this was a good idea?

Here's the story. It's nineteenth-century Italy—why Count Frankenstein (he's a count rather than a baron in this film) lives there is anybody's guess—and the villagers discover a bunch of Neanderthal men living in a nearby cave. That's right, Neanderthal men who dress in furs and grunt a lot. What are they doing there? Where did they come from? Who knows? Who cares?

The locals attack and kill one of the Neanderthals for no particular reason, but the thugs who work for Frankenstein (Brazzi) grab the body and bring it to the lab where the count operates on him and brings him back to life. Frankenstein names his enormous creature Goliath.

Frankenstein's hirelings include a big guy named Igor (very creative), a hunchback, a dwarf named Genz (Michael Dunn), and Hans the butler. Genz is always getting into trouble—he spends a lot of time during this film peeping at naked girls and looking under the blouses of female corpses he and the guys dig up at the local cemetery. After a while, the count gets so tired of his antics that he fires him. With nowhere to go, Genz

99

Goliath, Count Frankenstein's creation.

wanders in the hills and comes upon another Neanderthal, named Ook, played by Boris Lugosi (I bet that isn't his real name). The two become friends, and Genz teaches Ook how to kidnap village girls, take them back to the cave, strip them, and feel them up, though Ook always gets carried away and kills them.

Meanwhile, Frankenstein's daughter, Maria (Simone Blondell), her fiancé, Eric (Alan Collins), and her friend Krista (Christiane Royce) arrive for a visit. Krista and the count hit it off, and he starts filling her in on his experiments. He even introduces her to Goliath, and, of course, the monster takes an instant liking to her.

Genz is still angry about losing his job ("I'll get my revenge on Dr. Frankenstein"), so he sneaks back into the castle and sets Goliath free. The Neanderthal kills just about everybody, including Count Frankenstein. While this is going on, Ook has kidnapped Krista and taken her back to the cave for a bit of fun. Goliath ends up in the cave, too, and when he sees his beloved Krista in danger, he and Ook fight it out, and Ook dies.

The villagers complain to the prefect of police (Purdom) about all the craziness that has been going on at the castle, and he decides to investigate. Armed with the usual torches, the locals descend on the Frankenstein home, where they run into Goliath and burn him alive.

Obviously, this is a hopelessly stupid film. That, in itself, isn't really a problem. After all, most of the films discussed in this book are stupid, but at least they're fun.

Maria (Simone Blondell) and Krista (Christiane Royce) go mud-bathing in one of the sleazier scenes from *Frankenstein's Castle of Freaks*.

Ook (Boris Lugosi) grabs Krista (Christiane Royce) in *Frankenstein's Castle of Freaks*.

Frankenstein's Castle of Freaks isn't fun, however, because it assumes that we are stupid, too. There is no humor here—everything is played straight, as if the people who made this atrocity were hoping we wouldn't notice how idiotic it is.

Even worse, the film relies on the oldest and most offensive stereotypes imaginable, and it fully expects viewers to go along with them. All of the attractive people here are good—even Count Frankenstein—and all the "freaks" of the title are bad: the evil dwarf, the brutal hunchback, the savage and brainless giants. The presence of the late Michael Dunn in this movie really hurts because he was a fine actor who occasionally got roles worthy of his talent *(Ship of Fools)*, but here he is relegated to the status of a sideshow attraction, and that is a waste.

The original *Frankenstein* of 1931 is a classic because it argues that we cannot judge people—in this case, Frankenstein's creation—on the basis of physical appearance. We cannot assume someone is a monster because he fits the stereotype. *Frankenstein's Castle of Freaks* says just the opposite—that physical imperfection is a sign of evil and that the villagers are right to attack and to kill anyone who is different.

As a result, *Frankenstein's Castle of Freaks* is more than just a stupid film. It is a thoughtlessly cruel and offensive film, and it is certainly worth passing up.

Cleopatra (Olga Baclanova) flirts with Hans (Harry Earles) in Tod Browning's classic *Freaks*. *(Courtesy MGM/UA Home Video)*

Freaks

ALTERNATE TITLES:

*Forbidden Love,
Nature's Mistakes,
The Monster Show*

1932

Director/producer: Tod Browning; *Screenplay:* Willis Goldbeck, Leon Gordon, Edgar Allan Woolf, Al Boasberg; based on the story "Spurs" by Ted Robbins.

CAST:
Wallace Ford, Leila Hyams, Olga Baclanova, Henry Victor, Harry Earles, Daisy Earles, Daisy and Violet Hilton

ORIGINAL RELEASE: MGM
VIDEO: MGM/UA Home Video

Unlike most of the films included in this book, *Freaks* has received a lot of critical attention over the years, and this one deserves it. It is a unique and exciting piece, directed by a master of horror who also did the original *Dracula*, two versions of *The Unholy Three*, and *The Devil Doll*. Even so, I think that *Freaks* warrants another careful look, if only because it is a film that people talk about and write about but that many have never actually seen.

The setting is a circus, and Browning, a former carnival man himself, uses actual sideshow stars as his actors—Johnny Eck, the living half-boy; Prince Randian, the living torso; Josephine Joseph, the half-man, half-woman; dwarf Angelo Rossitto, who would appear in any number of horror films over a period of some thirty years; and Siamese twins Daisy and Violet Hilton, who later starred in *Chained for Life,* the infamous 1951 exploitation film. The plot of *Freaks* involves Hans the midget (Harry Earles), who is engaged to another midget, Frieda (Harry's sister Daisy), but who becomes infatuated with Cleopatra (Olga Baclanova), the beautiful aerialist. She teases him until she learns that he has inherited a fortune. Then she and the circus strongman, Hercules (Henry Victor), plan that she will seduce Hans into marriage, then poison him for his money.

Hans and Cleo are married, but at the wedding feast,

Hercules (Henry Victor), the circus strongman, gets a dirty look from Angelino (Angelo Rossitto) and the Half Boy (Johnny Eck). (*Courtesy MGM/UA Home Video*)

103

The Bird Girl (Elizabeth Green) performs at the wedding feast for Hans (Harry Earles) and Cleopatra (Olga Baclanova). (*Courtesy MGM/UA Home Video*)

the drunken bride belittles the groom and his friends, calling them "dirty, slimy freaks" when they offer to make her part of their circle. Eventually, Hans's cohorts discover the plot to kill one of their own, and they attack Hercules and Cleo during a rainstorm in the absolutely chilling and unforgettable climactic scene of the film. The strongman is killed, and beautiful Cleo is horribly mutilated, transformed into a freak herself, and she becomes part of the sideshow.

Critics have been congratulating *Freaks* on its humane depiction of so-called "human oddities" for decades, and in part those congratulations are warranted. After all, in this film, the "monsters" are depicted as sensitive and honorable people, and the beautiful, normal people (Cleo and Hercules) are the monsters. Still, you have to wonder about the scenes that show armless, legless Randian rolling and lighting his own cigarette or the woman without arms eating and drinking with her feet—scenes that allow us in the audience to gawk at the freaks in the darkness of a movie theater or the comfort of our own home while at the same time feeling superior to those who gawk at exactly the same performances in sideshows.

You also have to wonder about the humor in the movie, most of which is insulting to the very people the film is supposed to champion. For example, actor Roscoe Ates, who spent his entire career making fun of people who stutter, is a stammering clown who is married to one of the Hilton sisters, thus giving rise to a string of Siamese-twin jokes. And when the bearded lady (Olga Roderick) has a baby, Phroso the clown (Wallace Ford) notes that it's a little girl and "it's gonna have a beard."

There is a sense in which *Freaks* exploits the very people it also champions, and perhaps that is unavoidable. The very nature of any film is that it gives us something to look at, and what this movie offers to our eyes is . . . freaks. At least in the sideshow, the freak can look back at the gawker. Watching *Freaks* on film or on video, we can gawk all we like in complete safety, without being seen.

The question is, do we watch *Freaks* in order to see the lowly elevated, or do we watch it only to stare at those who are not like us? There probably is no easy answer to this question.

From Beyond the Grave

ALTERNATE TITLES:

The Creatures From Beyond the Grave, Creatures

1974

Director: Kevin Connor; *Producers:* Max J. Rosenberg and Milton Subotsky; *Screenplay:* Robin Clarke and Raymond Christodoulou

CAST:

Peter Cushing, Diana Dors, Donald Pleasence, Nyree Dawn Porter, David Warner, Ian Carmichael, Ian Bannen, Angela Pleasence, Margaret Leighton, Ian Ogilvy, Jack Watson, Lesley-Anne Down

ORIGINAL RELEASE: Amicus Productions/Warner Brothers
VIDEO: Warner Home Video

The comic books *Tales From the Crypt, Vault of Horror,* and *Haunt of Fear,* all published by William M. Gaines's

The party turns nasty when Venus (Leila Hyams) insults the wedding party after the "Freaks" have invited her to become one of them. (*Courtesy MGM/UA Home Video*)

105

Entertaining Comics Company (EC, for short) were driven out of the marketplace in the 1950s by those during the McCarthy era who believed that violence in comics was the cause of juvenile delinquency. Admittedly, these were very nasty little books, full of graphic dismemberment, cannibalism, and rotting corpses walking through graveyards—enough to give any kid plenty of vivid nightmares. But the EC comics were also well drawn, well written, and very funny, and they were produced by some of the comics industry's best artists and writers—Johnny Craig, Wally Wood, Graham Ingels, Harvey Kurtzman, and others. Perhaps more importantly, these comics affected many of the most significant members of today's horror industry, who read them as kids. Stephen King and director George Romero admit to having loved such trash—their collaborations on the movies *Creepshow* and *Creepshow 2* are proof of that—and it's safe to say that horror today wouldn't be what it is if it hadn't been for EC.

After 1972, Amicus Productions in England turned out a series of anthology films based on the EC comic stories and style. *Tales From the Crypt* and *Vault of Horror* used actual stories from the original comics, and others such as *Dr. Terror's House of Horrors* (1965), *The House That Dripped Blood* (1971), and *Asylum* (1972) followed the same basic EC format with new tales, usually featuring British performers such as Peter Cushing, Christopher Lee, Patrick Magee, Ralph Richardson, Margaret Leighton, and Joan Collins in her pre-*Dynasty* days.

Though it isn't as well known as *Tales From the Crypt* and *Vault of Horror*, *From Beyond the Grave* is one of the best anthologies Amicus produced. Cushing is an antique dealer, owner of Temptations, Ltd., and his shop provides the point of departure for four separate stories with a related theme.

In the first tale, a man named Edward (David Warner) looks at an ornate mirror in the shop and buys it for much

Edward (David Warner) introduces a new victim to the mirror that possesses him in *From Beyond the Grave*.

106

less than it is worth after convincing the owner that it is not a real antique. Proud of having cheated the old man, Edward takes the mirror home where, at a party, he and his friends hold a mock séance. A figure appears in the mirror, and that same night, the corpselike creature returns to tell Edward, "You must feed me." Under the mirror's control, Edward begins to kill young women and "feed" their souls to the figure until it becomes strong enough to leave the glass and enter the real world. Eventually, the creature kills Edward, who takes his place in the mirror and waits for a new victim.

The second story features a retired military officer named Christopher Lowe (Ian Bannen) whose nagging wife, Mabel (Diana Dors), is driving him crazy. He meets another ex-serviceman, Underwood (Donald Pleasence), who is down on his luck, and to impress his new friend, Christopher goes to Temptations, Ltd. and steals a Distinguished Service Cross, which he passes off as his own. Christopher takes a liking to his friend's daughter Emily (Angela Pleasence, Donald's daughter), who is the opposite of Mabel. "I wish to serve you," she says. "I will do anything you ask, anything at all." Emily has supernatural powers, and at Lowe's command, she makes a voodoo doll of Mabel and uses it to kill her. Afterward, Christopher and Emily are married, but Lowe learns too late that the groom on the wedding cake is another voodoo doll—his.

The third tale is a typical EC comedy. Wealthy Reginald Warren (Ian Carmichael) goes to Temptations, Ltd. where he switches price tags on two snuffboxes, then buys the more expensive one for much less than its original price. That same day, on the commuter train, he meets Madame Orloff (Margaret Leighton), a psychic who tells him that there is a killer spirit on his shoulder— "His main objective is to get inside you, to take over." Warren doesn't believe in such nonsense, but when the spirit tries to kill his wife, Susan (Nyree Dawn Porter), he summons Orloff, who conducts a ridiculous exorcism

Madame Orloff (Margaret Leighton) performs a hilarious exorcism for Reginald Warren (Ian Carmichael).

Sir Michael Sinclair (Jack Watson) plans to sacrifice his captive (Lesley-Anne Down) in the blue room in *From Beyond the Grave*.

that destroys the entire house, but it works. Unfortunately, it only drives the spirit from Warren to his wife, who ends up killing him.

In the final story, William Seaton (Ian Ogilvy) buys an elaborate antique door at Temptations, Ltd., and unlike the other victims of the shop, he pays the asking price. At home, he uses it as a door to a cupboard, but one night when he opens it, he discovers that it leads to an ancient blue room where he finds an eighteenth-century portrait of Sir Michael Sinclair (Jack Watson) and a book entitled *An Experiment in Darkness*, which is a record of Sinclair's occult practices. The room itself needs human sacrifices, and the door is a means of trapping souls. Seaton even meets the walking corpse of Sinclair, who eventually enters the house and kidnaps Seaton's wife (Lesley-Anne Down). William takes an ax to the door, breaking the magic spell, and the room collapses, destroying Sinclair before he can sacrifice the young woman.

The lesson here is obvious. Edward, Lowe, and Warren are damned for their petty crimes, but Seaton and his wife are saved because they are innocent—William did not try to cheat the old man at Temptations, Ltd., which turns out to be a sort of testing ground for clients' moral fiber.

Like the original EC comic book tales, these stories offer plenty of violence, carnage, and rotting corpses, but even so, there is something wonderfully comforting about them. The classic EC stories are revenge tales, usually about revenge taken from beyond the grave. Somebody does something wrong but pays for it in the end, usually thanks to some kind of supernatural intervention. This suggests that there is a universal principle of justice, that bad guys always get what's coming to them, that the innocent always triumph.

Wouldn't that be nice?

The Fury

1978

Director: Brian De Palma; *Producer:* Frank Yablans; *Screenplay:* John Farris, based on his novel

CAST:
Kirk Douglas, John Cassavetes, Carrie Snodgress, Charles Durning, Amy Irving, Fiona Lewis, Andrew Stevens

ORIGINAL RELEASE: 20th Century-Fox
VIDEO: CBS/Fox Home Video

Unlike most of the movies in this book, this is a real film with real actors, a real script, and a real director. It's still weird enough to find a place here, however—try not to let the fact that it is well made prejudice you against it.

In Israel, Peter Sandza (Kirk Douglas) and his son, Robin (Andrew Stevens), are having fun on the beach with Peter's longtime friend and associate Mr. Childress (John Cassavetes). Peter and Childress both work for "a government agency you never heard of," but Peter is ready to retire and return to the States to spend more time with his son.

A sudden Arab attack marks the end of the fun. Robin is spirited away by Childress for his own protection, and it seems that Peter has been killed. But Peter is still alive, and when he realizes that Childress is responsible for the attack, that he staged it so he and the organization could kidnap Robin, he shoots his old friend and escapes, vowing to reclaim his son.

Childress is not killed, though his arm is rendered useless by Peter's attack. It seems that Robin has tremendous psychic abilities, and Childress wants to use the boy as a new kind of secret weapon—"The Chinese don't have one, the Soviets don't have one." He is more than willing to kidnap and murder in the name of national security.

In Chicago a year later, Peter tracks down a college student named Gillian Bellaver (Amy Irving), also psychic, who he hopes can help him locate Robin. At the Paragon Institute for psychic research, headed by Dr. Jim McKeever (Charles Durning), Gillian is undergoing tests of her telekinetic abilities, which have begun to frighten her. In stress situations, she can make people bleed uncontrollably without knowing what she is doing.

At Paragon, Gillian sees visions of Robin and realizes that he was once there, too. She wants to contact him because, in a way, they are brother and sister, sharing the same powers. Unfortunately, McKeever is one of Childress's contacts, and when the government man hears about Gillian, all he wants to know is: "Will the girl be another Robin Sandza?"

It seems that Robin hasn't worked out very well. In their efforts to use his psychic powers as a secret weapon, Childress and his crew have "pushed him too far," as the evil Dr. Susan Charles (Fiona Lewis) puts it. Now Robin is a psychotic monster who uses his abilities to kill on the slightest provocation. Childress is hoping to do better with Gillian.

Peter manages to break Gillian out of Paragon, and she leads him to where Robin is being kept. In the attempt to get his son back, however, Peter and Robin are killed, and Childress captures Gillian. He tries to sweet-talk her—"You're the only one who counts now"—but Gillian knows what he's up to, and focusing

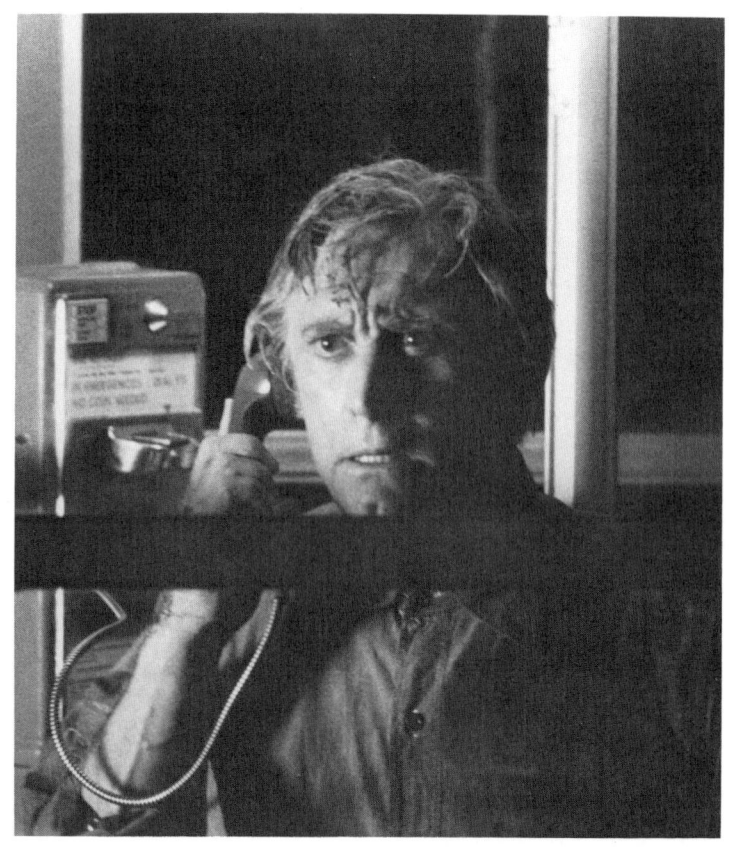

Peter Sandza (Kirk Douglas) is a secret agent in search of his son in *The Fury*.

all her psychic energy, she makes Childress explode. The scene of his body flying into pieces is repeated in slow motion at least half a dozen times before the closing credits, just to make sure we don't miss anything.

After the revelations of the Watergate scandal in the mid-1970s, the secret agent who had been a hero for so many years—James Bond, *The Man From U.N.C.L.E.*—suddenly became a villain as we realized what some of these people had been up to. It was a time when those at the highest level of authority had run roughshod over people's civil rights and had used "national security" as an excuse to commit crimes and to cover up criminal activities. Watergate suggested that our CIA and FBI, which were supposed to be protecting us from the bad guys, could use their special techniques against us, too.

The Fury addresses these concerns directly. Like Robin Sandza, Childress is a madman, obsessed with power, and because he is a high-ranking government official, he is free to do whatever he wants. The "national security" agency he heads is really concerned only with itself, not with us. As Peter explains, "It's a frightening power these people have. They can make anybody disappear anytime. . . . If they can make me disappear, they can make you disappear." No wonder everyone in the theater cheers when Childress is blown to smithereens.

The Fury is a good indicator of how completely we had lost faith in our government leaders after Vietnam and Watergate. And the movie still works, probably because that crisis of faith is still not resolved.

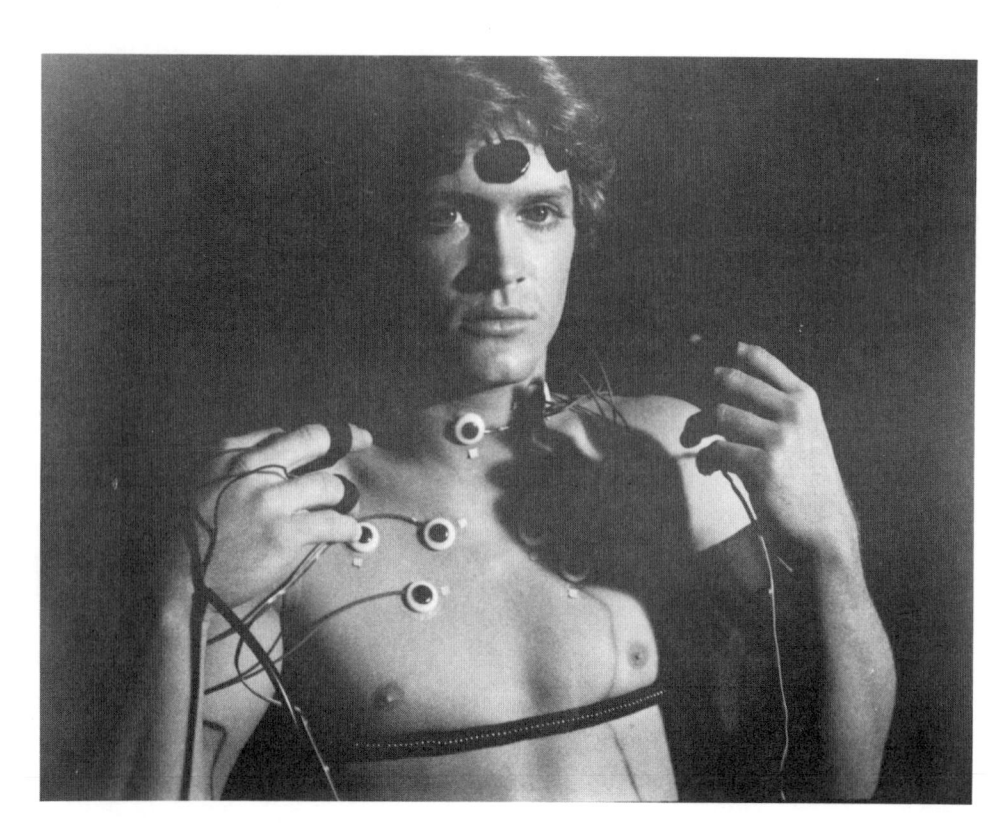

Robin Sandza (Andrew Stevens) is transformed into a psychic monster by "a government agency you never heard of."

Childress (John Cassavetes) is the evil head of the agency that wants to use Gillian's (Amy Irving) psychic powers as a new secret weapon in *The Fury*.

The Giant Gila Monster

1959

Director: Ray Kellogg; *Producer:* Ken Curtis; *Screenplay:* Ray Kellogg and Jay Sims

CAST:
Don Sullivan, Lisa Simone, Shug Fisher, Fred Graham

ORIGINAL RELEASE: McLendon Radio Pictures
VIDEO: Burbank Video and Sinister Cinema

Kellogg's best-known film is probably the controversial pro-war feature *The Green Berets* (which he codirected with John Wayne), but this was his first, and it played generally on a double bill with his second, *The Killer Shrews*. *The Giant Gila Monster* has everything a 1950s

Mr. Compton, Chase Winstead (Don Sullivan), and the sheriff (Fred Graham) check out the site of a strange highway accident in *The Giant Gila Monster*. (Courtesy Hollywood Book and Poster)

Chase (Don Sullivan) and Nicki (Lisa Simone) explore the wilderness in search of friends who have disappeared. (*Courtesy Hollywood Book and Poster*)

rock-'n'-roll horror flick is supposed to have—music, kids, hot rods, and a monster—what more could you want?

Chase Winstead (Don Sullivan) has a lot of responsibilities for a teenager. Since his father died in an accident on a Texas oil rig, the kid has been working at the local gas station to support his mom and his baby sister, who needs a lot of operations and new braces for her legs. Fortunately, Chase still has enough time and money left over to soup up his hot rod, date the local foreign-exchange student (Lisa Simone), and track down the monster that has been devouring his friends.

Somewhere, somehow, in the Texas wilderness, a giant Gila monster has come into being, and during the course of the film, it eats some teenagers, a traveling salesman, an oil truck, and a train, but when it invades the kids' dance party out at the old barn, that's going too far. Winstead loads his hot rod with nitro and drives it into the monster, blowing the thing to bits. As a reward, he gets the girl, a new hot rod from the railroad, and a job with the same oil company that killed his father.

This is a really neat movie. The special effects are pretty good (at least it's a real Gila monster), veteran stuntman Fred Graham is wonderful as the crusty old sheriff who really likes the kids, and Sullivan gets to perform a truly senseless song entitled "The Lord Said Laugh, Children, Laugh," accompanying himself on the ukulele. The teenagers are good, fun-loving kids, not juvenile delinquents, and best of all, the monster is not the product of nuclear weapons testing, atomic radiation, or the Communist conspiracy. In fact, no one ever finds out where it comes from. It's just there.

Beginning in the early fifties, horror movies started telling us that the problems we faced in the postwar era—from nuclear weapons to overpopulation to polio to giant grasshoppers and alien invasions—were simply too big for us to handle. We were supposed to trust the government, the military, and the scientists to deal with these horrors for us. But *The Giant Gila Monster* says that one teenage kid can make a difference in the world, that, if he's brave enough and inventive enough, he can solve the community's problems without having to rely on the authorities, and that's kind of refreshing.

The sheriff (Fred Graham) takes off after the Gila monster. (*Courtesy Hollywood Book and Poster*)

Chase (Don Sullivan), Nicki (Lisa Simone), and the gang from the malt shop find a car that was destroyed by the giant Gila monster. (*Courtesy Hollywood Book and Poster*)

The teens are ready to riot after *The Giant Gila Monster* breaks up the Saturday-night hop. (*Courtesy Hollywood Book and Poster*)

Godzilla on Monster Island

ALTERNATE TITLES:

*Gojira Tai Gaigan,
War of the Monsters,
Godzilla vs. Gigan*

1971

Director: Jun Fukuda; *Producer:* Tomoyuki Tanaka; *Screenplay:* Shinichi Sekizawa

CAST:
Hiroshi Ishikawa, Yuriko Hishimi, Tomoko Umeda, Minoru Takashima, Kunio Murai, Susumu Fujita

ORIGINAL RELEASE: Toho Productions
VIDEO: Sinister Cinema, New World Home Video

Let's get one thing straight right at the beginning. Most Godzilla movies are for kids. Admittedly, the first two—*Godzilla, King of the Monsters* (1954) and *Gigantis, the Fire Monster* (1955)—were for grown-ups, but by the time *King Kong vs. Godzilla* appeared in Japan in 1962, Toho Productions had found its true audience. Kids love Godzilla and his huge buddies, probably because the scaly heroes are always making messes and never have to clean up afterward. In *Ghidrah, The Three-Headed Monster* (1965), Godzilla finally becomes a good guy and a fine role model for young people everywhere. So it is unfair to judge Godzilla flicks as if they were failed adult films when, for the most part, they are very successful children's films.

Godzilla on Monster Island is a good example. Kotaka (Hiroshi Ishikawa) is a young and unsuccessful comic book artist whose girlfriend, Tomoko (Yuriko Hishimi), convinces him to take a job at Children's Land designing monsters for their rides and exhibits in the Godzilla Tower, a life-size replica of Japan's most famous monster. Children's Land is a kind of Disney World project that is still under construction, and when Kotaka reports for work, he suspects that something is not right there. For one thing, the chairman of the project (Susumu Fujita) is only about sixteen years old, and everybody involved keeps making cryptic comments about "perfect peace."

While snooping around, Kotaka meets Machiko (Tomoko Umeda) and her boyfriend, Shosaku (Minoru Takashima). Machiko's brother, Takishi (Kunio Murai), also worked for Children's Land as an electronics expert, but he has disappeared, and his sister thinks he is being held prisoner there.

Eventually, Kotaka, Tomoko, Machiko, and Shosaku uncover the whole plot. Children's Land is being built by aliens from another planet. The amusement park is merely a cover for their real project, world conquest. On top of that, the invaders aren't even human. They inhabit human bodies, which they call "uniforms," but in fact they are enormous intellectual cockroaches who have developed an elaborate technology. Their home planet became so polluted by the dominant species ("They were a lot like you") that all life there simply died out except for the species that was most adaptable—the cockroaches. In time, though, their world died completely, and they were forced to look for a new home. They came to Earth, a planet much like their own and polluted, too, but not yet beyond hope, if the source of pollution can be eliminated. The cockroaches are only looking for perfect peace—for themselves, of course—but first they must get rid of the dominant species here.

They bring the super space monsters Ghidrah and Gigan to Earth to wipe out everything and everyone—beginning with Tokyo, of course. But on Monster Island, home of all the Earth monsters, Godzilla and Anguirus know what's going on, and they head for Tokyo, too, to head off the alien invaders. This makes for a terrific final

Godzilla (for trivia buffs, that's Haruo Nakajima in the costume) and Gigan (Kengo Nakayama) go at it in *Godzilla on Monster Island*.

The battle between Godzilla and Gigan all but destroys Children's Land, the headquarters of the evil aliens.

tag-team battle between the good monsters and the bad monsters, which looks like touch-and-go for a while but which Godzilla and Anguirus eventually win, sending Ghidrah and Gigan packing into outer space again. Meanwhile, Kotaka and his gang manage to blow up the Godzilla Tower where the Children's Land plot is being hatched. This kills all the cockroaches and puts an end to their nefarious scheme.

If this sounds silly, it is, but that's the point. Besides, *Godzilla on Monster Island* has something special going for it. Along with *Godzilla vs. the Smog Monster*, also released in 1971, this is one of the first ecological horror films.

It shouldn't be surprising that Japan produced this early "fear of pollution" flick. After all, with its industrial economy and its huge population crowded into a small geographical area, the problems of pollution have been serious there for a long time. What is a bit more surprising is the fact that *Godzilla on Monster Island* is highly critical of technology. The invading cockroaches are "hypnotized by machinery," and this proves to be their downfall, because they rely too heavily on computers to do their work and their thinking for them. This antitechnology message might seem very strange, coming from a high-tech nation such as Japan, but after all, it is technology that has caused our present ecological

The monster cast is assembled: Godzilla, Anguirus (Yukeitsu Omiya), Gigan, and King Ghidrah (Kanta Ina).

It's tag-team action in Tokyo with Anguirus, Ghidrah, Godzilla, and Gigan.

117

problems, and the film suggests that, unlike the cockroaches, we can't trust technology to solve those problems for us.

The antipollution theme in *Godzilla on Monster Island* is very strong, with shots of belching smokestacks, scum-covered waterways, and lectures delivered by the invaders, who claim to be here to save our planet—from us. It's a convincing argument.

Gorgo

1961

Director: Eugene Lourie; *Producers:* Wilfred Eades and Frank and Maurice King; *Screenplay:* John Loring and Daniel Hyatt

CAST:
Bill Travers, William Sylvester, Vincent Winter, Martin Benson

ORIGINAL RELEASE: King Brothers/MGM
VIDEO: United Home Video, Sinister Cinema, and others

After the success of *Godzilla, King of the Monsters*, almost every major city in the world was destroyed by some kind of prehistoric creature. *Reptilicus* wrecked Stockholm, *Yongary* battered Seoul, South Korea, and of course nearly everybody took a shot at knocking down Tokyo. When it was London's turn to go, *Gorgo* got the honors.

Actually, director Lourie's *Beast From 20,000 Fathoms* predates the original *Godzilla,* and so, if you want to blame someone for all those silly Japanese monster flicks, Lourie is probably the guy. The special effects and the monster costume in *Gorgo* really aren't as good as those found in the Toho productions, but the British-made film does have a lot to recommend it.

Sam Slade (William Sylvester) and Joe Ryan (Bill Travers) operate a salvage boat that gets caught in a huge storm near an island off the coast of Ireland. There, during an underwater dive, they spot a sixty-five-foot prehistoric monster, apparently resurrected by the storm, that comes out of the sea to attack the town. Joe and Sam manage to capture the thing alive and plan to take it to London and make a fortune by selling it to the circus. Sean (Vincent Winter), a local orphan kid, objects to this mistreatment of the beast—"It's a bad thing you're doin', a terrible bad thing, Mr. Ryan"—and when the salvage ship sets sail with its valuable cargo, Sean stows away.

In London, Joe and Sam unofficially adopt Sean and strike a deal with Dorkin (Martin Benson) of the Dorkin Circus, who names his new attraction Gorgo. British scientists are furious at the abuse of this important discovery, but the media eat it up, especially after Gorgo

kills a couple of its handlers. Because of these deaths, Sam begins to agree with Sean that they have done a terrible bad thing, but Joe still sees only the commercial side of their enterprise.

Then scientists make a remarkable discovery. Gorgo is only a baby monster. The adult of his species would be more than two-hundred feet tall. Nobody pays much attention to this news until Mama Gorgo appears, de-

Fishermen from an island off the coast of Ireland are surprised to see the claw of *Gorgo* rise out of the ocean.

119

stroys the island where she misplaced her baby, then heads toward London. Sam insists that they set Baby Gorgo free, but Joe refuses, and the British military leaders insist that they can handle the situation.

An aircraft carrier is dispatched to deal with the mother, but she sinks it. No weapons are effective

Young Sean (Vincent Winter) tries to set Gorgo free on board the ship that is taking the creature to London. Joe Ryan (Bill Travers) tries to stop him.

Gorgo is paraded through London on his way to the circus.

against the creature, and in the final destruction sequence, Mama Gorgo wrecks London Bridge, Big Ben, the underground, etc. She finally sets her baby free, and the two go into the sea once more, turning their backs on puny mankind.

The theme here is nature vs. civilization, one of the major themes in Western literature. *Gorgo* is basically *Moby Dick*, if Captain Ahab had captured the white whale alive and sold it to P. T. Barnum. In most giant-creature-attacks-civilization films, however, civilization wins, at least temporarily. In *Gorgo*, however, the monsters win, and that's enough to make you think about

Mama Gorgo comes to save her baby, destroying Big Ben and most of London in the process.

In the opening film-within-a-film sequence of *He Knows You're Alone*, the mad slasher (Tom Rolfing) stabs his victim through the back of her theater seat. (*Courtesy MGM/UA Home Video*)

the ways in which we have exploited the natural world and the ways in which that exploitation might come back to haunt us in the future. In this sense, *Gorgo* is an intelligent and disturbing film, an early warning of ecological crisis, and even if you've seen it before, it is well worth another look.

He Knows You're Alone

1980

Director: Armand Mastroianni; *Producers:* George Manasse, Robert Di Milia, and Nan Pearlman; *Screenplay:* Scott Parker

CAST:
Don Scardino, Caitlin O'Heaney, Elizabeth Kemp, Patsy Pease, Lewis Arlt, Tom Hanks, Tom Rolfing

ORIGINAL RELEASE: United Artists
VIDEO: MGM/UA

In the opening sequence, two young lovers are making out in their car parked in the woods when, to the surprise of absolutely no one who's ever seen a mad-slasher film, a guy shows up with a knife to kill them. What is surprising is that, when the camera moves back a bit, we learn that this familiar scene is only part of a movie being shown in a neighborhood theater. Two young women are watching in the audience, but one of them can't take it. She escapes to the bathroom where she stops to admire her engagement ring, but then becomes frightened because she thinks someone is following her. She returns to her friend and asks to leave, but suddenly, someone comes into the row behind her and stabs her through the theater seat just at the moment when another young woman is being slaughtered on the screen.

From here on, *He Knows You're Alone* offers two parallel stories. One follows Len Gamble (Lewis Arlt), a police detective whose bride-to-be was killed three years before by a man who is responsible for the deaths of a number of engaged women. The other story is about Amy (Caitlin O'Heaney), who is to be married in two weeks. Throughout the film, she is stalked by the same crazed bride slasher who killed Len's fiancée, and he in turn is stalked by Len.

The other characters include Marvin (Don Scardino), Amy's former boyfriend who works at the city morgue, and Amy's friends Nancy (Elizabeth Kemp) and Joyce (Patsy Pease of *Days of Our Lives* soap opera fame), who are planning to spend the weekend at Amy's house while her parents are out of town. Amy's fiancé is also away, for a bachelor's party, but in fact Amy isn't very sure about this wedding business; she might still be in love with Marvin, who really does seem like a nice guy. But she soon forgets this little problem when she realizes she is being followed by the knife-wielding maniac, who kills Nancy and Joyce and who certainly has Amy on his list.

It all ends in the morgue where Amy goes to get help from Marvin. Len follows the killer there but is killed, and it is up to Amy and Marvin to put an end to the bridal slaughter, which they do.

We all know that almost every mad-slasher movie ever made is a mindless copy of John Carpenter's *Halloween*. *He Knows You're Alone* is a copy of Carpenter's film, too, but director Mastroianni (actor Marcello's cousin) is very deliberate in his borrowings. The music, for exam-

The engagement ring on her finger marks Amy (Caitlin O'Heaney) as the bride killer's next victim. (*Courtesy MGM/UA Home Video*)

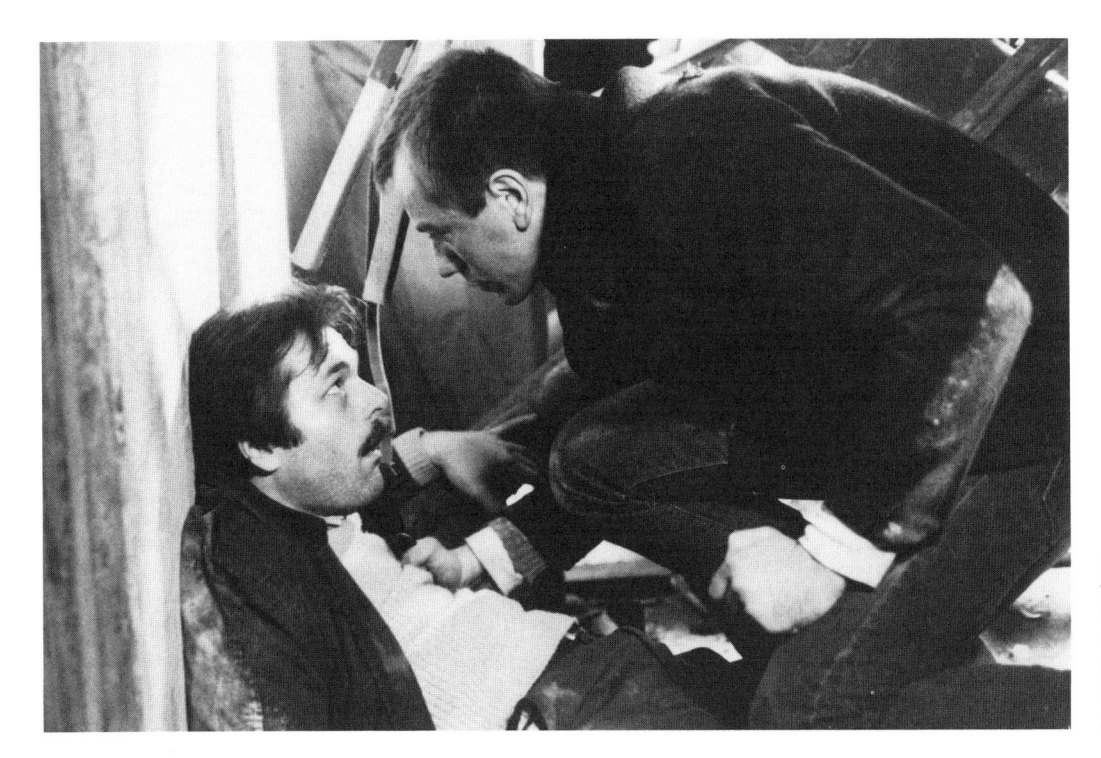

Len (Lewis Arlt), the cop who has been on the trail of the bride killer (Tom Rolfing) for years, finds him at last but ends up being killed himself. (*Courtesy MGM/UA Home Video*)

The killer (Tom Rolfing) has Amy (Caitlin O'Heaney) just about where he wants her in *He Knows You're Alone*. (*Courtesy MGM/UA Home Video*)

ple, is almost identical to Carpenter's score for *Halloween*. The camera angles are the same. Like Laurie in *Halloween*, Amy keeps seeing the killer everywhere, though no one else seems to notice him. Also like Laurie, Amy is not the helpless victim; she is very resourceful when faced with the possibility of a nasty death. And like Dr. Loomis in *Halloween*, Len is a fanatic intent on getting the murderer, and he sometimes seems to be as crazy as the killer himself.

In *Halloween*, Carpenter quotes from his sources—*Psycho, The Thing From Another World,* and *Forbidden Planet*. Mastroianni uses quotations, too, but only from *Halloween*. Even in the shower scene in *He Knows You're Alone*, Mastroianni isn't quoting from Hitchcock; he's quoting Carpenter quoting Hitchcock.

Mastroianni *wants* us to recognize his source and to realize that *He Knows You're Alone* is only a movie based on another movie. That's what the opening film-within-a-film sequence is all about; it's a reminder that what we are seeing is only a movie, that no one is really being killed, that these are actors doing their job. If that weren't enough, there's a psychology major named Elliot, played by Tom Hanks (yes, *the* Tom Hanks), who delivers a mini-lecture on the horror film to Amy and Nancy: "You can leave the movie . . . with a vicarious thrill and a feeling that you've just conquered death . . . . People pay to be scared. When you think about it, it's ridiculous." He is talking about the very movie we are watching, of course. This might be the only film ever made that actually contains an argument against itself.

Mastroianni seems to be poking fun at the mad-slasher genre by self-consciously copying what other slasher films mindlessly copy. But there are problems with the way he goes about this. For one thing, *He Knows You're Alone* is not a perfect copy of *Halloween*. Again following Carpenter's lead, most mad-slasher films offer punishment to promiscuous young people, and it is usually only the chaste and/or the monogamous who survive. Mastroianni's bride killer, on the other hand, seems to be punishing marriage, monogamous fidelity, and it hardly seems fair to be punished for doing what you're supposed to do.

Besides, Mastroianni's killer doesn't stick to his own rules. He kills Nancy, who isn't engaged to anyone. He kills promiscuous Joyce while she is in bed with one of her married professors. Is this guy a bride killer or not? He can't seem to make up his mind.

He Knows You're Alone (shot on Staten Island in New York) is unique among mad-slasher films because at least it knows where it came from. In the end, though, the film is unnecessarily confused and doesn't really have a lot going for it. Mastroianni surely had something interesting in mind when he made this film of quotations and quotations-within-quotations, but he might have been better off simply doing another brainless imitation of *Halloween* and hoping we wouldn't notice.

The Hideous Sun Demon

ALTERNATE TITLES:

*Blood on His Lips,
Terror From the Sun,
the Sun Demon*

1959

Director/producer: Robert Clarke; *Screenplay:* E. S. Seeley Jr. and Doane Hoag

CAST:
Robert Clarke, Patricia Manning, Nan Peterson, Patrick Whyte

ORIGINAL RELEASE: Pacific International
VIDEO: Rhino Home Video

Here's a great idea. Werewolf movies are wonderful, right? And a guy who's a werewolf only becomes a werewolf when the full moon comes out, right? So suppose we just reverse that and have a guy who only becomes a monster when the *sun* comes out. It's a surefire winner, right?

Well, not necessarily.

Dr. Gilbert McKenna (Robert Clarke) has a drinking problem. On top of that, he's an atomic scientist who handles radioactive materials all day. Drinking and atomic science don't mix, and when Gil causes an accident at the lab that exposes him to a megadose of weird radiation, it looks like he's done for. But at first it seems he's okay. Unfortunately, the incident has left him with a kind of allergy. When he is exposed to sunlight, he becomes a violent and hideous sun demon—actually, a kind of iguana on two legs.

Gil's coworkers Ann Russell (Patricia Manning) and Dr. Frederick Buckell (Patrick Whyte) try to get him to take it easy and stay indoors until they can get a specialist in radiation sickness to come and treat him. But McKenna is his own man, willful and stubborn, and he goes out one evening and starts a relationship with a sleazy

A little girl finds Dr. Gil McKenna (Robert Clarke) hiding in her playhouse. She doesn't know, of course, that he is the hideous sun demon. (*Courtesy Hollywood Book and Poster*)

125

Gil (Robert Clarke) learns why overexposure to sunlight can be dangerous. (*Courtesy Hollywood Book and Poster*)

The hideous sun demon (Robert Clarke) arrives home after a hard day. (*Courtesy Hollywood Book and Poster*)

nightclub singer, Trudy Osborne (Nan Peterson), only to be caught by the sun on the beach the next morning.

Ann really loves Gil despite the fact that there seems to be nothing to recommend him, but McKenna is too stupid to realize this, and so, even when she tries to take care of him, he sneaks away—again at night—to meet Trudy. Again, he gets caught out in the sunlight—again, he becomes the demon and kills a gangster named Georgie, Trudy's former boyfriend. In the end, the demon is chased by the police and falls from a high tower, putting an end to his misery.

This one is pretty bad. Werewolf movies work because we know that the guy who is a werewolf didn't ask to be one and can't do anything about it—when the full moon comes out, he changes into a monster and he can't control what happens. But McKenna is clearly responsible for his problem, and he can easily keep himself from becoming a hideous sun demon—all he has to do is stay inside or at least get back home before dawn. The fact that he keeps getting caught out in the light just makes him seem stupid, not sympathetic.

Also, werewolf movies are scary because all the action happens at night, in the dark, when you can't see the monster coming until it's too late. But you can see a hideous sun demon coming from a mile off because it's broad daylight. The idea simply doesn't work.

Like so many horror and sci-fi movies of its time, *The Hideous Sun Demon* expresses a real concern about atomic radiation, but also like many such films, the message is mixed. Sure, atomic radiation is dangerous, but none of this would have happened if Gil had been more careful. He shouldn't have been so independent; he should have been more of a team player—a typical message for the conformist fifties.

Hillbillys in a Haunted House

1967

Director: Jean Yarbrough; *Producer:* Bernard Woolner; *Screenplay:* Duke Yelton

CAST:

John Carradine, Basil Rathbone, Lon Chaney Jr., Ferlin Husky, Joi Lansing, Don Bowman, Richard Webb, George Barrows

ORIGINAL RELEASE: Woolner Brothers
VIDEO: Goodtimes Home Video

Wow! John Carradine, Basil Rathbone, and Lon Chaney Jr., all in the same film. This must be a horror classic! Sorry. *Hillbillys in a Haunted House* could very well be in fact the worst movie ever made by anybody about anything. It certainly shows that, by 1967, Carradine, Rathbone, and Chaney had fallen a long way since their early appearances in such films as *Bluebeard, Tower of London,* and *The Wolf Man.* Ape imitator George Barrows didn't have far to fall, however—you might remember him as Ro-man in the grade-Z movie *Robot Monster.* Most of the other actors are country singers from the days before country music was respectable. One exception is busty Joi Lansing, who used to do occasional guest spots on *The Beverly Hillbillies* TV show, so I suppose that's how she managed to find a place for herself in this masterpiece.

Hillbillys in a Haunted House is a country music remake of director William "One Shot" Beaudine's *Ghosts on the Loose,* which managed to team up Bela

Basil Rathbone as Gregor and John Carradine as Dr. Himmel—both appeared in some truly dreadful films but none quite so bad as *Hillbillys in a Haunted House.*

127

Maximillian (Lon Chaney Jr.) enjoys playing with his iron maiden—everyone should have one in the basement.

Jeepers (Don Bowman) discovers a werewolf in the closet. It's only a dummy—but, in this film, who isn't?

Lugosi with the East Side Kids, and if ever there was a movie that didn't deserve to be remade, *Ghosts on the Loose* was it. But, for some reason, the Woolner brothers decided to produce it anyway. This was journeyman director Jean Yarbrough's last film; his first was *The Devil Bat* with Bela Lugosi—not exactly a distinguished career.

The plot here is pitiful. Country singers Woody Weatherby (Ferlin Husky) and Boots Malone (Joi Lansing), along with their manager Jeepers (Don Bowman), are driving to Nashville for a jamboree when a storm approaches, and they have to seek shelter in the abandoned Beauregard mansion, which, of course, has the reputation of being haunted.

Once inside, the trio starts seeing weird things and hearing eerie noises. Weatherby and Jeepers are terrified, but Boots says, "Well, I for one do not believe in ghosts, and I think we ought to investigate." When she sees an ape wandering through the halls, however, she starts screaming, too. They all run out to the car to escape, but what do you know, it won't start, and they are stuck.

It seems that there are spies operating in the basement of the mansion, trying to steal secrets from the nearby missile plant. Dr. Himmel (Carradine), Gregor (Rathbone), Maximillian (Chaney), and an ape named Anatole (Barrows) are working for Madame Wong

George Barrows played the Robot Monster in the grade-Z movie of the same name. His role in *Hillbillys in a Haunted House* was definitely a step down.

(Linda Ho), and they have the house rigged to scare off intruders.

Gregor and Himmel think the country singers upstairs are agents for the Master Organization to Halt Enemy Resistance—that's right, M.O.T.H.E.R. Remember that, at about this time, *The Man From U.N.C.L.E.* was one of the top-rated TV shows. In any case, when Anatole captures Boots and brings her down to the basement, the enemy agents decide to interrogate her. When they accuse her of being an agent for M.O.T.H.E.R., she doesn't know what they're talking about and says, "My mother's in Las Vegas." That's about the level of humor throughout the flick.

Jim Meadows (Richard Webb), a real agent from M.O.T.H.E.R., shows up and saves Boots. Anatole kills Himmel for stealing one of his bananas, and Meadows shoots the ape. Then the real ghost of Colonel Beauregard shows up, too, and scares the remaining enemy agents so badly they give up and Meadows arrests them. Now Woody, Boots, and Jeepers are free to travel on to

Boots (Joi Lansing) puts a stop to Maximillian (Lon Chaney Jr.) and saves Agent Jim Meadows (Richard Webb), the man from M.O.T.H.E.R., in *Hillbillys in a Haunted House.*

Nashville—somehow, their car has repaired itself. The last twenty minutes of the movie feature the jamboree with songs by Molly Bee, Merle Haggard, Husky, Bowman, Lansing, and others. Yippee!

What makes *Hillbillys in a Haunted House* so awful is that the tissue-thin plot exists only to get from one country song to the next. Boots keeps saying again and again, "Sing a song, Woody," and Woody does. At one point, a bunch of neighbors show up to see who is in the mansion, and they turn out to be Sonny James and his band—that's good for another song or two. Later, Jeepers can't sleep, so he turns on the TV, and lo and behold, he gets the local country music hour with Merle Haggard and some other people. Even if you love country music, that probably won't help, because most of the performers are people you've never heard of, and none of the songs from this film ever became hits.

What makes *Hillbillys in a Haunted House* particularly offensive is its reliance on the old stereotype of Southerners as ignorant, stupid bubbas. Of the trio of stars, Boots is the one who is smart and courageous; she is also the only one who doesn't speak with a Southern accent. The real hero of the movie turns out to be Agent Meadows (played by Webb, who was Captain Midnight in the 1950s TV show of the same name); he, too, has no accent and is clearly a Northerner.

So *Hillbillys in a Haunted House* is a bad film on every conceivable level. If, however, you're a connoisseur of bad cinema—and the fact that you're reading this book indicates that you might be—check this one out. You couldn't do much worse.

House of Whipcord

1974

Director/producer: Pete Walker; *Screenplay:* David McGillivray

CAST:
Barbara Markham, Patrick Barr, Ray Brooks, Ann Michelle, Penny Irving, Robert Tayman, Sheila Keith, Dorothy Gordon

ORIGINAL RELEASE: American International Pictures
VIDEO: Monterey Home Video

This British entry is a strange, nasty, and horrifying variation on the "women in prison" theme that I, for one, can't quite figure out.

Ann-Marie (Penny Irving) is a nineteen-year-old French girl trying to make it as a model in London. One night at a party she meets Mark (Robert Tayman)—he gives his full name as Mark E. Desade—and they start going out together. When he invites her to the country to meet his mother, she accepts. They arrive at an enormous walled house where Ann-Marie is taken into custody by two brutal female guards named Walker (Sheila Keith) and Bates (Dorothy Gordon), stripped, bathed, checked for lice, put into a prison uniform, and presented to dotty Judge Bailey (veteran actor Patrick Barr) and Warden Wakehurst (Barbara Markham). It seems that Bailey and Mrs. Wakehurst have been running their own legal system for years in what was once a county jail. As the judge explains, "This court exists outside the statutory laws of the land. It is a private court." And what is Ann-Marie doing there? According to Wakehurst, "You are here to serve sentence according to the proper moral and disciplinary standards."

The "prison" houses only female inmates—about a dozen of them—and it exists to punish "moral depravity." Ann-Marie is there because she posed nude in public. Bailey really is a retired judge, and Mrs. Wakehurst is a former prison governor who lost her position after accusations of brutality. The two decided that the real legal system was becoming too lenient, and they have since taken the law into their own hands. In fact, it is Wakehurst who runs the show; the judge is wimpy and senile and, like justice itself, blind, so he is totally dependent on her. Mark, the one who lures their victims to the estate, is their illegitimate son.

The rules at this prison are simple. A first offense of any sort gets you solitary confinement for two weeks. A second offense gets you a whipping. After a third offense, you are hanged. During the course of the film, we get a liberal dose of all three, including the sadistic whipping of a couple of the inmates—Ann-Marie among them—at the hands of Walker while Wakehurst looks on with a sinister grin.

Meanwhile, Julia (Ann Michelle), Ann-Marie's roommate in London, is worried about the disappearance of her friend. With the help of her boyfriend Tony (Ray Brooks), she tracks her to the old county prison, but arrives to find that Ann-Marie has been executed for attempting to escape. This comes as quite a shock to us viewers, because we've been led to believe that Ann-Marie was the heroine who was going to survive in the end. Julia is also taken prisoner and sentenced to death, but Tony brings the police and saves her. Mark is killed in the scuffle, Wakehurst hangs herself, and everybody else is taken into custody, though, if Bailey and Wakehurst have been correct in their assessment of the legal system, Walker, Bates, and the judge will probably get off with light sentences for their crimes.

At first, *House of Whipcord* seems to be another one of those horror films that revels in the very cruelty it

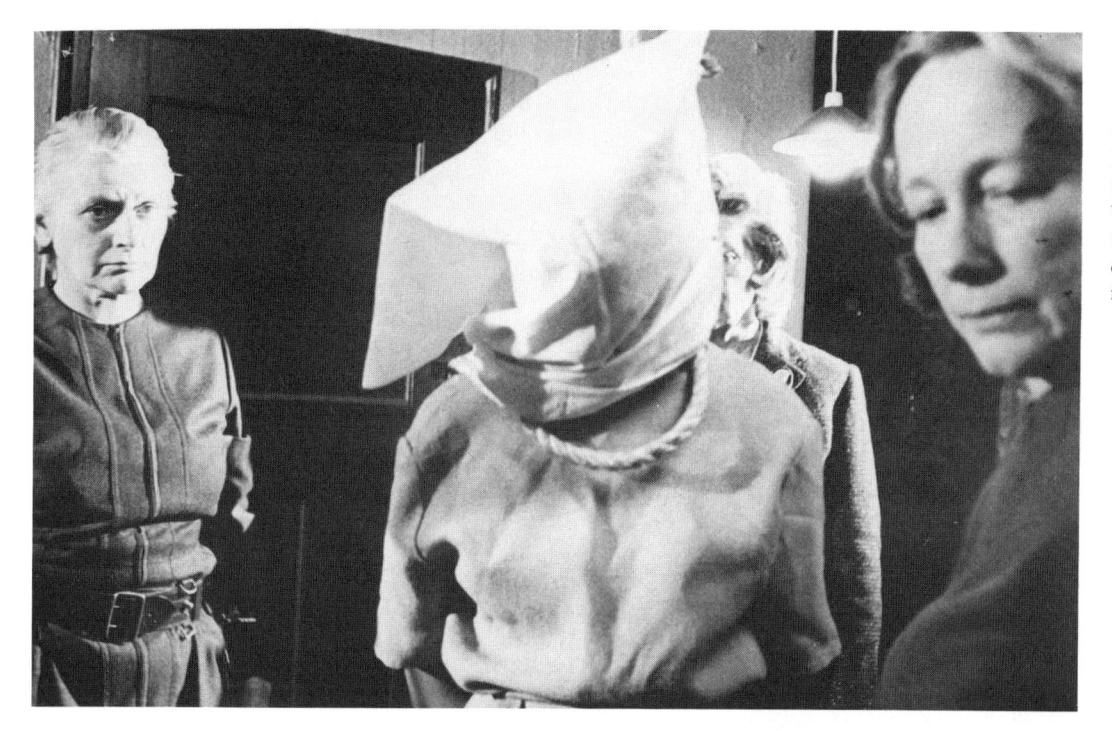

Guards Walker (Sheila Keith) and Bates (Dorothy Gordon) and Warden Wakehurst (Barbara Markham) prepare to execute a difficult prisoner in *House of Whipcord*.

The newspaper ad for *House of Whipcord*.

pretends to criticize. Certainly, director Walker is asking us to disapprove of what Bailey and Wakehurst are doing, right? But then why does he pay such careful attention to the sadistic whipping scenes and the general violence against women whose only crime seems to be the fact that they are attractive while Wakehurst and the guards are not? Why does he give his own name—Walker—to the brutal and inhuman guard who actually administers the whippings and the hangings? And why does the film open with the following statement:

"This film is dedicated to those who are disturbed by today's lax moral codes and who eagerly await the return of corporal and capital punishment."

That's supposed to be ironic, isn't it? Surely, the film isn't really intended for the enjoyment of the Baileys and the Wakehursts of the world. Or is it? Is Walker trying to have it both ways? Is the film trying to appeal, on the one hand, to those who deplore the abuse of justice and, on the other, to those who get off on seeing women whipped and brutalized? There is no way of knowing, and the result is a film that is impossible to like but equally impossible to get out of your mind once you've seen it.

I Eat Your Skin

ALTERNATE TITLES:

Voodoo Blood Bath, Zombies

1964/1971

Director/producer/screenplay: Del Tenney

CAST:
William Joyce, Heather Hewitt, Walter Coy, Robert Stanton, Betty Hyatt Linton, Dan Stapleton

ORIGINAL RELEASE: Cinemation Industries
VIDEO: Rhino Home Video

Don't take the title too seriously because, in fact, nobody eats any skin in this film. In 1971, producer Jerry Gross bought the movie and gave it a new name so he could use it on a double bill with *I Drink Your Blood*. The original

The natives on Voodoo Island don't seem to do much except dance in the deceptively titled *I Eat Your Skin*.

title was *Voodoo Blood Bath,* but don't look for any bloodbaths either. Truth in advertising has never meant much to the makers of horror films.

There *is* voodoo in the movie, however, as fun-loving, womanizing American writer Tom Harris (William Joyce) finds out when he visits Voodoo Island to do research for his new novel. His agent, Duncan Fairchild (Dan Stapleton), and Fairchild's wife, Coral (Betty Hyatt Linton), come along for the ride, and they meet Charles Bentley (Walter Coy), overseer of the island plantation, Dr. August Biladeau (Robert Stanton), the resident mad scientist, and his lovely daughter, Jeanine (Heather Hewitt). Dr. Biladeau is trying to find a cure for cancer, using venom from snakes on the island and testing his formula on the local population—they're only natives, after all.

Harris soon discovers that there is an army of zombies on the island, as well as a thriving voodoo cult that practices human sacrifice and does a lot of dancing. The cult is led by a mysterious masked figure who, in the end, turns out to be Bentley, who has been using native superstitions to his advantage.

It seems that Dr. Biladeau's research hasn't been going well. Instead of curing cancer, his formula transforms his human guinea pigs into ugly, bug-eyed automatons. Seeing his opportunity for world conquest, Bentley has been forcing Biladeau to create an army of these zombies. At the end of the movie, Biladeau kills Bentley, and then, while Harris, Jeanine, and the others escape, he throws the switch that will blow up his lab and all of Voodoo Island.

Voodoo has been a reviled religion in horror films for decades, and as in *I Eat Your Skin*, it is usually depicted as a barbaric practice reserved for those savages who live in third-world countries and who, if they were only more civilized, would be practicing Christianity. There is no recognition that voodoo is a religion like any other, practiced by many believers who are certainly not primitives. But then horror films are not noted for their tolerance of difference. *I Eat Your Skin* adds to the insult by suggesting that nonwhite voodooists wouldn't even be capable of practicing their own religion if they didn't have a white man (in this case, Bentley) leading them along every step of the way.

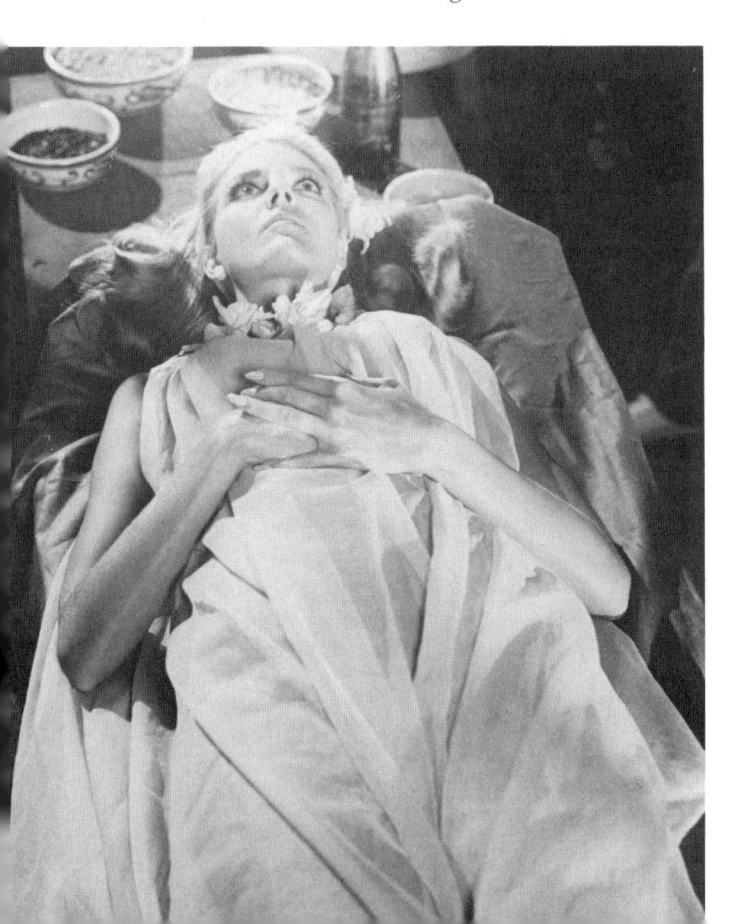

I Was a Teenage Werewolf

1957

Director: Gene Fowler Jr.; *Producer:* Herman Cohen; *Screenplay:* Ralph Thornton

CAST:
Michael Landon, Whit Bissell, Yvonne Lime, Barney Phillips, Tony Marshall

ORIGINAL RELEASE: American International Pictures
VIDEO: Columbia/Tristar Home Video

The late Michael Landon of TV fame is wonderful in his starring screen debut as the teenage werewolf. This is a real classic that holds up very well, even after more than thirty-five years. It has its low points, but the performances are still strong, and the werewolf makeup is still striking.

Tony (Landon) is a maladjusted teen—"I burn easy"—who gets into so much trouble that his high school principal, his girl, and Sergeant Donovan (Barney Phillips) of the local police talk him into seeing Dr. Alfred Brandon (Whit Bissell), a psychologist who delivers interminable lectures on pure science and who has some strange notions of therapy. Through hypnosis and injections of his homemade serum, Brandon sends Tony back into his animalistic past. The kid goes on the rampage, killing a couple of teens and Brandon himself before being shot down by the police, thus giving Donovan the opportunity to say, "It's not for man to interfere with the ways of God."

The issue here is juvenile delinquency. In the fifties, a host of psychologists, psychoanalysts, and sociologists made careers for themselves by discussing and writing

Jeanine Biladeau (Heather Hewitt) is prepared to make the ultimate sacrifice in *I Eat Your Skin*.

Before *Bonanza*, before *Little House on the Prairie*, before *Highway to Heaven*, Michael Landon made his debut in *I Was a Teenage Werewolf*. (*Courtesy Hollywood Book and Poster*)

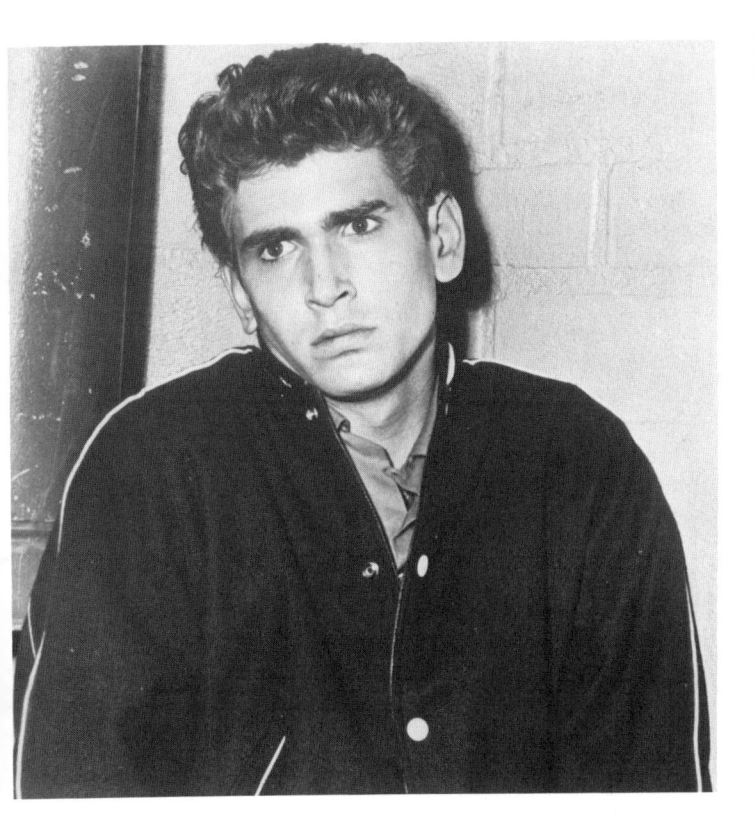

Landon sans makeup, as a mixed-up, misunderstood James Dean-type fifties teen.

Landon and girlfriend Yvonne Lime in *I Was a Teenage Werewolf*...

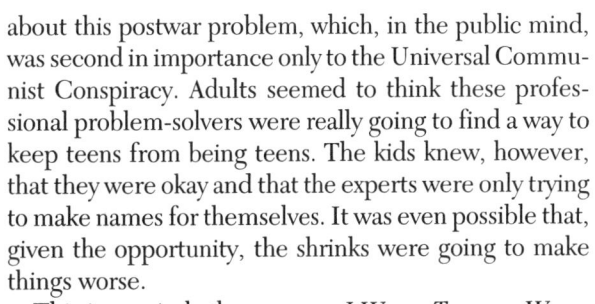

...and later after undergoing a rather hairy transformation, menacing Dawn Richards.

about this postwar problem, which, in the public mind, was second in importance only to the Universal Communist Conspiracy. Adults seemed to think these professional problem-solvers were really going to find a way to keep teens from being teens. The kids knew, however, that they were okay and that the experts were only trying to make names for themselves. It was even possible that, given the opportunity, the shrinks were going to make things worse.

This is precisely the message *I Was a Teenage Werewolf* addresses to teens—that the so-called experts are the cause of the problem, not its solution—and it does so with wit and good old-fashioned scary stuff. If you have the chance, see this one again. And look for Guy Williams, from TV's *Zorro* and *Lost in Space*, in a small part as a sympathetic cop.

Invasion of the Body Snatchers

1978

Director: Philip Kaufman; *Producer:* Robert Solo; *Screenplay:* W. D. Richter

CAST:
Donald Sutherland, Brooke Adams, Jeff Goldblum, Art Hindle, Leonard Nimoy, Veronica Cartwright

ORIGINAL RELEASE: United Artists
VIDEO: MGM/UA Home Video

Some horror film remakes are every bit as good as the originals, and some are even better. Unfortunately, Philip Kaufman's remake of Don Siegel's 1956 classic is not as good as the original, though it is still a fine film. Certainly the special effects are better than what was possible in the midfifties, and the remake has the same bizarre premise that made the first *Invasion of the Body Snatchers* a winner—Earth is being invaded by plants from outer space.

Matthew Bennell (Donald Sutherland) works for the Los Angeles Department of Health. So does Elizabeth Driscoll (Brooke Adams), who lives more or less unhappily with Jeffrey (Art Hindle). One day, Elizabeth finds a strange plant, brings it home, and things start to change.

She develops the idea that "Jeffrey is not Jeffrey," that he is some kind of impostor. Matthew becomes aware of similar cases, and his psychiatrist friend David (Leonard Nimoy) says, "I've heard the same damn story from six patients this week." Elizabeth is convinced that some kind of plot is taking shape in the city. "I keep seeing these people, all recognizing each other. It's a conspiracy, and I know that." Jack (Jeff Goldblum), another of Matthew's friends, agrees.

Jack: "It's a big conspiracy."
Matthew: "What's a conspiracy?"
Jack: "Everything."

Are Jack, his wife, Nancy (Veronica Cartwright), and Elizabeth only being paranoid, as David suggests? And even if they are, does that necessarily mean they are wrong? What is going on here?

Well, if you've seen the original *Invasion of the Body*

Elizabeth Driscol (Brooke Adams) shows coworker Matthew Bennell (Donald Sutherland) a strange flower in the 1978 remake of *Invasion of the Body Snatchers*. (Courtesy MGM/UA Home Video)

Psychiatrist David Kibner (Leonard Nimoy) explains to Jack Bellicec (Jeff Goldblum, left), his wife, Nancy (Veronica Cartwright), Matthew (Donald Sutherland), and Elizabeth (Brooke Adams) that their theory about people being taken over by some alien force is only a paranoid delusion. (*Courtesy MGM/UA Home Video*)

Snatchers—and who hasn't?—you know exactly what's going on. Seeds from outer space have produced pods with the power to duplicate any living being perfectly— even people. While you sleep, the pods suck out your memories, your personality, everything, until your dried-up body disintegrates into dust, and you become a new you. But not quite. The duplicates are devoid of emotion, and they are no longer individuals with differing beliefs and convictions. At bottom, pod people are all alike. As Elizabeth explains, "People are being duplicated, and once it happens to you, you're part of this thing."

So, yes, there is a conspiracy. The pod people are out to convert everyone, to eliminate humans from Earth and take over. First Los Angeles, then the world.

Matthew becomes convinced and tries to get help from the authorities. Some of them think he's crazy, though others seem to be sympathetic. But are they? Or are they only more of the pod people? Whom can you trust? Jeffrey is a pod person, David is one, and Jack becomes one. Soon Matthew, Elizabeth, and Nancy are running for their lives as more and more of the population of Los Angeles is taken over by the pods.

Eventually, Elizabeth falls asleep and becomes a pod person, too. Matthew finds a greenhouse and distribution center that is growing pods and shipping them out to who knows where. He tries to destroy it, but he is discovered.

Later, we see Nancy wandering through the city, still human but trying to pass for a pod. She spots Matthew and runs to him, but he points at her and begins to shriek—the signal pod people have to warn that a human is in their midst. Yes, Matthew is now a pod person himself, and we know that, by the time the final credits are finished rolling, Nancy will be one, too. Apparently, there are no human beings left in Los Angeles. The pods have won.

This is a good solid film with a very talented cast, but it often lacks suspense because—let's face it—we've seen it before in the original, so we have a pretty good idea of what's going to happen next. Director Kaufman gives credit to his source. Don Siegel, director of the 1950s version, has a bit part here as a cabdriver, and the man who runs through the streets shouting "They're here already. You're next!" in the early moments of the film is Kevin McCarthy, star of the first *Invasion of the Body Snatchers*. But, of course, Kaufman doesn't have to remind us that we are watching a remake. We are well aware of that from the opening theme, which sounds remarkably like the sound track from the original.

But Kaufman's version is not a mindless copy. For one thing, it is set in a big city, while the original was set in a small town. That's a problem, though, because, in a small town, everybody knows everybody, and so the loss of lifelong friends and neighbors becomes tragic in Siegel's film. This tragic sense is missing in the remake because,

Matthew (Donald Sutherland) discovers the plants that are duplicating human beings. (*Courtesy MGM/UA Home Video*)

in a big city, no one knows anyone and so there is little to lose.

Kaufman's film also tries to instill a sense of paranoia in the viewer, but Siegel's film doesn't even bother with that. In the 1950s, thanks to the Cold War, the Red scare, HUAC, and Joseph McCarthy, there was more than enough paranoia to go around. The remake has to create a kind of artificial paranoia. The first version merely tapped into a sense of paranoia that was already there, and that was what made it powerful and timely.

The pod version of Jack (Jeff Goldblum, left) and his pod buddies capture Matthew (Donald Sutherland) and prepare to snatch his body in *Invasion of the Body Snatchers*. (Courtesy of MGM/UA Home Video)

Without question, the 1978 film is very good because it addresses some basic fears we all share—the fear that our personalities might somehow be distorted by outside forces and that those we know and care about might suddenly become different from what we need them to be. The fundamental problem, though, is that *Invasion of the Body Snatchers* is very much a film of the fifties, not of the seventies.

Note: Both versions of *Invasion of the Body Snatchers* are based on Jack Finney's novel of the same name that was serialized in *Collier's* magazine in the midfifties and that differs quite a bit from the original film and the remake. If you haven't read this book, do it. It is still available and it's one of the finest sci-fi/horror novels ever written.

It Came From Beneath the Sea

1955

Director: Robert Gordon; *Producer:* Charles H. Schneer; *Screenplay:* George Worthing Yates and Hal Smith

CAST:
Kenneth Tobey, Faith Domergue, Donald Curtis, Harry Lauter

ORIGINAL RELEASE: Columbia Pictures
VIDEO: Goodtimes Home Video

The poster from *It Came from Beneath the Sea*. (Courtesy Hollywood Book and Poster)

This one premiered in San Francisco where audiences got to watch their Golden Gate Bridge get crushed by the tentacles of a giant octopus. What a thrill!

The atomic submarine commanded by Pete Mathews (Kenneth Tobey, who appeared in virtually every horror film made in the 1950s) runs into something big while on maneuvers in the Pacific, and scientists Lesley Joyce (Faith Domergue) and John Carter (Donald Curtis) are called in to investigate.

It seems that a giant octopus is lurking in the sea, and it's on its way to San Francisco. Interestingly enough, the monster was not caused by nuclear weapons testing—or at least not directly. Apparently, such creatures already existed in the depths of the ocean, but this one became radioactive after exposure to fallout from nuclear tests, and now the fish it usually preys upon can sense it coming. If it wants to eat, it must start preying on something that isn't as smart as fish—in this case, human beings. The thing crushes a few boats, a hick sheriff (Harry Lauter), and most of the San Francisco dock area before Mathews and Carter manage to torpedo it from the atomic sub and put an end to the threat.

This is a nice little movie, mostly due to Ray Harryhausen's special effects, which, as usual, are wonderful (even though, for some reason, the octopus is three tentacles short of a full load, making it merely a pentapus). Domergue—who appeared in almost as many fifties horror films as Tobey—is impressive as Dr. Joyce, a 1950s version of the liberated woman who confounds Mathews, her love interest, again and again, despite Carter's repeated efforts to fill the navy commander in on what "modern women" are really like. In any case, whenever there's trouble, she still screams her head off and needs to be rescued by one of the male heroes, so the notion of women's liberation in this film doesn't really go very far.

As happens so often in fifties films, there's good news and bad news here. The bad news is that nuclear weapons can give rise to monsters, though this comes as no shock if you're a fan of horror flicks. The good news, however, is that the very same atom that brought us the bomb can be used to defeat those monsters, in this case in the form of an atomic submarine. So everything works out in the end, and the bomb isn't really so bad after all. Right?

It Conquered the World

1956

Director/producer: Roger Corman; *Screenplay:* Lou Rusoff

CAST:
Peter Graves, Beverly Garland, Lee Van Cleef, Sally Fraser, Charles B. Griffith, Russ Bender

ORIGINAL RELEASE: American International Pictures
VIDEO: Columbia/Tristar Home Video

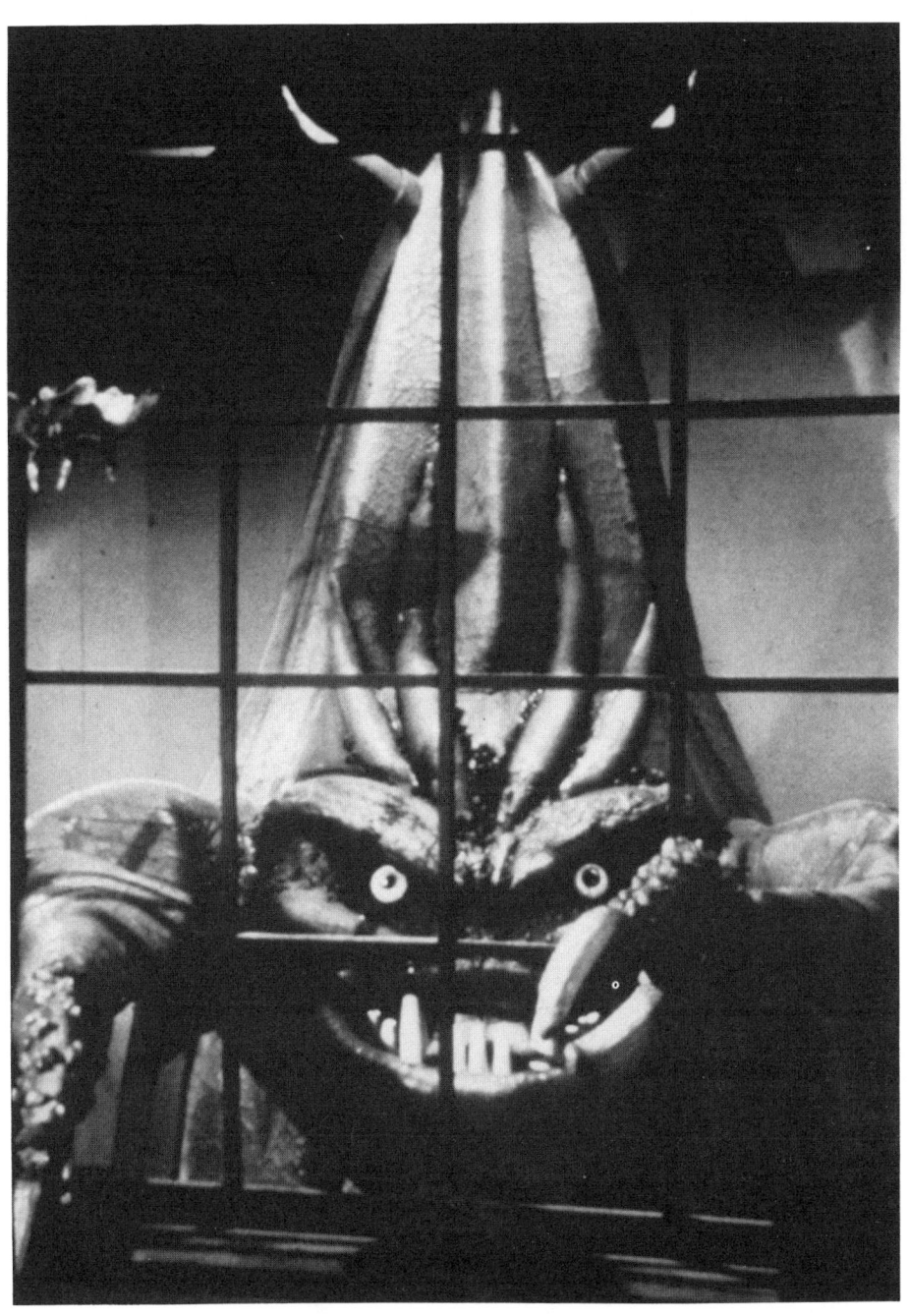

The "it" from *It Conquered the World*. (*Courtesy Hollywood Book and Poster*)

In fact, it does not conquer the world, but it makes a real effort to do so. It is a thing from Venus that looks like an upside-down ice cream cone with tentacles and fangs, and it comes here on one of our satellites, guided to Earth by misguided Dr. Tom Anderson (Lee Van Cleef) who is sure the alien is coming to help us solve our problems. "I believe he's here to rescue mankind," Anderson says, "not to conquer it."

But rocket scientist Paul Nelson (Peter Graves) knows that it means to take over, and he is not going to let that happen. When the Venusian uses flying batlike creatures to plant mind-control devices in the brains of the police chief (Charles B. Griffith), an army general (Russ Bender), and other important locals, Nelson shoots them down without a thought. He even kills his own wife, Joan (Sally Fraser), when he finds out that she has been taken over.

Eventually, Dr. Anderson sees the error of his ways after the thing kills his wife, Claire (Beverly Garland), and he sacrifices himself to put an end to the Venusian's plan for world conquest.

The cast here is a who's who of 1950s horror films. Peter Graves *(Killers From Space, Beginning of the End)* went on to TV in *Fury* and *Mission Impossible,* as did Beverly Garland *(Curucu, Beast of the Amazon; The Alligator People)* with her role in *My Three Sons.* Lee Van Cleef *(The Beast from 20,000 Fathoms)* became the superheavy in a variety of Italian westerns, ninja movies, and on television, and now and then he even got to play the good guy. The film also features Dick Miller *(Bucket of Blood)* as a helpless sergeant and Jonathan Haze *(Little Shop of Horrors)* as a stereotypical chick-stealing Latino. With this cast of professionals, it shouldn't be surprising that this early Roger Corman effort is particularly well done.

It is, however, a fairly straightforward Red-scare flick, with the Venusian playing the part of the Commie who would convert us all through brainwashing and Van Cleef as the intellectual dupe who is so caught up in his theories that he can't see the threat coming. Graves is the skeptic who can see through the "promise" of Venusianism/Communism. "I'd have to take a long, hard look," he says, "at anything that was going to change the world and me so completely." Once he's taken that look, of course, he realizes that anyone infected with the Communist plague cannot be allowed to live.

This kind of propaganda made perfect sense during the paranoid fifties, but today it seems a lot scarier than the cardboard monster in *It Conquered the World*.

It Lives Again

ALTERNATE TITLE:

It's Alive II

1978

Director/producer/screenplay: Larry Cohen

CAST:
Frederic Forrest, Kathleen Lloyd, John P. Ryan, John Marley, Andrew Duggan, Eddie Constantine

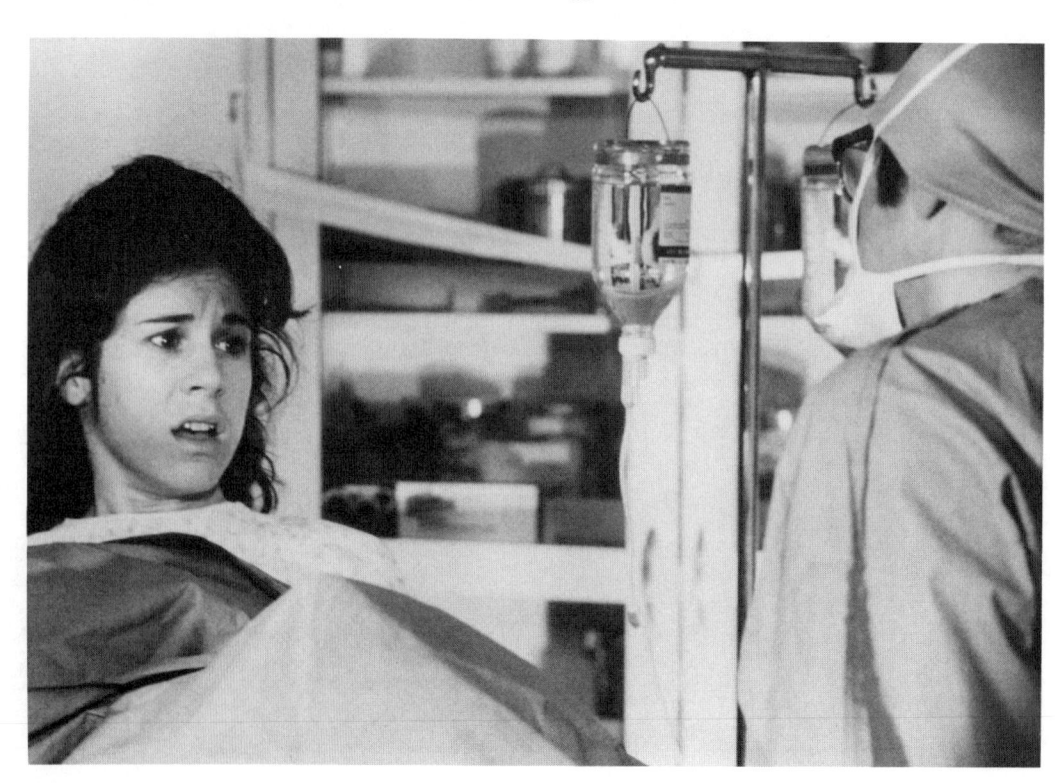

Jody Scott (Kathleen Lloyd) is about to give birth to . . . something in *It Lives Again*.

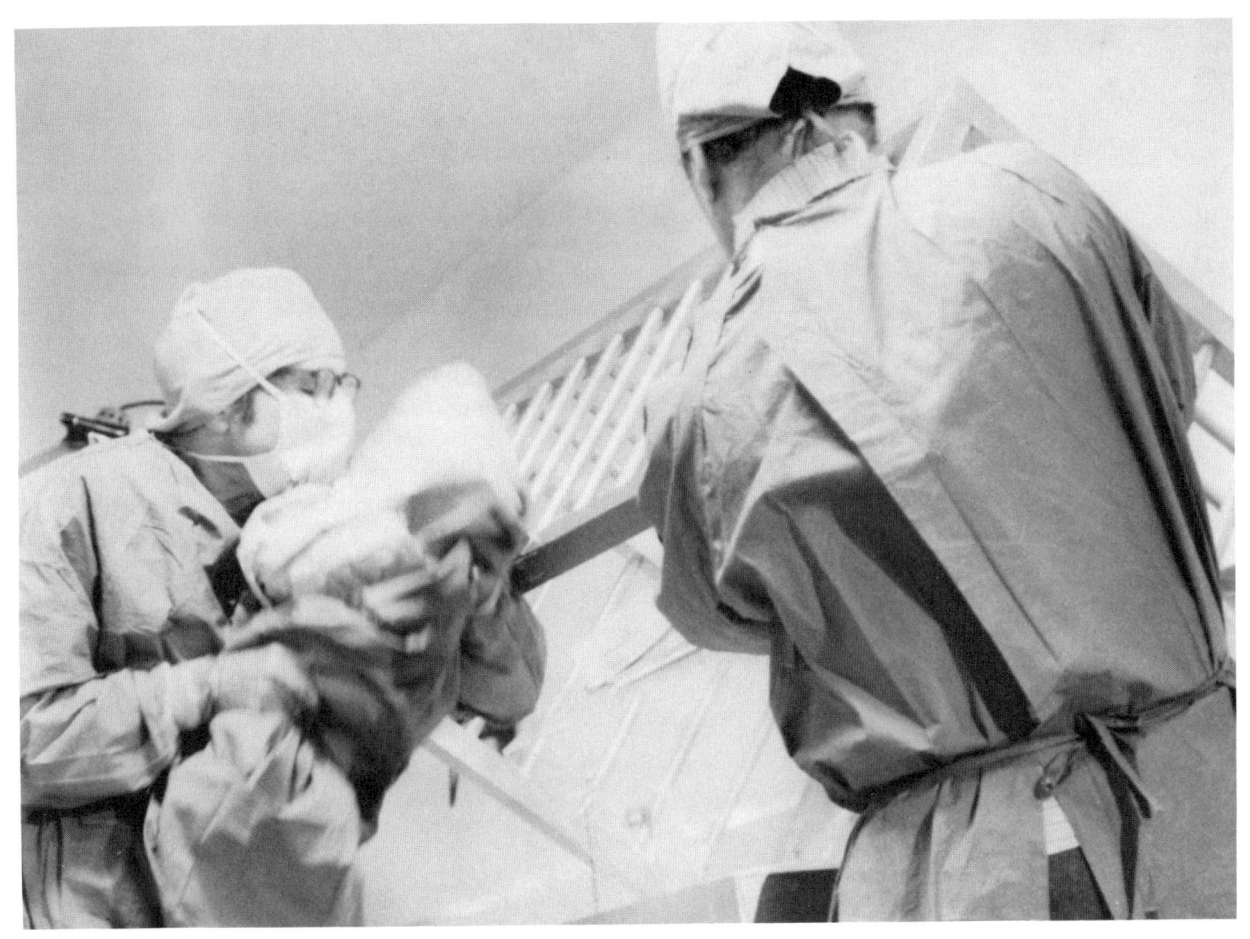

The doctors put the killer baby in an incubator cage.

ORIGINAL RELEASE: Warner Brothers
VIDEO: Warner Home Video

Somehow, director/producer/screenwriter Larry Cohen manages to take the weirdest ideas imaginable and turn them into real movies that work. His film *Q* is about a giant flying serpent in New York City. *The Stuff* is about an addictive low-calorie dessert that takes over people's minds and bodies. In *It's Alive,* you might remember, the premise is a killer baby that wipes out its entire delivery crew at birth, then goes on a murderous rampage until it is hunted down by the police.

Needless to say, *It Lives Again* is the sequel to *It's Alive,* and by now, there are lots of killer babies being born—"It's happening, and it's going to continue happening." Two nationwide conspiracies are also at work. On the one hand, the police and the government are trying to track down the babies at birth and kill them, though of course they don't want the public to know that they are massacring infants, no matter how dangerous the little tykes might be. On the other hand, a group of parents, doctors, and scientists is trying to save these children from the authorities and give them a chance to live.

Friends are having a baby shower for Jody Scott (Kathleen Lloyd), and among the guests is someone they don't know. It turns out to be Frank Davis (John P. Ryan), the father from the first film, who says that the police are watching them. Jody and her husband, Gene (Frederic Forrest), fit the profile for parents likely to give birth to a mutant kid, and a special squad is in place to kill the child at birth if it is "abnormal."

Gene and Jody don't believe their child is "abnormal" and write Davis off as a crank, but at the hospital they are stopped by police, headed by a fanatic named Mallory (John Marley), and they soon realize Davis was right. Fortunately, Frank manages to get the Scotts out of the hospital to a waiting mobile delivery room where Jody gives birth to a mutant baby boy.

The child is taken to a facility in Los Angeles where two other killer babies are being cared for under the direction of Drs. Perry (Andrew Duggan) and Forrest (Eddie Constantine). Perry explains that these new children are, of course, superstrong, but they are also superintelligent and capable of survival under the most

143

Adam, the killer baby, leaves his mark on a cake at an outdoor birthday party.

extreme conditions. They are, according to Frank Davis, "the beginning of a new race of humanity that will finally eclipse our own." They kill because they are frightened and can sense when people mean them harm. Under the watchful eyes of Perry, Forrest, and their staff, however, the three babies in their care seem to be thriving.

Jody loves her baby, no matter what, but Gene is far from convinced. Meanwhile, with the help of Jody's mother, the police find Perry's facility and close in. Thinking they have been betrayed, the babies attack and kill Perry, Frank Davis, and a few extras. Mallory and his team shoot two of the infants, but the Scott baby manages to escape.

Gene agrees to help the police in their effort to kill his son, but when the baby returns to them—these kids have an uncanny ability to home in on their parents—he regrets what he has done. "Please forgive me," Gene says to the kid, who really only wants his mom and dad. Gene and Jody snuggle with the baby. Then, when Mallory charges in, gun drawn, the kid attacks him, and Gene shoots the child to save the cop and to spare his son what might be a more horrible death. In the end, Gene Scott is in San Francisco, contacting an expectant couple, carrying on Frank Davis's work.

Like most of Cohen's films, *It Lives Again* addresses some tricky issues. Modern medical technology makes it possible to detect genetic defects in the fetus, and a pregnancy can be terminated if the child is going to be "abnormal." But, Cohen asks, who is to determine what is "normal" and "abnormal?" What is the difference between a genetic "defect" and the next step in human evolution? Who has the right to make these choices? The parents? The authorities? There are no easy answers to these questions.

The film also addresses a more personal issue. Those of us who are parents fear for our kids, but we are also a bit afraid of them. After all, babies have no sense of morality and are capable of extreme fits of anger. If an infant were six feet tall and weighed a coupled hundred pounds, it could probably destroy a good-sized city.

Also, if you've ever spent sleepless nights cradling your screaming baby, you know the real meaning of the saying "This child will be the death of me." Sometimes it does seem that our kids are out to get us. The *It's Alive* films merely take these basic fears and make them literal.

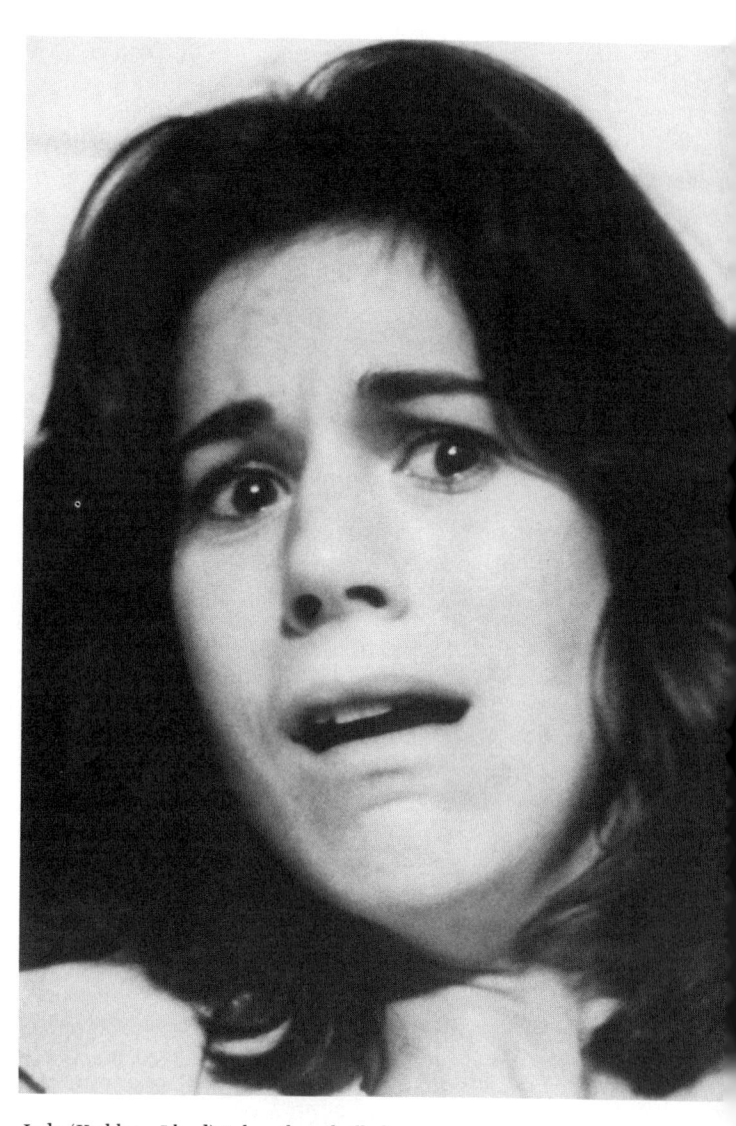

Jody (Kathleen Lloyd) is less than thrilled when her baby comes back home in *It Lives Again*.

Wisely, Cohen never shows the killer babies very clearly in either *It's Alive* or *It Lives Again*—when we do see them briefly, we realize how stupid this whole idea really is. And yet, for the most part, these movies work because they tap into fears we have but are hardly aware of—which is exactly what the best horror flicks ought to do.

Lady Frankenstein

ALTERNATE TITLES:

*La Figlia di Frankenstein,
Madame Frankenstein,
The Daughter of Frankenstein*

1971

Director/producer: Mel Welles; *Co-producer:* Harry Cushing; *Screenplay:* Edward di Lorenzo

CAST:
Joseph Cotten, Sarah Bay (Rosalba Neri), Mickey Hargitay, Paul Mueller, Peter Whiteman

ORIGINAL RELEASE: New World Pictures
VIDEO: United American Video

Mel Welles is wonderful as Gravis Mushnick in the original *Little Shop of Horrors*, but as the director of this made-in-Italy production, he is less than brilliant. Joseph Cotten is Baron Frankenstein, though his performance is a long way down the cinematic scale from his work in Welles's *Citizen Kane* (Orson, not Mel).

Frankenstein is up to the usual thing, though this time he has a daughter, Tania (Sarah Bay), who is also a scientist and surgeon and who wants to help out around the lab. Working with his assistant Charles (Paul Mueller), the baron creates life, but once again, he uses a bad brain and the results are less than satisfactory. Fortunately for Joseph Cotten's reputation, the maniacal creature kills its creator early in the film, leaving Charles and Tania to carry on the good work.

Baron Frankenstein (Joseph Cotten) conducts one of his unholy experiments in *Lady Frankenstein*.

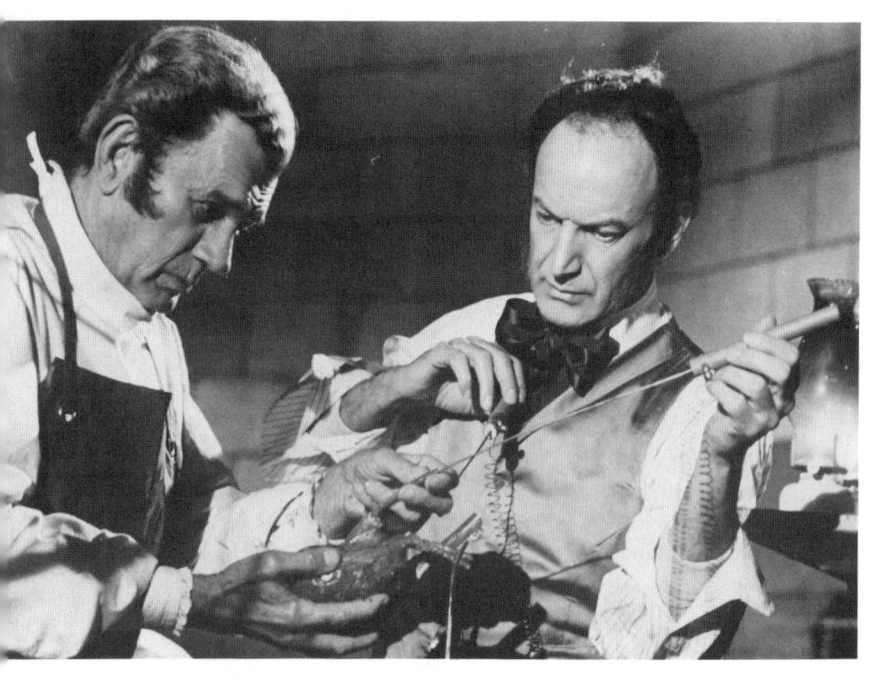

Frankenstein (Joseph Cotten) and his assistant Charles (Paul Mueller) revive a dead human heart.

Tania Frankenstein (Sarah Bay) meets her father's monster.

Charles (Paul Mueller) confesses his love for Tania (Sarah Bay) and agrees to let her give him a body she likes better than the one he has now.

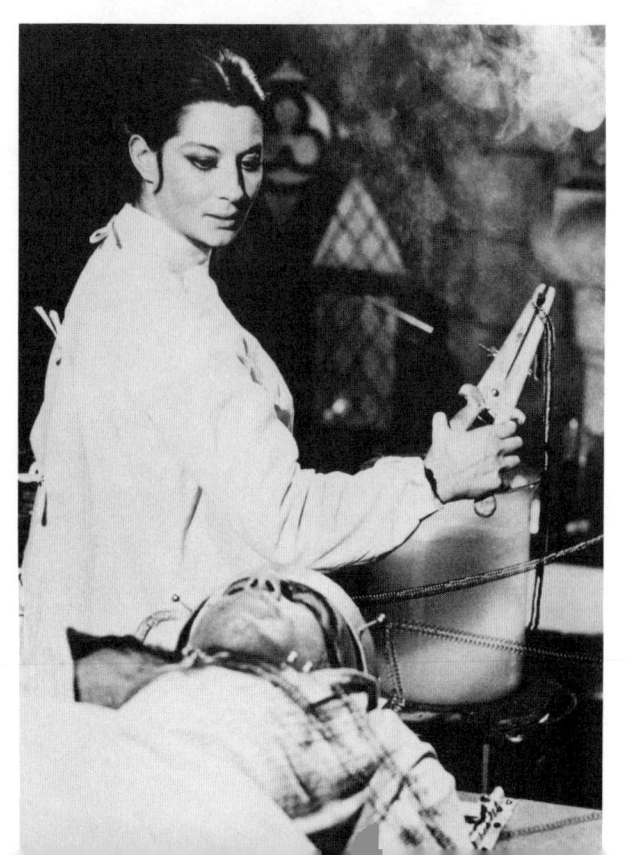

Lady Frankenstein (Sarah Bay) prepares to transfer Charles's brain into the body of Thomas (Peter Whiteman), the simpleminded but good-looking handyman.

stein is an open assault on the educated, liberated woman. When Tania complains to her father, "The professors [at the university] have a lot of old-fashioned ideas about a woman's place," we can see that the filmmakers have a lot of old-fashioned ideas, too. Tania does not know her place and will have to pay for it. The fact that she is open about her sexuality makes things even worse. As educated, liberated, and sexually aggressive, she is clearly evil and must be destroyed—according to the film. No doubt this is why her creation kills her at the end—because, as an independent woman, she cannot be permitted to live.

Land of the Minotaur

ALTERNATE TITLES:

*The Devil's People,
The Devil's Men,
Minotaur*

1976

Director: Costa Carayiannis; *Producer:* Frixos Constantine; *Screenplay:* Arthur Rowe

CAST:
Peter Cushing, Donald Pleasence, Luan Peters, Costas Skouras

ORIGINAL RELEASE: Crown International Pictures
VIDEO: Interglobal Video Promotions

Looking for revenge, Lady Frankenstein decides to create a second being to hunt down and kill the first. Her idea is to take the brilliant brain of assistant Charles—who is not particularly attractive—and put it into the good-looking body of Thomas, the village idiot, thus creating the perfect mate for herself at the same time. Muscleman Mickey Hargitay, widower of Jayne Mansfield, plays Captain Harris of the local police, who is trying to solve the murders committed by the creature with the bad brain.

Thomas/Charles, now superstrong, defeats the original monster and earns his closing nude scene with Tania. Meanwhile, the local peasants attack the castle and set it on fire, as peasants are wont to do. Before perishing in the flames, Thomas/Charles strangles Tania for no apparent reason, and everyone gets what's coming to him/her.

Horror films usually do not look kindly on people who are too smart and/or too educated, but *Lady Franken-*

Made and set in Greece, the scenery here is quite beautiful, but the film itself pretty much falls flat, despite the presence of horror veterans Peter Cushing and Donald Pleasence. In fact, its single high point is a remarkable electronic-music sound track by Brian Eno.

Father Roche (Pleasence) is a local priest who, it seems, has been battling the forces of evil in a small Greek community for years. There, villagers worship a statue of the legendary minotaur that snorts fire through its nose, and they even offer human sacrifices of captured outsiders, all under the leadership of Baron Corofax (Cushing), who, for some reason, has come to Greece from the Carpathian Mountains.

When some young friends of his disappear, however, Roche apparently feels he has had enough, and he calls on a New York private detective named Milo (Costas Skouras) to help find the missing kids and ferret out the

New York detective Milo (Costas Skouras, left), Father Roche (Donald Pleasence), and Laurie Gordon (Luan Peters) wonder about the young Greek girl who seems possessed by some evil force in *Land of the Minotaur*.

Baron Corofax (Peter Cushing) is the head of the local satanic cult.

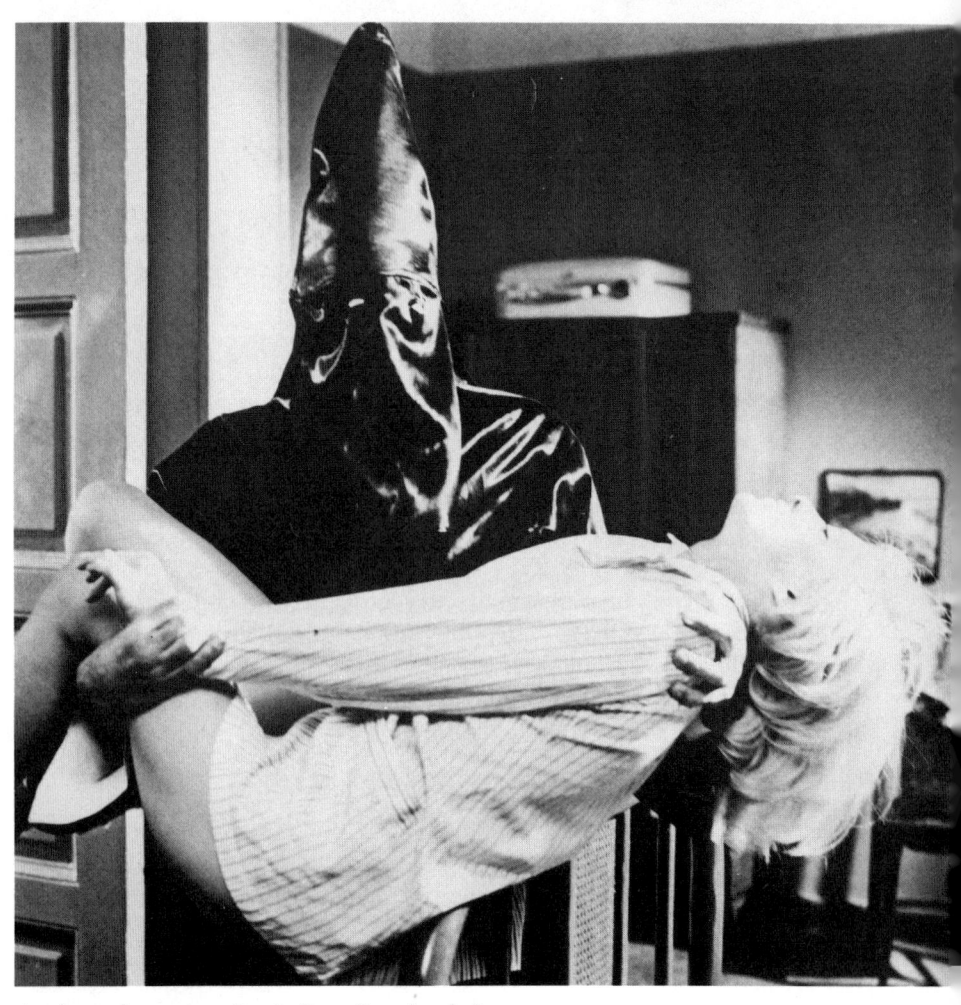

A cult member captures Laurie (Luan Peters) and plans to sacrifice her to the minotaur god.

The sacrifice begins in the *Land of the Minotaur*.

evildoers. Roche is always spouting off about evil and devil worshipers, but Milo is not a believer ("There you go again, demons and devils, heh, heh") until he sees the proof with his own eyes.

The worshipers themselves dress in black Klan uniforms, except for Cushing, who gets to wear a really neat red robe and hood. Milo and Roche follow the evil townsfolk to their meeting place in one of the local ruins where they are about to carry out another of their pagan rituals, and Father Roche proclaims, "There is one force that has the power to stop it." We all know what he has in mind—we *have* seen *The Exorcist,* after all—but it is still a surprise when he throws holy water on the practitioners and they literally explode. It's enough to make you wonder (a) why he didn't do this years ago if it was that easy and (b) what he needed the New York detective for.

Land of the Minotaur makes a couple of outrageous claims. First, according to the film, Christianity is clearly the only true and effective religion—practitioners of other religions, please take note. Second, even though ancient Greece is the source of Western culture and thought, including Christian theology, the film says that the ancient Greeks—like Corofax and his modern-day followers—were really only a bunch of pagan intellectuals and murderers, and that all vestiges of them, including their ancient ruins ("The ruins are sites of evil"), ought to be eradicated.

I wonder how Socrates, Plato, and Aristotle would have felt about that.

Irena (Andrea Scotti) and her husband, Fabian (Elio Zamuto), go at it in a typical scene from *Legend of the Wolf Woman*.

Legend of the Wolf Woman

ALTERNATE TITLES:

*La Lupa Mannera,
Werewolf Woman,
Daughter of a Werewolf,
She-Wolf*

1977

Director/screenplay: Rino Di Silvestro; *Producer:* Diego Alchimede

CAST:
Anne [Annik] Borel, Tino Carraro, Fred Stafford, Elio Zamuto, Howard Ross, Andrea Scotti

ORIGINAL RELEASE: Dimension Pictures
VIDEO: K-Beech Video

This Italian production didn't make it to the States until 1981 when Joe Dante's remarkable film *The Howling* made werewolves a going concern again. In fact, though, this really isn't a werewolf movie in the usual sense. The only transformation scene is in the opening sequence, and that's just as well, because the makeup is pretty bad. *Legend of the Wolf Woman* is the only film I know of dealing not with the usual full-moon/silver-bullets/hair-and-fangs werewolf story but with the actual mental disease of lycanthropy, and that's interesting—or it might have been if this weren't such a shoddy, aimless, pointless movie.

The opening scene shows a woman (Anne Borel) dancing naked in the forest in a circle of fire under a full moon. While she transforms into a werewolf, the voice-over narrative delivers a little lecture on lycanthropy and tell us that what we are witnessing happened one hundred years ago—later on in the movie, we find out that it happened two hundred years ago, so there must be some sort of translation problem here. The peasants show up with their torches in search of the werewolf, who kills one of them before they manage to tie her to a stake and burn her alive.

Now the scene shifts to the present day when Daniela Nasari (Borel again), the daughter of an Italian count (Tino Carraro), discovers a portrait of her lycanthropic ancestor and reads the legend of the family curse. Needless to say, this is enough to give her nightmares. Then a voice begins speaking to her, a voice no one else can hear: "We're waiting for you. You belong to us."

Daniela Messeri (Anne Borel) has one of her hysterical fits in the mental institution.

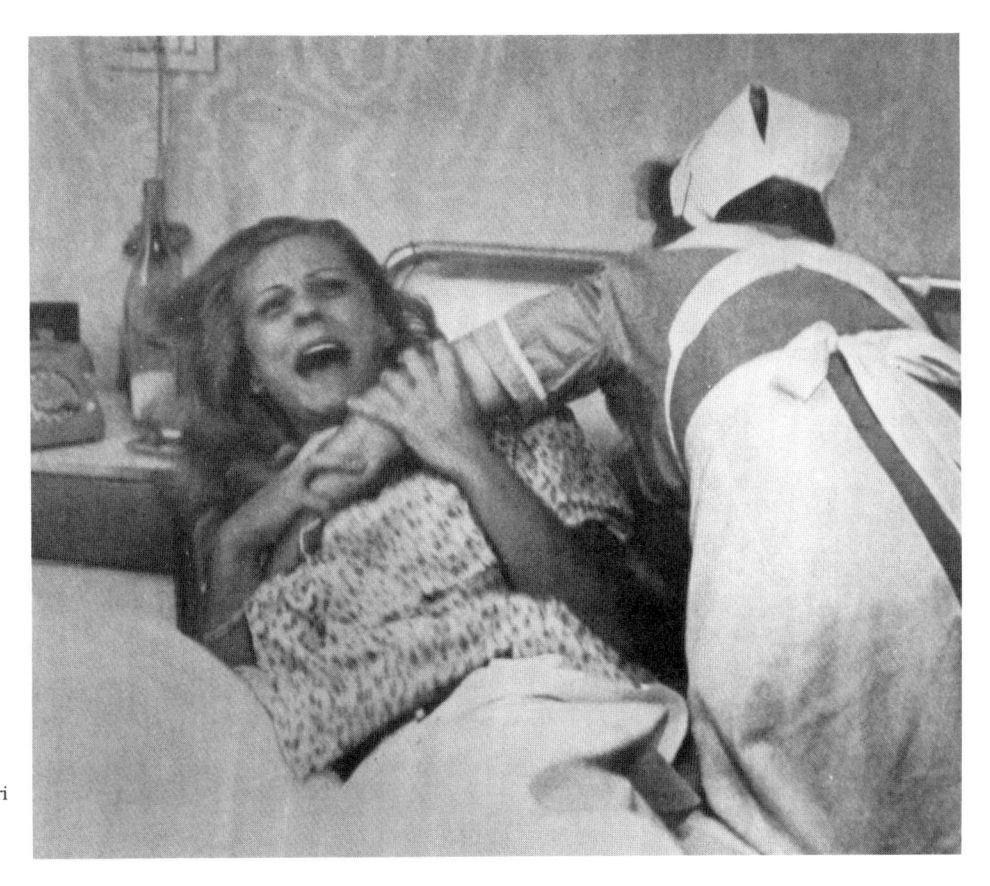

Daniela's father, Count Messeri (Tino Carraro), and her sister, Irena (Andrea Scotti), visit the hospital.

151

Daniela's sister, Irena (Andrea Scotti), arrives with her new husband, Fabian (Elio Zamuto), who looks exactly like the peasant who was killed by the wolf woman in the opening sequence. That night, Daniela meets with the spirit of her ancestor, who tells her that she bears the family curse of the werewolf. With this information, Daniela lures Fabian out of the house, pretends to seduce him, then rips his throat out with her teeth. She dumps the body into a ravine, and the police assume his death was an accident.

No one suspects Daniela of murder, but she is acting pretty strangely, so her father has her committed to a mental institution where she keeps having violent fits, so violent that she has to be tied down. Finally, after murdering another patient and a doctor, she manages to escape, and Inspector Montica (Fred Stafford) is called in: "I have to find her before she can do any more harm."

According to her psychiatrist, Professor Travel (Howard Ross), Daniela suffers from lycanthropia, brought on by her "repulsion for the sex act," which is a result of having been raped at age thirteen. "Now," he says, "she is convinced her ancestor and she are one and the same."

Daniela goes on killing people—anyone who seems to find her sexually attractive—until she meets the man of her dreams. She is even tempted to kill him, but she gets over it, and they settle down together. He doesn't know that she is still in hiding from the law, but she seems to be cured . . . that is, until three guys break into the house one night, rape her, and kill her boyfriend.

Now Daniela has more work to do; she has to get revenge for herself and her lover. And she does, killing all three of her attackers and even taking time to cook and eat the last one. It must be obvious by now that the people who made this film were taking no chances. *Legend of the Wolf Woman* begins as a standard werewolf movie, but in the hospital scenes, Daniela's fits are more like demonic possession *(The Exorcist)* than lycanthropy, and, of course, there is also the reincarnation angle—she is possessed by the spirit of her she-wolf ancestor. Once these plots run thin, though, the movie turns into a woman's-revenge/*I Spit on Your Grave* sort of film. But even this "new" twist can't keep the movie going for much longer.

The inspector tracks Daniela down to the forest where her original ancestor died, and though she tries to burn herself alive in a circle of fire, the cops capture her. Another voice-over narrative informs us that this is a true story and that the real Daniela Nasari is still institutionalized.

It is commonplace in horror films for sexually aggressive women to be depicted as monsters—vampires,

Daniela (Anne Borel) eats her last victim in *Legend of the Wolf Woman*.

witches, etc.—who are evil and dangerous because they are out of control. *Legend of the Wolf Woman* moves in the opposite direction by showing us that women who are sexually inhibited are also dangerous because they, too, are out of control. The only good woman, again according to horror movie lore, is the one who settles down with one man. If a woman wants more than one lover, or none at all, she is sure to be homicidal. This is certainly the case in *Legend of the Wolf Woman*. Daniela kills until she meets her one true love, a man who brings her under control. Then she is cured until she loses that man, and she starts killing again.

Like so many seventies horror flicks, though, this one offers the occasional nod to feminism—"You men will never understand us women," Daniela says. But given the amount of time this movie devotes to the gratuitous study of Borel's body—she is undressed or partially dressed for at least half the film and should get an award for the most screen time spent naked by a horror movie heroine—this feminist message is hard to believe.

Legend of the Wolf Woman pretends to explore new horror movie territory—lycanthropy as a mental disorder—but in fact it's only the same old stuff: a sleazy nudie film that warns women to know their place and stay there or face some disastrous consequences.

Mania

ALTERNATE TITLES:

*The Flesh and the Fiends,
The Fiendish Ghouls,
Psycho Killers*

1960

Director: John Gilling; *Producers:* Robert S. Baker and Monty Berman; *Screenplay:* John Gilling and Leon Griffiths

CAST:

Peter Cushing, Donald Pleasence, June Laverick, Dermot Walsh, George Rose, Billie Whitelaw, John Cairney

ORIGINAL RELEASE: Pacemaker Films/Valiant Films
VIDEO: United American and Sinister Cinema

Despite the various lurid titles under which this film has appeared, it is a fine piece, a darkly effective reworking of the true story of "resurrectionists" Burke and Hare,

Hare (Donald Pleasence) and Burke (George Rose) are grave robbers, murderers, and not very nice guys in *Mania*.

Dr. Knox (Peter Cushing) and his niece, Martha (June Laverick), seem happy enough, but the good doctor has a dark secret.

William Burke (George Rose) gets another corpse for the anatomy room the easy way.

Dr. Mitchell (Dermot Walsh) and Dr. Knox (Peter Cushing) accept another delivery from Hare (Donald Pleasence) and Burke (George Rose).

the grave robbers and murderers who supplied bodies to physicians in early nineteenth-century Britain.

Cushing is at his best as the dispassionate Dr. Knox, lecturer in anatomy at the medical academy and the resurrectionists' best client. Despite all his talk about medicine and humanity, he is cold and cruelly distant: "Emotion is the drug that dulls the intellect."

When one of the lodgers at Burke's (George Rose) house dies, he and Hare (Donald Pleasence) come up with the idea of selling the body to Knox. Being good entrepreneurs, they continue to supply the doctor by creating bodies themselves. Knox knows what's going on, but he doesn't care, as long as he's getting what he needs for his anatomy classes: "I neither condone nor condemn. I accept."

Finally, Burke and Hare are found out. Hare testifies against his partner in return for his own freedom, and Burke is hanged, but Hare is tracked down by vigilantes and his eyes are burned out. Knox sees the error of his ways and, thanks to his friend Dr. Mitchell (Dermot Walsh), is exonerated by the law and by the local medical council.

Burke (George Rose) and Hare (Donald Pleasence) kill medical student Chris Jackson (John Cairney) and sell the body to his profesor in *Mania*.

Though there is nothing supernatural here, *Mania* is full of terrifying scenes, from the graphic depiction of corpses being dragged out of their graves to the brutal murder of Jamie (Melvyn Hayes), the village idiot, in a pigsty. The film is a study in class differences, showing the poverty, exploitation, and everyday cruelty that produce the Burkes and Hares of the world and contrasting this with the genteel society of Dr. Knox, his niece Martha (June Laverick), and her lover, Mitchell.

Chris Jackson (John Cairney) is a poor medical student, struggling to compete with his more privileged classmates, who falls in love with Mary (Billie Whitelaw), a lower-class barfly. In most films, they would be the young lovers who would survive and thrive because, as we all know, love conquers all adversity. In the dark world of *Mania*, however, Burke and Hare murder Mary and sell her body, then kill Chris when he finds out what happened. Again, the underprivileged die while Knox, Mitchell, and Martha live happily ever after.

What does the film have to say about these conditions? Like Dr. Knox, it neither condones nor condemns. That judgment is left up to us.

The Manitou
1978

Director/producer: William Girdler; *Screenplay:* William Girdler, Tom Pope, and Jon Cedar; *based on the novel by* Graham Masterson

CAST:
Tony Curtis, Michael Ansara, Susan Strasberg, Stella Stevens, Jon Cedar, Ann Sothern, Burgess Meredith

ORIGINAL RELEASE: Avco Embassy Pictures
VIDEO: Charter Entertainment

Take a little bit of *The Exorcist,* a bit of sixties psychedelic flash, and a bit of trumped-up Native American folklore and you get this wild, often senseless, and sometimes very funny film about the reincarnation of a

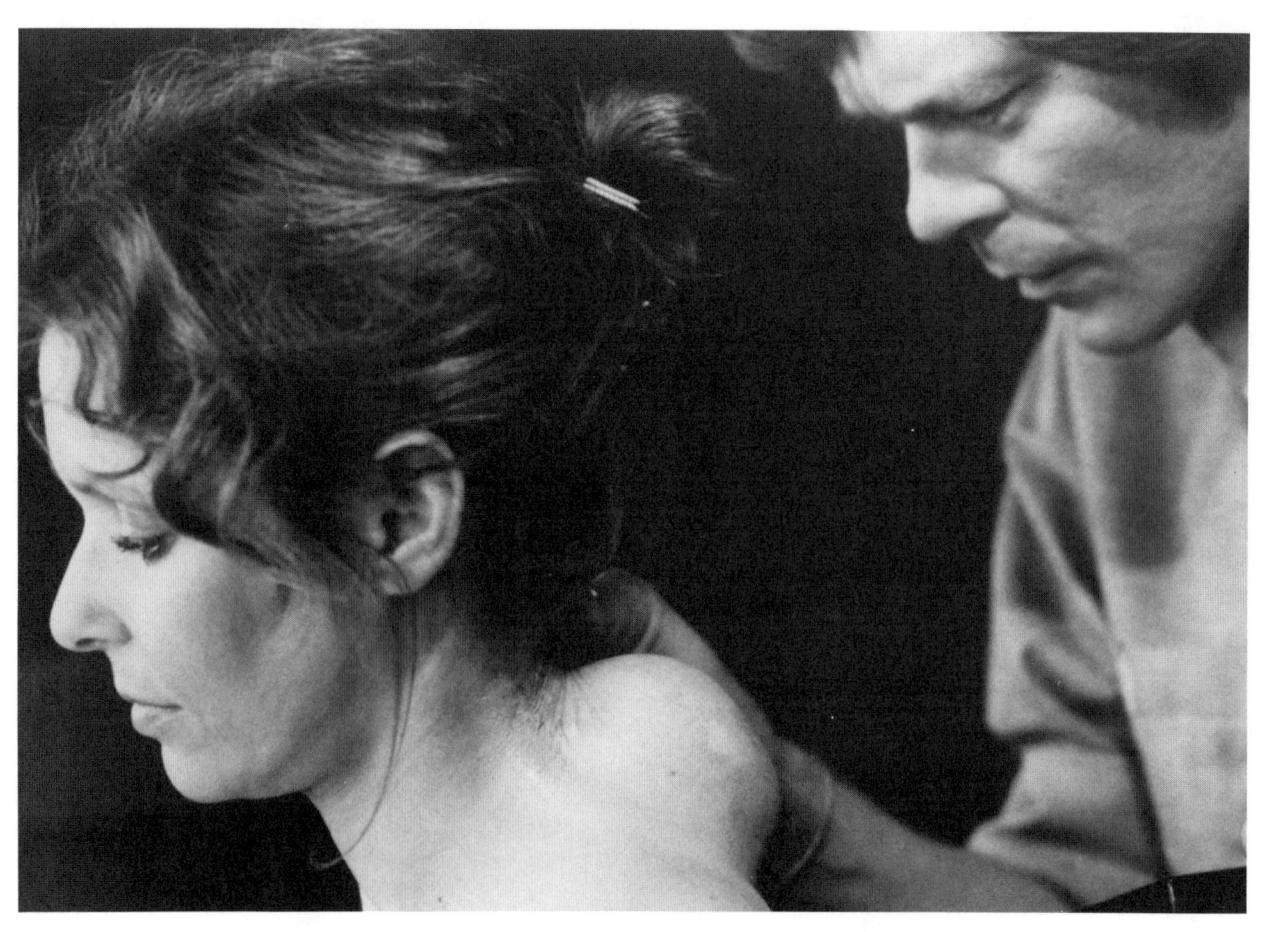

Karen Tandy (Susan Strasberg) goes into the hospital to be treated for the tumor that is growing on her back in *The Manitou.*

Harry Erskine (Tony Curtis) goes to anthropologist Ernest Snow (Burgess Meredith) for advice about Native American magic.

four-hundred-year-old medicine man and the trials he faces in the modern world.

Karen Tandy (Susan Strasberg) has a tumor on the back of her neck that is growing at an extraordinary rate. X rays show that it contains something that looks like a human fetus, which baffles even experts like Dr. Jack Hughes (Jon Cedar), who finds that, when he tries to operate, some kind of force stops him while his patient murmurs a strange phrase in a strange language over and over.

Harry Erskine (Tony Curtis) is a fake spiritualist who is Karen's ex-lover, and when she calls him, he comes running to help. Despite the fact that he is not a believer in the supernatural—"I'm a seller, not a buyer"—he becomes convinced that something has taken control of the woman he still loves.

Harry calls on true spiritualists Amelia Crusoe (Stella Stevens) and Mrs. Karmann (Ann Sothern), who hold a séance and raise the manitou—or eternal spirit—of an Indian medicine man. This seems to be what is possessing Karen, but Harry still doesn't know what to do about it.

In horror films, when the heroes are in doubt, they usually call in a college professor. In this case, it is anthropologist Ernest Snow (Burgess Meredith), who tells Harry to "fight fire with fire." This advice sends Harry to South Dakota to get John Singing Rock (Michael Ansara), another medicine man, who finally explains what's been going on.

It seems that really powerful medicine men can reincarnate themselves from the bodies of living human beings and thus continue their lives, gaining strength with each new birth. Singing Rock figures the one who is developing in Karen's tumor/womb is probably on his fourth or fifth time around.

When Singing Rock goes to Karen's hospital room and confronts the as-yet-unborn medicine man, though, he quickly realizes that it is "Misquamacus, the greatest medicine man of all." Still, John agrees to try to send Misquamacus back to "where he came from," over the objections of Dr. Hughes, who thinks the whole thing is ridiculous.

In a particularly gross scene, Misquamacus is born from the now-gigantic tumor on Karen's back, but he comes out ugly and deformed, thanks to the X rays that bombarded him while he was still a fetus, and he isn't very happy about that. John calls upon all the elemental spirits, but this is old stuff to Misquamacus, and he simply laughs them off.

Then Harry gets an idea. Singing Rock has explained that all beings have manitous, even man-made objects. Couldn't they use the manitou of the hospital's high-tech equipment against the medicine man, spirits that Misquamacus has never confronted before? They crank up all the computers and lasers in the place, but John can't channel their manitous against the evil Misquamacus—"It's white man's medicine." It turns out, though, that Karen can direct these computerized spirits against the little monster, and in a fantastic light show worthy of a sixties rock concert, she zaps the medicine man back into limbo.

Tony Curtis has always been a masterful comedian, and it is his tongue-in-cheek delivery that saves *The Manitou* from being nothing more than a string of special effects loosely tied together with plot. In the end, however, there is something hypocritical about this movie.

The Manitou pretends to respect Native Americans and their culture and notes how unfairly Indians have been treated and continue to be treated by the government and big business. There is even the suggestion that Native beliefs are correct and stronger than the faith of the whites. As John says to Erskine and Hughes, who hope to defeat Misquamacus, "Your god won't help you. Nothing in your Christian world will help."

But Singing Rock is wrong. It was white technology—the gun—that crushed American Indian cultures in the first place. In this film, white technology defeats the most powerful Native medicine man, who, it seems, cannot be beaten by Indian methods. In short, despite its phony tribute to Indians and Indian beliefs, *The Manitou* insists that white culture is still superior to Indian culture and that, if Native Americans get out of hand, whites can use their technology to crush them all over again.

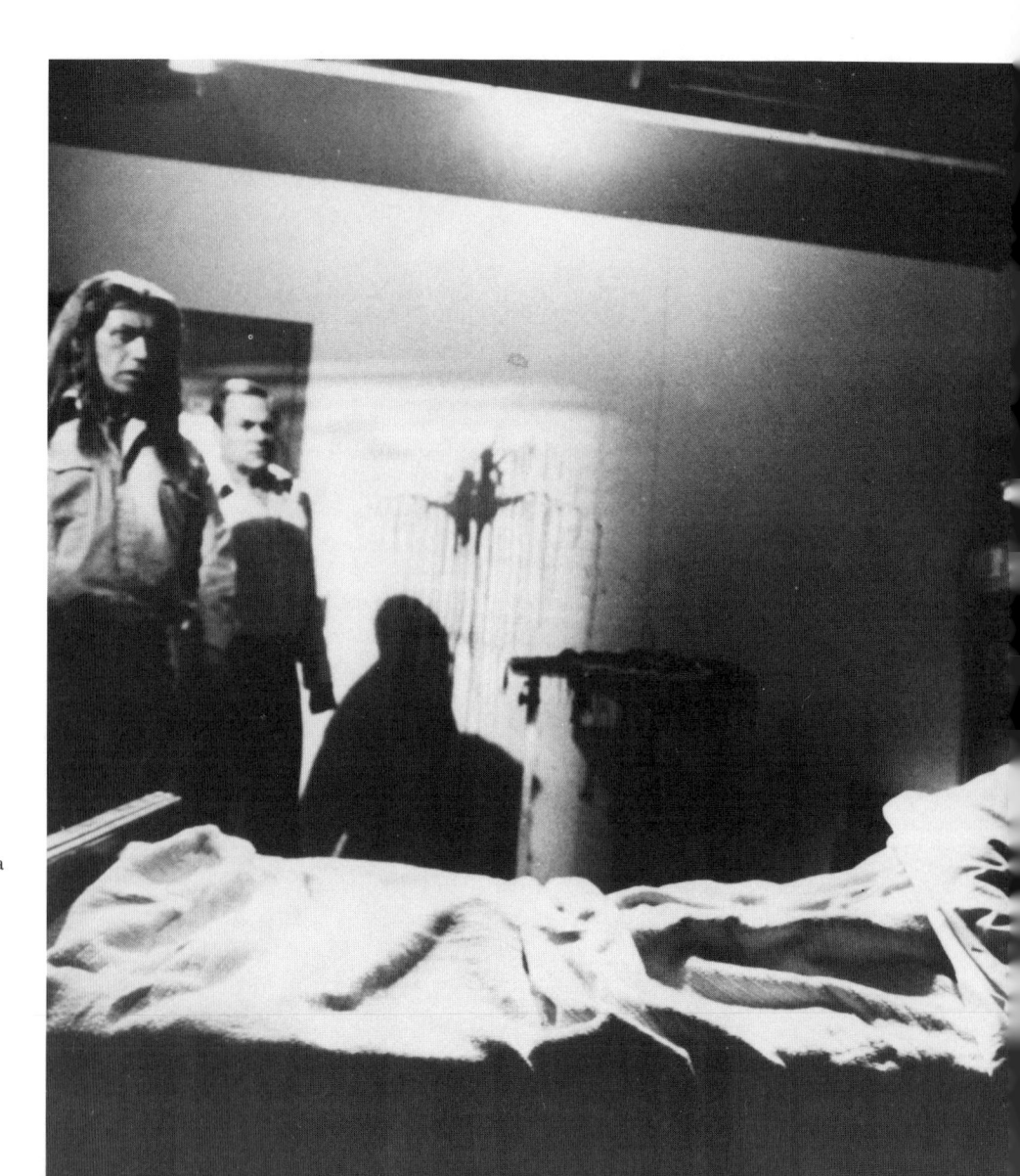

John Singing Rock (Michael Ansara, left) and Harry (Tony Curtis) look on in horror as Karen (Susan Strasberg) "gives birth" to a four-hundred-year-old Indian medicine man from the enormous tumor on her back.

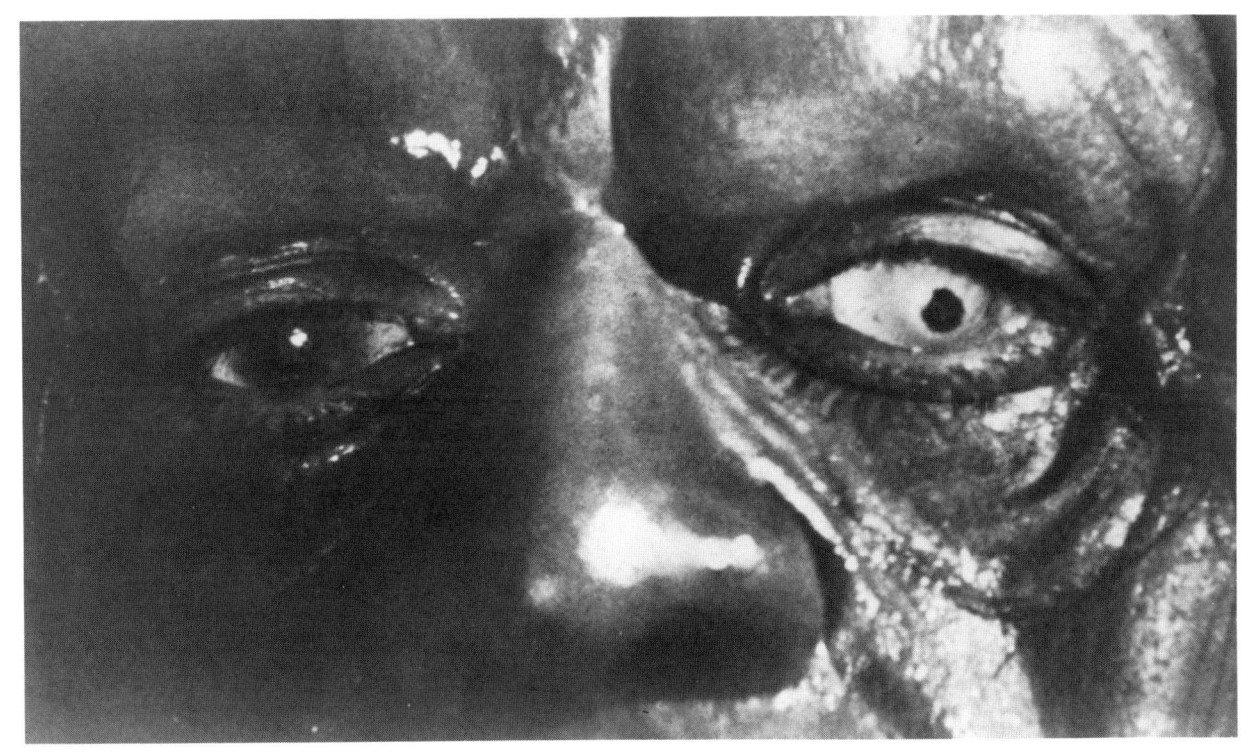

Misquamacus, the evil medicine man of *The Manitou*.

Mansion of the Doomed

ALTERNATE TITLE:

The Terror of Dr. Chaney

1976

Director: Michael Pataki; *Producer:* Charles Band; *Screenplay:* Frank Ray Perilli

CAST:
Richard Basehart, Gloria Grahame, Trish Stewart, Lance Henriksen, Vic Tayback

ORIGINAL RELEASE: Group 1
VIDEO: Bingo, Inc.

Michael Pataki is one of those fine character actors you've seen frequently in movies and on TV, though you probably don't know him by name. Maybe it was this lack of recognition that led him to try his hand at directing during the 1970s. Unfortunately, films such as this one

159

are not likely to make a significant place for him in the annals of cinema. And don't be fooled by the presence of such excellent performers as Richard Basehart, Gloria Grahame, and Lance Henriksen in *Mansion of the Doomed*. This is junk. Worse, it isn't even original junk.

One of the true classics of the horror film is the 1959 French production *Les Yeux Sans Visage* (*Eyes Without a Face*). In that movie, a surgeon sacrifices young women in the effort to restore the face of his once beautiful daughter, who was horribly disfigured in an auto accident. Now of course *Mansion of the Doomed* has a completely different plot line because, here, a surgeon sacrifices others in the effort to restore the sight of his daughter whose face is okay but whose eyes were destroyed in an auto accident. Maybe they should have called this movie *A Face Without Eyes*, just to show how very different it is from the French masterpiece.

Basehart is Dr. Leonard Chaney (*Len* Chaney?), an eye surgeon who decides that he can restore sight to his daughter, Nancy (Trish Stewart), by transplanting whole living eyes into her sockets. With the assistance of his longtime nurse and housekeeper, Katherine (Gloria Grahame), he performs the operation, using Nancy's boyfriend, Dan (Lance Henriksen), as an unwilling donor. The procedure seems to be successful at first, but then Nancy goes blind again. Chaney locks the now-eyeless Dan in a cell in the basement of his mansion—I assume most respected eye surgeons have similar facilities in their homes for imprisoning their patients when necessary—and decides to try it once more.

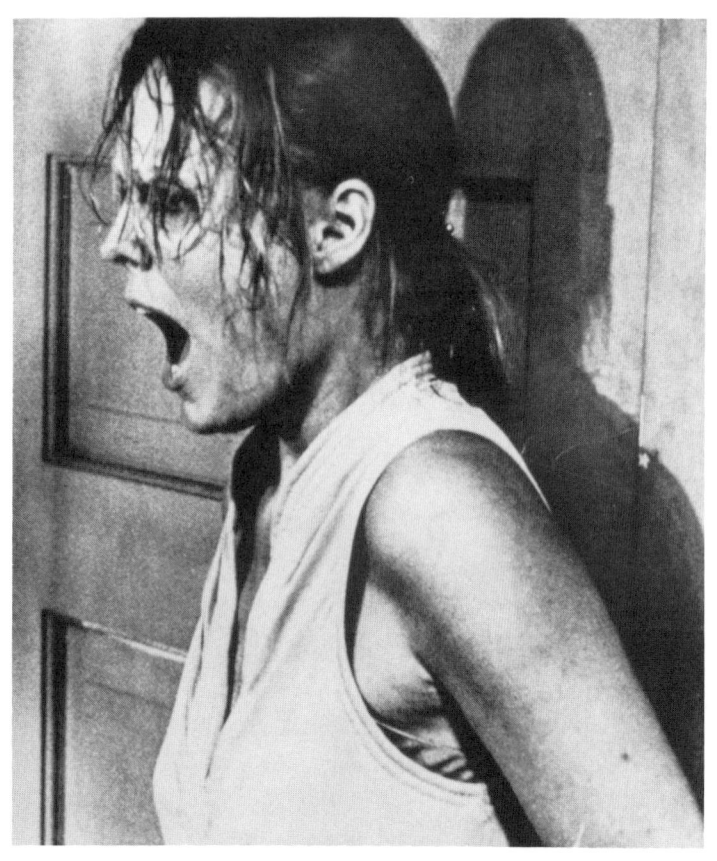

Nancy Chaney (Trish Stuart) doesn't take it very well when she realizes that her most recent eye transplant operation has failed in *Mansion of the Doomed*.

Nancy's boyfriend, Dan (Lance Henriksen), and his fellow eyeless prisoners plan their escape from the *Mansion of the Doomed*.

The police investigate the death of an eyeless woman in a traffic accident near the house of eye surgeon Dr. Len Chaney.

He picks up a female hitchhiker (Libbie Chase) and she soon joins Dan in the lockup, eyeless as well. More victims follow, and nothing seems to work, though the scar tissue around Nancy's eyes is beginning to look pretty bad. Curiously, Miss Chaney never seems to wonder where all the eyes are coming from, though she does ask her father what Dan's been up to lately.

The good doctor is not one to give up—as he tells Nurse Katherine, "I have not run out of donors." The basement cell is filling up pretty quickly, and Dan has been plotting an escape attempt, although that is not going to be easy, since all the inmates are blind. Eventually, however, one of the young women does manage to get out, though she is struck by a car and killed. This brings the police, who wonder why the dead woman's eyes are missing. Detective Simon (Vic Tayback) talks to Chaney as an expert on eye surgery, but the cops don't put it together, even though the eyeless woman was killed right in front of Chaney's mansion.

Eventually, of course, Nancy finds out the truth and sets the prisoners free. They kill Katherine and, in a riot of poetic justice, gouge out Chaney's eyes.

The word *mansion* in the title says a lot about how we are supposed to respond to this movie. Chaney is a doctor and he's rich—and in popular culture, doctors and rich people are bad. Physicians have a particularly evil image in horror films because, let's face it, we don't like them. They have complete control over whether we live or die, they keep poking and prodding our bodies,

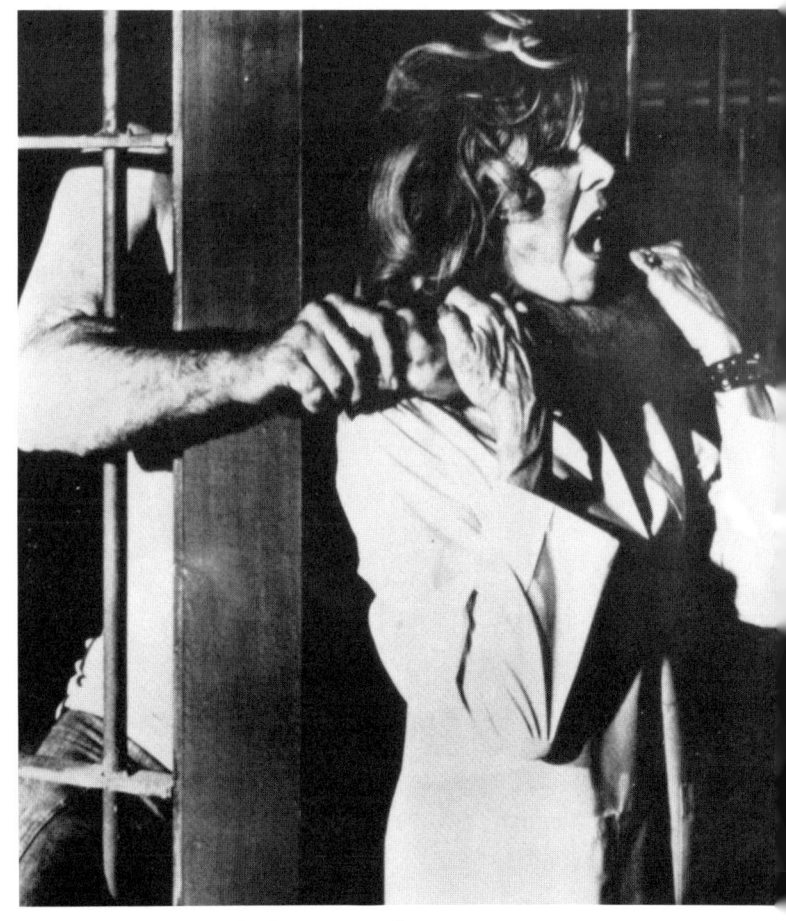

The eyeless prisoners in the basement get their revenge against Katherine (Gloria Grahame) in Mansion of the Doomed.

161

they use words we don't understand, and they make too much money. Films like *Mansion of the Doomed* are one way in which we can get a bit of revenge against the medical profession.

But the evil-doctor routine is not enough to bring this movie to life. Neither are the gross scenes of gruesome eye operations in tight close-up. That's too bad, because this film could have had a lot going for it. In our culture, sight is our most valuable sense, the one we would most fear losing. And the very fact that we are *watching* this film proves that we have something to lose—movies, after all, are about seeing. But, for some reason, *Mansion of the Doomed* never takes advantage of the fear all sighted people have about losing their eyes. As a result, it manages to be pretty disgusting at times, but it never really manages to be frightening.

Mary, Mary, Bloody Mary

1975

Director: Juan Lopez Moctezuma; *Producer:* Proa Films; *Screenplay:* Malcolm Marmostein

CAST:

Cristina Ferrare, John Carradine, David Young, Helena Rojo, Arthur Hansel, Enrique Lucero

ORIGINAL RELEASE: Translor
VIDEO: Summit Video

Mexican director Moctezuma has made some very strange films in his time—*Sisters of Satan* and *Dr. Tarr's*

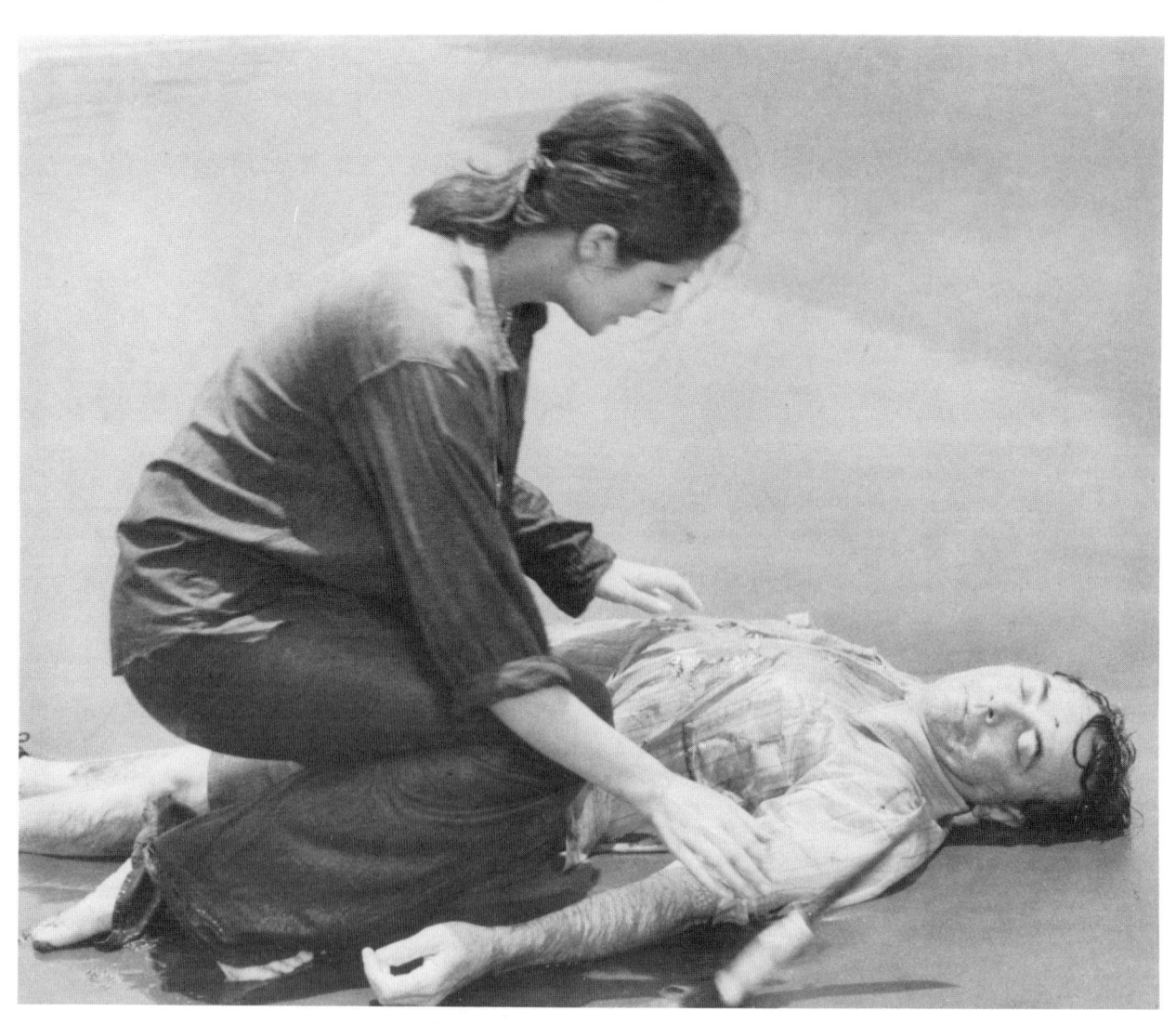

Mary (Cristina Ferrare) prepares to drink the blood of the fisherman she has killed on the beach.

Mary (Cristina Ferrare) the artist and gallery owner Greta (Helen Rojo) meet for drinks, but Greta won't last the night.

Torture Dungeon, to name only two. Certainly, *Mary, Mary, Bloody Mary* is one of the strangest vampire films ever, if only because it isn't really a vampire film.

Played by fashion model Christina Ferrare, Mary kills people and drinks their blood, but there are no fangs, coffins, stakes, crosses, holy water, or any of the other trappings of the good old vampire movie here. Mary is not a supernatural being; she's just a nice American girl traveling in Mexico who has this thing for human blood and who kills using a hairpin especially designed for that purpose.

Early on, she kills a sleazy American-embassy employee who has been coming on to her and drains him dry. This nearly causes an international incident as FBI agent Congrove (Arthur Hansel) is called in to help local inspector Pons (Enrique Lucero) investigate. The two discover that there have been a dozen or more such blood killings in Mexico in the past few weeks.

Meanwhile, Mary—who is an artist and a drifter—picks up hitchhiker Ben Ryder (David Young) on her way to Mexico City. The two become lovers and spend

Mary's father (John Carradine), who taught her bad habits in the first place, returns to threaten his daughter.

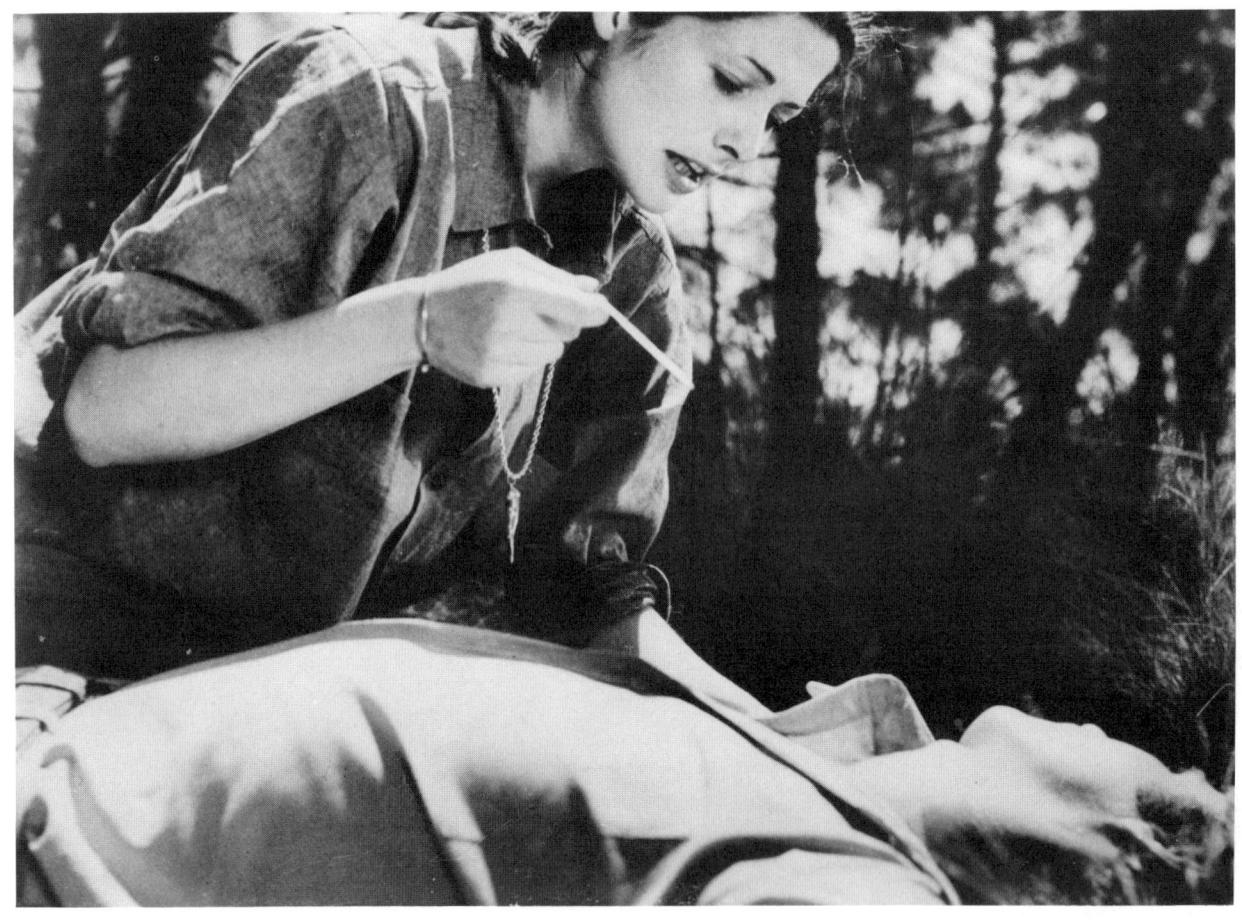

Mary (Cristina Ferrare) consumates her relationship with Ben (David Young) by drinking his blood in *Mary, Mary, Bloody Mary*.

the day at a beach where, in a particularly brutal scene, Mary knocks off a vacationing fisherman while Ben is exploring on his own.

In the city, Mary attends a gallery opening featuring her paintings, and the gallery owner, Greta (Helena Rojo), a lesbian who has been after Mary for some time, tries to separate her from Ben. Mary allows Greta to take her home, then kills her, too. The body count is rising.

Interestingly enough, it seems that Mary is not the only blood drinker on the loose. She finds out about her rival when she reads of another murder in the papers, a murder she did not commit. In fact, the other killer is a man in a black cape and mask (John Carradine), and he is on Mary's trail, which she discovers when he tries to run her down with his car, then stalks her at a festival and chases her through a graveyard. She narrowly escapes with her life.

One night while Ben is sleeping, the need comes on Mary again, but for the first time, her emotions interfere with her habits, and she cannot bring herself to kill him. It's a good thing, too, because when the man in black finally catches up with her, it is Ben who comes to the rescue.

The guy in the cape is Mary's father, the one who first taught her to drink blood as a child. Mary thought he was long dead, and in all honesty, he looks it—his face is decayed and rotting—but he's still spry enough to put up a good fight. He explains that he has been trying to kill Mary for her own good, to save her from a lifetime of horrible addiction: "This is your future, Mary, if I permit you to live."

Ben shoots Dad before he can do the deed, but the young lover is shocked to see Mary pounce on her father's body and start drinking his blood—she's been doing without for a long time, it seems. Mary kills Ben and drains him, too. In the end, Inspector Pons blames her father for all the killings, and Mary is free to pursue her interests.

This film is remarkably well made, even beautiful in parts, but what is most astonishing about it is that we find ourselves rooting for Mary all the way. Normally in a film like this, the vampire is evil, and this is particularly true when the vampire is a woman. But here we understand what Mary is doing. Most often, she kills people who are trying to take advantage of her, but even when this is not the case, we know that she is only doing what she must.

During the early scene on the beach, Mary and Ben witness the aftermath of a shark attack. A young man has been bitten on the arm, and his friends are in the water, stabbing the shark with spears and knives, killing it simply for being what it is. Mary, of course, is like the shark; she is simply doing what she does. That is why she has to kill Ben in the end; to let him live and to continue to love him, Mary would have to cease to be herself.

The theme song of *Mary, Mary, Bloody Mary* is entitled "Do You Know Who You Are?" The answer is, yes, for better or worse, Mary knows.

The Mask

ALTERNATE TITLES:

Eyes of Hell,
The Spooky Movie Show

1961

Director/producer: Julian Roffman; *Screenplay:* Frank Taubes and Sandy Habner

CAST:
Paul Stevens, Claudette Nevins, Bill Walker, Anne Collings, Martin Lavut, Norman Ettlinger

ORIGINAL RELEASE: Warner Brothers
VIDEO: Rhino Home Video

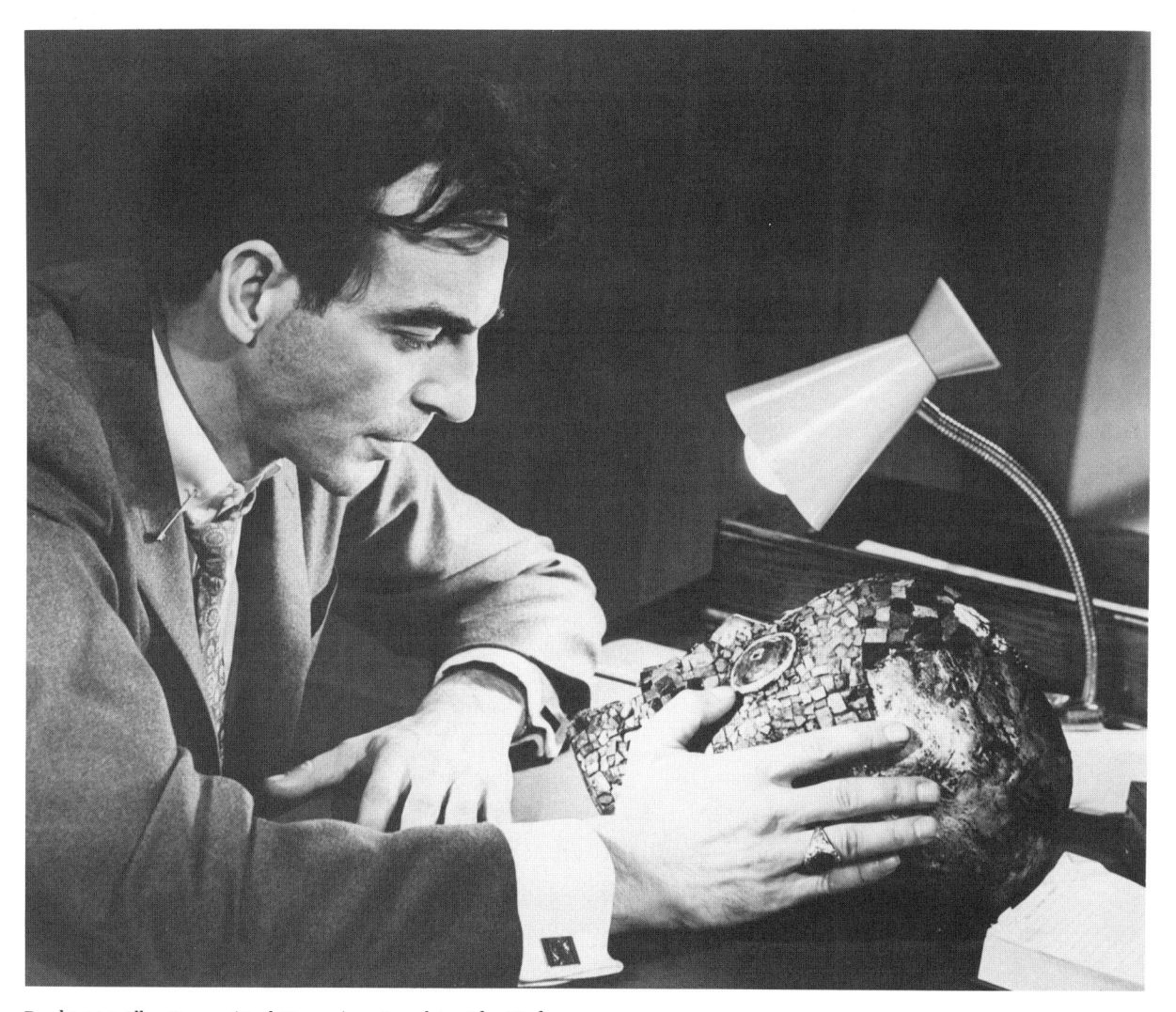

Psychiatrist Allen Barnes (Paul Stevens) contemplates *The Mask*.

When Barnes (Paul Stevens) puts on the mask, he has strange hallucinations. These scenes in the film are in 3-D.

The Mask came along after the fifties 3-D craze had passed and Hollywood had figured out that the revolutionary three-dimensional process wasn't going to win viewers away from their television sets and back to the theaters. That's unfortunate, because this Canadian production is an effort to make intelligent use of 3-D and to use the necessary red-and-green glasses as a gimmick for audience participation in the action of the film itself.

166

Allan Barnes (Paul Stevens) is a psychiatrist who has a problem patient. Michael Radin (Martin Lavut), who works for the Museum of Ancient History, is having nightmares in which he kills young women and does other despicable deeds. But Radin doesn't think they are nightmares. He thinks he really is committing crimes over which he has no control. On top of that, he blames these crimes on an ancient South American mask that is part of the museum's holdings. According to Radin, donning the mask puts its wearer into a kind of trance and causes his most evil, subconscious thoughts to come to the surface. The mask demands blood sacrifices, and the person wearing it is forced to carry out those ritual murders. Apparently, the wearing of the mask is also habit-forming. "I'm like an addict," Radin claims.

Barnes tries to convince Radin that the mask has no power over him, that the problem is all in his mind, but Radin gets frustrated and storms out of his shrink's office. That same evening, Radin mails the mask to Barnes, then shoots himself.

Barnes is devastated by the unexpected death of his patient, but when he receives the mask, he feels a strange fascination for it. He keeps hearing a voice that says, "Put the mask on now," and so he does.

Up to this point, the film has been in regular 2-D, but when Barnes wears the mask, the movie switches to three dimensions. When the film was shown in theaters, viewers were given cardboard copies of the mask with built-in 3-D glasses, and when Barnes was told to "put the mask on now," viewers were supposed to don their masks, too.

The 3-D sections are weird hallucinatory segments involving strange landscapes, sacrificial altars, Aztec architecture, priests in robes, human sacrifices, and fireballs and snakes flying out of the screen. There's a guy who looks like Barnes in a tattered suit, and Radin also appears now and then with one eye dangling down on his cheek. In short, these 3-D dream sequences make no sense at all, but they are lots of fun.

In any case, after his first experience, Barnes goes back to two dimensions convinced that the mask offers insights into the deepest secrets of the human mind, "even deeper than the subconscious." Pam Albright (Claudette Nevins), his girl, doesn't think he should be tampering with such things, but it seems Barnes is already hooked. When he tells her, "It's ordering me to pick it up," she runs off with the mask and returns it to the museum where it belongs.

Barnes steals it back—"It's mine now"—but when an urge comes over him to kill his secretary Jill Goodrich (Anne Collings), he becomes frightened enough to call on Dr. Quincy (Norman Ettlinger), his old college professor. The good doctor tells Barnes the same things Barnes told Radin only a couple of days before—that the problem is in his mind, not in the mask. But Quincy is concerned; he confides to Pam that Barnes "is on the verge of a complete breakdown."

Under the influence of the mask, Barnes goes after his secretary again—"I must experience the greatest act of a human mind, to take another human life"—but Pam calls the cops, who capture him and put him away. In the closing sequence, the mask is back in the museum, but now there is another guy hovering around it, fascinated as Barnes and Radin were, and we know the whole cycle is about to begin again.

This is a wonderful and effective little film that, in a sense, was ahead of its time. Long before we all learned to "just say no," *The Mask* was warning us about the use of drugs and the dangers of addiction to nice, ordinary people like Michael Radin and Allan Barnes. When Barnes says of the mask, "I tried to stop. I can't. I don't want to," we know what his problem is. But just in case we've somehow missed the point, Pam makes the connection between the wearing of the mask and the use of drugs absolutely clear when she says, "Do you have to take the drug again, Allan? . . . And when you put it on

The woman who waits for Barnes when he wears the mask.

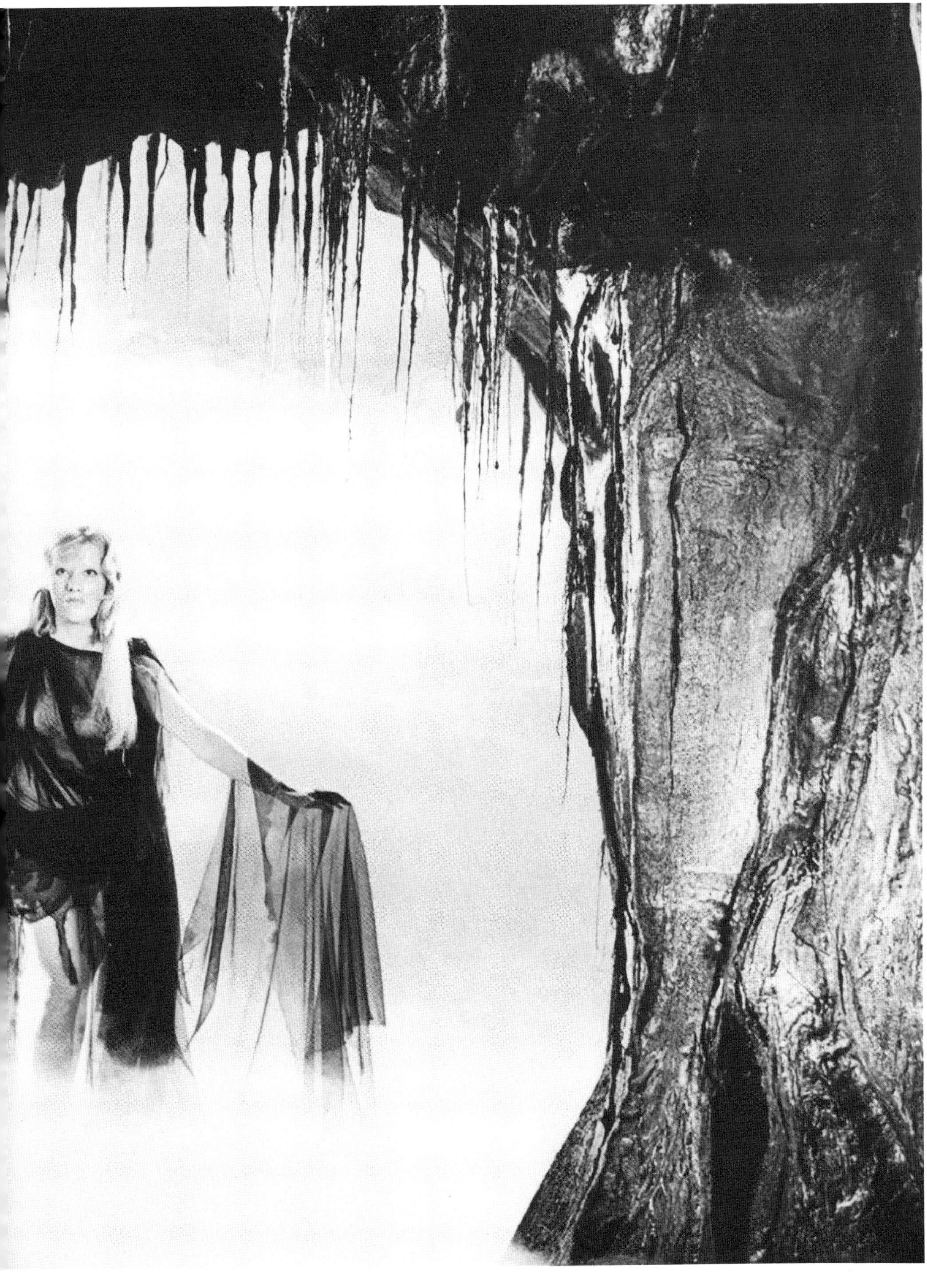

Pam (Claudette Nevins) and Professor Quincy try to save Barnes from himself.

again, what will it be like? A shot? A jolt?"

Like a lot of other horror films, *The Mask* is a cautionary tale that tells us what not to do. Also like a lot of other horror movies, the message here is mixed. The weird 3-D hallucination scenes are certainly the best parts of the movie; they are otherworldly and attractive, like the "trip" scenes from the LSD films of the late sixties and early seventies. So, on the one hand, *The Mask* says, "Don't take drugs." On the other hand, though, it says, "Look how cool this is." The 3-D sequences make you want to "put the mask on now," and so the messages of *The Mask* seem to cancel each other out.

By the way, in the Rhino Home Video print of *The Mask*, the dream sequences are in 3-D, and the video-cassette even comes with 3-D glasses (sorry, no mask) so you can enjoy Barnes's hallucinations in the comfort of your own home.

Far out, man!

Preparations are made for a human sacrifice to the god of *The Mask*.

Pvt. James Reese (Christopher Walken) of the U.S. Army seems to be a prisoner in a luxurious medical facility in West Germany in *The Mind Snatchers*.

The Mind Snatchers

ALTERNATE TITLES:

*The Happiness Cage,
The Demon Within*

1972

Director: Bernard Girard; *Producer:* George Goodman; *Screenplay:* Ron Whyte; based on the play by Dennis Reardon

CAST:
Christopher Walken, Joss Ackland, Ralph Meeker, Ronny Cox, Bette Henritze

ORIGINAL RELEASE: Cinerama Releasing
VIDEO: Congress Video Group and others

Back in the 1960s, scientists located the pleasure center in a monkey's brain and discovered that, if an electrode was planted in that area and if the monkey learned to press a button that would send an electrical charge to stimulate that center, it would pass up sex and food—even die—rather than give up the chance to press the button. These experiments inspired Dennis Reardon's

Sergeant Miles (Ronny Cox) and Reese (Christopher Walken) are fellow patients but usually don't get along.

stage play *The Happiness Cage,* which served as the basis for *The Mind Snatchers.* Filmed in Denmark, this movie features a remarkable cast—including a very young Christopher Walken—and an intelligent script that never lets up.

Corp. James Reese (Walken) is a difficult young soldier stationed in West Germany who is always getting into trouble with the military police. When MPs break his arm during an arrest, he is sent to a maximum-security hospital/mansion where he meets two Vietnam vets, both terminal. Lieutenant Rhodes is suffering from combat wounds, while Sergeant Miles (Ronny Cox) has lung cancer. Reese also meets Dr. Frederick (Joss Ackland), a German doctor who seems to run the place.

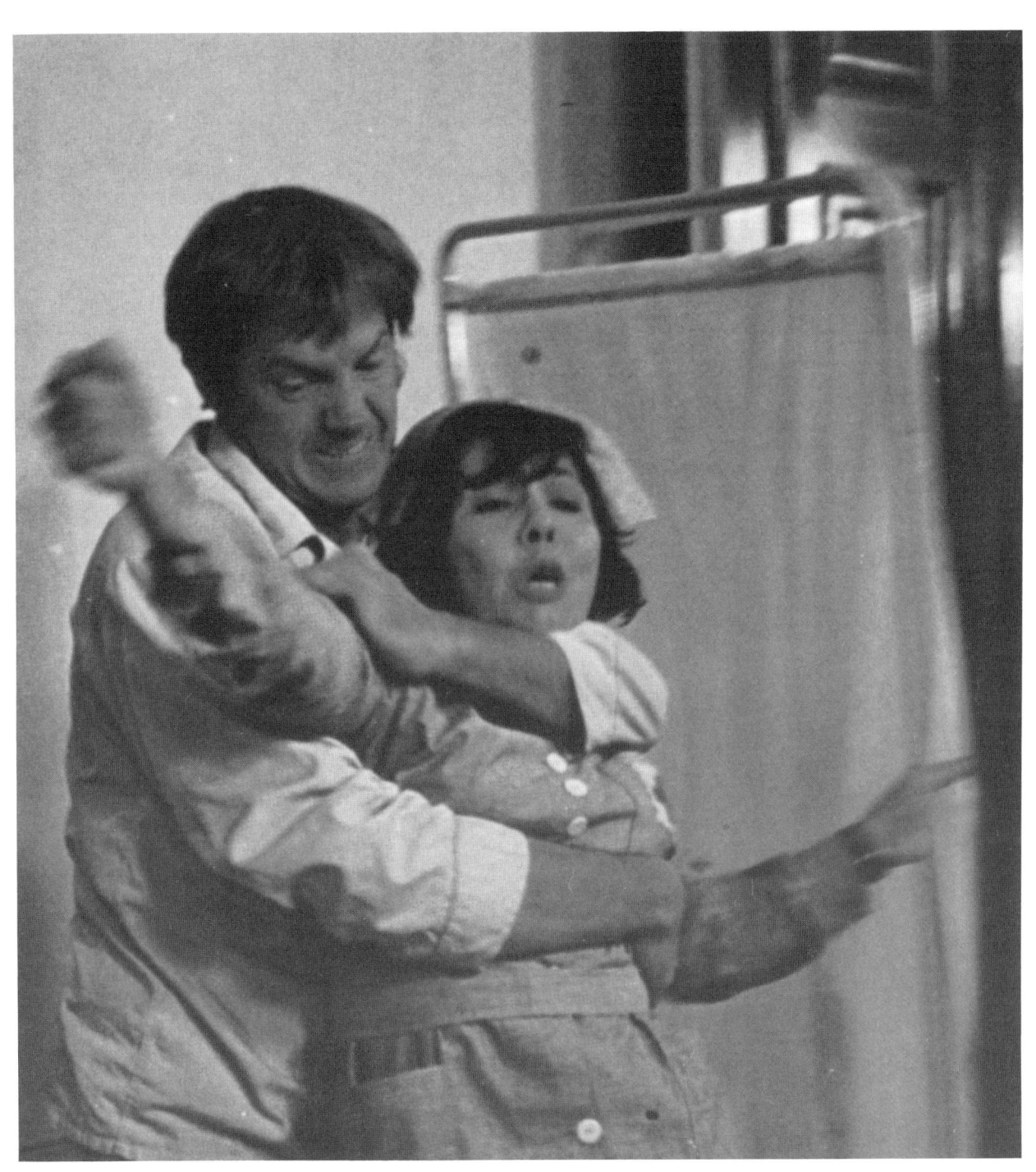

The sergeant (Ronny Cox) rapes Red Cross worker Anna Krauss (Bette Henritze).

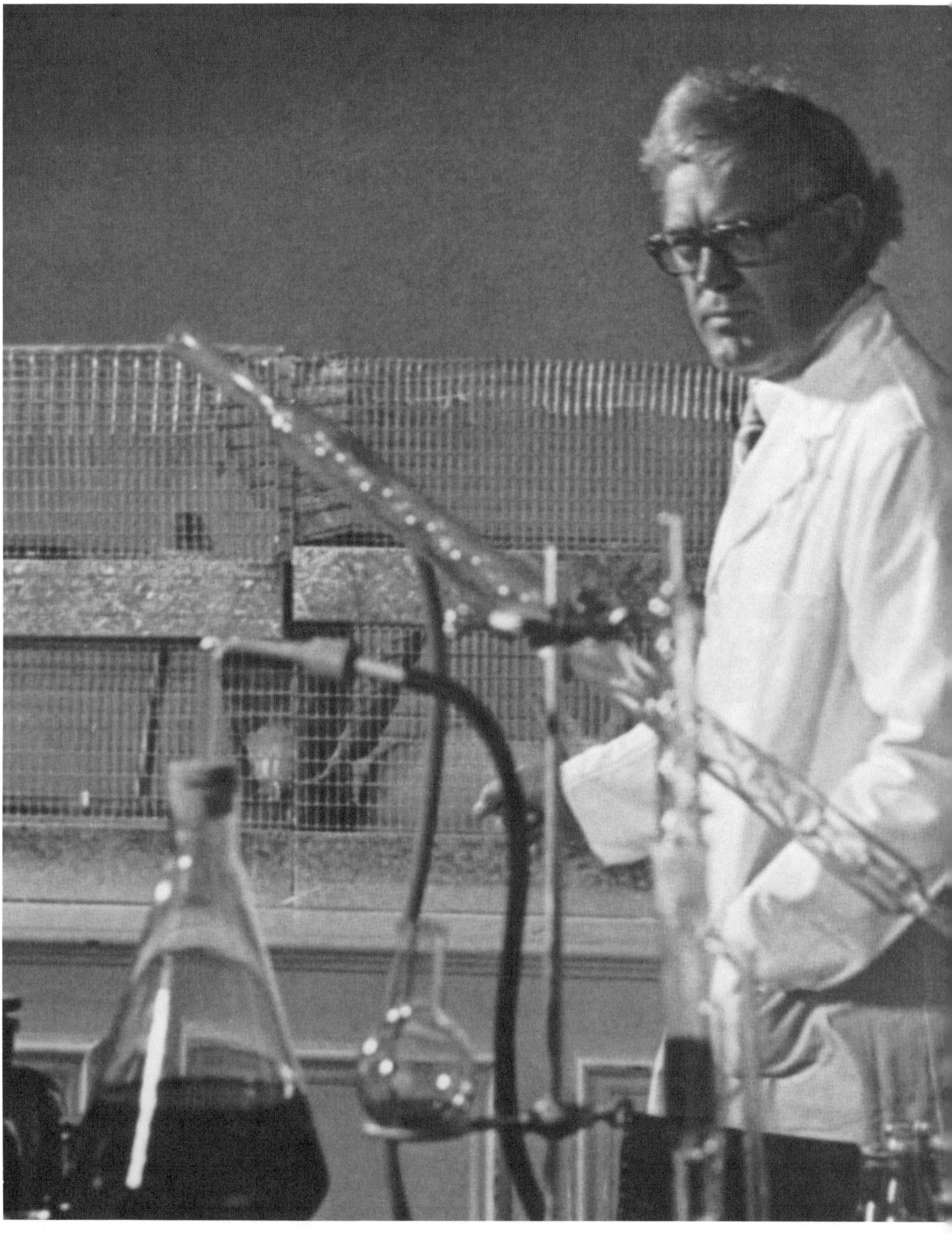

While exploring the facility, Reese finds a lab and a monkey in a cage, its head covered in bandages. He also discovers that the hospital is surrounded by barbed wire and guard dogs—"What is this place, Auschwitz?" Needless to say, he becomes suspicious, particularly when high-ranking military officials and members of the United States Congress come to visit the installation. Something is going on.

He soon finds out what it is. Miles begins coughing up blood, and Frederick offers him relief from his pain. One brain operation later, Miles is bandaged like the monkey and has wires coming out of his skull. He is given a button and told to push it whenever he feels pain, but he quickly becomes addicted to the stimulation, just like the monkeys in the real experiments of the sixties. When Reese tries to free his companion by disconnecting him, Miles goes wild. Frederick's human experiment has failed.

It seems that the good doctor only wants to relieve human suffering, make people happy, and eliminate their pain and hostility. In the case of Miles, however, the experiment went too far. The major (Ralph Meeker) who is really in charge of the hospital and who, like the congressmen, is only interested in the military potential of the experiments, insists that Frederick try again, this time with Reese.

The private is forced to undergo the operation, and when he wakes up, Frederick gives him the button, but Reese refuses to push it. He doesn't want to give up his suffering; he doesn't want to be mindlessly happy. "I don't love pain," he says, "but it defines me. It's part of what I am." Frustrated, the major takes the button and presses it for him.

The final scene is a press conference where the major is introducing the new, happy, docile Reese to the world. He is now the model soldier, willing to follow orders blindly as long as he can press the button that is never out of his hand.

Horror films have always been suspicious of science, and since the Vietnam era, they have been suspicious of the military and government as well. From the mid-1960s until the mid-1970s, every American male of draft age had good reason to fear that the military was "out to get him," and *The Mind Snatchers* taps directly into that fear by suggesting that the army and the government want to turn every man into the perfect soldier, no matter what it takes to bring that about, even if it means robbing every inductee of himself.

In the 1950s, at the beginning of the Cold War, horror films usually said that science could be a good thing if it worked in the service of the military, and that is exactly what happened in countless alien-invasion and giant-insect films of the era. By the late sixties, though, science and the military no longer seemed like such a good team, and that is what *The Mind Snatchers* is all about.

Dr. Frederick (Joss Ackland) is conducting strange experiments on U.S. servicemen in *The Mind Snatchers*.

In this film, the military in the person of the major is downright evil, with no regard for human life. The members of Congress aren't any better. Dr. Frederick, on the other hand, seems like a decent guy who is really sincere about ending human suffering, though he is willing to compromise his principles in order to get the funding he needs. In other words, he is a good man who can be corrupted, and that is one of the most frightening aspects of the film. Reese is corrupted, too, but not by his own choice. The doctor has a choice, but he chooses badly and he knows it.

We can identify with Reese as a victim of the authorities, but we can also identify with Frederick, who is a victim of his own desire and ambition and who, like Reese, has also lost himself. Neither of these possibilities are attractive, of course, but they are real possibilities for all of us, and that fact is what makes *The Mind Snatchers* such a powerful and effective film.

Mother's Day

1980

Director/producer: Charles Kaufman; *Co-producer:* Michael Kravitz; *Screenplay:* Kaufman and Warren D. Leight

CAST:
Nancy Hendrickson, Deborah Luce, Tiana Pierce, Holden McGuire, Billy Rae McQuade, Rose Ross

ORIGINAL RELEASE: United Film Distribution
VIDEO: Media Home Entertainment

This is another one of those "special day" movies (*Halloween, Friday the 13th, My Bloody Valentine, Happy Birthday to Me, April Fool's Day, New Year's Evil,* etc.), though it is a bit more ambitious than most.

Abbey (Nancy Hendrickson), Jackie (Deborah Luce) and Trina (Tiana Pierce) were roommates at Wolfbreath University, and now each year they get together for a little reunion. Things have gone very well for Trina since

Another victim pleads with Mama (Rose Ross) for her life in *Mother's Day*.

graduation; she's a rich, Beverly Hills type, though we never find out exactly what she does there. Jackie and Abbey haven't been so lucky. Jackie lives with and supports a guy who treats her like dirt. Abbey takes care of her sick, nagging mother. Needless to say, Trina's beginning to get tired of these reunions, but Jackie and Abbey have almost nothing else in their lives to look forward to.

This year, they're camping in the New Jersey Pine Barrens where a yokel at the general store plays the banjo just as in *Deliverance,* so we know what to expect. And sure enough, the three friends are kidnapped, tortured, and raped by two brothers, Ike (Holden McGuire) and Addley (Billy Rae McQuade), who operate under the watchful eye of their domineering mother (Rose Ross).

The violence against the women in this film is particularly savage. The brothers toy with Jackie, forcing her to play out scenes from movies with them—in one, she dresses like Shirley Temple—but each scene ends with repeated rapes and beatings, until Jackie is beaten to death. Abbey and Trina escape and vow, "We'll get them."

Addley (Billy Ray McQuade) is just a mama's boy at heart.

Mama (Rose Ross) shows her boys how to do it as she strangles a young woman.

keeps showing. If there are good intentions lurking somewhere in this film, that doesn't change the fact that the movie is cruel, repulsive, and completely lacking in the redeeming social value it pretends to have.

Nightmare in Wax

ALTERNATE TITLES:

Crimes in the Wax Museum,
Monster of the Wax Museum

1969

Director: Bud Townsend; *Producers:* Martin B. Cohen and Herbert Sussan; *Screenplay:* Rex Carlton

CAST:
Cameron Mitchell, Anne Helm, Scott Brady, Berry Kroeger, Victoria Carroll, Phillip Baird, John Cardos

ORIGINAL RELEASE: Crown International Pictures
VIDEO: Interglobal Video Promotions Ltd.

For Mama, every day is Mother's Day.

And they do. Addley gets a TV antenna through the throat, an ax to the groin, and a rag stuffed in his mouth till he suffocates. Ike has Drāno poured into his mouth, a television smashed over his head, and then he gets cut to pieces with an electric kitchen knife. Abbey smothers Mom with an inflatable pillow shaped like an enormous pair of breasts, all the while pretending it's her own mother she's putting to death.

This sounds pretty nasty, and it is, but *Mother's Day* clearly has something to say. Ike and Addley's mom notes, "With TV and all, I keep in touch with everything," and this seems to be true. Her kids are named for Eisenhower and Stevenson, who ran the first televised presidential campaigns in the fifties, and her house is a tribute to TV culture with its Elvis posters, Big Bird alarm clock, and Star Trek and G.I. Joe dolls. The televisions in her home are never turned off and play in the background of every scene. In fact, Ike and Addley claim to have learned everything they know from watching the tube—probably from watching movies like *Mother's Day.*

Obviously, this film is supposed to be a satirical indictment of violence in the media. The problem is that it's also an *example* of violence in the media, and it seems perfectly possible to watch the graphic beatings and rapes presented here and never catch on to the idea that the film is trying to be critical of the very violence it

Not another wax-museum horror flick? Yes, and a particularly silly one at that.

Vince Rinaud (Cameron Mitchell) used to be a makeup man for Paragon Pictures. He used to be engaged to starlet Marie Morgan (Anne Helm). He used to be happy. But that was before studio chief Max Black (Berry Kroeger), Marie's former lover, got jealous and set Vince's face on fire. Now Marie is engaged to movie heartthrob Tony Deane (Phillip Baird), and Vince—just like Vincent Price in *House of Wax*—is a hideously scarred sculptor and owner of a Hollywood wax museum where he roams around dressed in an ominous black cape, plotting revenge and saying things like, "Marie is the kiss of death."

Recently, a number of Paragon stars have disappeared quite mysteriously, and their images have been turning up in Vince's museum. Detective Haskell (Scott Brady) is on the case, but there are no clues. Amazingly, no one seems to suspect Vince—you'd think the cape alone would be enough to give him away. I guess Haskell never saw *House of Wax.*

It seems that Vince is really an accomplished guy. Not only is he a professional makeup man and a skilled wax sculptor, but also he has perfected a serum that can paralyze a human being, putting him in a catatonic state so he resembles a wax dummy. On top of that, the serum also acts as a kind of hypnotic drug, forcing the victim to

Vince Renard (Cameron Mitchell) is the makeup man turned evil wax sculptor turned murderer in *Nightmare in Wax*.

Sergeant Carver (John Cardos, left) and Detective Haskell (Scott Brady) study the "wax" head of actor Tony Dean (Phillip Baird).

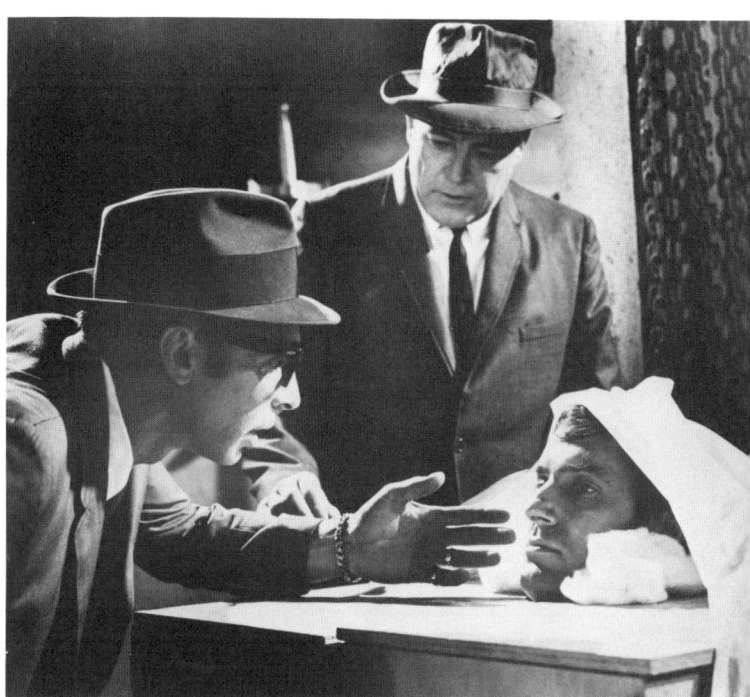

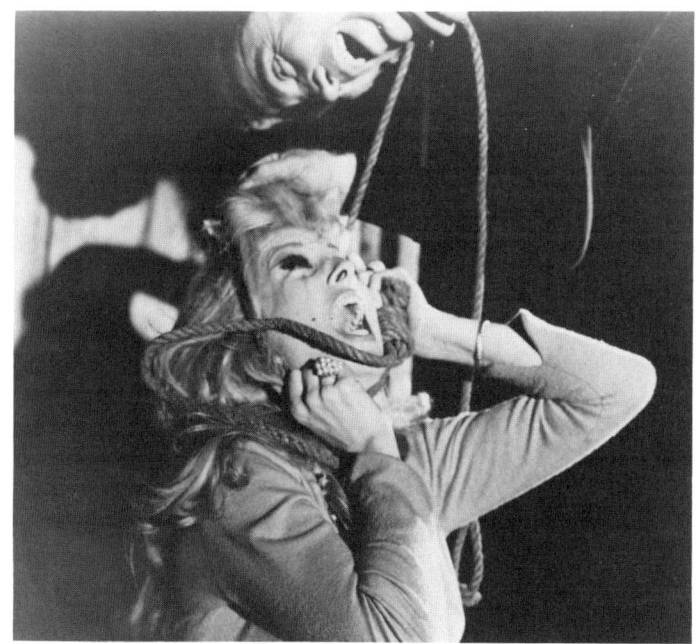

A maniacal Vince Renard (Cameron Mitchell) puts an end to Carissa (Victoria Carroll).

Carissa (Victoria Carroll) knows too much for her own good about Vince's operations.

do whatever he is told to do. And on top of that, Rinaud has developed vitamin injections powerful enough to keep his paralyzed subjects alive indefinitely, even though they can't eat, drink, breathe, or even sweat. It's really amazing, isn't it? Oh, if Vince had only used his genius for good instead of evil.

Well, in case you haven't caught on by now, the images of the Paragon stars in Vince's museum aren't images at all—they *are* the Paragon stars, frozen into zombies by Vince's serum. Marie is next on the list for an injection of zombie juice, but no plan is perfect. Electricity neutralizes the effects of the stuff, and during an electrical storm, Vince's zombies return to normal and foil the plot. Vince ends up falling into his vat of molten wax—just like Vincent Price in *House of Wax*.

Is this a put-on? It's hard to tell. All the actors seem to be playing it straight except for Mitchell, and there's no way to know whether his overacting is on purpose or just his usual style. There are some inside gags here. Paragon Pictures really is one of the companies responsible for *Nightmare in Wax*. In the film, director Alfred Herman (James Forrest) (clearly based on Alfred Hitchcock) plans to make a horror movie in Vince Rinaud's museum, about a madman who hypnotizes his victims, just as real-life director Townsend has used the real-life Movieland Wax Museum in Los Angeles as the setting for his horror movie about a madman who hypnotizes his victims, the very movie we've been watching. And as a nod to *House of Wax* fans, Mitchell's character's name *is* Vincent. So maybe we're supposed to understand that, like so many horror films of the past thirty years, *Nightmare in Wax* is not intended to be taken seriously, that it's just a kind of self-reflexive insider's joke.

But aren't jokes supposed to be funny?

Phantom From Space

1953

Director/producer: W. Lee Wilder; *Screenplay:* Bill Raynor and Myles Wilder

CAST:
Ted Cooper, Rudolph Anders, Harry Landers, James Seay, Noreen Nash, Dick Sands

ORIGINAL RELEASE: United Artists
VIDEO: Goodtimes Home Video

A woman tells Lieutenant Hazen (Ted Cooper) that her husband has just been attacked by a phantom from space. (*Courtesy Hollywood Book and Poster*)

Hazen (Ted Cooper) and his men try to locate the source of radio and TV interference in *Phantom From Space*. (*Courtesy Hollywood Book and Poster*).

Billy Wilder's lesser-known director brother offers another low-budget quickie from outer space that, despite its many shortcomings, turns out to be a rather sensitive, intelligent film.

Phantom From Space is presented in a documentary style with a narrative voice-over and lots of stock footage. A UFO is sighted off the coast of California, and shortly after, Lieutenant Hazen (Ted Cooper) of the Communications Commission is called in to track down some unexplained TV and radio interference. At the same time, Lieutenant Bowers (Harry Landers) is faced with two apparent murders committed by a man witnesses describe as wearing a diving suit and helmet. Hazen and Bowers get together with Major Andrews (James Seay) and Dr. Wyatt (Rudolph Anders), who are investigating the UFO and discover that they are not after a Commie agent but an alien who has crash-landed on Earth.

During a chase scene, the alien abandons his suit and helmet, and his pursuers realize that he is invisible. They also discover that he needs to don his helmet periodically in order to breathe and that the air in his tanks is running out. They take the helmet back to Dr. Wyatt's institute, hoping to trap the alien when he returns for it. The plan fails, and though the spaceman tries to communicate with the earthlings using a tapping code, they never manage to figure out what he wants to say. In the end, the alien suffocates, becomes visible (he is a musclebound actor named Dick Sands dressed in tights), and evaporates before their eyes.

What saves this film is certainly not its ridiculous special effects or its complete lack of characterization but its attitude toward the alien. In the 1950s, during the Red scare, most science fiction and horror films insisted that whoever was not like us was a menace and had to be destroyed. *Phantom From Space,* on the other hand, views the alien sympathetically. He is frightened, lost, and alone on Earth, and though he causes some damage and kills two people, this is done in self-defense, because others have assumed he is dangerous simply because he is different. This film asks the 1950s viewer to put aside his or her paranoia and consider the very real possibility that those who seem to be different are not so very different at all—a remarkably intelligent notion to find in an otherwise pedestrian, low-budget sci-fi/horror film.

The Pit

ALTERNATE TITLE:

Teddy

1981

Director: Lew Lehman; *Producer:* Bennet Fode; *Screenplay:* Ian A. Stuart

CAST:

Sammy Snyder, Jeannie Elias, Laura Press, Laura Hollingsworth, Lillian Graham, Andrea Schwartz, Paul Grisham, Gerrard Jordan, Wendy Schmidt

ORIGINAL RELEASE: Amulet Pictures/New World

VIDEO: Prism Entertainment

This little film was shot in Beaver Dam, Wisconsin, on next to nothing, and it is proof that low-budget movies are not necessarily bad movies. In fact, this one is wonderful—well acted, well paced, funny, creepy. It's got everything going for it.

Everybody in town seems to think twelve-year-old Jamie Benjamin (Sammy Snyder) is weird, a problem child, but he is really just like any other boy his age—he's obsessed with sex and women's bodies, he plays stupid pranks and gets into trouble, his mother mothers him too much, his father ignores him, and he has a crush on his baby-sitter. But the people around him give him a hard

Jamie Benjamin (Sammy Snyder) gives nasty Mrs. Oliphant (Lillian Graham) the ride of her life on her way to *The Pit*.

Jamie tries to save Sandy (Jeannie Elias) from the Trogs, but she ends up as their lunch.

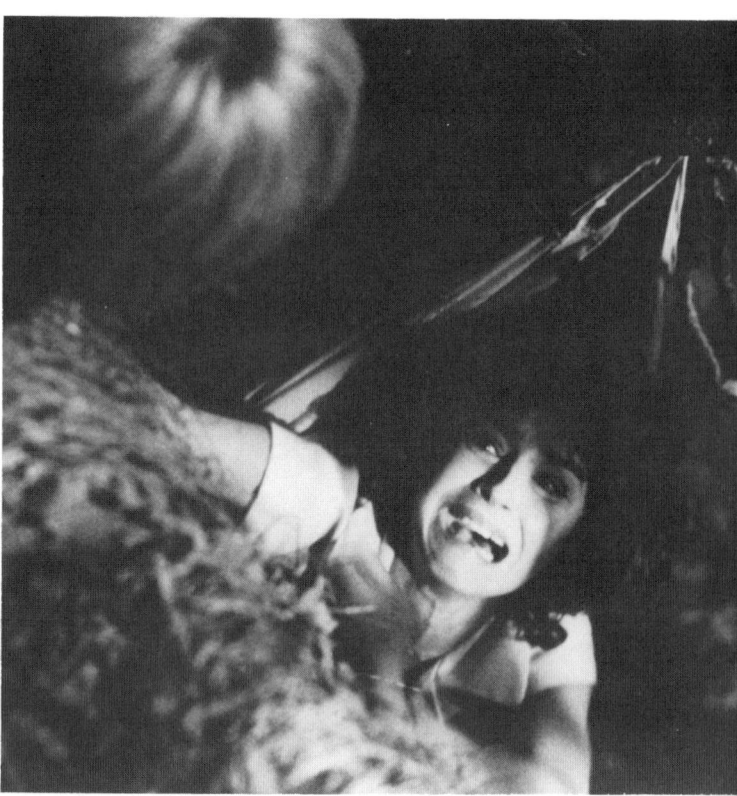

time. Mrs. Oliphant (Lillian Graham), the blind lady in the wheelchair who lives down the street, is always saying, "Just not right, that boy." The bully at school picks on him. Pretty girls laugh at him. Nobody wants to be his friend. So he spends a lot of time by himself, talking to his raggedy old teddy bear, appropriately named Teddy, and it talks back to him. Well, maybe he is a little weird, after all.

The Benjamins are moving to another town, and while Father and Mother are away house-hunting, they hire college student Sandy O'Reilly (Jeannie Elias) to be a live-in caretaker for Jamie. He likes her. As he tells Teddy, "She's not like the others. She's pretty. Really pretty." In fact, Jamie likes Sandy so much that he decides to tell her his secret. "I know where there's a huge hole in the ground. . . . And at the bottom of the hole, down in the dark, there are some things."

Sandy doesn't believe him, of course. Jamie is a very imaginative kid, but in this case he isn't imagining. There is an enormous pit in the woods about a mile from Jamie's house, and living in the pit, trapped there, are four hairy humanoid things. Jamie calls them Trogs. He often goes to the forest, sits on the edge of the pit, and talks to them, though they do nothing more than grunt back.

Jamie's relationship with the Trogs is going well enough, but otherwise his life is a mess. Sandy has a college football-player boyfriend, and Jamie is a bit angry about that. His teacher makes him stay after school when she finds him with a stolen library copy of a book entitled *Creative Nude Photography*. Now the town librarian is mad at him, too. And Freddy, the school bully, gives him a bloody nose for no reason at all.

Meanwhile, Jamie is beginning to worry about the Trogs because they don't seem to be able to get anything to eat down in the pit. He brings various foods from the house, but they don't like anything until he tries raw meat. Jamie spends all the money he can find on cheap stew meat at the local butcher's, and the Trogs gobble it all down. Then he tries to coax some chickens and a cow out into the woods, hoping he can get them into the pit, but that doesn't work. Finally, he discusses his problem

The police find mutilated victims after Jamie helps the Trogs to escape from the pit.

The Trogs—played by Harris Kal, Alison McCuaig, Paul Martin, and Tom Martin.

183

The sheriff's posse finishes off the creatures living in *The Pit*.

with Teddy, who says, "Then there's only one thing left, isn't there?" Jamie knows exactly what Teddy has in mind. He replies, "Yeah, but not nice people."

Fortunately, Jamie knows lots of mean people he can feed to the Trogs. There's Abergail (Andrea Swartz), the librarian's niece, who is always nasty to Jamie and who won't let him ride her bike; he tricks her into following him into the woods and pushes her into the pit. There's Freddy (Paul Grisham), the bully, and his girlfriend, Christina (Wendy Schmidt). There's Sandy's boyfriend, Allan (Gerrard Jordan). And there's blind Mrs. Oliphant—the funniest scene in the film is the one in which Jamie pushes the screaming old lady's wheelchair over bumpy dirt paths and through the woods to the edge of the hole where he dumps her in.

At last, he manages to get Sandy to come to the woods with him. He has no intention of pushing her in, of course—he only wants her to share his secret. She is amazed when she looks into the pit and realizes that what Jamie has been telling her is true. She wants to inform the authorities, but Jamie thinks that wouldn't be right: "They'd put 'em in a zoo or lock 'em in a cage for sure."

Unfortunately, when Sandy leans over the edge to get a better look at the creatures, she slips. Jamie tries to hold on to her, but he can't, and the Trogs get her. This is the only scene of graphic gore in the movie, and it is really effective.

Jamie cries to Teddy and blames himself for what happened to his beloved Sandy. But that isn't his only problem. He can't think of anyone else mean enough to feed to the Trogs, so he lowers a rope into the pit and lets them escape to find their own food. The police begin discovering the partially devoured remains of the monsters' victims, and a posse tracks the Trogs back to their hole and guns them down.

The Benjamins return home, and Jamie goes to visit Grandma and Grandpa in the country. There he meets a pretty girl his own age named Alicia, and she really seems to like him. She takes him into the woods and shows him a pit, and when he looks over the edge, he sees Trogs living there, too. "They eat people," he tells her. "I know," she says, and she casually pushes him in.

This movie works beautifully because, as kids, we all knew somebody like Jamie. In fact, as kids, male or female, we all thought we *were* someone like Jamie. We were afraid that nobody liked us, that nobody understood us, that everybody wanted to pick on us. Just imagine how great it would have been to get revenge on all the bullies and the grown-ups who ever treated us badly. The truth is that, while we watch *The Pit*, we're cheering for Jamie every step of the way. Sure, he gets it in the end—the rules of the horror film say that you have to pay for your crimes—but he is still the hero of the movie because he does what heroes do, namely what we would like to do ourselves, if only we had the chance.

Plan 9 From Outer Space

ALTERNATE TITLE:

Grave Robbers From Outer Space

1959

Director/producer/screenplay: Edward D. Wood Jr.

CAST:
Bela Lugosi, Tor Johnson, Lyle Talbot, Criswell, Vampira, Duke Moore, Gregory Walcott, Paul Marco

ORIGINAL RELEASE: DCA
VIDEO: Sinister Cinema

Many critics claim that this is the worst movie ever made, but that judgment seems to slight Wood's other efforts. Indeed, *Plan 9* is the perfect example of what Woodian cinema is all about.

As with most of Wood's films, you get the sense, watching *Plan 9*, that you've walked in late and missed something very important, something you never figure out. This much seems certain, however. Aliens are here on Earth, seemingly trying to conquer us by implementing Plan 9, which involves raising the dead to kill the living. Airline pilot Jeff Trent (Gregory Walcott) stumbles upon the plot and breaks it up with help from the military and the local police.

But maybe the aliens aren't trying to take over Earth after all. As their representative Eros (?!) (Dudley Manlove) says, "We do not want to conquer your planet, only save it." What they want to save us from is the Solarmonite bomb, which explodes sunlight and, if detonated, would destroy the universe. Of course, we don't have the Solarmonite bomb yet, but we will, and when we do, we'll use it because, as Eros also points out, "All you of Earth are idiots." So, before we invent the sunlight bomb, Eros and his minions are going to save Earth by destroying it.

The plot might be a bit confused, but the film still has

The old man's wife (Vampira), Lt. Dan Clay (Tor Johnson), the old man (director Ed Wood's chiropractor serving as the late Bela Lugosi's stand-in), and Criswell (as himself)—only a few of the many stars in *Plan 9 From Outer Space*. (*Courtesy Hollywood Book and Poster*).

TV *Creature Feature* hostess Vampira comes back from the dead—she was buried in that dress?—in *Plan 9 From Outer Space*. (*Courtesy Hollywood Book and Poster*)

a lot going for it. For one thing, it features Tor Johnson (once a professional wrestler named the Swedish Angel) in one of his few speaking roles, though his Swedish accent is so heavy, you can't understand anything he says. Paul Marco is, once again, Kelton the dumb cop. Vampira, a fifties TV horror hostess, is one of the walking dead, as is Bela Lugosi, who appears here in his last film. In fact, *Plan 9* was made after he died, using old footage repeated again and again and a stand-in who, even with his cape drawn across his face, looks nothing like Lugosi. And there's B-movie fixture Lyle Talbot as Roberts, a Pentagon general, and TV psychic Criswell doing the narration. What more could you want?

As usual, Wood has a point to make in this film, and it seems to be that UFOs are real, that aliens have already contacted our governmental and military leaders, but that those in power refuse to acknowledge the extraterrestrials in our midst. As Jeff Trent says of the flying saucers, "These things have been seen for years. They're here, it's a fact, and the public ought to know about it." According to Wood, the government should end its conspiracy of silence and admit to the existence of the aliens, who, after all, are only here to save us. Or destroy us. Or something.

And what are the eight other plans?

Queen of Blood

ALTERNATE TITLE:

Planet of Blood

1966

Director/screenplay: Curtis Harrington; *Producer:* George Edwards

CAST:
Basil Rathbone, John Saxon, Dennis Hopper, Judi Meredith, Florence Marly, Forrest J. Ackerman

ORIGINAL RELEASE: American International Pictures
VIDEO: Star Classics

In the 1960s, Roger Corman acquired some impressive Soviet sci-fi footage, and Harrington shot this film in order to make use of some of it. More Soviet stuff appears in American International's *Voyage to the Prehistoric Planet* and *Voyage to the Planet of Prehistoric Women*.

As Dr. Farraday, Basil Rathbone (in one his last roles) heads an international space agency that receives a

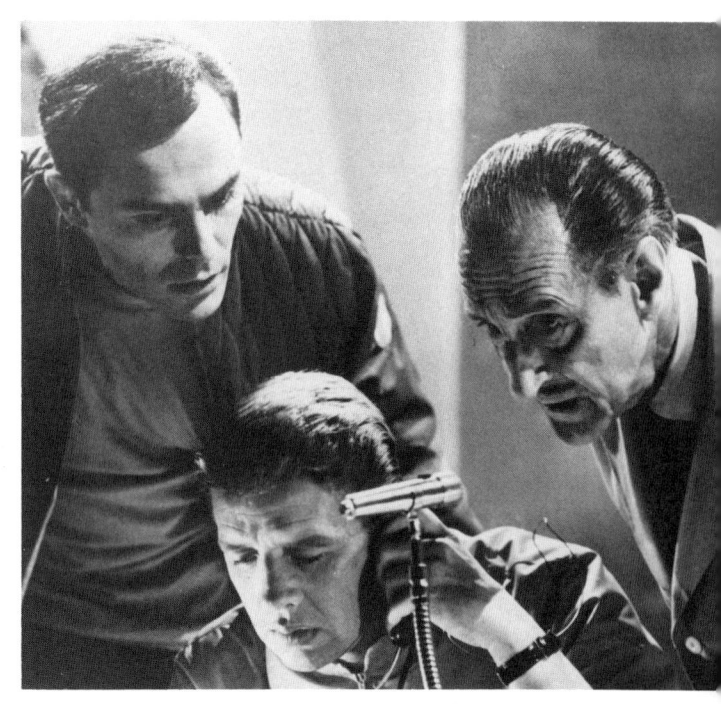

Allan Brenner (John Saxon, left) and Dr. Farraday (Basil Rathbone) listen to distress signals coming from Mars.

distress message from Mars. Alien ambassadors on a peace mission to Earth have crashed there, and Rathbone launches an effort to rescue them. The rescuers include John Saxon, a real veteran of the horror genre, as Allan Brenner; his girlfriend Judi Meredith, as Laura James; and a young Dennis Hopper, who shows all the promise that he would realize later in films from *Easy Rider* to *Blue Velvet*, as Paul Grant.

They find only one survivor, a greenish humanoid female, Velena (Florence Marly), and take her on board for the return trip to Earth where Farraday and his assistant, played by the legendary horror expert Forrest J. Ackerman, eagerly await the arrival of this specimen from outer space. Velena turns out to be a kind of bloodsucking insect, and she begins to kill off the crew one by one, beginning with Paul. Allan realizes the danger immediately: "She's a monster . . . . We ought to destroy her right now." But the scientists insist that she be kept alive and healthy, despite the danger.

Finally, when Velena tries to feed on Allan, Laura fights for her man, scratching the alien with her fingernails and causing her to bleed to death—it turns out that she has a case of alien hemophilia. Back on Earth, Allan and Laura discover that their guest has hidden hundreds of her eggs on board the ship, and though Allan repeats his warning ("We have to destroy them"), Rathbone is thrilled to have these little aliens-to-be for scientific study. The film ends ominously, with Ackerman smiling over a tray of disgusting, pulsating red eggs.

The movie really is pretty effective, and Marly is truly

Paul (Dennis Hopper) offers the alien (Florence Marly) a drink—but she isn't particularly fond of water.

After wiping out most of the crew, the alien (Florence Marly) goes after Allan (John Saxon).

Legendar horror-film expert Forrest J. Ackerman gloats over the alien eggs in *Queen of Blood*.

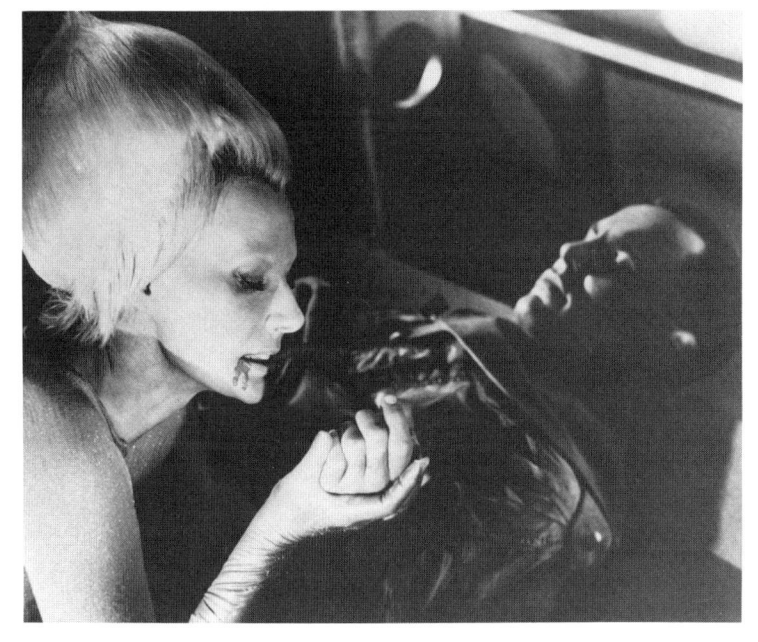

chilling and weird as the alien insect lady. *Queen of Blood* looks both forward and back. It is certainly a forerunner of Ridley Scott's *Alien* of 1979, but it is also a throwback to the fifties alien paranoia. Like so many films from that era, it is an essay in isolationism, saying, don't trust foreigners, even when they make overtures of peace, because they're really only out for the blood—not a particularly healthy message, then or now.

The Satanic Rites of Dracula

ALTERNATE TITLES:

Dracula Is Alive and Well and Living in London, Count Dracula and His Vampire Bride

1973

Director: Alan Gibson; *Producer:* Roy Skeggs; *Screenplay:* Don Houghton

CAST:
Christopher Lee, Peter Cushing, Michael Coles, Freddie Jones, Barbara Yu Ling

ORIGINAL RELEASE: Hammer Films/Dynamic Entertainment
VIDEO: Liberty Entertainment

With this film, Lee plays Dracula for the last time in the Hammer series that includes *Horror of Dracula, Dracula Has Risen From the Grave,* and other titles. Though he receives top billing here, he appears only briefly and speaks only a few lines, and so the interplay between Lee and Cushing that usually makes their coappearances so striking is missing in this later film.

The setting is 1970s London, and Dracula—resurrected once again—has put together a satanic cult of high-powered business executives, military and government leaders, and scientists who are planning to take over the world. The prince of darkness has other plans, however. He forces scientist Julian Keeley (Freddie Jones) to develop a superstrain of plague bacteria, which he plans to use to wipe out human life on Earth. Of course, as a vampire who needs human blood to survive, this would mean the end of Dracula as well. So why is he doing it? Lorimar Van Helsing (Cushing), descendant of the original Professor Van Helsing, explains, "Perhaps in the depths of his subconscious, that is what he really wants—an end to it all." It seems that even Dracula cannot avoid Dr. Freud.

The cult has its headquarters in a mansion outside of London where high-tech security, armed guards, and a vampire priestess named Chin Yang (Barbara Yu Ling) keep everything going. There is also a collection of vampire women kept chained to the walls in the basement for no particular reason.

Dracula has assumed the guise of D. D. Denham, reclusive Howard Hughes–like business tycoon whose holdings in oil and banking make him one of the most

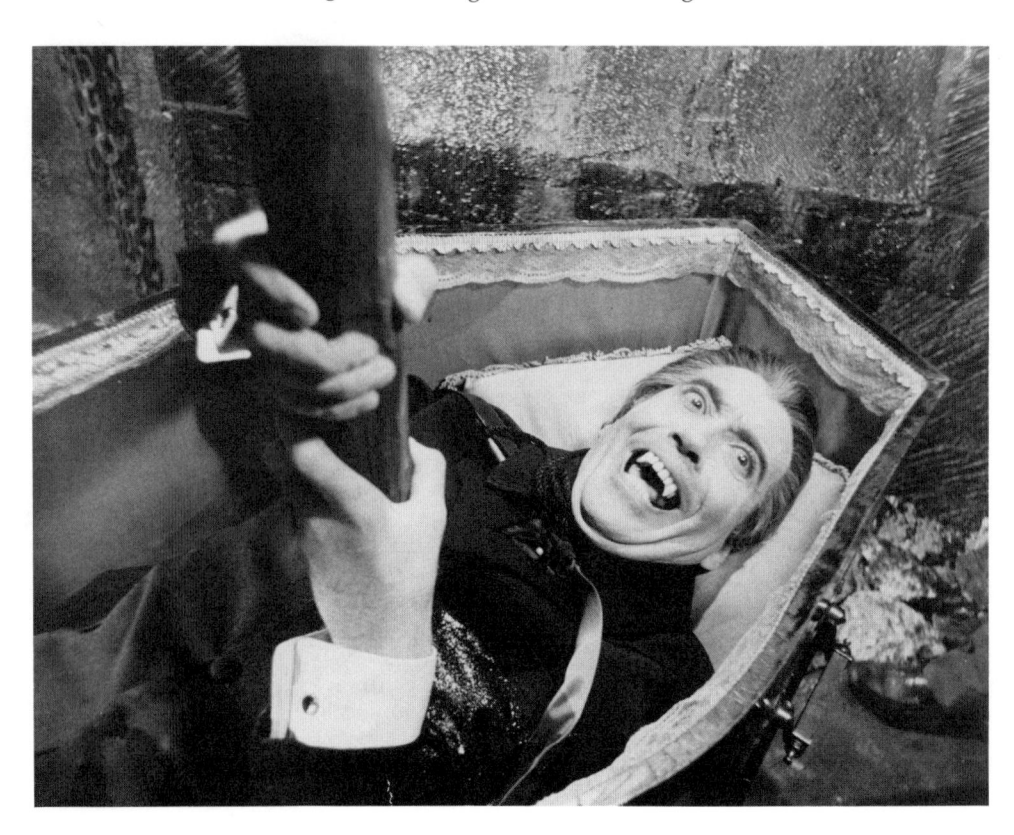

Christopher Lee—quite possibly the greatest Dracula ever.

Jessica Van Helsing (Joanna Lumley) is threatened by one of Count Dracula's vampire brides (Pauline Peart) in *The Satanic Rites of Dracula*. (Courtesy Hollywood Book and Poster)

powerful men in the world. Denham is a mystery—he never grants interviews, never appears in public, and never permits his picture to be taken (vampires cast no reflection in mirrors and leave no image in a photograph). With the help of Inspector Murray of Scotland Yard (Michael Coles), Van Helsing discovers Denham's true identity and once again puts an end to Dracula's plans by driving a stake through his heart.

Made at a time when we as a culture were beginning to mistrust big business and our military and political leaders (the military-industrial complex, as it was called during the Vietnam era), *The Satanic Rites of Dracula* provides the easy answers to the questions: Who are these powerful and wealthy people who run the government and the big corporations and who seem to rule the world? How did they get that way? What have they got that the rest of us don't? They are devil worshipers and vampires, of course, and they got their power and wealth through a kind of satanic networking. Talk about corruption in politics and business!

So if your boss seems hard to get along with, try shoving a cross under his nose. If he flinches, drive a stake through his heart, and that should solve the problem.

Satan's Cheerleaders

1977

Director: Greydon Clark; *Producer:* Alvin L. Fast; *Screenplay:* Greydon Clark and Alvin L. Fast

CAST:

John Ireland, Yvonne DeCarlo, Jack Kruschen, John Carradine, Jacquelin Cole, Kerry Sherman, Hillary Horan, Alisa Powell, Sherry Marks

ORIGINAL RELEASE: World Amusements
VIDEO: United Home Video

It takes a lot of nerve to give a film a title like *Satan's Cheerleaders*, but it takes even more nerve to make a movie like this one. The cast sounds impressive—Ireland, DeCarlo, Carradine—but in fact these Hollywood veterans are obviously trying to get it over with as quickly as possible.

Four high school cheerleaders—Patti (Kerry Sherman), Debbie (Alisa Powell), Sharon (Sherry Marks), Chris (Hillary Horan)—and their coach Ms. Johnson (Jacquelin Cole) are driving to the first big game of the season when their car breaks down in the sticks. They are taken in by Sheriff Bub (John Ireland) and his wife, Emmy (Yvonne DeCarlo, formerly Lily of *The Munsters*), who run a rural satanic cult. Sheriff Bub receives a command from Satan, calling for a human sacrifice of the one virgin among the group, so the cult members lock up the girls and their teacher. The five victims escape a couple of times and are recaptured a couple of times, but when midnight rolls around, all are present and accounted for, and the sacrifice is ready to begin.

The sheriff tries to figure out which of the girls is the virgin Satan wants as his sacrifice, but it isn't easy. As Debbie says: "An unsoiled maiden? You gotta be kidding, man. This isn't the Middle Ages."

And now for the big surprise. It seems that, while the sheriff and his cult are mere dabblers in the demonic arts, Patti is one of the chosen people of Satan, the reincarnation of an ancient and powerful witch, though she has never known about her special gifts until now. Emmy has suspected this all along, but when she tries to kill Patti with an incantation, the cheerleader turns the deadly spell back on her.

Patti informs the gathering that the only virgin in the group was Ms. Johnson, whom the sheriff raped earlier that day, thus despoiling Satan's prize. The devil de-

Emmy (Yvonne De Carlo), the sheriff (John Ireland), and Billy (Jack Kruschen) conduct a Black Mass in *Satan's Cheerleaders*.

stroys the sheriff, Patti takes over the coven, and in the end, the cheerleaders use their satanic powers to help their boyfriends win football games.

This is a very irritating movie. The cheerleaders are giggling teens who talk in dirty double entendres all the time, and it's really impossible to care whether they get sacrificed or not. They are stereotypes you've seen before—Patti is the smart one, Chris is outspoken, Debbie is slutty but nice, Sharon is busty and stupid, but not as stupid as Ms. Johnson, the coach. The acting is awful, and the disco theme "One for All and All for One" is guaranteed to get on your nerves.

Even so, there is something going on here. In the sixties and seventies, people talked a lot about the "generation gap," and that is precisely what this movie is about. Of course, horror films in the fifties knew all about the generation gap, too. In movies like *The Blob* and *The Giant Gila Monster*, it's the teens who know what's happening, though the adults don't believe them.

The local wino (John Carradine) does little to help the terrified Debbie (Alisa Powell).

Billy (Jack Kruschen) wants the virgin for himself, but the sheriff (John Ireland) wants to save her for the Master.

The sheriff (John Ireland) puts an end to dissension in the ranks by killing Billy (Jack Kruschen) in *Satan's Cheerleaders*.

190

But in the fifties teen movies, at least the kids and the grown-ups are on the same side.

That isn't the case in *Satan's Cheerleaders* where the adults don't simply ignore the problem—they *are* the problem. The authority figures here want to kill the kids, and the kids are smart enough to know it and to do something about it. The film says that, even when it comes to satanic rituals, teens do it better than the older generation.

The gap between the generations in this movie is fundamentally sexual. The cheerleaders are products of the sexual revolution, unlike Ms. Johnson, who is still a virgin at age twenty-six. The sheriff's big mistake is that, because he is of the old school of thought, he assumes that the girls are virgins because they're young. But as Debbie explains, "I'm no maiden. I've been a cheerleader for three years."

While most horror movies punish sexually active young women, in this film the fact that the girls are sexually active is what saves them—they can't be sacrificed to Satan because they are "soiled." It seems then that *Satan's Cheerleaders* is probably a lot more original than anyone involved with the film ever intended.

But while the movie seems to be in favor of the new generation's values, it also suggests that young people have a special connection to evil, to the demonic—something that is also suggested in *The Exorcist*, which was released in 1973 and which gave rise to hundreds of satanism movies like this one. *Satan's Cheerleaders* has something for everyone. To teens in the audience, it says, along with Ms. Johnson, "They're good kids." To any adults who would actually watch a film with a title like this, it says, the kids are possessed by Satan, which explains why they are the way they are and why you don't understand them.

Note: The script supervisor for this film was Debra Hill, who went on to coproduce and cowrite *Halloween*, *The Fog*, and other important John Carpenter films, so it seems the experience of making *Satan's Cheerleaders* wasn't wasted on everyone.

Scream and Scream Again

1970

Director: Gordon Hessler; *Producers:* Max J. Rosenberg and Milton Subotsky; *Screenplay:* Christopher Wicking

CAST:
Vincent Price, Christopher Lee, Peter Cushing, Alfred Marks, Christopher Matthews, Michael Gothard

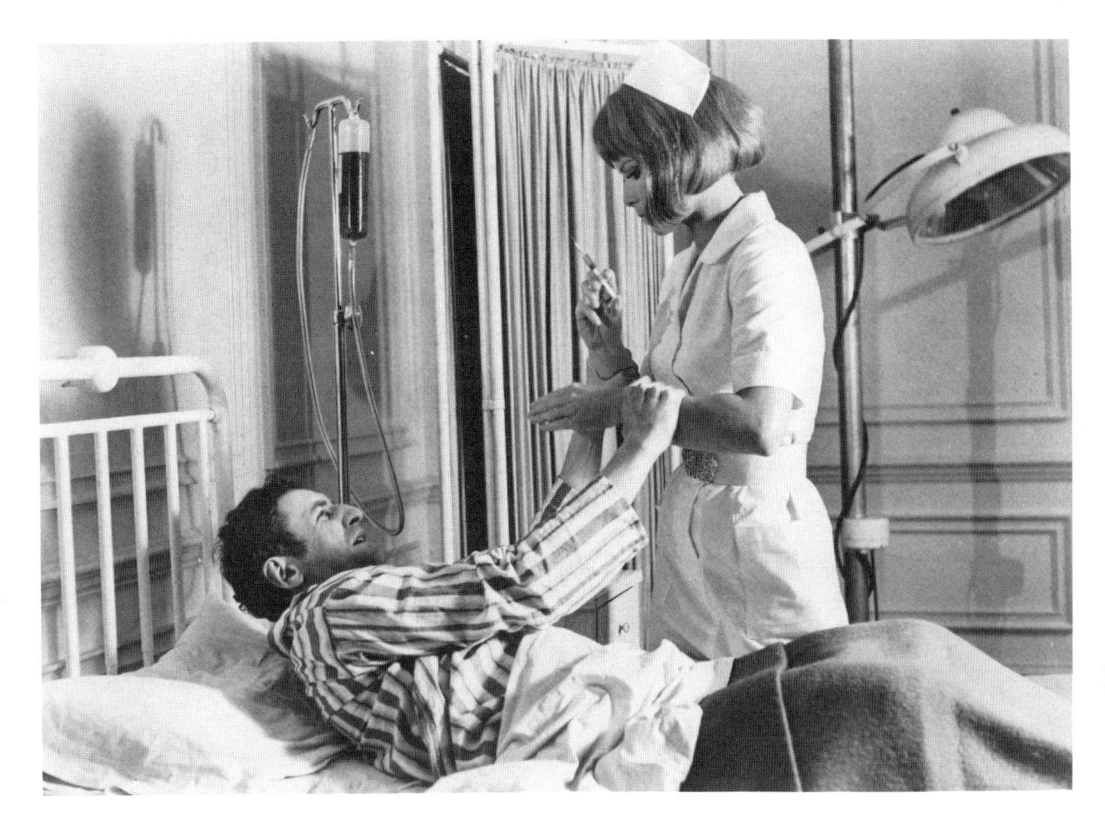

The jogger who keeps losing one limb after another throughout *Scream and Scream Again* tries to resist the nurse with the hypo.

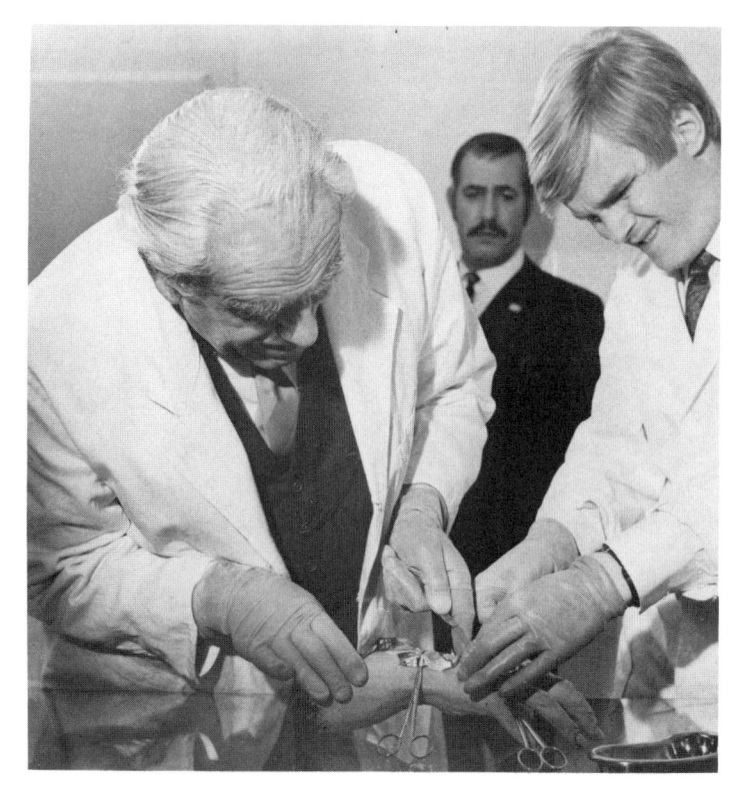

ORIGINAL RELEASE: Amicus Productions/American International
VIDEO: Vestron Home Video

This charmingly grotesque (or grotesquely charming) little British film brings together Price, Lee, and Cushing, all on the same bill—what a bonanza for horror fans. Of course, all three appear only briefly—Cushing for only a minute or two—but it's still worthwhile.

A rapist/serial killer named Keith (Michael Gothard) has been terrorizing London, and police superintendent Bellaver (Alfred Marks) and young Dr. Sorel (Christopher Matthews) are investigating. Meanwhile, in a military state behind the Iron Curtain, a chief inquisitor and secret agent is secretly killing off his superiors. The connection between these two events makes up the plot of the film.

Price is Dr. Browning, a scientist who is developing a superrace ("but not an evil superrace") by doing transplants and grafting synthetic muscles and tendons onto normal flesh and bone. All of his "composites" have superhuman strength, and, it appears, scientists and government officials all over the world are involved in this project. Keith, the serial killer, is one of Price's creations run amok, as is the foreign agent. In fact, Price

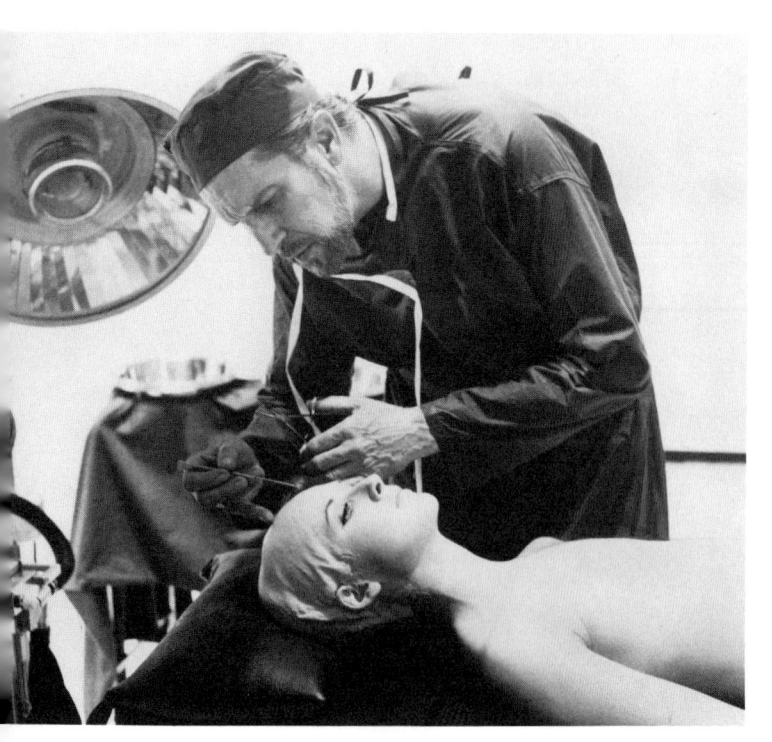

Under the watchful eye of Superintendent Bellaver (Alfred Marks), the chief pathologist, and his assistant David Sorel (Christopher Matthews) study the hand that the humanoid Keith has left behind.

Dr. Browning (Vincent Price) works on his most recent humanoid creation.

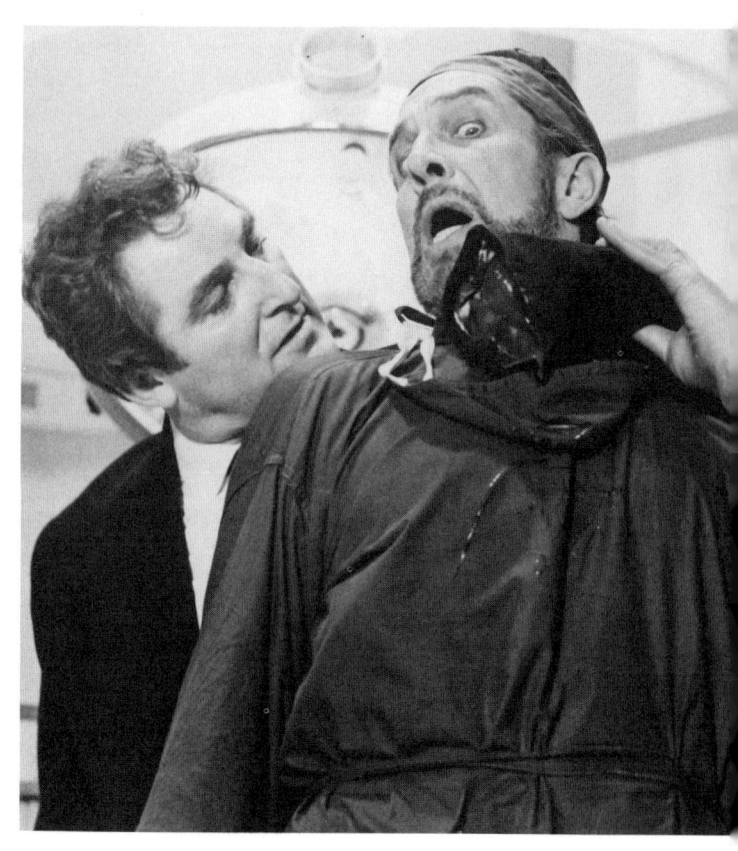

Konratz (Marshall Jones) threatens Dr. Browning (Vincent Price) in *Scream and Scream Again*.

himself is a superhuman, though he seems like a pretty good guy, if somewhat misguided.

Sorel figures the whole thing out and survives, though most of the cast members, including Price himself, end up in a vat of acid the doctor keeps handy for disposing of unnecessary materials. The end of the film is not comforting, however, for we learn that Mr. Fremont (Lee), a high-ranking intelligence officer with the British government, is also one of the superhumans and is part of a conspiracy to take over the world.

This is a zany film with a good if bizarre sense of humor. In one running gag, a young man who has seemingly had a heart attack keeps waking up periodically throughout the movie to find that another of his limbs has been amputated by Dr. Browning and his people. Eventually, Sorel discovers only the man's head in a refrigerator. Keith, the mad killer, is captured by the police and cuffed to a car, but a moment later he escapes after tearing off his own hand. This is very funny stuff—if you think this kind of stuff is funny.

Traditionally, horror films have been hard on the medical profession, and that makes sense because, the truth is, we don't like doctors. They stick us with needles, poke at our bodies, and sometimes cut us open. They make a lot more money than we do, use words we don't understand, and though we have to trust them with our lives, who knows what they're really up to? There are good doctors, of course, like young Sorel in *Scream and Scream Again,* but when Browning says to him, "As a doctor, I think you're going to be fascinated with what I'm trying to do," we know that Sorel is still one of the club, a club we don't belong to, and that means you can only trust even a good doctor so far.

Shock Waves

ALTERNATE TITLES:

*Death Corps,
Almost Human*

1977

Director: Ken Wiederhorn; *Producer:* Reuben Trane; *Screenplay:* John Harrison and Ken Wiederhorn

CAST:
Peter Cushing, John Carradine, Brooke Adams, Luke Halpin, Don Stout

ORIGINAL RELEASE: Cinema Shares
VIDEO: Prism

The SS commander (Peter Cushing) makes his way through the jungle, knowing that something is loose on the island in *Shock Waves.*

There are thousands of tiny islands scattered through the world's great oceans, and on every one of them, there is a crazed Nazi scientist still working on the evil experiments he just couldn't give up at the end of World War II. Well, that's the picture you might have of the world if you watch too many horror films like this one.

In fact, what sets *Shock Waves* apart from many similar films is that there is no crazed Nazi scientist living alone on a deserted island. Peter Cushing plays a crazed Nazi *SS officer* living alone on a deserted island. And he isn't conducting evil experiments—he's just sort of hanging out, waiting for something to happen. And as luck would have it, something does.

Shock Waves really is a pretty good movie. Certainly, it is the best of the Nazi zombie flicks (for further reference, see *Night of the Wehrmacht Zombies, Zombie Lake, Oasis of the Living Dead,* etc.). *Shock Waves* has a strong cast, a good script, and despite the fact that hardly a drop of blood is spilled, it is effectively scary.

A group of tourists are on a dive boat operated by a

193

crusty old captain (John Carradine), his first mate, Keith (Luke Halpin), and Dobbs the cook (Don Stout), and things aren't going well. The engine keeps breaking down, the weather isn't good, and suddenly an old wreck rises from the bottom of the ocean and slams into the boat, almost sending her to the bottom.

The captain dives to inspect the damage and dies mysteriously, but the others make it to the shore of an uncharted desert isle—this is beginning to sound like an episode of *Gilligan's Island*—where they find an abandoned hotel occupied only by a man named Scar (Cushing) who warns them away. "There is danger here—danger in the water." But of course they have nowhere to go, so they bed down for the night.

Meanwhile, from the recently risen wreck come a group of decayed, very blond guys in sunglasses and Nazi uniforms, and they start to kill off the tourists, beginning with poor Dobbs. Scar explains that "we Germans developed the perfect weapon" during the war, the perfect soldier, "not dead, not alive, but somewhere in between." The members of the so-called Death Corps were so homicidal, in fact, that they killed their own men and had to be "withdrawn for further study." About a dozen of them were on board a ship under Cushing's command, and at the end of the war, he sent them to the bottom, then went into exile on the island. Now they have returned.

The Nazi zombies kill their old commanding officer, then the used-car salesman and his wife, then the first mate, until only Rose (Brooke Adams) is left in a dinghy, floating away from the island where, it would seem, the

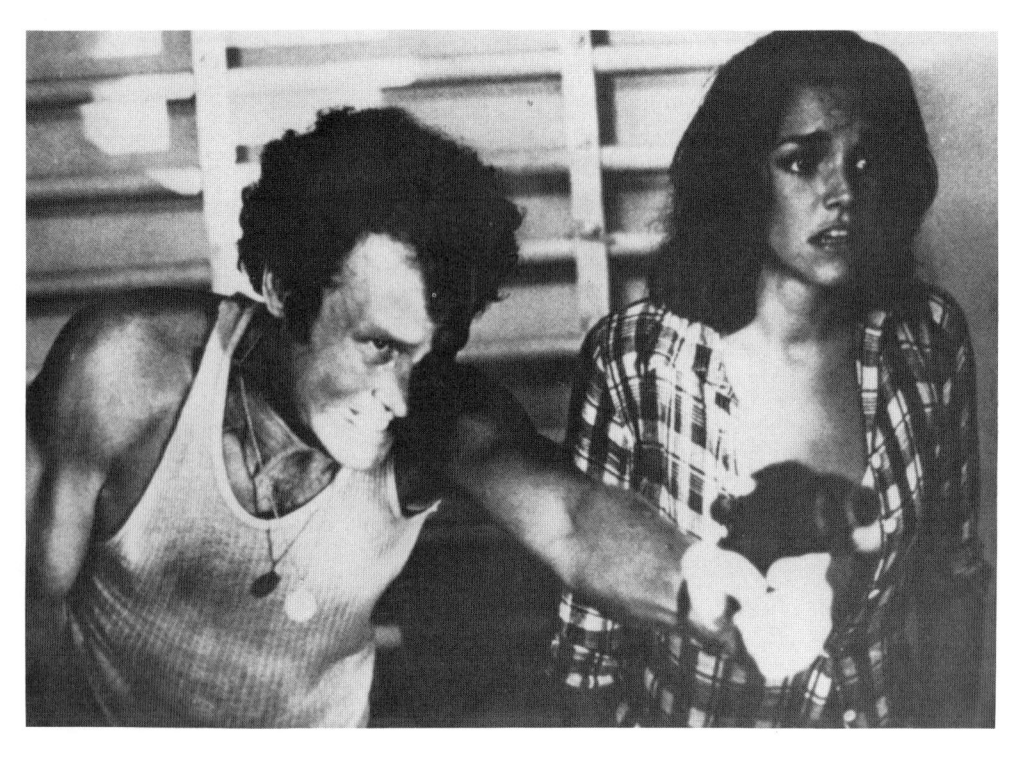

The commander (Peter Cushing) is killed by one of his own Nazi zombies.

A claustrophobic Chuck (Fred Buch) loses control in the meat locker where Rose (Brooke Adams) and the others hope to hide from the living dead.

Rose (Brooke Adams) and Keith (Luke Halpin) try to escape, but their plans are about to be foiled by a dead Nazi in sunglasses in *Shock Waves*.

zombies are still thriving. She is picked up by a fishing boat, and though she has been saved, it is clear that she has lost her mind as a result of her experiences with the Nazi undead.

This is a very engaging film, though it does have its problems. At one point early on, Rose is attacked by a zombie, and when she manages to pull its sunglasses off, it drops over dead. Now it seems that this "perfect weapon," which apparently took years for all those evil Nazi scientists to develop, shouldn't be so easy to kill, but there you have it. It doesn't matter anyway, because the tourists don't pay much attention to Rose's discovery, and they spend the rest of the film simply screaming and being choked to death when they ought to be ripping off sunglasses.

There is a clear connection between Nazis and horror films, from such low-budget quickies as *She Demons*, *The Frozen Dead*, and *They Saved Hitler's Brain* to such high-class movies as *The Boys From Brazil*. Hitler and his regime openly displayed the possibilities of real horror, a systematic evil that horror movies could never hope to match and would not want to, though, for better or worse, any numer of films have tried to come to terms with the unspeakable horror of Nazism, which, for a time, became reality.

Nazi zombie films such as *Shock Waves* are important because they remind us of what we must never forget: that although racism, genocide, and calculated cruelty should have died out long ago, they are still with us, and they can rise again at any moment like the Death Corps from the sunken wreck.

Slithis

ALTERNATE TITLE:

Spawn of the Slithis

1978

Director/screenplay: Stephen Traxler; *Producers:* Stephen Traxler and Paul Fabian

CAST:
Alan Blanchard, J. C. Claire, Dennis Lee Falt, Mello Alexandria

ORIGINAL RELEASE: Fabtrax
VIDEO: Media Home Entertainment

Strange things are going on in Venice, California—so what else is new? Someone or something is killing, multilating, and eating household pets. No one pays any attention until the same someone or something kills and partially devours an elderly couple in their home; then the police finally start to investigate.

Enter Wayne Connors (Alan Blanchard), high school journalism teacher who hates his job and his students and who really wants to be a high-powered investigative reporter. He decides to look into the murders on his own, and at the scene of the crime, he discovers a funny-looking patch of mud. His scientist friend John tells him that the substance is "slithis." It seems that,

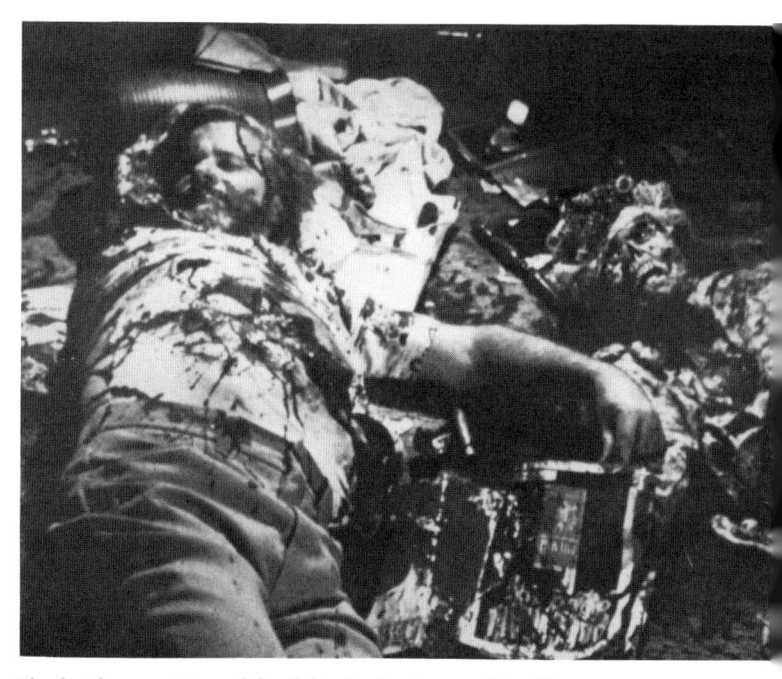

The first human victims of the slithis that has been stalking Venice, California.

about twenty years ago, in an early prototype of a modern nuclear power plant, some radioactive water leaked into a nearby lagoon, creating an organic mud that could take on the characteristics of whatever it ingested. Scientists working on the project called it slithis, for lack of a better term. Of course the power company and the government covered the whole thing up.

Wayne thinks he might be on to something big, a story important enough to gain him a new career. His wife tells him to forget it—"You have a good job at the high school." Naturally, he ignores her.

The killings of people continue, and the police are blaming the crimes on one of the many local cults. Then Wayne finds a wino named Bunky who has actually seen the thing: "It looked like somethin' that crawled out of the sewer."

The police don't believe Wayne's story, so he hires a boat and a local diver, Chris Alexander, to get samples of mud and water at the nearby nuclear power plant to see if there has been a leak. Scientist John finds traces of slithis, but of course the power company denies that there has been any problem at the plant.

There are even more killings, so Wayne and Chris get two other guys to help them, and they go out in the boat, using sonar to track down the monster, which looks like

Dr. Berg, one of the original discoverers of *Slithis,* knows a thing or two about the dangers of overexposure to radioactivity.

The *Creation* heads out to sea to track down the slithis monster.

The spawn of the slithis claims another victim.

a very unattractive Creature from the Black Lagoon. By this time, the thing is a humanoid—remember, it takes on the characteristics of whatever it eats. It is smart enough to know what is going on, so it hops onto Chris's boat and knocks off the two extras.

After a long and savage battle Chris and Wayne kill the beastie—or so it seems. But then, for no particular reason, the monster comes back to life and gets everybody. So it looks as if Wayne's wife was right; he should have stayed with his job at the high school.

Slithis is slow going at times, but it is still a lot of fun, mostly because it is so obviously a fifties film trying to find a place in the late seventies. Horror fans have long had a deep affection for "monster from the surf" flicks, which got started because somebody decided to combine the monster movies of the fifties with the *Beach Blanket Bingo* and *Gidget* films that were big hits at the drive-ins. This hybrid subgenre has given birth to movies like *Monster From the Ocean Floor* (Roger Corman's first production), *Horror of Party Beach,* and *Beach Girls and the Monster* in the fifties and sixties, and of course the ultimate ocean-monster/beach-party movie, *Jaws* of 1975, which gave us a whole new generation of films like *Humanoids from the Deep, Piranha, Blood Beach, Tentacles,* and *Slithis.*

Like so many seventies horror films, *Slithis* has an ecological message. While movies in the fifties were worried about atomic bomb testing, *Slithis* and its contemporaries were more concerned with nuclear power plants and the possibility for accidents—a possibility that, since the incident at Three Mile Island in 1979, is now all too real.

Otherwise, though, *Slithis* is a solid 1950s horror movie that just happened to come along a couple of decades late, and like all beach-party monster films, it warns us to stay away from the water. Why? Because if we keep spending our days at the beach, swimming and soaking up the sun, we won't have time to watch movies like *Slithis.*

Squirm

1976

Director/screenplay: Jeff Lieberman; *Producer:* George Manasse

CAST:
Don Scardino, Patricia Pearcy, R. A. Dow, Jean Sullivan, Fran Higgins, Peter MacLean, Carl Dagenhart

ORIGINAL RELEASE: American International Pictures
VIDEO: Vestron Home Video

When Hitchcock's *The Birds* was released in 1963, every species of creature on earth was given permission to try to destroy humankind. Of course, the giant-insect films of the 1950s had gotten the ball rolling, but after *The Birds,* the situation started to get serious. Civilization was threatened by rats in *Willard*, by frogs and other reptiles in *Frogs*, by bees in *The Swarm*, by dogs in *Dogs*, by almost everything in *Day of the Animals*, and in 1972 by giant man-eating bunnies in *Night of the Lepus* (a flick that must be seen to be believed). In *Squirm*, of course, the challengers for world dominance are the worms.

The time is 1975, and the place is Fly Creek, Georgia, where a storm has knocked down power lines and flooded most of the back roads. The electrical wires are sending "over three hundred thousand volts" into the ground and energizing the worms, turning them into carnivorous little monsters.

Meanwhile, a New Yorker named Mick (Don Scardino) is on his way to visit his friend Geri (Patricia Pearcy) at her backwater Georgia homestead. He is hopelessly out of place there, and he meets a weird group of folks: Roger (R. A. Dow, formerly Tony Dow of *Leave It To Beaver*), the near-idiot son of Willie Grimes

In *Squirm,* Mick (Don Scardino) arrives from the big city to visit Geri (Patricia Pearcy) in rural Georgia.

(Carl Dagenhart), the local worm farmer; Sheriff Reston (Peter MacLean), who takes an instant dislike to the city kid; Naomi (Jean Sullivan), Geri's mom, who is completely out of touch with reality and who acts like a genteel and spacey character in a Tennessee Williams play; and Alma (Fran Higgins), Geri's younger sister,

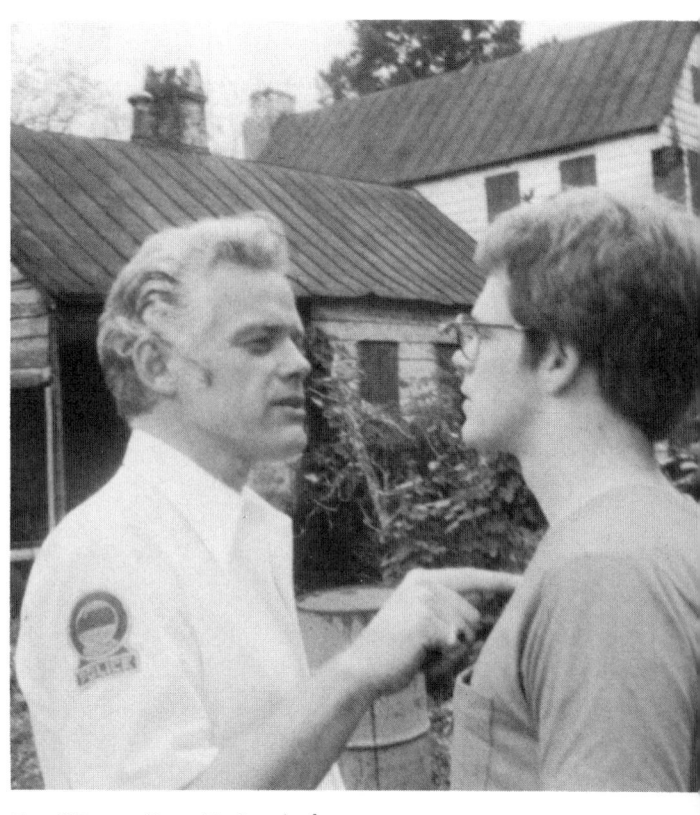

Sheriff Reston (Peter MacLean) takes an instant dislike to Mick (Don Scardino).

Mick (Don Scardino) shows Geri (Patricia Pearcy) and her sister, Alma (Fran Higgins), a skull he has found—the work of killer worms.

who has urban pretentions (she reads *Cosmopolitan*, smokes dope, and wears platform shoes).

Even though he's from out of town, Mick is smart enough to know that something is wrong in Fly Creek. First, he finds a worm in his chocolate soda at the local diner. Then, while he's out fishing with Geri and Roger, a worm bites him. Things get even worse when Roger, who is interested in Geri and jealous of Mick, is attacked by worms that burrow under his skin and send him screaming into the woods. Shortly after, Mick finds Roger's father dead and full of worms that are eating him from the inside out. The kid from the city concludes, "Something is making the worms go crazy."

Mick and Geri try to alert the sheriff, but of course he doesn't believe them, though he is convinced later that night when the worms come into his house and eat him. By this time, Mick has figured out the whole thing, including the fact that the worms don't like the light and

Roger (R. A. Dow) goes down for the third time in a sea of worms. It's enough to make you "squirm."

come out only after dark. The worms attack Geri's house and eat her mother, and Roger reappears with worms crawling out of every pore in his body, only to fall into an eight-foot pile of the creepy crawlies.

Mick and Geri climb a tree to wait for dawn while Alma hides in a trunk in the attic. By morning, the guys from the power company have repaired the fallen lines, and it seems that everything is back to normal—except that the kids are the only people left in Fly Creek. Everyone else has been devoured.

This movie is a lot more fun than most ecological-disaster films because it is so well made and because the special effects are so gruesomely convincing. The close-up shots of the worms are particularly eerie. Lieberman is a very good director—he also made the classic *Blue Sunshine*—and his skill shows here in the convincing performances and the excellent pacing.

Like every ecological disaster film, *Squirm* points out how tenuous our human grip on the earth really is and how easily we can fall victim to the natural world that we have misused and abused. During the fishing scene, when Geri plunges a hook into a fat, wriggling worm, we cringe, because we know the worms are about to get their revenge for this kind of mistreatment.

Most ecology films blame pollution or radioactivity for the upheaval in the natural world, but here the disaster is caused by simple electricity, suggesting that even the technology we most take for granted could backfire on us by having evil effects on nature's creatures. In other words, you don't have to live near a toxic waste dump, an A-bomb test site, or a nuclear power plant to be at risk. What happens in Fly Creek could happen anywhere. That's a nice touch, and it makes *Squirm* a lot more than just another nature-vs.-civilization flick.

Tentacles

ALTERNATE TITLE:

Tentacoli

1977

Director: Oliver Hellman (Olvidio Assonitis); *Producer:* E. F. Doria; *Screenplay:* Jerome Max, Tito Carpi, and Steve Carabatsos

CAST:
John Huston, Shelley Winters, Bo Hopkins, Henry Fonda, Cesare Danova, Claude Akins

ORIGINAL RELEASE: American International Pictures
VIDEO: Vestron Home Video

This newspaper ad makes it seem that *Tentacles* is a big-budget Hollywood production with lots of stars. It isn't.

It's time for a pop quiz. Here goes:
If *Jaws* = a giant shark, then *Tentacles* = _____.
    A. a giant leech
    B. the fifty-foot woman
    C. a killer shrew
    D. a giant octopus
    E. all of the above

If your answer to the question was D, you're at least as smart as the people who made this film. In fact, you could have made it yourself, and you would probably have done a better job. The odds are, though, that you wouldn't have been able to convince such big-name stars as Henry Fonda, John Huston, and Shelley Winters to appear in your low-budget rip-off of *Jaws*. How the people who really did make *Tentacles* managed to put together a cast like this is beyond me. Blackmail, maybe? Admittedly, the big names appear only briefly—they put in an afternoon's work and got out as quickly as possible.

Captain Robards (Claude Akins) and Ned Turner (John Huston) try to figure out what's been killing the locals in *Tentacles*.

John Corey (Cesare Danova) and Mr. Whitehead (Henry Fonda) are among the terrorized California citizens who are being threatened by the giant octopus.

The octopus has just claimed another victim in *Tentacles*.

But their presence makes this look like a major Hollywood production, which it definitely is not.

The production is Italian, and it is brought to you by Olvidio Assonitis, who has made a career out of mindlessly copying blockbuster horror films. His *Beyond the Door* is a nonsensical rip-off of *The Exorcist*, and *Tentacles*, of course, is his version of *Jaws*. Unlike *The Exorcist*, *Beyond the Door* is not the least bit frightening. Unlike *Jaws*, *Tentacles* is not the least bit exciting. But somebody is making a buck here, and that seems to be what matters.

There really isn't any reason to go into the plot of the film in any detail, because you already know it. A giant octopus that looks a lot like a mop is terrorizing the California coast, going after swimmers, boaters, and baby carriages. Among the terrorized locals are Mr. Whitehead (Fonda), Ned and Tillie Turner (Huston and Winters), and Captain Robards (Claude Akins wearing basically the same costume he used as the sheriff in his *Lobo* TV series). After a number of deaths and some efforts to get rid of the thing, the multi-armed monster is finally done in by two trained killer whales.

In all fairness, it's hard to fault Assonitis for making this shoddy imitation of *Jaws*. *Jaws* itself is, after all, an imitation, too. It owes its very existence to a whole string of "monster from the surf" stories, from ancient tales of sea serpents to *It Came From Beneath the Sea*, *Horror of Party Beach*, and beyond. But, of course, Steven Spielberg knows exactly what he is doing, and his imitations are quite conscious. This is why, in the course of *Jaws*, we see characters reading Herman Melville's *Moby Dick* or playing fishy video games. These are little reminders of where the story comes from. Spielberg's story is one we already know, and he knows we know it, just as he knows that, if we've ever seen one of those Saturday-matinee serials from the 1940s, we already know the story of *Raiders of the Lost Ark*. The fact that Spielberg can take this absolutely familiar story and make it unfamiliar, new, and exciting without losing sight of his sources is a tribute to his abilities as a filmmaker.

On the other hand, Assonitis pretends that his imitation is not an imitation at all, and so there is no effort here to transform something old into something new, to make the familiar unfamiliar again. *Tentacles* is presented as simply the same old junk, which is exactly what it is.

In fact, though *Tentacles* is a mindless imitation of an imitation, the Assonitis film and *Jaws* say very different things to us. *Jaws*, like the old sea serpent stories and *Moby Dick*, is a tale about civilization vs. nature. It warns that the natural world—in this case, a great white shark—can intrude on humanity at any time, and though we might be able to deal with the problem temporarily, nature is always there, and it doesn't particularly care about our needs and desires. The natural world in *Jaws* is superior to us, and we simply have to learn to live with that fact or perish.

With its trained killer whales, however, *Tentacles* suggests that we humans are so superior to the natural world that we can train nature to defeat itself. That is exactly the kind of thinking—or thoughtlessness—that has led to the ecological disasters we face today.

The Terror

1963

Director/producer: Roger Corman; *Screenplay:* Leo Gordon and Jack Hill

CAST:
Boris Karloff, Jack Nicholson, Sandra Knight, Dick Miller, Jonathan Haze, Dorothy Neumann

ORIGINAL RELEASE: Filmgroup/American International Pictures
VIDEO: Goodtimes Video, Sinister Cinema, and others

This legendary film was shot in three days, using the same sets and costumes as *The Raven*, which Corman had finished earlier than expected. Boris Karloff was still under contract, and not one to waste an opportunity, Corman had his crew throw *The Terror* together virtually overnight. Though Corman is listed as the director, in fact he shared those duties with Francis Ford Coppola (billed in the credits as associate producer), Monte Hellman, Jack Hill, Dennis Jacob, and costar Jack Nicholson. Needless to say, the result is often uneven. Given the quality of the people involved, this could have been a much better film, but surprisingly, it really isn't that bad.

Andre Duvalier (Nicholson) is a cavalry officer in Napoleon's army who has been separated from his regiment. He meets a beautiful young woman named Helene (Sandra Knight), who promptly disappears. His efforts to find her again lead him to the castle of Baron Von Leppe (Karloff) where he sees a portrait of the woman. The baron explains that this is a portrait of his wife, Ilsa, who has been dead for twenty years.

Andre stays at the castle and sees Helene several times on the grounds, at windows, and near the family crypt. Not one to believe in ghosts, he presses the baron for the real story, and he gets it. Ilsa was a peasant when Von Leppe met and married her. Then the baron was called away to war, and when he returned a year later, he found her with her lover Eric and, in a fit of rage, killed her. His servant Stefan (Dick Miller) took care of the lover. Von

Helene (Sandra Knight) appears in the graveyard near Castle Von Leppe in *The Terror*. Is she a ghost or a living woman?

Leppe has lived with his guilt ever since: "For twenty years, I've not set foot beyond the walls of this castle." The baron has also seen the woman Andre knows as Helene, and he believes she is the ghost of Ilsa, who has returned for him.

Ilsa/Helene keeps appearing to the baron and urging him to kill himself so they can be together, but Von Leppe hesitates to damn himself by taking his own life. Eventually, Andre discovers that Helene is involved in some kind of plot. An old village woman, Katerina (Dorothy Neumann), has a strange hypnotic control over Helene and is making her believe that she is possessed by the spirit of Ilsa. Katerina was Eric's mother, and she is using Helene to get her revenge against Von Leppe. There is also the suggestion that Helene is the daughter of the long-dead Ilsa and Eric.

Finally, the baron agrees to kill himself by flooding the crypt where Ilsa is buried. But just as Katerina is about to get her revenge, Stefan adds a new twist to the plot by telling her that the baron is not the baron at all. Twenty years before, when Von Leppe returned from the war, he did kill Ilsa, but Eric then killed the baron. To protect

Andre (Jack Nicholson) threatens the old witch woman (Dorothy Neumann) to get the information he wants.

Baron Von Leppe (Boris Karloff) and Stefan (Dick Miller) struggle as the servant tries to prevent his master from going into the crypt.

It's almost a happy ending for Helene (Sandra Knight) and Andre (Jack Nicholson) in *The Terror*.

himself, Eric took the baron's place and never again left the castle. But Eric's guilt drove him mad, and he became the baron in his own mind. Katerina's plot is about to result in the death and damnation of her own son.

In the end, Von Leppe/Eric does flood the crypt, and he and Stefan die there, though Andre rescues Helene. Once the baron is dead, however, Helene begins to decay before Andre's eyes until she is only a rotten corpse. It seems, then, that something supernatural has been going on all along.

Given the thousands of horror films that have been made over the years, it's surprising to notice how few ghost movies there are, but *The Terror* is one of them. In our rational culture, of course, we don't believe in ghosts. The living are the living and the dead are the dead. Like Andre, we say, "The dead cannot reach out from the grave." But the dead *do* influence us. Cultures that practice ancestor worship understand this. The ghost story understands it, too. Helene tells Andre, "I am possessed by the dead." Eric, too, is possessed by the dead baron. In fact, we are all possessed by the dead. We are who we are, at least in part, because of those who came before. Ghost stories such as *The Terror* remind us that we do not create ourselves as individuals or as a society. Like Baron Von Leppe, we owe a debt to the dead, and the ghost story is important because it reminds us of that debt.

Them!

1954

Director: Gordon Douglas; *Producer:* David Weisbart; *Screenplay:* Ted Sherdeman and Russell Hughes

CAST:
James Whitmore, Edmund Gwenn, Joan Weldon, James Arness

ORIGINAL RELEASE: Warner Brothers
VIDEO: Warner Home Video

This is fifties sci-fi/horror at its best. Giant mutant ants, products of the first atomic bomb test in New Mexico near the end of World War II, are plundering the Southwest for sugar and killing dozens of innocent victims in the process. Veteran actor James Whitmore stars as the New Mexico state trooper who first discovers the catastrophe, and James Arness (the Thing in *The Thing From Another World* and Matt Dillon on TV's *Gunsmoke*) is the FBI agent called in to help out. Edmund Gwenn (Santa in *Miracle on 34th Street*) and Joan Weldon are a father-daughter team of entomologists who help to diagnose and eventually solve the problem.

The police and the military manage to destroy the nest in the New Mexico desert, but not before two winged queen ants and their consorts escape to parts unknown. One queen lays her eggs on board a cargo ship, which the

Dr. Patricia Medford (Joan Weldon) almost becomes lunch for one of "them." (*Courtesy Hollywood Book and Poster*)

ants then sink at sea, destroying the crew and themselves as well. The other builds her nest in the drainage tunnels beneath Los Angeles, and our heroes track her there for the final showdown with the new colony in which, amazingly, top-billed Whitmore dies saving the lives of two kids.

This was the first of the giant-insects-attack-major-urban-area films, which flooded the market after *Them!* became the biggest money-making film of 1954. *Tarantula, The Black Scorpion, The Deadly Mantis,* and *The Beginning of the End* (giant grasshoppers attack Chicago, pursued by Arness's brother, Peter Graves), all followed in rapid succession. Almost invariably, of course, atomic radiation is to blame for the problem. What makes *Them!* unique among science-fiction/horror films of the fifties, however, is its absolute indictment of atomic weapons and atomic testing. Most films of the era say that, yes, nuclear weapons are a curse, but we need them, and more often than not, they can be used to destroy the monsters they have inadvertently created. But *Them!* does not compromise its antinuclear stance. At the end, Arness notes that the ants are the product of the very first atomic test and that many more such tests have been conducted since. What horrors might they bring? Scientist Gwenn replies, "Nobody knows. When man first entered the atomic age, he opened a door into a new world. What he will find in that new world, nobody can predict." This was an ominous and courageous message for its time, and it was clearly one that moviegoers wanted and needed to hear.

205

By the way, keep your eyes open for bit-part appearances by Fess Parker (Disney's *Davy Crockett*), William Schallert (veteran character actor and father on *The Patty Duke Show*), Leonard Nimoy (Mr. Spock of *Star Trek*), and Dub Taylor.

Tombs of the Blind Dead

ALTERNATE TITLES:

*La Noche del Terror Ciego,
The Blind Dead*

1972

Director/screenplay: Armando De Ossorio; *Producer:* Salvadore Romero

CAST:
Lone Fleming, Cesar Burner, Helen Harp, Joseph Thelman, Maria Sylva

ORIGINAL RELEASE: Hallmark Releasing
VIDEO: Paragon Video Productions

This is the first in a series of four movies Armando De Ossorio directed based on the Templars, a brotherhood of knights who took part in the Crusades. Apparently, according to history, the society of Templars amassed such wealth through their exploits that they threatened the power of the Vatican, and so they were excommunicated. Ossorio's tales don't have much to do with the historical facts of the case, but *Tombs of the Blind Dead* and the films that followed are really pretty good—atmospheric and creepy with just enough gore and nastiness to make them seem mildly perverse.

This Spanish/Portuguese production begins in the thirteenth century with Templars sacrificing a young woman and drinking her blood in a satanic ritual. Now that we know what these guys were like, the action moves into the 1970s when old school chums Betty and Virginia meet at a resort in Lisbon. Though this seems to have little bearing on the plot, Betty is a lesbian who once seduced Virginia when they were younger. Virginia is now with Roger, and the two invite Betty to join them on a train excursion and picnic the next day.

During the ride, however, Virginia becomes angry at the attention Roger is paying to her old friend, and so she jumps off the train and hikes to an abandoned monastery where she unrolls her sleeping bag and spends the night. As it turns out, this is the site where the Templars are buried. Centuries before, the local villagers became so angry at the Knights' satanic carryings-on that they executed all of them and left their bodies out in the open where the crows could peck out their eyes. This is why they are the blind dead.

But rumors of the Templars' passing have been greatly exaggerated, and that night they come out of their tombs and kill Virginia. The walking-dead scenes here are very effective. The Templars are little more than moldy skeletons in robes and hoods, with skull faces and empty eye sockets; some ride horses, and all of them move in slow motion, though they don't seem to have any trouble catching their victims. They are blind, of course, and so all you have to do to escape them is to be quiet. Scream, though, and they are all over you, as Virginia finds out.

When their friend doesn't return to the resort, Betty and Roger decide to go looking for her. Of course, the waitress at the restaurant and all the other locals warn them not to go out there into Templar country, but they ride to the monastery on horses anyway. There they meet some cops and learn that Virginia has been found, murdered. The police suspect a band of local smugglers.

Roger and Betty are beginning to suspect, however, that this has nothing to do with smuggling, and so they get the head smuggler, Pedro, and his gun moll, Ginger, to go to the monastery with them to find out what is really going on. While they are there, Pedro takes time out from their investigation to rape Betty—apparently, Ossorio really gets off on lesbians being raped because an identical scene appears in *Horror of the Zombies,* one of the Templar sequels.

That night, the Templars attack, killing Pedro, Roger, and Ginger, though Betty manages to avoid them by keeping her mouth shut. Just as dawn is breaking, she makes it to the train tracks where the old engineer doesn't want to stop for her—he, too, knows the stories about the blind dead—but his young fireman pulls the brake and gets Betty on board. The dead manage to board the train, too, however, and they kill everybody there, except Betty, who is hiding in the coal car. When the train gets to the station, the dead get off to invade the town. Betty screams, and that's the end.

Like *Tombs of the Blind Dead,* many horror movies have their roots in folklore—werewolf, vampire, and ghost stories are obvious examples. What is interesting about these movies is that they ask us to pay attention to people we might normally ignore in real life—gypsies, peasants, country folk, senile old women, the bearers of folklore—because these people have the information we need to survive. They know about silver bullets, stakes through the heart, and blind dead skeletons that prey on

The Templars prepare for a Satanic Mass in *Tombs of the Blind Dead*.

Nina, Betty's assistant, puts in a bit of overtime at the mannequin factory.

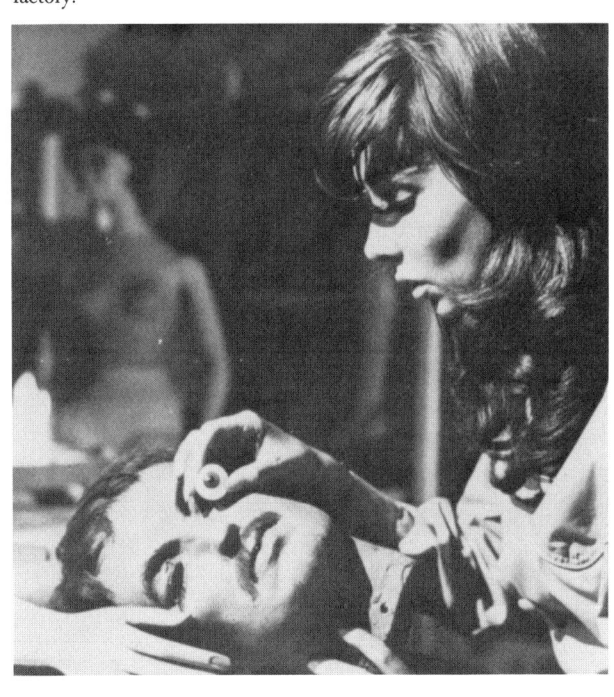

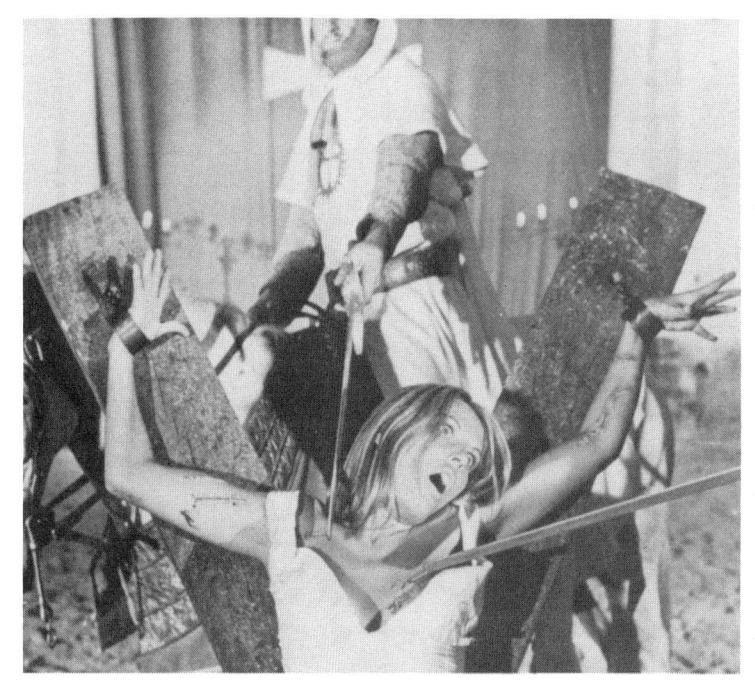

The demonic knights sacrifice a young woman to the devil.

The living-dead Templars kill the train's engineer in the closing moments of *Tombs of the Blind Dead*.

the living, stuff that we sophisticated urban types don't understand and usually refuse to listen to until it's too late.

So, in *Tombs of the Blind Dead*, when all the locals tell Roger not to go to the Templars' gravesite and he says, "Superstitition be damned," we know that the peasants are right and he is wrong, though, in fact, if we were in his place in real life, we probably wouldn't listen to the peasants either.

Tombs of the Blind Dead and many other horror films warn us never to think that we know it all and to pay attention to those people who might not seem fashionable or up-to-date but who might be bearers of ancient widsom that we need, whether we know it or not.

The Toolbox Murders

1978

Director: Dennis Donnelly; *Producer:* Tony Didio; *Screenplay:* Neva Friedenn, Robert Easter, and Ann Kindberg

CAST:
Cameron Mitchell, Pamelyn Ferdin, Wesley Eure, Nicholas Beauvy, Aneta Corsaut

ORIGINAL RELEASE: Cal-Am Productions
VIDEO: Video Communications Inc.

By 1978, Cameron Mitchell had fallen a long way from his first screen appearance back at MGM three decades before. Here, he plays Vance Kingsley, owner of an apartment building in which a number of murders are committed by someone in a ski mask wielding an electric drill, a hammer, a screwdriver, and a nail gun. Of course the victims are all young, attractive, single women, and, of course, Vance is the killer.

Kingsley also kidnaps fifteen-year-old Laurie (Pamelyn Ferdin) from the building and keeps her tied up in his house where she is to replace his own daughter, Kathy, who was killed in an automobile accident. In fact, it is grief over his daughter's death that has turned Vance into a murderer, though the film never explains what possible connection there might be between Kathy's accident, the women who are killed, and Vance's fixation on tools as weapons.

But things become even more confused. Joey (Nicholas Beauvy), Laurie's teenage brother, tries to find his sister, and his friend Kent (Wesley Eure) helps out. But Kent is Vance's nephew, and when Joey finds proof that Vance is the killer, Kent pours gasoline over his friend, torments him with matches, and finally sets him on fire, all to protect his uncle, though in fact the two are not shown to be particularly close.

Later, Kent stabs Uncle Vance to death and rapes Laurie. It turns out that Kent and Kathy were lovers, and her death has apparently driven him crazy, too. Laurie stabs Kent with a pair of scissors and escapes while the closing credits inform us that *The Toolbox Murders* was based on a "true story."

Why does Vance Kingsley kill young women? "They were all committing unnatural acts," he explains. These "unnatural acts" include undressing in their own homes, looking in mirrors, living alone, being divorced, and perhaps being sexually active. But why does Vance *really* kill these women? He does it because there is an

It's the hammer this time, but Kingsley (Cameron Mitchell) has a whole box full of weapons in The Toolbox Murders. (Courtesy Hollywood Book and Poster)

Vance Kingsley (Cameron Mitchell) pursues another victim in The Toolbox Murders. (Courtesy Hollywood Book and Poster)

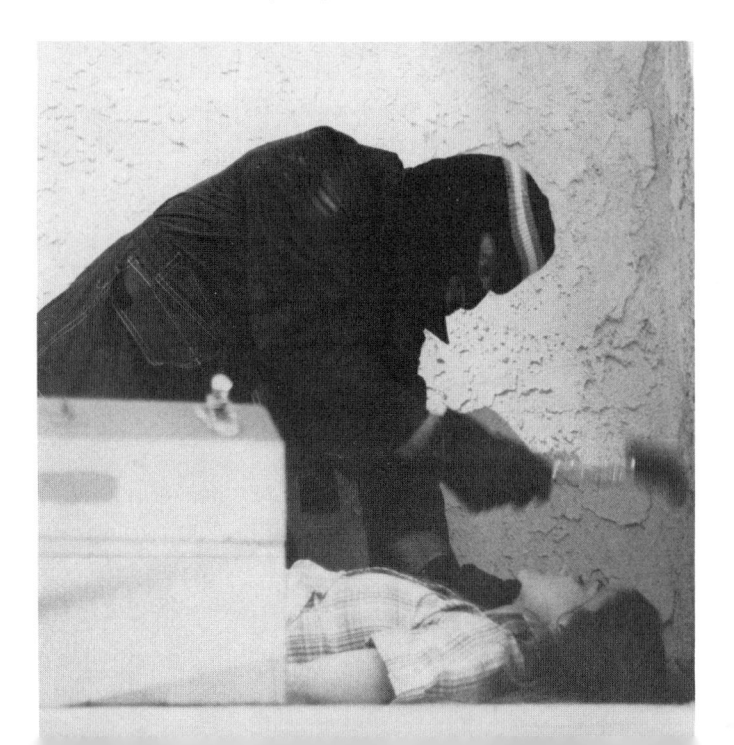

audience for this kind of thing, because this is what some of us want to see.

The very existence of a film such as *The Toolbox Murders* shows how deeply our culture fears and hates women, particularly women who are not "owned" by men and who, therefore, do not "know their place." The movie exists only to depict these women being brutally murdered. It is never anything but grim, the story line is senseless, there is no suspense or mystery—even in his ski mask, we know that Vance is the killer right at the beginning. And the film is not an amateur production. For all his failings, Mitchell is a seasoned professional; the same is true for Corsaut (she was Steve McQueen's girlfriend in *The Blob* and Sheriff Andy's girl on *The Andy Griffith Show*), and Ferdin and Eure (both graduates of Saturday-morning kids' TV). In short, this is not mindless entertainment put together by people who didn't know what they were doing. It is a carefully staged attack on women, and it ought to be an embarrassment to all of us who watch horror films.

Torso

ALTERNATE TITLES:

I Corpi Presentano, Tracce Di Violenza Carnale, The Bodies Showed Traces of Carnal Violence

1975

Director: Sergio Martino; *Producers:* Antonio Cervi and Carlo Ponti; *Screenplay:* Ernesto Gastaldi and Sergio Martino

CAST:
Suzy Kendall, Tina Aumont, Luc Merenda, John Richardson, Angela Cavello, Carla Brait

ORIGINAL RELEASE: Joseph Brenner Associates
VIDEO: Prism Entertainment

Italian gore films have been around for a long time, and like Mexican vampire films, they are an acquired taste. Watching a film like Lucio Fulci's *Zombie* or *Gates of Hell*, Francesco Martino's *Dr. Butcher, M.D.*, Antonio Margheriti's *Cannibals in the Streets,* or Umberto Lenzi's *Make Them Die Slowly* for the first time is like drinking your first cup of coffee—it seems pretty awful, but after a while, you develop a tolerance and even a certain need for the stuff. Now that's scary, because these are some of the most violent movies ever made, and yet there is something compelling about them,

Italian art student Carol allows herself to be groped and fondled by hippie bikers.

Kay (Suzy Kendall) finds her friend Dani (Tina Aumont) murdered.

maybe because they are unlike anything else you are ever apt to see.

As Italian gore flicks go, *Torso* is pretty tame. Most of the really nasty stuff is only hinted at or shown in quick bursts—blink and you've missed it. But *Torso* is nasty in its own way.

Kay (Suzy Kendall) is a sedate, virginal American student studying art in Italy with a professor named Franz (John Richardson). One night, her fellow students Flo and John are making it in the car when they are

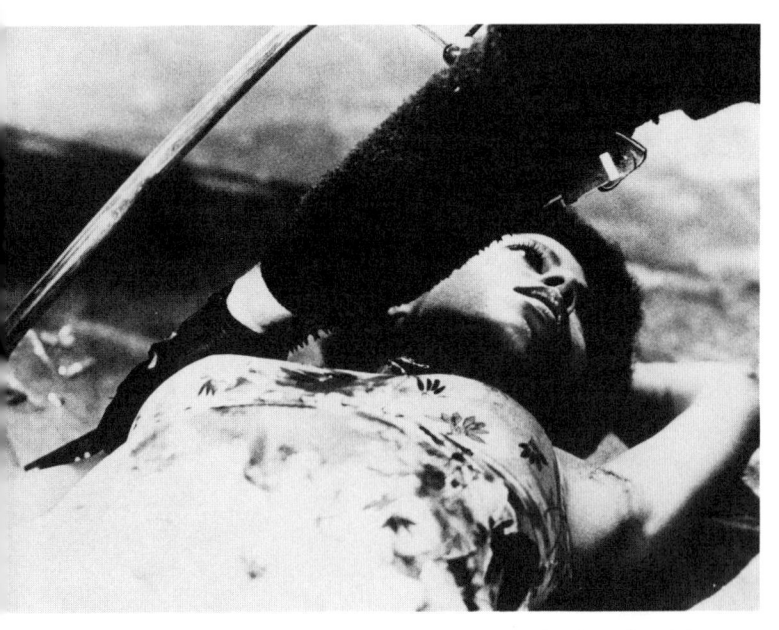

The killer uses a hacksaw to dismember the body of Ursula (Carla Brait).

attacked and killed by a homicidal killer in a stocking mask. Flo (Patricia Adiutori) is strangled with a striped scarf, then dismembered with a large knife; her head, arms, and legs are cut off, leaving only—you guessed it—the torso.

Kay and her friends Dani (Tina Aumont), Katia (Angela Cavello), and Ursula (Carla Brait) are shocked by the killings. When Inspector Martino asks them whether they have ever seen anyone wearing a scarf like the murder weapon, Dani thinks she has, but she can't remember who it was. But Dani has problems of her own. She is being pursued by a guy named Stefano (Roberto Bisacco) who is bugging her all the time, and she is a bit afraid of him. Could he be the killer?

The girls are also worried about their friend Carol (Cristina Airoldi), who has taken to hanging out with a gang of hippie bikers. One day at one of their drug parties, she lets herself be undressed and fondled by two of these punks, but when she refuses to go all the way, they chase her into the woods. There she meets the masked killer, who strangles her with a scarf, gouges her eyes out—this is really the only graphic scene in the film—and chops her up.

Dani decides that she and her friends have to get out of town, so they go to her uncle's country mansion while he is away. While they are there, Kay falls down the stairs and twists her ankle. Young, handsome town doctor Roberto (Luc Merenda) comes to call, and he seems quite taken with Kay. Could he be the killer?

There are a lot of shower-taking, nude-swimming, and lesbian scenes between Ursula and Katia just to keep us interested until Dani sees Stefano walking through the woods and realizes that he has followed her there. He must be the killer, for sure.

That night, while Kay is under sedation for her ankle, the killer murders Stefano—he wasn't the one after all—then comes into the house and slashes Dani, Katia, and Ursula. In the morning, Kay wakes up, makes her way painfully down the stairs, and finds her friends' bodies. Suddenly the killer returns, and from her hiding place, Kay watches as he dismembers the young women with a hacksaw.

Finally, the murderer discovers Kay and unmasks himself—it's Franz, the professor. It seems that he had a bad experience with a little girl when he was a kid, and that's why he is a psychopath today. In any case, he likes Kay, but now she is a witness, and he has to get rid of her.

Before he gets a chance to do her in, however, Roberto comes calling, fights with Franz, and kills him, putting an end to the terror.

There is nothing particularly new about a horror film that victimizes women, but *Torso* puts an extra spin on that old idea. Director Martino spends a lot of time in this movie doing precisely what Franz is doing—dismembering women. There are many shots of women's torsos, suggesting that the torso is the perfect sex object—it has no head, so it can't think or talk, and it has no arms or legs, so it can't respond or struggle. The torso alone is no longer a human woman, a person, and this is what Franz seems to enjoy—"They were only dolls," he says. Martino seems to think that we will enjoy that, too.

The embarrassing thing for male viewers is that perhaps we do. Admittedly, an enormous amount of popular culture (movies, TV, commercials, magazines,

Kay (Suzy Kendall) uses a mirror to signal for help while the killer stalks her in Torso.

etc.) is devoted to depicting women as objects, as dolls, and at some level, we males have learned to respond positively to that. In a way, no real woman in the real world can be as good as a model in a magazine layout because real women are people, and that always complicates matters. The model in the magazine is lifeless—we can do whatever we want with her.

The women in *Torso* are strikingly beautiful, and for that very reason, "those girls ain't for the likes of us," as one of the local boys says. They ain't for the likes of us male viewers either, and the movie says that what we can't have ought to be destroyed, rendered lifeless, made uncomplicated. So, although this movie poses as a mystery, it really doesn't matter in the end who killed the women, as long as somebody was doing it.

Flo, Katia, and Ursula are complicated because they are sexually active and because they take their clothes off before our eyes, even though we know "they ain't for the likes of us." That's why they die. Only Kay never appears naked or engages in any sexual activity. She is uncomplicated, and that's why she lives. As Franz says, "You're different. You're pure." In the end, though, she needs Dr. Roberto to save her life, because her refusal of sex really isn't sufficient to protect her. After all, Katia, Ursula, and Flo die because they do have sex, but Carol dies because she doesn't want to. So, women, take your choice, but if you are attractive, you're going to die anyway.

For male viewers, what is compelling about a film like *Torso* is that it is absolutely familiar. This movie only takes a single logical step beyond the centerfold or the TV beer commercial in its objectification of women. That's frightening, but not as frightening as thinking about the *next* logical step.

Torture Dungeon

1970

Director: Andy Milligan; *Producer:* William Mishkin; *Screenplay:* Andy Milligan and John Borske

CAST:
Jeremy Brooks, Susan Cassidy, Patricia Dillon, Richard Mason, Haal Borske, Donna Whitfield

ORIGINAL RELEASE: Mishkin Productions

VIDEO: Midnight Home Video

If you've never seen an Andy Milligan film, it's hard to imagine how really bad they are. The acting is ludicrous,

Jeremy Brooks (center) and a host of New Yorkers pretend they are in Elizabethan England in *Torture Dungeon*.

The duke's executioners put an end to young William by nailing his hands to the wall and stabbing him with a pitchfork.

the camera work is hopelessly incompetent—Milligan is his own cinematographer—and your neighbor's home videos have higher production values. It's almost impossible to believe that these movies actually showed in theaters on the big screen and that people actually paid to see them.

Still, films like *Bloodthirsty Butchers, Carnage, The Rats Are Coming, The Werewolves Are Here!* and *Torture Dungeon* have a certain charm, if that's the word. If nothing else, making something so awful and putting your name on it shows courage. And the truth is, Milligan always seems to be trying to do more than he

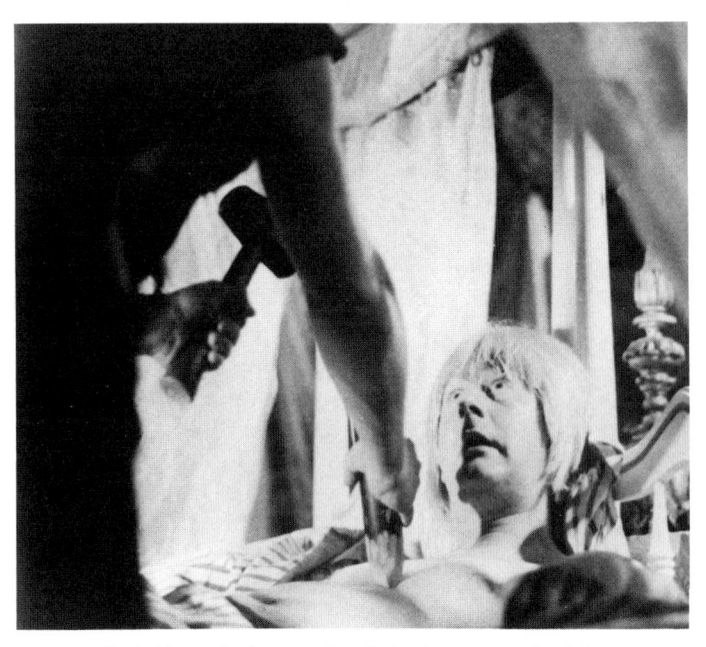

The half-witted Albert, Duke of Abathy, is put to death by Norwich's executioners the morning after his wedding night.

"Revenge! Revenge!" is what the one-eyed woman wants for herself and for the victims in the *Torture Dungeon*.

possibly can, given his lack of talent and shoestring budgets. You have to admire that, I suppose.

In *Torture Dungeon*, for example, he is trying to stage an Elizabethan drama on film, though this is hardly Roman Polanski's *Macbeth*. It is Milligan's goriest and sexiest movie, though it's marred by his insistence on showing fairly unattractive people naked and by the fact that some characters have fake British accents, some don't, and others have accents some of the time but not always.

The setting is England—it's really Staten Island—and Norman (Jeremy Brooks), the Duke of Norwich, is trying to get rid of the successors to the throne so he can become king. Norman is a strange and very bad guy. As he says, "I live for pleasure alone—only second to power, of course." But the duke has his problems, too. He has only one arm (the "missing" one is obviously under his cape), is subject to epileptic seizures, and is, as he explains, "try-sexual," because he'll try anything.

The film opens with the decapitation murder of Norman's half brother, leaving only his other half-siblings Albert, Lady Agatha, and Lady Jane standing between him and the throne. The governing council of the nation is eager to get Albert (Haal Borske) married so that he can provide a new heir, and following Norman's advice, they choose a peasant girl, Heather Mac-Gregor (Susan Cassidy), to be Albert's bride.

There are two problems with this plan. One is that Albert is a half-wit who eats bugs and things—it seems that someone, perhaps Norman, dealt him a head injury when he was a child. The other problem is that Heather is in love with William, a fellow peasant. Heather's adoptive father and his friend, an elderly one-eyed woman, explain to Heather that she has no choice but to marry Albert. Even so, she and William plan to run off together. Before they can do that, though, Norman's hooded executioners catch up with William, nail him to the wall of a barn, and finish him off with a pitchfork.

Heather goes to court where everybody warns her about the duke. Agatha (Donna Whitfield) and Jane (Patricia Dillon) even go so far as to take her down to Norman's torture dungeon where she sees people without legs, without tongues, etc., all victims of Norman's personal brand of evil.

Albert and Heather are married and consummate their union, though with some difficulty, since Albert never really understands what's going on. Afterward, Norman's executioners come into Albert's room and drive a stake through his heart.

Agatha and Jane know they are next on Norman's list, so they run for it, but Norman catches Agatha and stabs her to death, and the guys in the black hoods get Jane. Now it's Heather's turn, just in case she is carrying the late Albert's child.

Marvin, one of Norman's executioners and certainly the worst actor in the film, goes after Heather with an ax, but then he realizes that he loves her and can't carry out the duke's orders. Then Ivan (Richard Mason), Norman's hunchbacked court jester, confidant, and lover, tries to kill Heather, and he and Marvin end up killing each other. Then Norman tries to kill Heather himself, only to be killed in turn by the one-eyed lady, who has been cropping up from time to time throughout the flick and screaming "Revenge! Revenge!" at every opportunity.

This all seems very complicated, but it gets worse. Heather is safe, but the old woman has been kicked by a horse and lies dying. In an extended predeath monologue, however, she explains that she is really the queen, mother to the late Albert, Agatha, and Jane—not to Norman, though, because he is illegitimate. Years before, when she was pregnant yet again, little Norman set fire to the chapel where she was praying, killing her servant and almost killing her. Everyone believed that the queen was dead, and because she had amnesia at the time, she couldn't tell them any different.

She gave birth to a baby girl, who was put up for adoption. Now get this. Apparently, that kick to the head has given the old woman her memory back, because now she recalls that the baby girl was—you guessed it—Heather, who is the rightful heir to the throne. This also means that Heather was married to and might be pregnant by her own brother, Albert, but royalty does that kind of thing all the time.

If this plot seems confusing, that's because it is. The story is unnecessarily convoluted, and there are so many people cluttering up the cast that it's hard to tell them apart—there are actually three characters named Peter and two named Jane in this film.

But *Torture Dungeon* provides an answer to the question that has been haunting cult horror film fans for years: Why, given Milligan's minuscule budgets, does he usually insist upon doing period pieces that call for special costumes, sets, etc., all of them obviously fake? In this case, at least, the answer seems to be that Milligan is trying to do his own version of Shakespeare. *Torture Dungeon* contains an array of plot devices from the classic Shakespearean tragedies and comedies, along with the sex and violence that used to pack them into the Globe Theatre in Elizabethan times.

Well, let's face it, Shakespeare provided the popular culture of his day. But if Andy Milligan is his modern-day equivalent, then we are probably in very serious trouble.

Trap Them and Kill Them

ALTERNATE TITLES:

Emanuelle e gli Ultimi Cannibali,
Emanuelle and the Last Cannibals

1977

Director: Aristide Massaccesi (Joe d'Amato); *Producer:* Gianfranco Gouyoumdjian; *Screenplay:* Aristide Massaccesi and Romano Scandariato

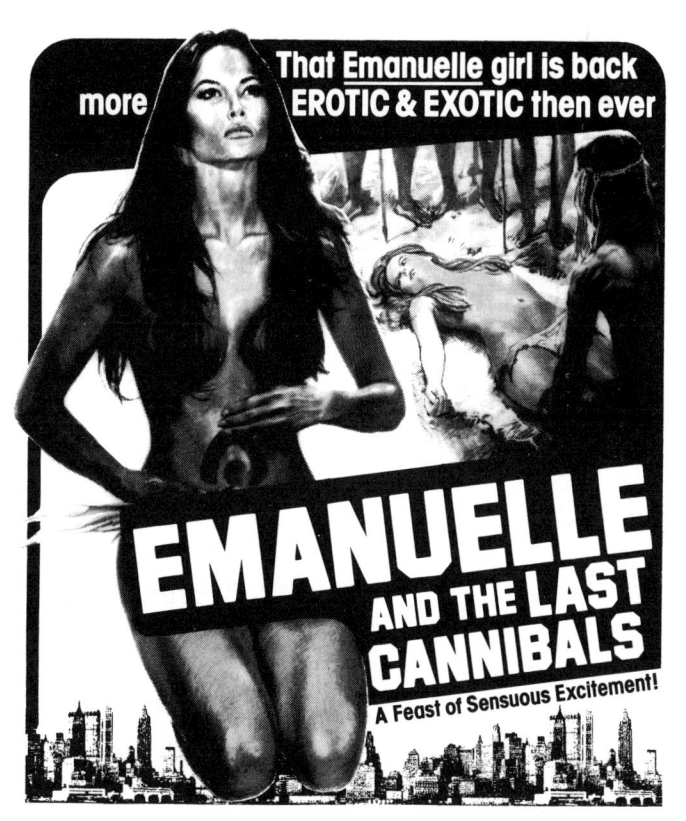

Emanuelle and the Last Cannibals was rereleased under the title *Trap Them and Kill Them* to cash in on the success of Umberto Lenzi's *Make Them Die Slowly.*

CAST:
Laura Gemser, Gabrielle Tinti

ORIGINAL RELEASE: Fulvia Cinematografica
VIDEO: Gorgon Video

This is what the world really needs—a soft-core porno cannibalism film. Massaccesi directed a number of the *Emanuelle* films in the seventies, and Gemser appeared in the title role in some of them, but those were just nice, dirty movies. Why these people thought this 1977 entry in the *Emanuelle* series was a good idea is anybody's guess, but here it is: one of the most repulsive movies you are ever likely to see.

The Italian cannibal film has become a horror subgenre of sorts, and this one, like so many of the others shot in South America, tries to pass itself off as a true story "as reported by Jennifer O'Sullivan," whoever she is. In the opening sequence, a white female patient in a mental institution in New York City bites off a nurse's breast and eats it. It seems the young patient was found in the Amazon where she was held prisoner by a tribe of cannibals, and apparently the food agreed with her.

213

Emanuelle (Laura Gemser) is a journalist who has been posing as an inmate of the hospital on assignment, and she gets the whole story. Her editor offers to fund an expedition to the Amazon to get a piece on the cannibals, so Emanuelle contacts Prof. Mark Lester (Gabrielle Tinti, Gemser's real-life husband) to ask him to lead it. He takes her back to his place and shows her his cannibal films—sort of the equivalent of showing her his etchings—and it works, because they end up in bed.

In the Amazon region, Lester mounts an expedition with a couple of native guides, and he also agrees to escort Sister Angela and young Isabelle Wilks to Father Morales's mission in the jungle. On the way, after some nude bathing scenes and more sex, they meet Donald McKensey, his wife, Maggie, and their guide, Salvador. Donald claims to be on a hunting trip and he explains that Father Morales's mission has been wiped out. "All of the bodies were horribly mutilated," Maggie informs them.

Mark and Emanuelle decide they should turn back, but the cannibals kill one of their native guides and steal their boats and supplies. The group starts off over land, but Sister Angela is captured by the cannibals and eaten, putting a damper on the whole expedition.

The McKenseys in fact are searching for a plane that went down in the jungle carrying a shipment of diamonds, but of course they don't share this information with the others. Donald and Maggie actually find the plane and the diamonds, but unfortunately they take time out to have sex in the jungle because—well, because that's what people in these movies do—and the cannibals attack them, wounding Donald and capturing Maggie.

The expedition goes out looking for Maggie and finds the cannibal tribe's island home, but Salvador is killed and Donald and Isabelle are captured, leaving only Emanuelle and Mark to save everybody.

They don't do a very good job of it. Maggie is disemboweled and eaten, Donald is cut in two, but the cannibals keep Isabelle for later. Ever the professor, Mark explains that they are going to sacrifice her to the goddess of the waters. This ritual begins with Isabelle's being gang-raped by the entire clan—apparently, the tribe consists only of males, which might explain why they are the last cannibals.

Finally, after watching the slaughter of Maggie and Donald and the rape of Isabelle without doing anything, Emanuelle gets an idea. She strips down, enters the water, and appears to the tribe, posing as the goddess of the waters. This works long enough to allow her to escape with Isabelle, and the survivors get away at last.

This is a confused and confusing movie. On the one hand, it offers up women's bodies to be gawked at, abused, multilated, and devoured. On the other, Emanuelle is presented as a strong, independent woman—"I'm a free woman and I behave as such"—and she *is* the heroine of the piece. It is she, not Mark, who solves the problem at the end of the film. Still, it is unlikely that anybody who would choose to watch *Trap Them and Kill Them* would be influenced very much by what tries to pass as a feminist message.

Trap Them and Kill Them is a throwback to the racist jungle movies of the thirties, forties, and fifties. The suggestion that there are third-world people who eat other human beings as casually as we go to McDonald's is both inaccurate and insulting. But the movie has other problems, too.

The plot of a pornographic film is just an excuse to move from one sex scene to the next. The plot of a gore movie is an excuse to move from one scene of ultraviolent slaughter to the next. *Trap Them and Kill Them* tries to move in both directions at once, and as a result, it ends up working against itself and going nowhere.

This explains how a movie with so much sex and violence can be so boring.

The Undying Brain

ALTERNATE TITLES:

*Brain of Blood,
The Creature's Revenge,
The Brain*

1971

Director: Al Adamson; *Producers:* Al Adamson and Sam Sherman; *Screenplay:* Joe Van Rodgers and Kane W. Lynn

CAST:
Grant Williams, Reed Hadley, Kent Taylor, John Bloom, Regina Carrol, Vicki Volante, Angelo Rossitto, Zandor Vorkov

ORIGINAL RELEASE: Hemisphere Releasing
VIDEO: New Horizons Video

The Undying Brain is the video title for this one, which was originally released to theaters as *Brain of Blood*, and it brings together actors who have seen better days—1940s serial star Reed Hadley, Grant Williams of *The Incredible Shrinking Man*, Angelo Rossitto of Tod Browning's *Freaks*—and the Adamson/Sherman company regulars: Kent Taylor (*Blood of Ghastly Horror*),

Dr. Trenton (Kent Taylor) and his assistant Dorro (Angelo Rossitto) prepare for another of their evil operations in *The Undying Brain*.

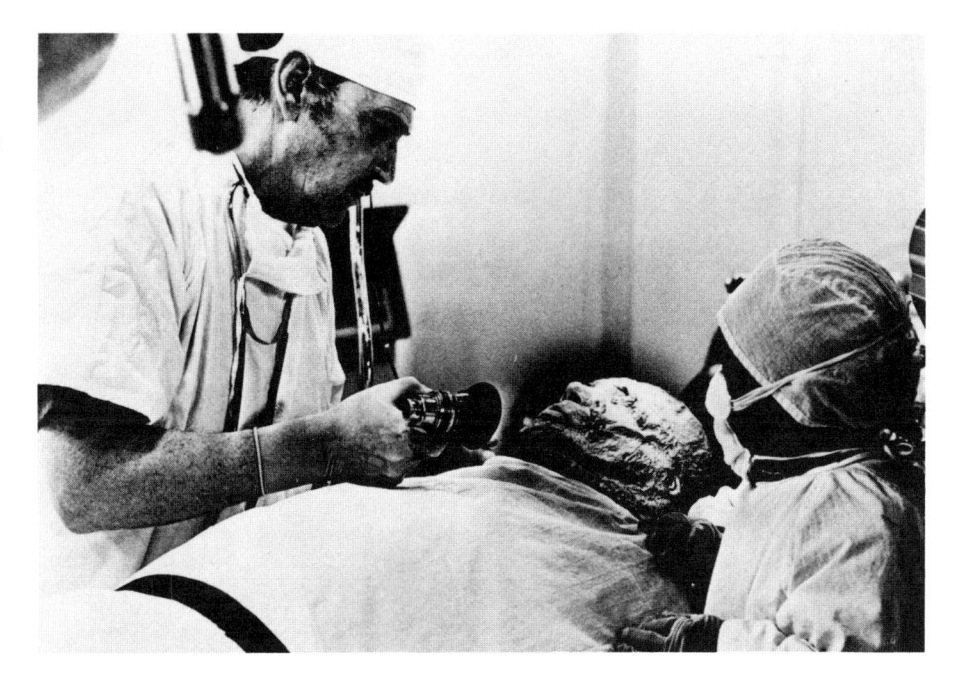

Katherine (Vicki Volante) is held prisoner in the basement where she provides the blood needed for the operations conducted upstairs.

Vicki Volante *(Blood of Dracula's Castle, Horror of the Blood Monsters)*, and John Bloom, Zandor Vorkov, and Adamson's wife, Regina Carrol *(Dracula vs. Frankenstein)*.

The aged emir of a Middle Eastern country (Hadley) is dying, and there is only one way to save him. His doctor, Bob (Williams), his aide Mohammed (Vorkov), and his fiancée, Tracy (Carrol), plan to take his body to the States after his death to have his brain transplanted by renegade scientist Dr. Lloyd Trenton (Taylor). His new body will then undergo plastic surgery to make him look more like himself, and he will be returned to his throne.

Dr. Trenton (Kent Taylor) and Bob (Grant Williams) remove the brain of the dead emir (Reed Hadley).

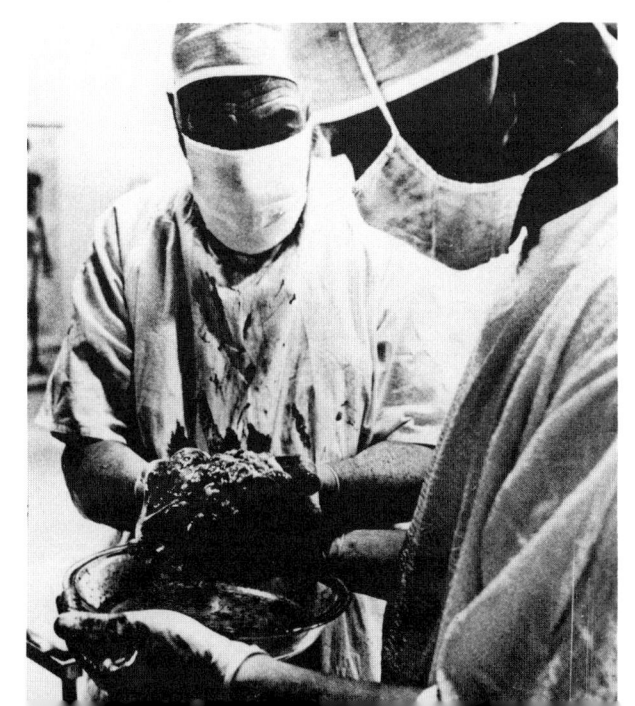

Gor (John Bloom) goes after Dr. Trenton (Kent Taylor) in *The Undying Brain*.

Dr. Trenton is, of course, a total lunatic, who is assisted by the maniacal Dorro (Rossitto) and a disfigured giant named Gor (Bloom). The emir's body arrives at the lab wrapped in aluminum foil, and in a very nasty, gory operation, Trenton removes the brain and stores it in blood he gets from young women he keeps chained in the basement. Meanwhile, Gor is out trying to round up a suitable body for the transplant.

The giant does his job too well, however, and by the time he is finished, the body he got is so mangled that Trenton can't use it. The doctor is pressed for time—he can only keep the emir's brain alive for a little while longer—so he decides to do the transplant using Gor's body as a temporary dwelling place for the gray matter until he can find something more suitable.

Meanwhile, a killer hired by Trenton knocks off Mohammed and almost gets Bob, too. Then Dorro kills the assassin. Bob realizes that something is up, so he and Tracy return to Trenton's lab in time to see Gor wake up speaking in the emir's voice. When the emir/Gor sees what he has become—"I'd rather be dead"—he tries to kill Trenton, then runs off with Tracy.

Trenton has Bob tossed into the basement, then pursues the emir and Tracy, using a kind of signal gun that zaps an electrode planted in the emir's brain, causing him great pain. For some reason, the emir is now a homicidal maniac and still has some of Gor's memories and personality traits, and that's only the beginning of his problems. It turns out that Trenton and Tracy are in cahoots; their plan is to control the emir, using the electrode in his brain, and take over his small but wealthy country.

With help from Katherine (Volante), one of the women in the basement, Bob escapes and sees the error of his ways: "This whole experiment was a horrible mistake." He also sees that the emir is willing to sell out to anybody, just to keep himself alive. He tries to put an end to things, but Gor kills him at the command of Dr. Trenton. Conveniently, Tracy falls off a cliff, thus getting her out of the way.

In the closing sequence, the emir is back in his own nation, only now, of course, his brain is in Bob's body—he still looks like the emir, though, thanks to plastic surgery. He names Dr. Trenton to a high post as one of his most trusted advisers, and we know that Trenton is now the true ruler of the emir's nation.

There is something zany and wildly demented about most of Adamson's films. They don't make much sense, and they're not supposed to. But *The Undying Brain* isn't as much fun as, say, *Blood of Dracula's Castle* or *Horror of the Blood Monsters,* and there's a good reason for that.

There is a big difference between films that inspire national pride and films that exploit and even encourage our fear and dislike of foreigners. *The Undying Brain* is one of the latter. It's an example of Arab bashing, made before Arab bashing really became popular. The Middle Eastern characters are always saying Middle Eastern things like, "We pray that Allah will spare our leader," just as reminders that they are not like us. And, of course, the emir himself, who is supposed to be the beloved and benevolent ruler of his nation, is really a self-serving villain who will sell out in a second, just to stay alive and in power.

Trenton is the monster here, of course, but he is only able to operate thanks to the rich and powerful foreigners who support him. The problem with *The Undying Brain* is that it is a hate film, and by the time the final credits roll, we hate everybody in it. We hate the foreigners, we hate Trenton, we hate Dorro and Gor. We also hate Tracy and Bob, both Americans who have been bought by foreign money. In the end, *The Undying Brain* is a meanspirited film, and that's too bad, because Adamson can do much better.

The Unearthly

1957

Director/producer: Brooke L. Peters; *Screenplay:* Geoffrey Dennis and Jane Mann

CAST:
John Carradine, Myron Healey, Allison Hayes, Tor Johnson, Marilyn Buferd, Sally Todd, Arthur Batanides

ORIGINAL RELEASE: Republic Pictures
VIDEO: Rhino Home Video

Carradine (*House of Frankenstein, Billy the Kid vs. Dracula, Wizard of Mars, Blood of Dracula's Castle,* and countless other horror films) plays his best mad scientist, Dr. Charles Conway, and Myron Healey (*Varan, the Unbelievable, Attack of the Claw Monsters*) makes a rare appearance as a good guy in this one. Tor Johnson (*Plan 9 From Outer Space, Bride of the Monster*) is, once again, Lobo the mindless giant.

Conway and his coldly evil assistant, Sharon Gilcrest (Marilyn Buferd), are trying to make human beings immortal by implanting an artificial gland of Conway's own design. Thus far, however, the operation has turned their patients into hideous, insane mutants whom Conway keeps locked up in a basement dungeon (no mad scientist should be without one).

The pair run a kind of rest home for neurotics as a cover and use their patients as guinea pigs—"In science, there's always been some necessary sacrifices." Following what she calls a "nervous breakdown," Grace Thomas (Allison Hayes) arrives as a new patient and meets

Her doctor tricks Grace Thomas (Allison Hayes) into spending some time at Dr. Conway's clinic to relax after her nervous breakdown in *The Unearthly*. (*Courtesy Hollywood Book and Poster*)

Dr. Charles Conway (John Carradine) tries to discover the secret of eternal life. (*Courtesy Hollywood Book and Poster*)

Director Brook L. Peters positions Marylyn Bufred and John Carradine for one of the more tender scenes in *The Unearthly*. (*Courtesy Hollywood Book and Poster*)

Danny Green (Arthur Batanides), a feisty drug addict, and Natalie (Sally Todd), a flirtatious young woman who wears low-cut blouses and reads sleazy romance novels. Grace also meets Mark Houston (Healey), an undercover cop who has infiltrated Conway's operation.

Eventually, Grace and Mark discover that Conway has used his synthetic gland on Natalie, turning her into a deformed and ugly though possibly immortal version of her former self, and working with Danny, they manage to put an end to Conway's nefarious activities. Not surprisingly, Conway is done in by one of his own creations, and Sharon is hauled off to jail, while the mutants in the basement are incarcerated in a suitable state institution, where, if they really are immortal, they're going to run up a hell of a bill at the expense of taxpayers.

This is another one of those sexist "women be warned" horror movies, though it's a bit more obvious than most, and the character Grace is the target of the lesson. Early in the film, Grace—like Natalie—is unattached, wears low-cut blouses, and runs around the rest home in a flimsy nightgown. After Natalie is zapped by Conway, however, Grace appears only in dark-colored dresses that cover her body from neck to wrist to ankle, and she hooks up with Mark, the male hero who will save her. The film ends with them kissing and living happily ever after, with him firmly in control of the relationship.

Grace has gotten the point. *The Unearthly* offers women three possibilities. Natalie, who is single and overtly sexual, is bad and gets what she deserves. Sharon, who is cold and sexless, is bad and gets what *she* deserves. Grace learns to save herself for one man, and she is getting married. Needless to say, she survives to be a housewife and mother.

Women, know your place.

Dr. Conway (John Carradine) is comforted by his assistant, Dr. Gilcrest (Marylyn Bufred), but his mad-scientist racket is rapidly falling apart. (Courtesy Hollywood Book and Poster)

Undercover cop Mark Houston (Myron Healy) gets the drop on Dr. Conway (John Carradine) in *The Unearthly*. (Courtesy Hollywood Book and Poster)

The Vampire Lovers
1970

Director: Roy Ward Baker; *Producers:* Harry Fine and Michael Style; *Screenplay:* Tudor Gates

CAST:
Ingrid Pitt, Pippa Steele, Madeleine Smith, Peter Cushing, Kate O'Mara, Douglas Wilmer, Jon Finch, George Cole

ORIGINAL RELEASE: Hammer Films/American International
VIDEO: Embassy Home Video

Vampire Lovers is a film version of J. Sheridan Le Fanu's midnineteenth-century novella *Carmilla*, a truly shock-

The vampire appears in its burial shroud in the opening sequence of *Vampire Lovers*.

ing vampire tale that predates Bram Stoker's more famous *Dracula*. Though some of the names are changed, the movie follows the story rather closely. As the title suggests, the eroticism that was implicit in Le Fanu's tale is explicit in the film.

Somewhere in Austria, Baron Joachim Von Hartog (Douglas Wilmer) tries to wipe out the Karnstein family—vampires all—to get revenge for the death of his sister. Unfortunately, he misses one Karnstein, a young woman (Ingrid Pitt) who is known by a number of aliases—Mircalla, Marcilla, Carmilla—but who is dangerous by any name.

Laura (Pippa Steele), niece of General Von Spielsdorf (Peter Cushing) and friend of Emma Morton (Madeleine Smith), is the first victim of the lovely vampire, who seems to seek out only women as her consorts. Emma is next on the list, and Carmilla stages a coach accident on the road near the Morton estate so the family will take her in and care for her. Once she has infiltrated the household, she captivates young Emma and her governess (Kate O'Mara) and kills any man who tries to interfere with her plan.

Laura (Pippa Steele) and Carmilla (Ingrid Pitt) become very good friends.

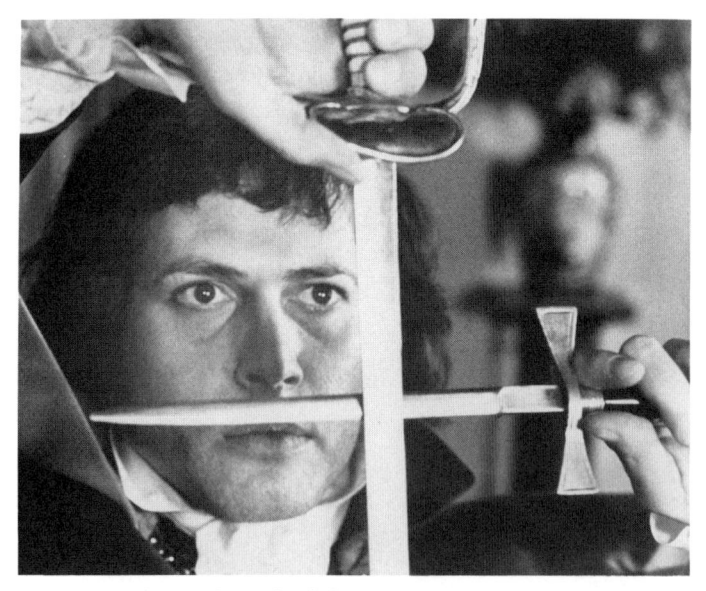

Carl (Jon Finch) fends off the vampire with an improvised cross.

Morton (George Cole), Gen. Von Spielsdorf (Peter Cushing), and the other vampire hunters discover the grave of Mircalla/Marcilla/Carmilla in *Vampire Lovers*.

Emma falls ill—the doctor calls it "anemia"—and she has dreams about a huge gray cat that leaps into her bed each night and bites her in the breast. She is going downhill rapidly when her father (George Cole) catches on to what's happening and joins forces with the general and the baron (who, after all, has experience in such matters). Together, the men track Carmilla down, drive a stake through her heart, and decapitate her, thus setting Emma free to marry Carl Ebhardt (Jon Finch), the best-looking young nobleman in the district.

The Vampire Lovers is not the first lesbian vampire story. *Dracula's Daughter* of 1936 had lesbian overtones, as did Le Fanu's original novella. But here lesbianism is clearly the main theme. When Emma asks Carmilla, "Don't you wish some handsome young man would come into your life?" her new friend replies, "No, and neither do you, I hope."

In the real world, lesbians are a threat to a male-dominated society because they say, in effect, that they don't need men. The lesbian vampire is a double threat because she has no need or desire for men and she can, in a sense, reproduce herself without male participation by creating new female vampires. Vampirism is, of course, inherently sexual—there is the penetration of the body by another, the exchange of fluids, etc. The female vampire, however, usurps the male role as sexual aggressor. Carmilla rejects men as superfluous, and so it is no wonder that, at the end of *Vampire Lovers*, it is the men who must band together to destroy her in an effort to win back their dominant position and defeat this supernatural advocate of women's liberation. The men succeed, and henceforth they can be secure in their positions as fathers and husbands, generals and noblemen, the ones in control—at least until the sequel, *Lust for a Vampire*, when the whole thing starts all over again, suggesting that the men's "right to rule" may not be as secure as they would like to think.

Werewolf of Washington

1973

Director/screenplay: Milton Moses Ginsberg; *Producer:* Nina Schulman

CAST:
Dean Stockwell, Biff McGuire, Jane House, Michael Dunn

ORIGINAL RELEASE: Diplomat Pictures
VIDEO: Monterey Home Video

Dean Stockwell is a fine actor, but he appeared in a lot of movies like this one before he finally got nominated for an Oscar. His performance in *Werewolf of Washington* really is excellent, however, and the movie itself—while hardly a classic—isn't nearly as bad as you might think.

Jack Whittier (Stockwell) has a problem. He is press secretary to the president of the United States (Biff McGuire), and on a side trip to Hungary, he is bitten by a werewolf. On his return to Washington, he discovers

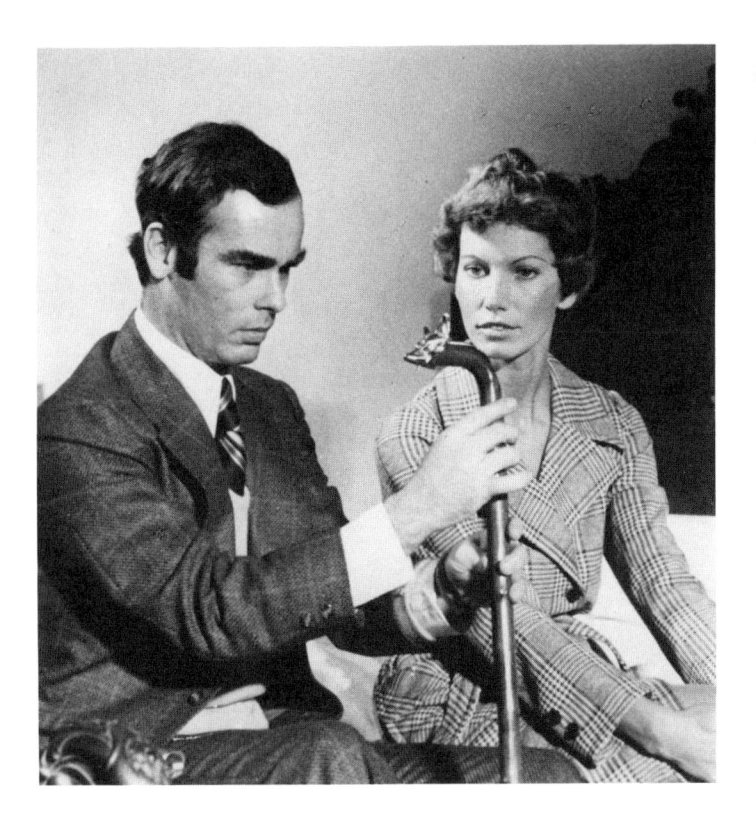

In *Werewolf of Washington,* presidential press secretary Jack Whittier (Dean Stockwell) and his love interest, Marion (Jane House), contemplate the wolf-headed cane as if they never saw the same gimmick in the original *Wolf Man.*

A victim of the *Werewolf of Washington.* Note the cans of Alpo that the canine monster has overlooked.

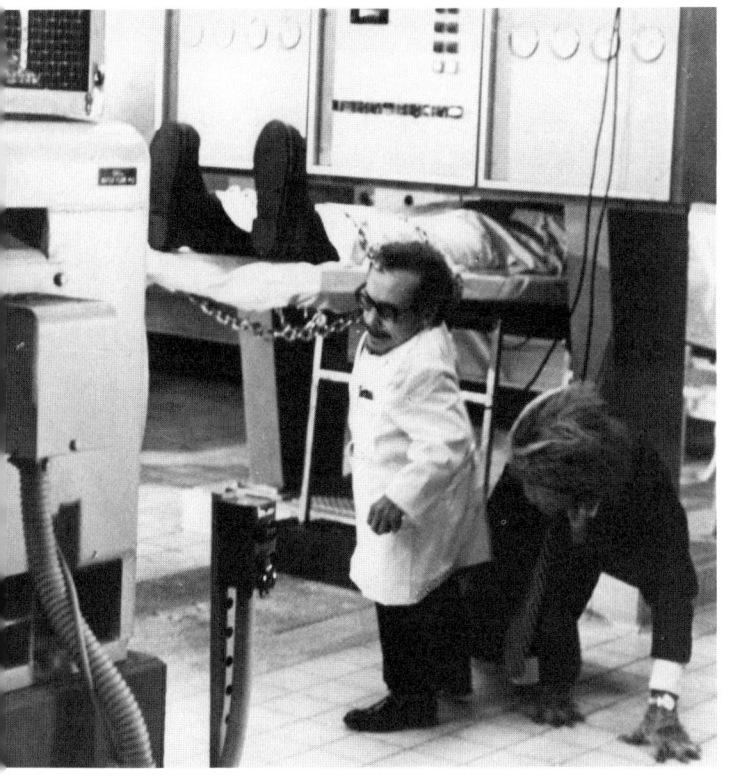

The werewolf (Dean Stockwell) runs amok in the secret laboratory hidden behind a White House men's room where diminutive Dr. Kiss (Michael Dunn) performs monstrous experiments for the good of the nation.

that he is now a werewolf himself, and when the moon is full, he ravages the city, attacking people in phone booths, dumping bodies into shopping carts, and generally making a nuisance of himself until at last he attacks the president during a flight aboard Air Force One.

Does lycanthropy provide grounds for impeachment?

There really isn't any reason to dwell on the plot here, because you already know it. *Werewolf of Washington* is a parody of every werewolf movie you've ever seen, and it pumps every lycanthropic cliché for all it's worth—full moon, wolfbane, the cane with a wolf's head, etc.

Werewolf of Washington is more than just a spoof of such classic films as *Werewolf of London* and *The Wolf Man,* however. This movie was made during the Watergate era when, for the first time in American history, we the people got a look at the kind of dirty deals and nasty horrors that go on at the highest levels of American politics. Like any good political satire, *Werewolf of Washington* takes the facts and exaggerates them to give us a new perspective on what we already know, suggesting, in this case, that some of our elected leaders and their appointees might very well be monsters in real life.

As a horror film, *Werewolf of Washington* isn't a bit frightening. What is really scary about this film, though, is how much the dialogue sounds like the things we heard back in the seventies during the televised Water-

Jack (Dean Stockwell) attacks the president (Biff McGuire) on board Air Force One while a Chinese ambassador (Stephen Cheng) looks on in horror in *Werewolf of Washington*.

gate hearings. Whittier goes to a psychiatrist for help, but the good doctor only tells him to keep his problems to himself. "There is no doubt the press would seize on your present tragedy to discredit the president," he says, and we recognize immediately that there is a cover-up in the works. The powers-that-be in the executive branch are more than willing to allow a werewolf to roam the city, killing dozens of people, rather than risk embarrassing the administration by trying to deal with the problem.

Sometimes, though, the satire here gets too broad, as in the sequence featuring Dr. Kiss (Michael Dunn), a mad scientist whose job seems to be to create monsters for the good of "national security" and who enters his laboratory through a secret door hidden in a White House men's room.

In fact, *Werewolf of Washington* often seems to be pushing too hard to get laughs. When the president's daughter, Marion (Jane House), Jack's love interest, says things like, "You're an awful wolf, aren't you?" or "Will you please not bark at me?" you quickly realize that this is as good as the jokes are going to get. A lot of this stuff just isn't funny—and yet it is often so unfunny that it *is* funny, if that makes any sense.

I have to admit that the first time I saw *Werewolf of Washington*, I hated it, but the more often I watch it, the better I like it. So if you haven't seen this one, give it a try. If you have seen it, try it again.

Wolfen

1981

Director: Michael Wadleigh; *Producer:* Rupert Hitzig; *Screenplay:* David Frye and Michael Wadleigh

CAST:
Albert Finney, Diane Venora, Edward James Olmos, Gregory Hines, Tom Noonan

ORIGINAL RELEASE: Orion/Warner Brothers
VIDEO: Warner Home Video

New York police detective Dewey Wilson (Albert Finney) has been off the job for some time because of a drinking problem, but he is called in to investigate the brutal killing of wealthy coke-snorting socialites Christopher (Max M. Brown) and Pauline Vanderveer (Anne Marie Photamo). The police department suspects terrorists—the Vanderveers were old money, long involved in third-world exploitation—but Dewey isn't so sure. When more bodies turn up in the South Bronx—this time, the bodies of derelicts and homeless people—the case becomes even more baffling.

Working on the theory that wild animals did the killings, Dewey and his partner, police psychologist Rebecca Neff (Diane Venora), contact zoologist Dr. Ferguson (Tom Noonan), who identifies hairs found at the crime scenes as belonging to a wolf. But of course there are no wolves in New York City: "They went the way of the Indian and the buffalo."

True, there are no buffalo left in New York, but there *are* Indians, and Dewey contacts Eddie Holt (Edward James Olmos), a Native American radical he once helped send to jail. Holt speaks mysteriously about shape-shifting but then tells Dewey, "It's not wolves. It's Wolfen." The Wolfen, it seems, are a twenty-thousand-year-old race of superwolves who are still living on their old hunting grounds, even though urbanization has all but put them out of business. They live in abandoned buildings and survive by hunting down and eating terminally ill derelicts. Using information he gets from his morgue attendant friend Whittington (Gregory Hines), Dewey figures out that the same kind of killings have been going on in Newark, Philadelphia, New Orleans, and many other American cities for years.

Native Americans have known about the existence of Wolfen for generations and have even worshiped them as gods. Dewey figures out that the Wolfen killed Christopher Vanderveer to stop his plans to demolish much of the South Bronx and build luxury condos on the Wolfen hunting grounds.

Before he can get any evidence to prove his theory, however, the Wolfen kill Ferguson and Whittington, his two best witnesses. Dewey and Rebecca try to track the Wolfen without success, but eventually they themselves are hunted down by the ultracanines and trapped in Vanderveer's office. There, before the eyes of the ancient, godlike Wolfen, Dewey destroys the model of Vanderveer's development project as a promise never to tell anyone who really committed the murders, and the Wolfen let them go free. Then, just in case we've missed the point, Dewey's voice-over at the end informs us that "in arrogance, man knows nothing about what exists."

The idea here—that intellectual superwolves have been living in New York City and other major urban areas for generations without ever being discovered—is ridiculous, of course. But this movie is so beautifully made and so well paced that you probably won't notice how zany it is until you sit down and think about it later.

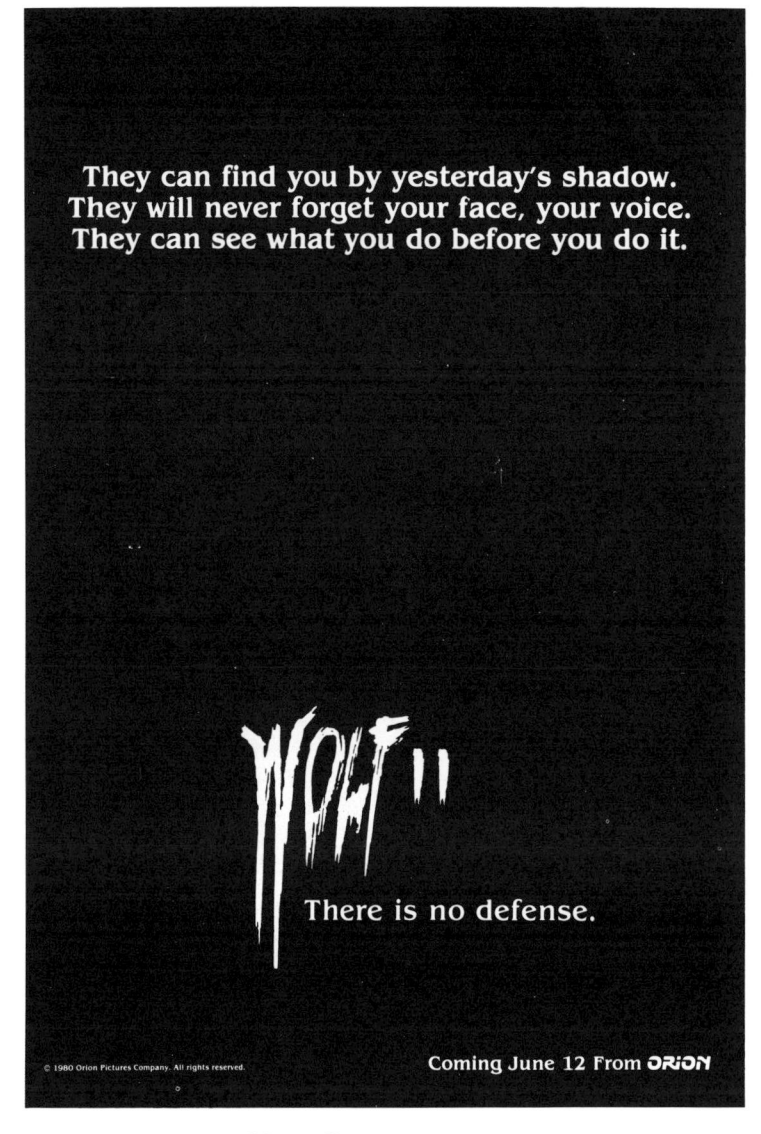

The original newspaper ad for *Wolfen*.

Finney is wonderful as the marginal cop who realizes that Native American wisdom is truer than the white, European-based culture that only wants to exploit and develop, and performances by Hines, Venora, and Olmos are every bit as solid. *Woodstock* director Michael Wadleigh has made a very effective film here, arguing against the Vanderveers of the world—with an old Dutch name like that, they were probably the ones who bought Manhattan from the Indians in the first place.

Generally speaking, horror films are antiprogress, favoring ancient wisdom over modern notions of what is good for us. *Wolfen* clearly champions the ancient wisdom of the Indians over the progressive ideas of the urban developers. On the other hand, the movie finds itself in the curious position of arguing in favor of slums

Detective Dewey Wilson (Albert Finney) climbs across a bridge cable to talk to an iron worker who might have some information about the recent murders in *Wolfen*.

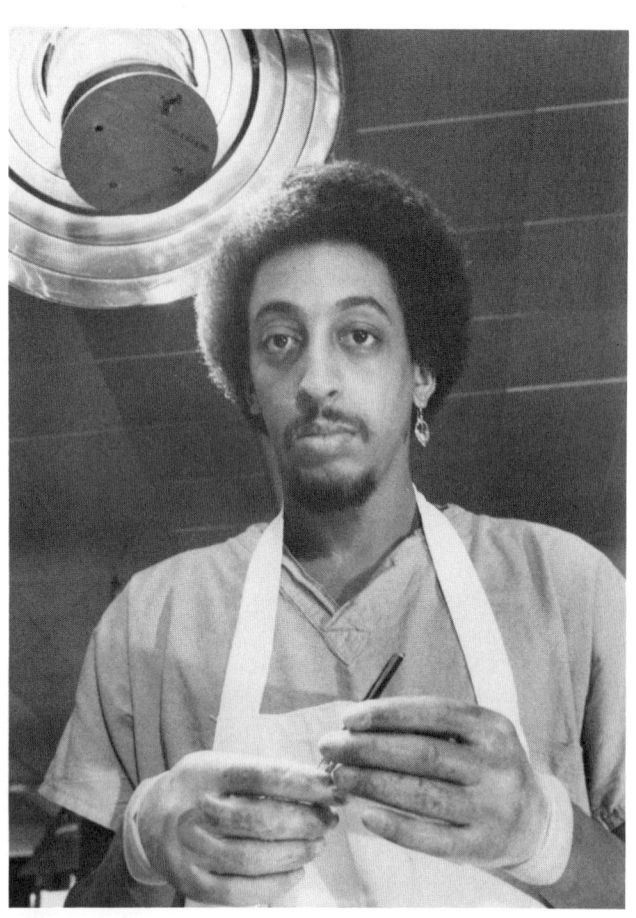

Dancer Gregory Hines is an unlikely candidate for the role of morgue attendant Whittington in *Wolfen*.

Dewey (Albert Finney) and police psychologist Rebecca Neff (Diane Venora) track the Wolfen to their lair in an abandoned building.

Dewey (Albert Finney) senses that the *Wolfen* are on their way.

and abandoned buildings and even of maintaining a population of poverty-stricken homeless people so the Wolfen can have a place to live and someone to prey upon.

That seems a bit much.

Zombies of Mora Tau

ALTERNATE TITLE:

The Dead That Walk

1957

Director: Edward Cahn; *Producer:* Sam Katzman; *Screenplay:* Raymond T. Marcus

CAST:
Gregg Palmer, Allison Hayes, Autumn Russell, Morris Ankrum, Joel Ashley, Marjorie Eaton

ORIGINAL RELEASE: Columbia Pictures
VIDEO: RCA/Columbia Home Video

The scene is Africa—though there are no blacks featured in the film—and Jan Peters (Autumn Russell) is returning to her great-grandmother's house after being away at school for the past ten years. At the same time, a boatload of American treasure hunters arrives at Mora Tau, hoping to salvage some diamonds that went to the bottom of the sea at the end of the nineteenth century aboard the ship *Susan B*. Legend has it that the *Susan B's* crew stole the sacred diamonds from local natives, who got their revenge by transforming ten crewmen into zombies condemned to guard the treasure forever.

Grandma Peters (Marjorie Eaton) warns the newcomers about the zombies and takes them to the graveyard where members of earlier salvage crews are buried. But George Harrison (Joel Ashley), leader of the expedition and a greedy, sleazy guy, is not to be stopped. Neither is the hero, diver Jeff Clark (Gregg Palmer), until it becomes clear to him that Grandma is right. The zombies start knocking off members of the crew and kidnap and zombify Harrison's sleazy wife, Mona (Alli-

Mrs. Peters (Marjorie Eaton) welcomes her great-granddaughter Jan (Autumn Russell) to the old homestead while the driver Sam (Gene Roth) looks on in *Zombies of Mora Tau*. (*Courtesy Hollywood Book and Poster*)

George Harrison (Joel Ashley) and Jonathan Eggert (Morris Ankrum) rescue Mona Harrison (Allison Hayes) from the zombies, unaware that she is now one of the living dead. (*Courtesy Hollywood Book and Poster*)

George (Joel Ashley) and Jeff Clark (Gregg Palmer) prepare to dive for the lost diamonds that are guarded by the zombies. (*Courtesy Hollywood Book and Poster*)

son Hayes), who kills her husband and goes off with her new undead friends. Jeff finally gets the diamonds and gives them to Grandma, who tosses them into the sea where no one will ever find them, thus ending the curse and putting the zombies to rest.

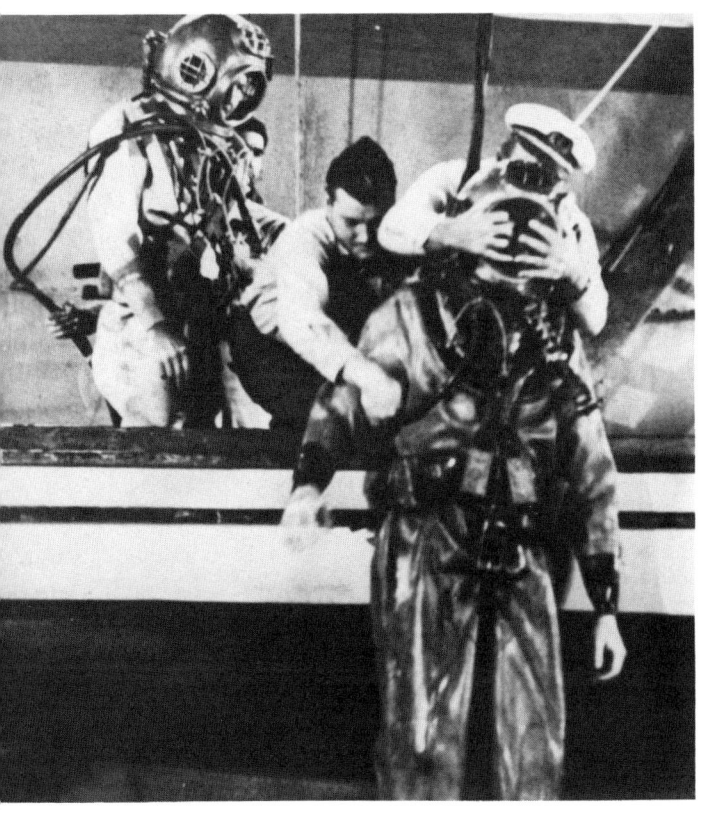

This seems to be a more or less forgettable film with mediocre acting and abysmal special effects—the "underwater" scenes clearly do not take place underwater—but there *is* something interesting going on. In *Zombies of Mora Tau*, white North American entrepreneurs do what white North American entrepreneurs do—invade and plunder a third-world country. But the film warns against this and suggests that, in other cultures, North Americans are out of their element and can only survive if—like Grandma Peters and Jeff—they stop trying to impose their values where they do not belong and accept the fact that they are uninvited guests in someone else's home and must behave accordingly.

This is a pretty strong message addressed to a 1950s America that had business interests all over the world and that faced anti-American sentiments and revolutions in many third-world nations. For this reason alone, *Zombies of Mora Tau* is probably worth another look.

Jeff (Gregg Palmer) has had a hard day underwater. (*Courtesy Hollywood Book and Poster*)

Jan (Autumn Russell) and Jeff (Gregg Palmer) have the diamonds, but these don't do them much good when the zombies attack. (*Courtesy Hollywood Book and Poster*)

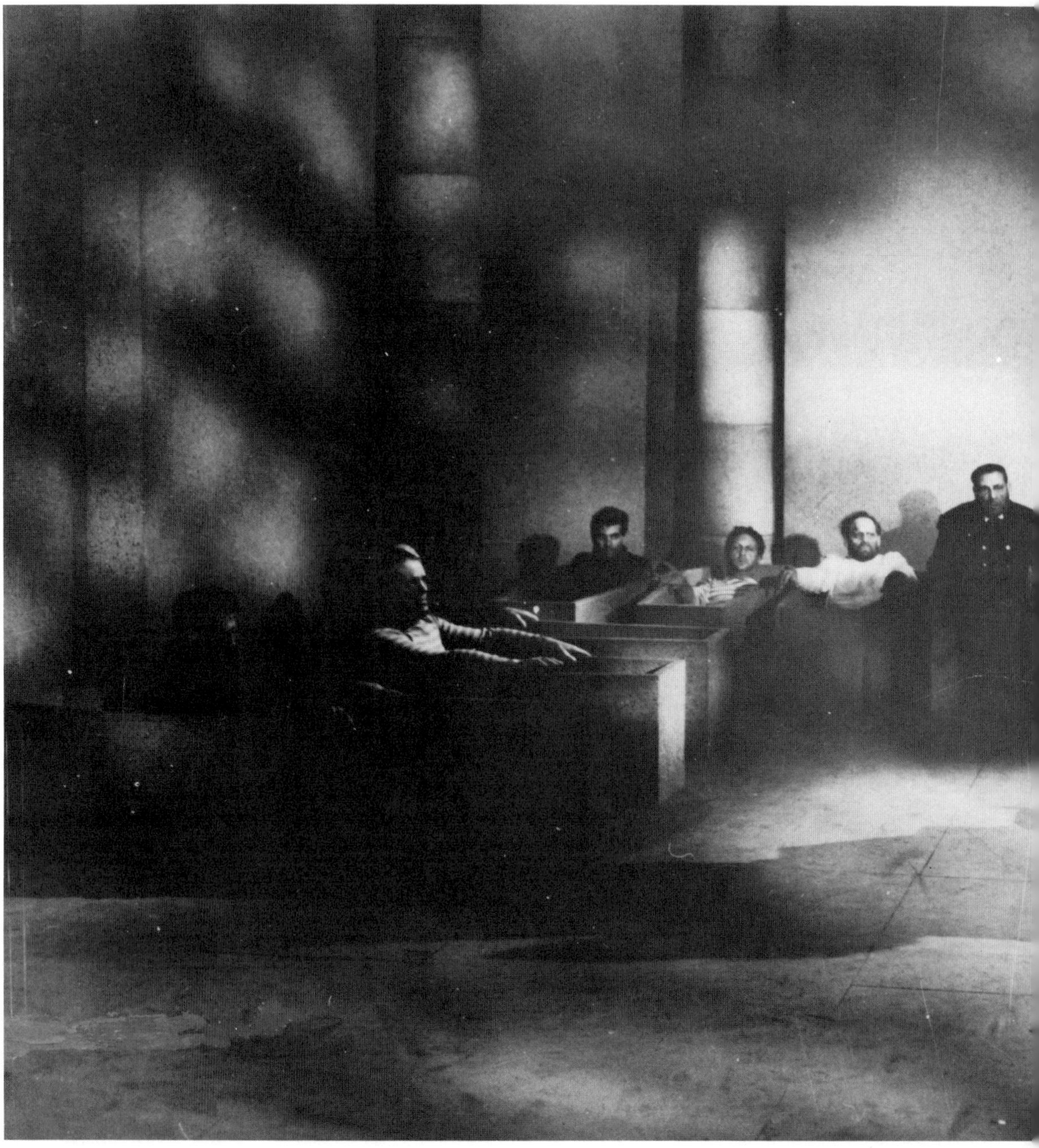

In the crypt, the living dead prepare to make Jan one of the zombies of Mora Tau. (*Courtesy Hollywood Book and Poster*)

ORDER NOW!
More Citadel Film Books

If you like this book, you'll love the other titles in the award-winning Citadel Film Series. From James Stewart to Moe Howard and The Three Stooges, Woody Allen to John Wayne, The Citadel Film Series is America's largest and oldest film book library.

With more than 150 titles--and more on the way!--Citadel Film Books make perfect gifts for a loved one, a friend, or best of all, yourself!

A complete listing of the Citadel Film Series appears below.
If you know what books you want, why not order now!
It's easy! Just call 1-800-447-BOOK and have your MasterCard or Visa ready.

STARS
Alan Ladd
Arnold Scwarzenegger
Barbra Streisand: First Decade
Barbra Streisand: Second Decade
Bela Lugosi
Bette Davis
Boris Karloff
The Bowery Boys
Buster Keaton
Carole Lombard
Cary Grant
Charles Bronson
Charlie Chaplin
Clark Gable
Clint Eastwood
Curly
Dustin Hoffman
Edward G. Robinson
Elizabeth Taylor
Elvis Presley
Errol Flynn
Frank Sinatra
Gary Cooper
Gene Kelly
Gina Lollobrigida
Gloria Swanson
Gregory Peck
Greta Garbo
Henry Fonda
Humphrey Bogart
Ingrid Bergman
Jack Lemmon
Jack Nicholson
James Cagney
James Dean: Behind the Scene
Jane Fonda
Jeanette MacDonald & Nelson Eddy
Joan Crawford
John Wayne Films
John Wayne Reference Book
John Wayne Scrapbook
Judy Garland
Katharine Hepburn
Kirk Douglas
Laurel & Hardy
Lauren Bacall
Laurence Olivier
Mae West
Marilyn Monroe
Marlene Dietrich
Marlon Brando
Marx Brothers
Moe Howard & the Three Stooges
Norma Shearer
Olivia de Havilland
Orson Welles
Paul Newman
Peter Lorre
Rita Hayworth
Robert De Niro
Robert Redford
Sean Connery
Sexbomb: Jayne Mansfield
Shirley MacLaine
Shirley Temple
The Sinatra Scrapbook
Spencer Tracy
Steve McQueen
Three Stooges Scrapbook
Warren Beatty
W.C. Fields
William Holden
William Powell
A Wonderful Life: James Stewart

DIRECTORS
Alfred Hitchcock
Cecil B. DeMille
Federico Fellini
Frank Capra
John Ford
John Huston
Woody Allen

GENRE
Bad Guys
Black Hollywood
Black Hollywood: From 1970 to Today
Classic Foreign Films: From 1960 to Today
Classic Gangster Films
Classic Science Fiction Films
Classics of the Horror Film
Cult Horror Films
Divine Images: Jesus on Screen
Early Classics of Foreign Film
Films of Merchant Ivory
Great French Films
Great German Films
Great Romantic Films
Great Science Fiction Films
Harry Warren & the Hollywood Musical
Hispanic Hollywood: The Latins in Motion Pictures
The Hollywood Western
The Incredible World of 007
The Jewish Image in American Film
The Lavender Screen: The Gay and Lesbian Films
Martial Arts Movies
The Modern Horror Film
More Classics of the Horror Film
Movie Psychos & Madmen
Our Huckleberry Friend: Johnny Mercer
Second Feature: "B" Films
Sex in Films
They Sang! They Danced! They Romanced!: Hollywood Musicals
Thrillers
The West That Never Was
Words and Shadows: Literature on the Screen

DECADE
Classics of the Silent Screen
Films of the Twenties
Films of the Thirties
More Films of the 30's
Films of the Forties
Films of the Fifties
Lost Films of the 50's
Films of the Sixties
Films of the Seventies
Films of the Eighties

SPECIAL INTEREST
America on the Rerun
Bugsy (Illustrated screenplay)
Comic Support
Dick Tracy
Favorite Families of TV
Film Flubs
Film Flubs: The Sequel
First Films
Forgotten Films to Remember
"Frankly, My Dear"
Hollywood Cheesecake
Hollywood's Hollywood
Howard Hughes in Hollywood
More Character People
The Nightmare Never Ends: Freddy Krueger & "A Nightmare on Elm Street"
The "Northern Exposure" Book
The Official Andy Griffith Show Scrapbook
The 100 Best Films of the Century
The "Quantum Leap" Book
Rodgers & Hammerstein
Sex In the Movies
Sherlock Holmes
Son of Film Flubs
Those Glorious Glamour Years
Who Is That?: Familiar Faces and Forgotten Names
"You Ain't Heard Nothin' Yet!"

For a free full-color brochure describing the Citadel Film Series in depth, call 1-800-447-BOOK; or send your name and address to Citadel Film Books, Dept. 1425, 120 Enterprise Ave., Secaucus, NJ 07094.